Antiblackness and the Stories of Authentic Allies

Antiblackness and the Stories of Authentic Allies

Lived Experiences in the Fight Against Institutionalized Racism

Edited by

NORMAN KIM, PHD

CAROLYN COKER ROSS, MD, MPH

MAZELLA FULLER, PHD, MSW, LCSW

CHARLYNN SMALL, PHD

OXFORD
UNIVERSITY PRESS

OXFORD
UNIVERSITY PRESS

Oxford University Press is a department of the University of Oxford. It furthers
the University's objective of excellence in research, scholarship, and education
by publishing worldwide. Oxford is a registered trade mark of Oxford University
Press in the UK and certain other countries.

Published in the United States of America by Oxford University Press
198 Madison Avenue, New York, NY 10016, United States of America.

CIP data is on file at the Library of Congress

ISBN 978-0-19-777085-6 (pbk.)
ISBN 978-0-19-764253-5 (hbk.)

DOI: 10.1093/oso/9780197642535.001.0001

Paperback printed by Marquis Book Printing, Canada
Hardback printed by Bridgeport National Bindery, Inc., United States of America

MIX
Paper | Supporting
responsible forestry
FSC
www.fsc.org   FSC® C103567

Contents

PART VIII: WHITE PRIVILEGE

Foreword

This anthology on the history and consequences of antiblackness in America was born of the revolution ignited by the murders of George Floyd, Breonna Taylor, and Ahmaud Arbery in 2020. It is the revolution that author and biblical scholar Esau McCaulley describes in his guest essay in the *New York Times* on Martin Luther King Jr. Day (McCaulley, 2023) when he recounts the message of Dr. King's final Sunday Sermon, *Remaining Awake Through a Great Revolution*. He corrects the misimpression that King was "color-blind" in his policy aims and stresses that the aims were "unapologetically color-conscious." He emphasizes: "Injustice leaves a legacy. It creates inequalities that do not simply disappear" (McCaulley, 2023).

This terrible legacy that will not disappear is brought into powerful, new light in *Antiblackness: White Privilege, Allyship, and Psychology*, an important and unique text. The authors unabashedly describe the ultimate injustice of chattel slavery in which Black people were not recognized as human and probe the vast physical and mental health consequences from the entire historical continuum of antiblackness. This collection contains an impressive range of voices and styles, weaving together research, historical overviews, and personal narratives. The scope of this work illuminates the entirety and informs our next steps. This quilt of topics means a reader can open to any chapter and find a valuable resource immediately. It is a book worth returning to, a reference book on the shelf.

Now you may be asking: Why am I writing this foreword, a White man of privilege who is both a physician and a CEO? I was asked, I believe, because of my role leading the Arnold P. Gold Foundation, a nonprofit that champions humanism in health care for all. Our mission is deeply connected to equitable care and to ensuring that care for all people is inclusive and antiracist (Arnold P. Gold Foundation, 2020). One of our trustees, Karen Watson, has a chapter here, Chapter 14, and helped make the initial connections to Dr. Carolyn Coker Ross, who represented the editors. Their high achievements and their conception of the text made the decision for me. The coeditors are all founders of the Institute for Antiracism and Equity in Mental Health (http://www.antiracismandequity.com), which is dedicated to focusing a lens on the social determinants of inequity and of health and providing training and consultation for the wide spectrum of mental health professionals and organizations.

The need for this work and the risks if the work is not done are real. Another Gold trustee, Dr. George Thibault, described the dangers of antihumanistic behaviors and policies, emphasizing, "It will be hard to have humanism in medicine if there is no humanism in the world around us" (Thibault, 2019, 1077) . The Gold Foundation has since made explicit a fundamental principle of our mission, that true humanistic care must be inclusive of all and that "humanism in healthcare demands we address racism" (Arnold P. Gold Foundation, 2020) . Floyd's death took place only 2 months after the World Health Organization's declaration of the COVID-19 global pandemic, and thereafter the foundation began speaking of the "two pandemics," emphasizing the biologic and social plagues confronting us.

In the Preface by Norman Kim and the Introduction by Kim and his coeditors, Carolyn Coker Ross, Mazella Fuller, and Charlynn Small, there is an exceptionally lucid description of the problem of racism—antiblackness in particular—and its consequences for mental health and health care in general. The reader should begin with these two sections, which include this concise focus on the health consequences:

> Our history of chattel slavery, the subsequent and pervasive race-based trauma that continues to affect our communities, and the codifying of antiblackness in our laws, our institutions, and our collective consciousness have all combined to result in our current state of health inequities. These inequities in access to care, appropriateness of care, and quality of care, among other factors, necessitate an exploring of the myriad ways in which antiblackness permeates health care and, by definition, our mental health care.

The idea that history informs the present is at least as old as the nation. Though some may blithely choose to *ignore* the past, few of us live in a bubble of "now." We carry with us personal histories that not only are our own but also are shaped by other histories, bigger histories—histories of systems and institutions that have helped create the world as it is, for better or for worse.

These histories permeate many chapters in this book, as authors examine racism through various lenses, including slavery, religion, politics, law enforcement, the military, and academia. Some essays probe the big picture, exploring how racism became embedded in systems and structures. Others are deeply personal accounts by authors—doctors, educators, soldiers, and psychologists among them—who share disturbing and soul-bruising stories of their experiences. As Dr. Colleen Ramsey asks in Chapter 5, "So how do you know if you matter in the bigger scheme of things when on a regular basis you are expending so much energy dodging landmines, microaggressions, racial undertones and defiance of recognition?" Perhaps most devastating is the exploration of how experiences of racism become embedded in *bodies*, forcing people to carry this trauma with them in ways that directly affect their health, both mental and physical.

Within this book and its 34 chapters reside a vast kaleidoscope of perspectives and insights, in which the authors share intimate, harrowing stories; examinations of critical theory; overviews of areas of intersectionality, such as disability and race; illuminating dives into such topics as food marketing and allyship; and even a vivid allegory to bring home the disparities in White and non-White lives. The collection relies heavily on the potency of storytelling to reveal hard and heavy truths. Many chapters also contain questions offered as points of reflection, ways to begin to explore unfamiliar areas of both our inner and outer worlds. This is perhaps one of the great gifts of this book, the way each author shares a piece of the landscape and provides a flashlight for exploration, tools, and handholds to begin widening our understanding.

There is considerable focus on the concept of being an authentic White ally. *Antiblackness* understands that equality requires intentionality. Weaving in concepts of psychology throughout, the book imparts a message to readers that allyship is not just what we do unto others, but also what we do unto ourselves. Racism, like all societal ills, is viscerally felt. The legacy of traumas past is in us.

In the chapter "Between Us: A Black and White Woman's Conversation About Friendship," Janie Victoria Ward and Becky Thompson speak to the authentic and intentional aspects of allyship, saying, "Compassion is imperative for fostering trust and repair, allowing us to connect by empathizing with another's experience. Without empathy and care, there cannot be a proper motive. Without proper motive, authentic allyship cannot exist. When authenticity is present, actions come from a place of responsibility rather than a place of guilt. This requires continuous mindfulness and internal examination of motive and intentions."

Antiblackness can be, to be honest and clear, an uncomfortable book to read. And it must be—there is no way it could be a comfortable, easy read *and* a successful book that illuminates the obstacles, journeys, and lives of people of color in our modern society.

One of the most important points of the book is the pervasive centering of White people in our society, which is so entrenched that most White people don't see it at all. You might wonder: What does that even mean? Think about it this way, if you are White: Do you notice when a scene has only people of color? When a movie has only Black characters? And yet, a scene with only White people doesn't raise the same noticing—it passes by, as if it were "normal."

In Chapter 4, "Before Race. After Race. Post Racial," Dr. Nerine Tatham references Plato's allegory of the cave, noting that "people tend to believe what they are raised to believe. Unless some random event happens to move us out of our cave, many won't spend time questioning their reality. That is why to be an ally, you must turn your head. This is one of the most significant things you can do, imagine that the reality you have experienced isn't the only version."

This won't be easy. It's not as simple as having empathy, the way we might for someone who is ill. We have all experienced illness, if not in ourselves, then through a friend or family member. But White people cannot *truly* understand the experiences that Black and Brown individuals have faced. A willingness to acknowledge that—to turn our heads and see that our reality is not the only reality—is the first step.

Richard I. Levin, MD
President and CEO, The Arnold P. Gold Foundation, Emeritus Professor of Medicine, NYU Grossman School of Medicine, Emeritus Professor of Medicine, McGill University

Acknowledgments

The author recognizes the important contributions of Brianne Warner Alcala, Stacy Bodziak, and Irene Zampetoulas to the development of the Foreword.

References

Arnold P. Gold Foundation. (2020, June 3). *Humanism in healthcare demands we address racism*. https://www.gold-foundation.org/newsroom/news/humanism-in-healthcare-demands-we-address-racism/

McCaulley, E. (2023, January 15). The kind of revolution that Martin Luther King Jr. envisioned [Guest Essay]. *New York Times*.

Thibault, G. E. (2019). Humanism in medicine: What does it mean and why is it more important than ever? *Academic Medicine, 94*, 1074–1077.

Preface

There is no health without mental health.
—Dr. David Satcher, the 16th U.S. Surgeon General, in 1999

My coeditors and I embarked on this collection in the turbulent wake of the murders of George Floyd, Breonna Taylor, and Ahmaud Arbery, who became some of the named among the tragic, countless legions of Black, Brown, and Asian individuals whose lives have been marred by racism and systemic discrimination. We are living in a time of escalating physical and psychological violence targeting people of color, folx in the LGBTQIA+ communities, immigrants and refugees, and people with other historically disenfranchised identities. This violence, like the racism of which it is indicative, is neither new nor aberrational.

Our history of chattel slavery, the subsequent and pervasive race-based trauma that continues to affect our communities, and the codifying of antiblackness in our laws, our institutions, and our collective consciousness have all combined to result in our current state of health inequities. These inequities in access to care, appropriateness of care, and quality of care, among other factors, necessitate an exploring of the myriad ways in which antiblackness permeates health care and, by definition, our mental health care.

The COVID-19 pandemic revealed just how paper thin the alluring fiction of equality and equity was in reality. While not a surprise to those who were already impacted by these inequities, the pandemic, and its disproportionate level of devastation in minority and marginalized communities, made long-standing socioeconomic disparities much harder to ignore by the general public. The most vulnerable and the marginalized (or, to put it more directly, the Blacker and Browner among us) became the very people we were asking to also step up and take care of and protect the rest of us, even though as a society we have not adequately protected them.

Despite an initial flurry of protests, concern, and "awareness," it also did not take long to return to the comfort of the status quo. This furious drive toward complacency and reliance on performative actions rather than genuinely impactful systemic change remains our greatest obstacle to leveling this increasingly uneven playing field. This systemic quicksand, wherein whiteness is the default and proximity to whiteness the ultimate goal, is the context for this collection of narratives and analyses by writers with the lived experience of antiblackness and those with the lived experience of White privilege.

While it might seem self-evident that those who have more resources get more and better care, it also bears repeating because our systems do not recognize this fundamental injustice as such. Current systems are set up to maintain these inequities, not dismantle them, and it is evident in our very models of disease and treatment, the ways we train clinicians, and ultimately the care provided. The lack of centering of the experiences of Black people, along with the historical and contemporaneous systemic racism within our health care systems, lies at the root of the barriers to care, let alone the provision of culturally attuned and competent care.

The Jesuit scholar and psychologist Ignacio Martín-Baró proposed the construct of liberation psychology in the 1970s (Martín-Baró, 1994) to challenge the Eurocentric bias of mainstream psychological doctrines that did not adequately center the experiences of those peoples who have been excluded and marginalized. Liberation psychology sought to decolonize our conceptualization of pathology and trauma from their narrowly individualistic frameworks and instead emphasized the impacts of the social systems and structures within which traumas were occurring and amplified the experiences of the oppressed who were most affected. In our current context, it elucidates the limitations and futility of attempting to isolate mental health struggles, and indeed psychopathology, from the sociocultural structures and cultural milieu from which they emanate.

Liberation psychology is a direct and pointed critique that continues to be relevant and that has had profound impacts on how we are trained to conceptualize and treat mental health issues. There is a clear problem and illogic to the prima facie assumption, and the continued basis of how most mental health providers are trained, that the ideas developed by two European men (Austrian Sigmund Freud and Swiss Carl Jung)—contemporaries in a specific period of time (late 1800s to the early 1900s) and from a similarly privileged social class—are ideas relevant to all peoples of any background and cultural context. The presumptive universality of their developmental theories and conceptualization of pathology has been problematic at best, and at worst actively harmful to many people from backgrounds and with identities that have been minoritized and marginalized.

The resulting disparities in mental health care utilization have long been known. Black Americans, Latinx Americans, and Asian Americans have consistently underutilized mental health care services (Hall et al., 2021) compared to their White peers. People from minority communities experience greater difficulty in accessing mental health care, report multiple barriers to care, and are significantly more likely to receive poorer quality care (Satcher Health Leadership Institute at Morehouse School of Medicine, 2022; U.S. Department of Health and Human Services, 2001).

Indicative of the overall bias with which we are interested in examining in this volume, much of the focus of the efforts that have been made to increase utilization rates have been on changing something in minority communities, namely increasing education around mental health issues and services within identified communities. Again, while this is undoubtedly important, there is an underlying presumption that the source of underutilization is a lack of understanding in minority communities and that the goal is to have them come to us in our existing systems. Understanding this as a systemic problem, in contrast, would at least imply some need for us to look at our own systems to ensure that we are providing care in a manner that is appropriate for, and acceptable and relevant to, the communities we are trying to serve. Not changing our Eurocentric, individualistic systems to more directly meet the needs of non-European communities means that we are accepting White centeredness as the default and presuming its superiority.

Among the many limitations of these White-centered approaches have been the lack of a framework to incorporate an understanding of the impacts of systemic oppression, generations of racism and discrimination, and the chronic stress and demoralizing effects of existing in multiple systems that have been designed to maintain, privilege, and advantage largely White power structures. This has led to us collectively pathologizing the understandable, survival-related responses of Black people and Black communities to the pervasive traumas directly resulting from their experiences of systemic racism and the continuing consequences of chattel slavery.

We expressly have not pathologized racism, privilege, or White supremacy while at the same time pathologizing responses to racism and privilege and, in effect, blackness. In fact, one of our axiomatic admonitions as clinicians of maintaining clinical neutrality all but guarantees that racism and White supremacy go unchallenged and unaddressed. For many people who do not find relevance for themselves within the context of mainstream mental health care, it often seems that this questionable value of clinical neutrality takes precedence over our ethical obligations of beneficence and nonmaleficence. Continuing to ignore these systemic issues, inequities, and injustices causes demonstrable harm, especially when care providers, as part of these very same systems, benefit from the marginalization and exclusion of others.

It is imperative that we move beyond simply acquiring additional cultural knowledge as the be-all and end-all of cultural competency. While knowledge acquisition is obviously important, systemic problems require systemic changes. In the context of mental health care, this means a paradigm shift in how we think about mental health issues and, therefore, how we approach their amelioration. In addition to understanding the history and breadth of racism, an adequate foundation of antiblackness in mental health necessitates a collective continual and rigorous self-examination on implicit bias and the ways in which we benefit from privilege. Bias and privilege alter our behaviors, form the basis for our assumptions about others as well as ourselves, and ultimately are the mechanisms through which systemic racism becomes the everyday, the banal, and the ordinary.

In the United States we are on the verge of becoming a majority "minority" country (U.S. Census Bureau, 2021). This is already true for the population of those under 18. So what does it mean when providers and all those who are responsible for making decisions and granting power and privilege within our health care systems, businesses, organizations, and institutions are not nearly reflective of the demographics of our population? What are we actually asking when we regularly put the burden of racism education, training, and ultimately making systemic changes squarely on the worn shoulders of the very people who are experiencing the consequences of racism on a daily basis, rather than on those who are benefiting from and, intentionally or not, supporting White-focused systems? How can we even begin to provide adequate culturally attuned and intelligent care to all of our diverse communities to meet the ethical obligations implicit in *primum non nocere* ("First do no harm") when our paradigms of care are not set up to account for the most pressing issues impacting the mental health of Black people and Black communities?

These are just some of the pressing questions that started us on this journey. Through the insights of the contributors in this collection, we are endeavoring to enrich our understanding of the seminal role of experiences of antiblackness as a driving factor in mental health inequities. We explore the specifically problematic nature of the ubiquitous messages about the relative values of Black and Brown bodies and lives.

True healing in our communities is not possible without justice and equity as the driving forces of our approaches. When providers work with people from Black communities, the sine qua non of competency and ethical service provision must be a deep understanding of the history and continued impacts of racism, a recognition of the ways that racism is embedded in our institutions and our society at large, and humility about how limited our models of mental health and their amelioration are. Finally, for these interrelated systems to start to change, the mantle of reversing systemic racism must be taken up by White allies, starting with introspection on privilege and bias. Only then can we start to move toward a truly equitable praxis necessary for addressing the impacts of antiblackness.

Norman H. Kim, PhD

References

Hall, G. C. N., Berkman, E. T., Zane, N. W., Leong, F. T., Hwang, W. C., Nezu, A. M., Nezu, C. M., Hong, J. J., Chu, J. P., & Huang, E. R. (2021). Reducing mental health disparities by increasing the personal relevance of interventions. *American Psychologist, 76*(1), 91.

Martín-Baró, I. (1994). *Writings for a liberation psychology*. Harvard University Press.

Satcher Health Leadership Institute at Morehouse School of Medicine. (2022). *The economic burden of mental health inequities in the United States report*.

U.S. Census Bureau. (2021, August 12). *2020 U.S. population more racially and ethnically diverse than measured in 2010*. https://www.census.gov/library/stories/2021/08/2020-united-states-population-more-racially-ethnically-diverse-than-2010.html

U.S. Department of Health and Human Services. (2001). *Mental health: Culture, race, and ethnicity—A supplement to mental health: A report of the Surgeon General*. U.S. Department of Health and Human Services, Substance Abuse and Mental Health Services Administration, Center for Mental Health Services.

Acknowledgments

We want to thank our ancestors, our community, and our White allies. We want to thank our editor, Marisa Solis, because of whose efforts this book has come to fruition.

Contributors

Ashley Acle, MBA, MFT, LMFT
Consultant, Clinical Supervisor, &
Advocate
Private Practice
San Francisco, CA, USA

Tiffany Benford, MSW, LICSW
Clinical Coordinator/Diversity
Specialist
Counseling Department
Springfield College
Springfield, MA, USA

Gail C. Christopher, DN
Executive Director
National Collaborative for
Health Equity
Washington, DC, USA

Jennifer A. Coleman, PhD, MA
Assistant Professor
Department of Psychiatry and
Behavioral Sciences
Rush University Medical Center
Chicago, IL, USA

Jacqueline A. Conley, PhD, MA
Professor of Psychology
Department of Natural, Social, &
Behavioral Sciences
Edward Waters University
Jacksonville, FL, USA

Betty Neal Crutcher, PhD, MPH
Cross-Cultural Mentoring Consultant
Harvard University School of Medicine
Boston, MA, USA

Alyssa Davis, MS, RDN
Dietitian
California State University
Los Angeles, CA, USA

Cy'Tique T. Davis, PhD
Visiting Professor
Department of Natural, Social, &
Behavioral Sciences
Edward Waters University
Jacksonville, FL, USA

Kenneth Davis, PhD
Assistant Professor
Department of Natural, Social, &
Behavioral Sciences
Edward Waters University
Jacksonville, FL, USA

Alonzo C. DeCarlo, PhD, MSW
Vice President for Academic and
Student Affairs
Northwest Suburban College
Rolling Meadows, IL, USA

Gabrielle M. del Rey, MMFT
Graduate Research Assistant
Challenging Racism & Empowering
Communities Through Ethnocultural
Research
Department of Educational and
Psychological Studies
University of Miami
Miami, FL, USA

Felecia Dix-Richardson, PhD
Associate Professor of Criminology
Department of Sociology and Criminal
Justice
Florida A&M University
Tallahassee, FL, USA

Joelle Dorsett, BS
Counseling Psychology PhD Student
University of Miami
Miami, FL, USA

Renée Evans, PhD
Practice Owner, Clinical Counselor,
Professional School Counselor, and
Diversity and Inclusion Specialist
Private Practice
Raleigh, NC, USA

Alexis R. Franklin
Graduate Research Assistant
Challenging Racism & Empowering
Communities Through Ethnocultural
Research
Department of Educational and
Psychological Studies
University of Miami
Miami, FL, USA

**Mazella Fuller, PhD, MSW,
LCSW, CEDS-C**
Clinical Associate Counseling and
Psychological Services
Duke University
Co-founder and Principal, Institute for
Antiracism and Equity
Durham, NC, USA

Melissa A. Gutierrez, MSEd
Graduate Research Assistant
Challenging Racism & Empowering
Communities through Ethnocultural
Research
Department of Educational and
Psychological Studies
University of Miami
Miami, FL, USA

Kisha B. Holden, PhD, MSCR
Professor and Director
Morehouse School of Medicine
Atlanta, GA, USA

Rebecca Hurst, PhD
Associate Director of Clinical Services
Counseling Center
North Carolina State University
Raleigh, NC, USA

Mardy S. Ireland, PhD
Psychologist and Psychoanalyst
Private Practice
Raleigh, NC, USA

Janelle A. Johnson, LMFT-S
Doctoral Student and Graduate
Research Assistant
TELS Educational Equity
North Carolina State University
Raleigh, NC, USA

Shannon Z. Jones, PhD
Director of Biological Instruction
URISE Program Coordinator
University of Richmond
Richmond, VA, USA

Norman Kim, PhD
Diversity, Equity, and Inclusion Officer
Research Foundation for Mental
Hygiene and Center for Practice
Innovations
Columbia University Irving Medical
Center, Department of Psychiatry
Division of Behavioral Health Services
and Policy Research, Law, and Ethics
New York, NY, USA
Cofounder
Institute for Antiracism and Equity

Anh-Thuy H. Le, PhD
Clinical Psychologist
Virginia Commonwealth University
Richmond, VA, USA

Ceewin N. Louder, MA
Graduate Research Assistant
Challenging Racism & Empowering
Communities Through Ethnocultural
Research Lab
Department of Educational and
Psychological Studies
University of Miami
Miami, FL, USA

Liana Maneese, LPC, NCC, MA
Founder + Identity Navigation Specialist
The Good Peoples Group + Adopting
Identity
Pittsburgh, PA, USA

Brandon Wise Masters, MA
Graduate Research Assistant
Challenging Racism & Empowering
Communities Through Ethnocultural
Research
Department of Educational and
Psychological Studies
University of Miami
Miami, FL, USA

Keith W. McIntosh, EdD, MBA
Vice President and Chief Information
Officer
Information Services
University of Richmond
Richmond, VA, USA

Marisol L. Meyer
Graduate Research Assistant
Challenging Racism & Empowering
Communities Through Ethnocultural
Research
Department of Educational and
Psychological Studies
University of Miami
Miami, FL, USA

Randy B. Nelson, PhD
Director, Center for Law & Social Justice
College of Arts and Humanities
Bethune-Cookman University
Daytona Beach, FL, USA

Guerda Nicolas, PhD
Professor
Challenging Racism & Empowering
Communities Through Ethnocultural
Research
Department of Educational and
Psychological Studies
University of Miami
Miami, FL, USA

Camilla W. Nonterah, PhD
Assistant Professor of Health Psychology
Department of Psychology
University of Richmond
Richmond, VA, USA

Matthew Oware, PhD
Chair and Professor
Department of Sociology and
Anthropology
University of Richmond
Richmond, VA, USA

Colleen P. Ramsey, MD
Internal Medicine Doctor
Duke Health
Durham, NC, USA

Courtney E. Randolph, PhD, MHC
Professor of Psychology
Social and Behavioral Sciences
Edward Waters College
Jacksonville, FL, USA

Chateé Omísadé Richardson, PhD
Assistant Professor/Coordinator of
Field and Clinical Placements
Department of Education
Spelman College
Atlanta, GA, USA

**Carolyn Coker Ross, MD,
MPH, CEDS-C**
Addiction Medicine and Certified
Eating Disorder Specialist
CEO of The Anchor Program
Cofounder and Principal of the Institute
for Antiracism and Equity
San Diego, CA, USA

Ashanda Saint Jean, MD
Chair of Obstetrics and Gynecology
Health Alliance Hospitals of the Hudson
Valley/Westchester Medical Center
Health Network
Associate Professor
Department of OB/GYN
New York Medical College
Valhalla, NY, USA

Charlynn Small, PhD, LCP, CEDS-C
Assistant Director of Health Promotion
Clinical Psychologist
Counseling and Psychological Services
Co-founder and Principal, Institute for
Antiracism and Equity
University of Richmond
Richmond, VA, USA

Claire St. John, MPH, RDN, CEDS-C
Registered Dietitian in Private Practice
Los Angeles, CA, USA

Maisha Standifer, PhD, MPH
Director of Health Policy
Morehouse School of Medicine
Atlanta, GA, USA

Nerine Tatham, MD
Staff Psychiatrist
Counseling and Psychological Services
Duke University
Durham, NC, USA

Becky Thompson, PhD
Professor
Department of Sociology
Simmons University
Boston, MA, USA

Clare Twomey, MD
Ordained Minister and Copastor
Vista Grande, United Church of Christ
Colorado Springs, CO, USA

**Meyleen M. Velasquez, DSW, LICSW,
RPT-S, PMH-C**
Social Worker
Hummingbird Counseling PLLC
Seattle, WA, USA

Janie Victoria Ward, EdD
Professor Emerita
Departments of Education and Africana
Studies
Simmons University
Boston, MA, USA

Karen E. Watson
Communications Strategist
The Centre for Health Economics
& Policy Innovation, Imperial
College London
United Kingdom

Kris Watson, Esq, MD, JD
Cofounder and CEO
Nurturing Justice Inc.
New York, NY, USA

Delbert R. Wigfall, MD
Professor of Pediatrics and Associate
Dean of Medical Education
School of Medicine
Duke University
Durham, NC, USA

Joyce Woodson, MBA
Associate Director
Enterprise Production Operations
The Nature Conservancy
Arlington, VA, USA

Kideste Yusef, PhD
Associate Professor of Criminal Justice
Director of Center for Law and Social
Justice
Bethune-Cookman University
Daytona Beach, FL, USA

Introduction

Antiblackness and the Continuing Legacy of Systemic Racism in Mental Health Care

Norman Kim, Carolyn Coker Ross, Mazella Fuller, and Charlynn Small

> In August of 1619, a ship appeared on this horizon near Point Comfort, a coastal port in the British colony of Virginia. It carried more than 20 enslaved Africans, who were sold to the colonists. America was not yet America, but this was the moment it began. No aspect of the country that would be formed here has been untouched by the 250 years of slavery that followed.
>
> —The 1619 Project (Hannah-Jones et al., 2019).

So opens the groundbreaking reframing of American history by Nikole Hannah-Jones and the *New York Times*, written to commemorate the 400th anniversary of the arrival of the first "20 and odd" Africans who were captured, transported under horrific conditions, and then sold to the governor of Virginia. The 1619 Project justifiably and rightly centers the reality and subsequent consequences of slavery in the formation and subsequent growth of this country, a debt for which there has yet to be a full reckoning. The historical trauma of slavery continues to emerge and re-emerge through our lived experiences of mass incarceration, poverty, food and medical deserts, and poor educational systems. Black people are chronically grieving.

The foundational institution of slavery required a justification that allowed for the violent subjugation of Black people for the benefit of White people (Hannah-Jones, 2021). Maintaining the myth of American exceptionalism continues to rely on this subjugation and the accompanying elements of antiblackness that dictate that Black people remain at the bottom of the social hierarchy. Since the inception of the notion of blackness, antiblackness

Norman Kim, Carolyn Coker Ross, Mazella Fuller, and Charlynn Small, *Introduction* In: *Antiblackness and the Stories of Authentic Allies*. Edited by: Norman Kim, Carolyn Coker Ross, Mazella Fuller and Charlynn Small, Oxford University Press.
© Oxford University Press 2024. DOI: 10.1093/oso/9780197642535.003.0001

has been explicitly associated with numerous negative qualities reinforcing the racist ideas of the inferiority and savagery of the Black person. Likewise, it is equally explicitly associated with positivity, and by extension righteousness and enlightened nature, of whiteness. Anti-Black racism was thus established as justifiable prejudice in the United States. Antiblackness has become so embedded in all of our systems, organizations, and other elements of our society we are supposed to be able to rely on that even clear, quantifiable patterns of prejudice and bias are dismissed, and the recipients of that bias blamed.

For antiblackness to be made so ubiquitous, the Black person cannot be human and must instead be both dehumanized and othered. At a systemic level, this has gone beyond just dehumanizing Black people; there has been a rigorous, relentless, and continuing process of dehumanizing the recipients of this kind of discrimination. To conceptualize antiblackness as an ordinary conflict would imply that perspective, education, reason, or even legislation would be enough to ameliorate its impacts. Michael Dumas (2016) calls antiblackness "an irreconcilability between the Black and any sense of social or cultural regard" (p. 13). Antiblackness confers upon White people the right to both control and devalue Black bodies and lives for the purposes of advancing the economic interests of White people. Indeed, history has shown repeatedly that the systemic racism that evolved from chattel slavery is based in maintaining economic advantages to White people and White systems, which is also why it has proven so resistant to attempts at rectification.

Black people do not need this anthology to elucidate the systemic inequities in the health care system that continue to negatively impact their communities and families. Black people live with these inequities every day, they encounter them when they try to access care, and stories of these inequities are well quilted into the fabric of their collective family histories. These inequities are but some of the myriad lasting consequences of slavery and institutionalized racism. But equal access to health care is nevertheless an important bellwether of the true and genuine commitment of our society to social justice for all Americans.

This divide in the way that Black people versus White people are evaluated and cared for by our health care systems is very evident in the discrepancies with which mental health issues are treated. Indeed, psychiatry itself has been used as a justification for mistreatment of Blacks and the perpetuation of segregation. Stemming from the racist belief that Blacks were biologically inferior, antebellum physician Samuel Cartwright (1793–1863) codified these widely held beliefs into medical canon by devising *drapetomania*, a psychiatric illness characterized by the overwhelming desire of some slaves to escape the purported beneficence of slavery, and *dysaesthesia aethiopica*, a disease affecting "Negroes" characterized by cognitive dullness, laziness, and physiologic insensitivity. These abhorrent, racist notions based in pseudoscience were used to justify the maltreatment and lack of treatment of Blacks in the health care system and elsewhere.

These inequities are clearly not an artifact of history; they continue, and their impact on Black people and Black communities is as pervasive as it is vast. These disparities in both access and care are also not simply a matter of socioeconomic status, which is often cited as a proxy for race and ethnicity. In his book *Black and Blue: The Origins and Consequences of Medical Racism*, John Hoberman (2012) makes the point that while "the [B]lack middle class . . . has better access to medical services than the [B]lack or white poor" (p. 148), Black Americans of any socioeconomic status must still deal with the consequences of systemic racism when accessing and receiving health care.

Health care organizations and providers still exist within a system that does not treat all of its citizens equally and with equal regard, and those implicit biases are evident in the quality of care that Black Americans routinely receive. Black Americans are, for all intents and purposes, entering into a fundamentally different system than their White peers. Nowhere is this intersection of access and systemic barriers more evident than in mental health.

The disproportionate impact of mental health issues on those from marginalized communities who are affected mirrors their relative levels of privilege in society as determined by identity factors such as race and ethnicity, gender and gender identity, sexuality, disability, age, education, or socioeconomic status. People who exist in positions of disadvantage and who have been disenfranchised face significant barriers when attempting to access mental health care, and people existing with privilege have increased access and tend to receive better, more appropriate care (Office of the Surgeon General, 2001).

This asymmetry is hard-wired into the very systems that people from marginalized communities are attempting to access, and it has served to maintain and worsen existing inequities. Historically, in the context of mental health care, both diagnoses and treatments have been used to further disadvantage those people from marginalized identities. Our current disease model tends to be overly reductionistic, separating out mental health issues from the social contexts in which they are inculcated, develop, and thrive.

While the growing body of evidence from brain research, genetics, treatment outcomes, and other disciplines examining psychiatric illnesses has absolutely yielded an enormously beneficial understanding of psychiatric illnesses and their treatments, there is also an essential corollary conversation to be had about the limitations and implications of the disease model for many people from marginalized communities (Shim et al., 2014).

As a field, we continue to do a great disservice to people who have experienced systemic racism, discrimination, and harassment by focusing on the symptoms that result from chronic exposure to these traumatic experiences rather than the context in which these experiences are allowed to happen (Kirkinis et al., 2021). Treating the trauma reactions that result from chronic experiences of racism is tantamount to prescribing ibuprofen to treat a headache and calling it a day rather than addressing the tumor that might be the root cause of the headaches in the first place.

In effect, we are pathologizing Black and Brown people's understandable and survival-based reactions to discrimination, racism, and poverty. We pathologize the victims of racism rather than the racism itself. We focus on treating these symptoms rather than trying to prevent these "symptoms" from being necessary consequences in the first place, thus ensuring that racism and the legion of institutions and systems that have been developed to support inequity and discrimination continue to thrive. While there are many layers of beneficiaries to this status quo, the people who are experiencing these traumas are certainly not among them.

In fact, this focus on treatment rather than prevention is in and of itself discriminatory. In looking at our various treatment modalities, it is clear that medications, therapy, treatment programs, and other treatment approaches are all significantly more accessible to some than others. In addition, our psychotherapeutic approaches and structures were developed in a specific Western European context that focused on the individual and one's specific developmental trajectory. This context also establishes a clear "default" for what is still considered normative (namely whiteness, cis-maleness, heteronormativity) against which all other groups and identities ought to be measured to determine what is pathological.

Many people of color and their families come from more collectivistic cultures and communities, where the focus is much more on the group or collective (including families, extended family, community, ancestors, etc.) over the individual, and where greater focus and value are put on interconnectedness with others rather than individuation or individual needs. Not only do most of our theories of development and normative psychological functioning put greater value on individualistic traits over collectivistic ones, both also the mechanisms of change and the units of change in treatment tend to be at the level of the individual.

In contrast, a prevention-focused approach to mental health issues would, by definition, involve all members of the larger community, group, or society. Our relative lack of focus on prevention efforts, for which the goal would be to inoculate an entire community rather than just certain individuals, serves to maintain the status quo wherein Black people's mental health tends to be an afterthought rather than the primary focus. In the context of anti-Black racism, prevention would also mean addressing racism more directly as being rooted in the prevailing White supremacy of our culture and institutions, which itself would require a collective resolve by those who benefit to eradicate it despite the advantages it confers upon White people.

This focus on individuals rather than the larger contexts in which they exist is a significant limitation to our current approach to mental health, which reflects an ontological stance that, intentional or not, serves to support anti-Black efforts, namely that the presumed biological determinants of diseases are of greater importance than the social determinants (such as structural racism and discrimination). As long as this remains axiomatic, we risk continuing to believe that our role as mental health care providers does not include looking at the historical and structural roots of the distress Black people experience and does not include looking at providers' own biases and how they might impact upon the treatments offered to Black clients versus non-Black clients.

American psychiatrist and scholar of White identity Jonathan Metzl (2010) has written that the racist ideas that were encoded in our history of mental health diagnoses and practices have not improved much since the days of Cartwright's *drapetomania*. Clear footprints of this ignominious history can still be seen in mainstream psychiatric practice. The addition of the word "aggressive" into the definition of schizophrenia was quickly followed by the marketing of psychiatric medications for use in Black patients, who were seen as more "out of control" and, by implication, more in need of being controlled.

The long-term echoes of this continuing pattern of pathologizing Black people are still evident in disparities in the rates with which many psychiatric illnesses are diagnosed, despite the lack of an epidemiologic foundation. This pathologizing of blackness, the numerous barriers for Black people trying to access mental health care, and the overrepresentation of Black people in the prison system (which itself has become a de facto albeit ill-equipped mental health service provider; Meerai et al., 2016) intersect to lay the groundwork for the current mental health crisis in Black communities. Moreover, all three elements also have their roots in antiblackness and our history of slavery, further perpetuating racist notions of blackness. As a result of these systemic biases in mental health care, the mental health needs of the Black community continue not to be addressed.

The Human Genome Project (Collins & Mansoura, 2001) revealed that our human genetics are 99.9% the same from one individual to the next. Whether consciously or unconsciously, with complicity or through complacency, we nevertheless continue to operate with both explicit and implicit notions of the innate superiority of whiteness. Black people, along with legions of others whose identities have been marginalized and devalued by our society and those holding on to power, have a different daily existence as a result of being denigrated (from the Latin *denigrare*, meaning to blacken or darken, the Latin root of which is *niger*) and disenfranchised despite our genetic sameness. The racism and discrimination experienced due to these invented differences have had devastating impacts on the collective mental health of Black communities, a burden they will continue to bear for the foreseeable future.

Antiblackness is at its core a mental health issue, the mechanisms of which we are beginning to better understand. The Adverse Childhood Experiences (ACE) study (Felitti et al., 1998) vividly demonstrated that children who experience violence, sexual abuse, emotional abuse or neglect, poverty, and discrimination are significantly more likely to develop myriad health and mental health problems. Black children are at even greater risk of experiencing multiple adverse childhood experiences, and therefore Black people are at increased risk of experiencing the attendant negative consequences to their psychological and physical well-being. Given the overwhelming evidence of the long-term, enduring impact of experiencing discrimination and systemic racism on Black communities, one must wonder why this understanding is not reflected in how we conceptualize, and therefore treat, mental health issues.

Instead, the widespread impacts and chronicity of these experiences of antiblackness are currently exacerbated, rather than alleviated, by our mental health care systems due to lack of training, lack of appropriateness in our models of assessment and treatment, and, more pointedly, lack of will of mental health systems to more effectively address race-based issues and disparities. This is a complex situation that requires not only political and institutional resolve and resources but also clear guidelines and a paradigm shift in our overall approaches.

Given the complexities of the legacies of chattel slavery and racism, whose impacts continue to magnify rather than lessen over time, it is particularly concerning that there is a significant and disproportionate lack of diversity in mental health professions. According to data examining the racial and ethnic makeup of the mental health workforce, 64% of psychiatrists (Wyse et al., 2020) and 84% of psychologists are White people (American Psychological Association, 2022), along with 76% of counselors and 65% of social workers (U.S. Bureau of Labor Statistics, 2021). These data stand in stark contrast to the more than 42% of the overall U.S. population made up of people from various non-White ethnic minority groups. This discrepancy is even more concerning since the communities that have the greatest shortages of mental health professionals also tend to be communities with the highest proportions of racial and ethnic minorities. As the demographic makeup of the United States becomes increasingly diverse, this disparity will only widen.

Right now, the onus of the work of combating racism is on those who are impacted—people of color—which in no way addresses the roots of systemic racism and discrimination. We also need to treat mental health issues that impact Black and Brown communities as the social justice issues that they are. One way to address this imbalance is by starting with the lived experiences of those impacted by systemic racism, for these narratives live in the bodies of Black and Brown people. It is imperative that we listen to the stories and collective wisdom of the people who have been directly impacted and actively commit to doing our own internal work to educate ourselves on issues of bias and privilege.

If we are to treat racism as the root disease causing multiple negative health outcomes in Black communities, we must commit to understanding antiblackness and the lived experiences of systemic racism. To have any chance of success, we must also focus on the elements of antiracist work that most directly involve White communities, which directly and indirectly benefit from structural racism. A full picture of antiblackness requires an examination of the collective voices and stories of the lived experiences of whiteness and White privilege, assessing cultural, historical, political, and economic factors as well as White experiences and perspectives of social justice and equity. It is vital to highlight the connections between power and privilege to antiblackness to adequately begin to think about what an equitable and just society might look like.

Because it is the default, whiteness is the ultimate asset, allowing for more social mobility, greater opportunities, and fewer barriers. Being of and from the majority culture, White people can fear, critique, or ignore anything outside of the dominant culture, but they can also appropriate or steal what they wish from other cultures without fear of reprisal or reprimand. In her seminal paper *White Privilege and Male Privilege*, Peggy McIntosh (1989) asserted that being a White person in the United States consists of "unearned advantages" and "conferred dominance." It confers the power to minimize the worth of Black people, harm them, and deny them rights to life, liberty, and the pursuit of happiness.

We must stop pathologizing blackness and asking Black people to continue to shoulder the burdens of racism. It is instead incumbent upon the various systems addressed in this anthology to change to meet the challenges presented by antiblackness. This anthology aims to focus on narratives revolving around the lived experiences of antiblackness and how to activate that understanding into a commitment and readiness to dismantle systemic oppression. This collection of narratives recognizes that all our struggles are intimately connected and that we must work together to create and embody change.

The contributors to this anthology endeavor to challenge and make explicit for the purposes of critical analysis the presumptive virtue of prioritizing White people's comfort and well-being at the expense of other groups' manacled social and economic immobility, physical well-being, emotional distress, and attempted desolation. Ignoring or minimizing this trade-off, which acts as a powerful barrier to engaging in this essential work, prevents the honesty and humility that this work requires. Finally, the contributors herein hope to add to the stories and narratives of countless other Black people and communities who have demonstrated, despite the inability and unwillingness of our current systems, resolve in the face of attempted subjugation, honor in the face of dehumanization, and tremendous resiliency in the face of trauma.

References

American Psychological Association. (2022). *Demographics of U.S. psychology workforce* [Interactive data tool]. https://www.apa.org/workforce/data-tools/demographics

Collins, F. S., & Mansoura, M. K. (2001). The Human Genome Project: Revealing the shared inheritance of all humankind. *Cancer, 91*(1 Suppl), 221–225.

Dumas, M. J. (2016). Against the dark: Antiblackness in education policy and discourse. *Theory Into Practice*, *55*(1), 11–19.

Felitti, V. J., Anda, R. F., Nordenberg, D., Williamson, D. F., Spitz, A. M., Edwards, V., & Marks, J. S. (1998). Relationship of childhood abuse and household dysfunction to many of the leading causes of death in adults: The Adverse Childhood Experiences (ACE) study. *American Journal of Preventive Medicine*, *14*(4), 245–258.

Hannah-Jones, N. (2021). *The 1619 project: A new origin story*. One World.

Hannah-Jones, N., Elliott, M., Hughes, J., & Silverstein, J., New York Times Company Smithsonian Institution, & 1619 Project. (2019, August 18). The 1619 project. *New York Times Magazine*.

Hoberman, J. (2012). *Black and blue: The origins and consequences of medical racism*. University of California Press.

Kirkinis, K., Pieterse, A. L., Martin, C., Agiliga, A., & Brownell, A. (2021). Racism, racial discrimination, and trauma: A systematic review of the social science literature. *Ethnicity & Health*, *26*(3), 392–412.

McIntosh, P. (1989). *White privilege and male privilege: A personal account of coming to see correspondences through work in women's studies*. Wellesley College Center for Research on Women.

Meerai, S., Abdillahi, I., & Poole, J. (2016). An introduction to anti-Black sanism. *Intersectionalities: A Global Journal of Social Work Analysis, Research, Polity, and Practice*, *5*(3), 18–35.

Metzl, J. M. (2010). *The protest psychosis: How schizophrenia became a black disease*. Beacon Press.

Office of the Surgeon General. (2001). *Mental health: Culture, race, and ethnicity: A supplement to mental health: A report of the surgeon general*. US & Center for Mental Health Services.

Shim, R., Koplan, C., Langheim, F. J., Manseau, M. W., Powers, R. A., & Compton, M. T. (2014). The social determinants of mental health: An overview and call to action. *Psychiatric Annals*, *44*(1), 22–26.

U.S. Bureau of Labor Statistics. (2021, January 20). *Labor force statistics from the current population survey* [Data set]. https://www.bls.gov/cps/cpsaat11.htm

Wyse, R., Hwang, W. T., Ahmed, A. A., Richards, E., & Deville, C., Jr. (2020). Diversity by race, ethnicity, and sex within the US psychiatry physician workforce. *Academic Psychiatry*, *44*(5), 523–530.

PART I

ANTIBLACKNESS AND
THE LEGACY OF SLAVERY

1

Slavery and Race-Based Trauma

The Impact of Historical and Intergenerational Trauma on Health

Carolyn Coker Ross

Historical Trauma

> Historical trauma is multigenerational trauma experienced by a specific cultural, racial or ethnic group. It is related to major events that oppressed a particular group of people because of their status as oppressed, such as slavery, the Holocaust, forced migration, and the violent colonization of Native Americans.
>
> —Administration for Children and Families (2017)

Historical trauma is a phrase first used in the examination of trauma effects in offspring of Holocaust survivors and Japanese Americans interned during World War II. While many in such groups experienced no effects of historical trauma, others experienced low self-esteem, depression, self-destructive behavior, a marked propensity for violent or aggressive behavior, substance use disorders, and high rates of suicide and cardiovascular disease. Historical trauma can be magnified when superimposed on current lifespan individual trauma. Parental trauma can disrupt parenting skills, contributing to behavior problems in children. Historical trauma can also damage cultural identity (Sotero, 2006).

A review of the literature has shown that there are four assumptions that underpin historical trauma theory:

1. Trauma is deliberately and systematically directed at a target population by a subjugating, dominant population.
2. Trauma occurs not just as one catastrophic event, but continues for an extended period.

Carolyn Coker Ross, *Slavery and Race-Based Trauma* In: *Antiblackness and the Stories of Authentic Allies.*
Edited by: Norman Kim, Carolyn Coker Ross, Mazella Fuller and Charlynn Small, Oxford University Press.
© Oxford University Press 2024. DOI: 10.1093/oso/9780197642535.003.0002

3. The traumatic events affect an entire population, creating a widespread, universal experience of trauma.
4. The magnitude of the trauma hijacks the population from its natural trajectory, leaving behind a legacy of physical, psychological, social, and economic disparities that affect many generations (Sotero, 2006).

Slavery as Historical Trauma

The shameful paradox of continuing chattel slavery in a nation founded on individual freedom, scholars today assert, led to a hardening of the racial caste system.

—Hannah-Jones (2019)

From the time the first slaves arrived in the American colonies in 1619, every part of America was impacted by the enterprise of slavery. While slavery is not unique to the Americas, what is unique is the codification of slaves as "chattel" (defined as "a personal possession"), which meant the enslaved could be owned by other human beings.

The original justification for the enslavement of Africans was that they were un-Christian heathens, and it was the duty of the White man to save their souls. As antislavery movements began to emerge, proslavery forces began to construct new arguments to defend slavery, and the construct of race emerged along with the notion that Africans were an inferior race who were born to be enslaved. The right to continue bringing slaves from West Africa to the Americas as well as the right to keep their descendants enslaved was supported by pseudoscience that held that slaves were subhuman.

Before the 1830s, portrayals of BlackAmericans as inferior were rare, but by mid-century this thought dominated popular and scholarly thought (Smedley, 1997). The *Dred Scott* decision of 1857 lent support to this doctrine of White superiority by ruling that Black people come from a "slave race" (and are not part of the human race) and therefore could not be eligible to be citizens (Lee, 2019).

American chattel slavery was unique in other ways. It rarely allowed for a slave to be freed or to purchase his or her own freedom. In other societies where slavery existed, children born to enslaved individuals were born free, which was not the case in the Americas. In few societies were people deemed to be less than human based solely on physical appearance. This enabled slave owners to justify brutality, rape, and other atrocities and to continue the subjugation of slaves (DeGruy, 2005; Sotero, 2006).

Links Between Historical Trauma and Disease Prevalence and Health Disparities

> Trauma in a person, decontextualized over time, looks like personality. Trauma in a family, decontextualized over time, looks like family traits. Trauma in a people, decontextualized over time looks like culture.
>
> —Resmaa Menakem (Tippett, 2020)

Historical trauma theory is based on the synthesis between the physical, psychological, and social pathways linking historical trauma to the prevalence of disease and health disparities (Figure 1.1). Historical trauma requires the subjugation of a population by a dominant group. Successful subjugation, in turn, requires (Sotero, 2006):

1. overwhelming violence—physical and psychological
2. segregation or displacement of the population from its natural habitat
3. economic deprivation
4. the dispossession of the population's culture

In the historical trauma model, the first generation of the population directly experiences subjugation and loss, as did our African ancestors. An estimated 2 million African ancestors died in the middle passage crossing the Atlantic on the way to the colonies (Statista, 2021). Upon arrival at the colonies and through the generations that slavery continued, approximately 6 million Africans and their offspring died enslaved.

Families were separated from their husbands, wives, children, and grandchildren, which had the impact of cultural and family rupture, with Black women often raising children alone—a condition that continues in the Black community today wherein 30% of Black households (vs. 9% of White households) have no husband.

Throughout the period of slavery, enslaved people suffered numerous traumas, degradation, beatings, rapes, and other atrocities. They were

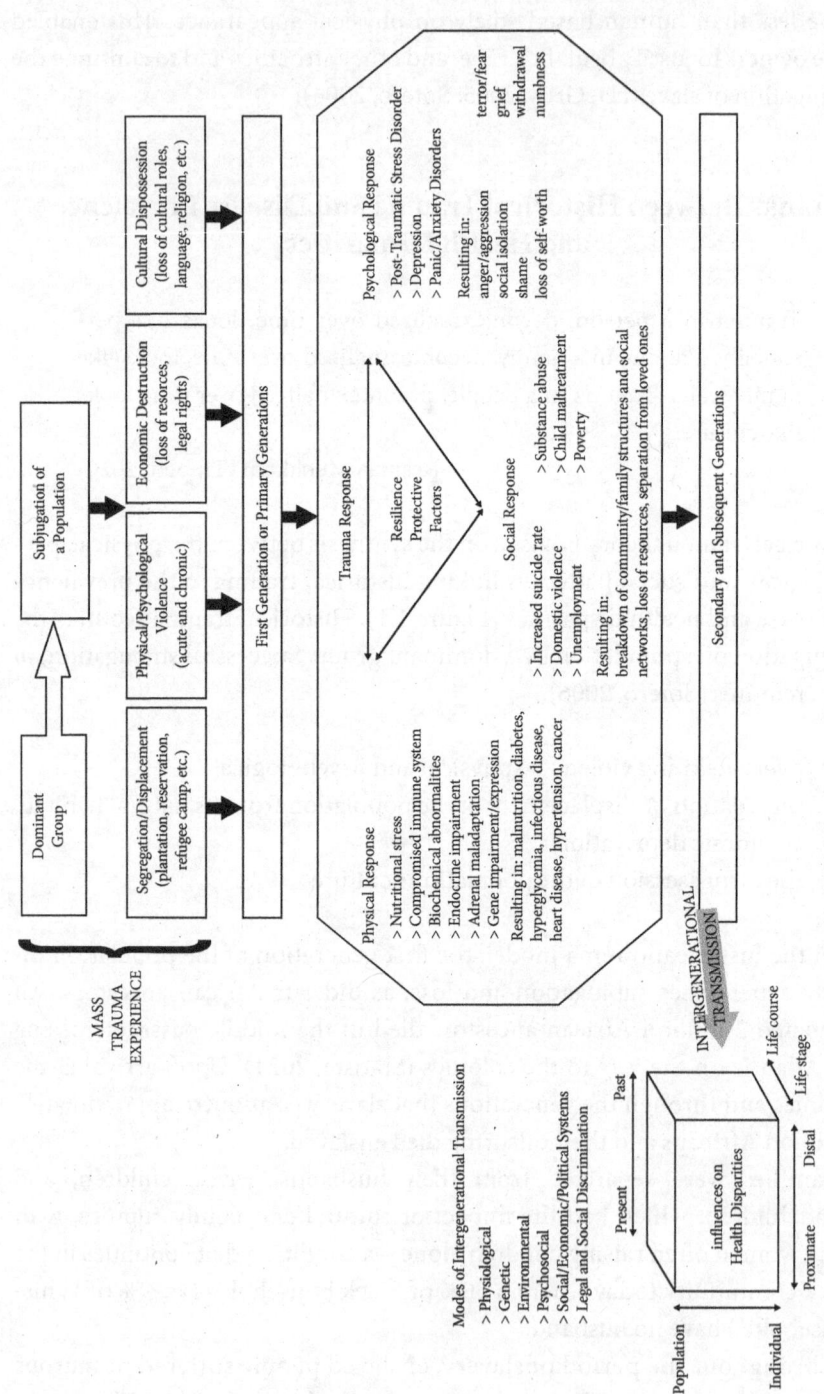

Figure 1.1 A Conceptual Model of Historical Trauma

denied access to medical care, forced to work all hours of the day and night, not allowed to learn to read or write, made to live on meager rations, housed in shacks, and forced to sleep on pallets on the floor. Mothers who had recently given birth were forced to return to the fields as soon as possible, often having to leave their infants without adequate care, causing up to 50% infant mortality by some estimates (Owens & Fett, 2019).

Due to extreme stress and grief from loss of family, loss of land and country, and loss of their original way of life, trauma manifested in this first generation in the form of posttraumatic stress disorder (PTSD), depression, self-destructive behaviors, suicide, anxiety, hostility, and chronic grief and could be transmuted into physical diseases and vice versa.

Second and subsequent generations were affected in multiple ways too. In many, the original trauma caused impairment in parenting or attachment insecurity. Maternal malnutrition impacted the quality of breast milk and caused low birth weight in infants. Prenatal metabolic adaptations to race-based traumatic stress (RBTS) have been linked to stress reactivity and diabetes risk in offspring. Maladaptive behaviors such as substance abuse, physical/sexual abuse, and suicide can directly traumatize offspring, and these effects can be transmitted to subsequent generations epigenetically.

Historical trauma effects can also be transmitted through oral tradition, storytelling, and collective memory, leading to "vicarious traumatization." Offspring are taught to share in their ancestors' pain, causing mistrust, unresolved grief, and feelings of persecution. The health disparities in historically traumatized populations can be understood as resulting from cumulative effects of social conditions and disease over multiple generations (Sotero, 2006).

Noted researcher Dr. Joy DeGruy has described these effects of the historical trauma of slavery as "posttraumatic slave syndrome"—the adaptive trauma responses seen in descendants of enslaved peoples that are exacerbated by the ongoing race-based trauma and microaggressions experienced by most Black Americans in their everyday lives. These include low self-esteem, a sense of a foreshortened future, self-destructive behaviors, vacant esteem (hopelessness, depression, and a general self-destructive outlook), a marked propensity for violence, and internalized racism (DeGruy, 2005).

Intergenerational Transmission of Historical Trauma Effects

Historical trauma is intergenerational trauma experienced by a specific cultural group that has a history of being systematically oppressed.
— Administration for Children and Families (2017)

Research has shown that despite their unique environments, lifestyles, and personal histories, historically subjugated populations consistently demonstrate poorer health outcomes compared to the general population (Conching & Thayer, 2019). The association between childhood adversity and adult health has been clearly shown by the Adverse Childhood Experiences (ACE) study, which reported an increased risk for over 40 mental and physical health conditions—including the top five causes of death in the United States (heart disease, diabetes, stroke, cancer, and lung disease) and now COVID—in adults with a history of childhood adversity. The ACE study also showed a negative relationship between number of adverse childhood experiences and adult education, employment, and income potential (Felitti et al., 1998; Metzler et al., 2017).

Studies have shown that environmental experiences such as exposure to trauma and toxic stressors can cause epigenetic changes, leading to changes in gene expression that can modify several physiological systems, including the hypothalamic–pituitary–adrenal axis, which governs stress management, the immune system, and the cardiovascular system (Conching & Thayer, 2019). Epigenetic changes can also change expression of genes for mental illness, depression, or PTSD, and these changes may be passed to subsequent generations.

Maladaptive behaviors and their resulting social problems, including substance use disorders, physical or sexual abuse, and suicidality, can directly traumatize offspring, perpetuating the intergenerational cycle of trauma (Sotero, 2006). African Americans are exposed to more trauma and stress than Whites throughout the lifespan, with 61% of Black children having at least one adverse childhood experiences compared to 41% for non-Hispanic White children (CAHMI, 2018). African Americans are twice as likely to live in poverty than the general population, increasing their risk for financial insecurity and other related stressors. Understanding the association between trauma and stress and its effect on the epigenome is important because epigenetic changes (unlike changes in DNA) can potentially be reversed (Waterland & Jirtle, 2003), which could interrupt the cycle of health risks of populations exposed to collective and systemic traumas.

The Impact of Race-Based Trauma on Health

A meta-analysis of studies on race-based trauma (Carter, 2007) found that negative race-based encounters produce extreme stress and that these negative RBTS events have a significant effect on an individual's mental and physical health. There is mounting evidence that the association between perceived experiences of racism and attendant psychological distress is robust and plays an important role in health disparities (Pieterse et al., 2012).

Race-based traumatic events tend to be internalized and may present as depression, which seems to occur whether the event is perceived to be stressful or not. Another unique factor related to RBTS is the likelihood that these events will reoccur multiple times over the lifespan, leading to chronic trauma reactions. As well, newer research has pointed to epigenetic changes that may have caused physiological changes in the stress response system from parents or grandparents whose gene expression was changed by their own experiences of RBTS, including from historical traumas such as slavery (Carter et al., 2020).

Legacy of Slavery: The Wealth Gap

> A vast wealth gap, driven by segregation, redlining, evictions and exclusion, separates black and white America.
>
> —Lee (2019)

Of all the forms of subjugation that were visited upon enslaved Africans and their descendants, perhaps the most persistent and long-lasting legacy of slavery was and continues to be economic subjugation, that is, the wealth gap between Blacks and Whites that continues to this day. African Americans paid the cost for building America with their labor, but the economic benefits derived from slavery accrued solely to White American slave owners whose states before the Civil War were the wealthiest in the nation. In fact, right before the Civil War, the Mississippi valley was home to more millionaires per capita than anywhere else in the United States (Craemer et al., 2020; Desmond, 2019)).

Whites living in the North also contributed to economic subjugation of African Americans. Many stores and factories refused to hire Blacks. Restaurants refused to serve them. Many midwestern towns forcibly evicted Black residents and became sundown towns (don't let the sun set on you in this town). Edward Baptist argues in his book, *The Half Has Never Been Told: Slavery and the Making of American Capitalism* (Baptist EE, 2014), that the forced migration and subsequent harsh treatment of slaves in the cotton fields were integral to establishing the United States as a world economic power (NPR, 2014).

The wealth gap between Blacks and Whites is the result of the intergenerational and systemic nature of racial disparities beginning with slavery and continuing with racial massacres and racial terror lynchings after the Civil War and discrimination during the Jim Crow era, during and after World War II, and after the civil rights movement. . There are many estimates on what it would take in reparations to close the wealth gap wherein White Americans hold eight times the wealth of Black Americans. One proporsal builds on the well-known link between life expectancy and wealth. A recent study (Himmelstein, Lawrence, et al., 2022) proposed that payments to Black Americans of $828, 055 would close the longevity gap between Black and White individuals by 65.0% to 102.5%. This would lead to an improvement in wealth and therefore, longevity, as well as improving housing, education, healthcare—overall allowing Black communities to thrive.

The descendants of enslaved people in America have, for the most part, not been able to benefit from intergenerational transmission of wealth, for example in the form of parental gifts of higher educations, cultural experiences, or social contacts that can be a launching ground for better jobs, higher pay, and increased savings. Nor can most Black families grow their wealth by inheritance (Craemer et al., 2020).

A rare example of restitution is the return of Bruce's Beach (a beach formerly for Black Americans in Los Angeles), which was taken from the family that owned it in 1924 for racist reasons. In 2022, this prime property, in what is now known as Manhattan Beach, was returned to the descendants of the original owners, but this could not make up for the loss of potential intergenerational wealth that resulted from the original seizure of the land.

Race-Based Terrorism

After slavery ended, lynchings were a vicious tool of control to re-establish White supremacy and to trample African Americans' civil rights. There were more than 4,000 racial terror lynchings that occurred from 1877 to 1950 in 20 states. The lynchings were public events that were meant to instill fear in the Black community and a technique to enforce racial exploitation—economic, political, and cultural—in an attempt to restore the subjugation of African Americans (Equal Justice Initiative [EJI], 2017).

The Role of Police and the Criminal Justice System in Perpetuating Violence

Often White mobs were aided by the police in perpetrating racial violence. Police violence against Black Americans was put in the spotlight in 2020 with the murder of George Floyd, which led to mass protests in over 60 countries and on all seven continents. This explosion of outrage was not just for one man's murder but also in response to the thousands of other Black men, women, and children murdered by police annually, most of whose deaths go unpunished. The criminal justice system in the United States is a historical stronghold for systemic racism and a legacy of slavery.

The EJI (n.d.) notes that ending mass incarceration is "the civil rights issue of our times." The United States represents 5% of the world's population but 25% of the incarcerated population. Spending for jails and prisons went from $7.4 billion in 1975 to $87 billion in 2015, and during that time the prison population grew from 200,000 to 2.2 million (Bronson & Carson, 2019). Racial disparities are found at every level of the prison system, and higher rates of incarceration have not been shown to reduce violent crime (Stemen, 2017). Mass incarceration policies have led to 10 million Americans having an immediate family member in jail or prison, more than 4.5 million Americans losing the right to vote, and a loss of $87 billion in gross domestic product. Black adults are 50% more likely to have a family member incarcerated than White adults and three times more likely to have a family member incarcerated for more than 1 year (FWD.us, 2014; Kelley, 2017). Most telling is the statement by former president Richard Nixon's domestic policy advisor, John Erlichman, who admitted in a 1994 interview that the War on Drugs began as a crusade to criminalize Blacks and the antiwar Left.

I'm sure I'm not alone in having members of my own family swept up in this crusade.

The Reckoning

Historical trauma has been called a "disease of time."
—Aboriginal Healing Foundation (2004)

There is a reckoning that is needed in American culture. The murder of George Floyd that sparked protests around the world was a sign that Black people around the globe expect and are willing to fight for this reckoning. The following section indicates some of the spaces where this reckoning must occur.

Medicine and Psychology

Racial and ethnic minorities experience a lower quality of health services and are less likely to receive even routine medical procedures than are white Americans.
—Institute of Medicine (2003)

Black Americans continue to die up to 5 years earlier than White Americans. Findings from the Institute of Medicine (2003) report, published 20 years ago, still hold true today—Black and Latinx Americans have higher rates of morbidity and mortality than White Americans, a fact highlighted by the COVID pandemic.

Currently medical systems rarely connect trauma of any kind with disease presentation or health outcomes. This lack of awareness and understanding of the critical role played by trauma has hurt people of color. One example is the way in which being in a larger body, which is more common to Black women, has been stigmatized and denigrated as being morally inferior and the cause of health inequities when, in fact, historical trauma is the original deepest root cause of these health disparities.

It is important that health care providers make it their individual mission to educate themselves about the health effects of trauma, especially race-based trauma, and that professional institutions own up to the extensive damage that has been done in the name of science to Black people around the globe.

The American Psychological Association has taken a step in this direction by admitting psychology's role in perpetuating racism and adopting a resolution to change that, and the American Medical Association has adopted guidelines to confront racism. However, this will make no dent in the power of systemic racism unless health professionals' education includes the same acknowledgment and information regarding the racist underpinnings of medicine and its complicity in the historical trauma of slavery.

This reckoning must not stop at education but should also include a focus on health care practitioners' attitudes and biases and a discussion of culture and racism and how it impacts the patient–provider interaction. Moreover, it is important that health care providers learn the importance of respect for their patients' culture. Cross-cultural training of health care providers should occur very early and teach skills and tools that can be used in practice, and there should be ongoing culturally specific education for anyone working in healthcare and mental or behavioral health.

Communities

Research has shown that educating people about historical trauma and enabling them to share their grief with others improves grief resolution and creates a release from blame and guilt about health status. These modalities may also empower individuals and communities to focus on addressing the root causes of health disparities in a way that is more culturally competent (Brave Heart, 2010; Sotero, 2006).

We need to fight for teachers and others who touch the lives of children to be educated about the impact of childhood trauma, to do mandatory universal screening of all children for trauma, and to be able to offer training and counseling for parents and children who have been traumatized. While this is a daunting expectation, imagine what impact preschool through high school teachers, pediatricians, therapists, and psychologists could have if they were educated and motivated to do this.

National

The national reckoning is unavoidable as the U.S. population is more multiracial and diverse than in the past. Black and Brown people around the world are crying out for change and are no longer willing to accept platitudes or have their viewpoints pushed aside. Systemic racism has played an active role in education, health care, housing and home ownership, the justice system, and the wealth gap. It is not enough to ignore the past or to make half-hearted attempts at correcting injustices. To make substantive change, we must hold our elected officials, schools, neighbors, friends, and family to new standards of systemic equality.

When the true history of the American people includes an accounting of slavery and the intergenerational transmission of race-based trauma to the descendants of the enslaved, when we admit to America's original sin of enslaving an entire group of people based on an invented social construct called "race" done out of greed, and when we no longer lie to justify this sin by using pseudoscience to blame the victims of this sin, Americans can begin to heal in earnest as well.

References

Aboriginal Healing Foundation. (2004). *Historic trauma and aboriginal healing.* Anishinabe Printing. http://www.ahf.ca

Administration for Children and Families. (2017). *What is historical trauma?* https://www.acf.hhs.gov/trauma-toolkit/trauma-concept

Baptist, E. E. (2014). *The half that has never been told.* New York. https://www.hachettebookgroup.com/imprint/basic-books/

Brave Heart, M. (2010). The return to the sacred path: Healing historical trauma and historical unresolved grief response among the Lakota through a psychoeducational group intervention. *Smith College Studies in Social Work, 68*(3), 287–305.

Bronson, J., & Carson, E. A. (2019, April). *Prisoners in 2017.* Bureau of Justice Statistics. https://bjs.ojp.gov/content/pub/pdf/p17.pdf

Carter, R. T. (2007). Racism and psychological and emotional injury: Recognizing and assessing race-based traumatic stress. *The Counseling Psychologist, 35*, 13–105. http://dx.doi.org/10.1177/0011000006292033

Carter, R. T., Kirkinis, K., & Johnson, V. E. (2020). Relationships between trauma symptoms and race-based traumatic stress. *Traumatology, 26*(1), 11–18. https://doi.org/10.1037/trm0000217

Child and Adolescent Health Measurement Initiative (CAHMI), Data Resource Center for Child and Adolescent Health. (2018). 2016 National Survey of Children's Health: Child and Family Health Measures and Subgroups, SPSS Codebook, Version 2.0. www.childhealthdata.org

Conching, A. K. S., & Thayer, Z. (2019). Biological pathways for historical trauma to affect health: A conceptual model focusing on epigenetic modifications. *Social Science & Medicine, 230*, 74–82. https://doi.org/10.1016/j.socscimed.2019.04.001

Craemer, T., Smith, T., Harrison, B., Logan, T., Bellamy, W., & Darity, W. (2020). Wealth implications of slavery and racial discrimination for African American descendants of the enslaved. *Review of Black Political Economy, 47*(3), 218–254. https://doi.org/10.1177/0034644620926516

DeGruy, J. (2005). *Post traumatic slave syndrome: America's legacy of enduring injury and healing.* Uptone Press.

Desmond, D. (2019). In order to understand the brutality of American Capitalism, you have to start on the plantation. The 1619 Project. *New York Times.* https://www.nyti mes.com/interactive/2019/08/14/magazine/slavery-capitalism.html.

Equal Justice Institute (EJI). (2017). *Lynching in America: Confronting the legacy of racial terror* (3rd ed.). https://lynchinginamerica.eji.org/report/

Equal Justice Institute (EJI). (n.d.). *Criminal justice reform.* https://eji.org/criminal-just ice-reform/

Felitti, V. J., Anda, R. F., Nordenberg, D., et al. (1998). Relationship of childhood abuse and household dysfunction to many of the leading causes of death in adults: The adverse childhood experiences (ACE) study. *American Journal of Preventive Medicine, 14,* 245–258.

FWD.us. (2014). *Every second: The impact of the incarceration crisis on America's families* [Fact sheet]. Rutgers University.

Hannah-Jones, N. (Host). (2019). Our democracy's founding ideals were false when they were written. Black Americans have fought to make them true. The 1619 Project. *New York Times.* https://www.nytimes.com/interactive/2019/08/14/magazine/black-history-american-democracy.html

Himmelstein, K. E. W., Lawrence, J. A., Jahn, J. L., Caesar, J. N., Morse, M., Bassett, M. T., Wispelwey, B. P., Darity, W. A., & Venkataramani, A. S. (2022). Association between racial wealth inequities and racial disparities in longevity among U.S. adults and role of reparation payments, 1992-2018. *JAMA Open Network, 5*(11), e2240519. https://doi.org/10.1001/jamanetworkopen.2022.40519

Institute of Medicine, Committee on Understanding and Eliminating Racial and Ethnic Disparities in Health Care. (2003). *Unequal treatment: Confronting racial and ethnic disparities in health care* (B. D. Smedley, A. Y. Stith, & A. R. Nelson, Eds.). National Academies Press. PMID: 25032386.

Kelley, E. (2017, May 9). *Racism & felony disenfranchisement: An intertwined history.* Brennan Center for Justice.

Lee, T. (2019, August 14). How America's vast racial wealth gap grew: By plunder. The 1619 Project. *New York Times Magazine.* https://www.nytimes.com/interactive/2019/08/14/magazine/racial-wealth-gap.html

Metzler, M., Merrick, M. T., Klevens, J., Ports, K. A., & Ford, D. C. (2017). Adverse childhood experiences and life opportunities: Shifting the narrative. *Child and Youth Services Review, 72,* 141–149.

NHPR. (2014, November 19). *Without slavery would the U.S. be the leading economic power?* https://www.nhpr.org/2014-11-19/without-slavery-would-the-u-s-be-the-leading-economic-power.

Owens, D. C., & Fett, S. M. (2019). Black maternal and infant health: Historical legacies of slavery. *American Journal of Public Health, 109,* 1342–1345. https://doi.org/10.2105/AJPH.2019.305243

Pieterse, A. L., Todd, N. R., Neville, H. A., & Carter, R. T. (2012). Perceived racism and mental health among Black American adults: A meta-analytic review. *Journal of Counseling Psychology, 59,* 1–9. http:// dx.doi.org/10.1037/a0026208

Smedley, A. (1997, November). Origins of "Race." *Anthropology News, 38*(8), 52. https://www.pbs.org/race/000_About/002_04-background-02-09.htm.

Sotero, M. M. (2006). A conceptual model of historical trauma: Implications for public health practice and research. *Journal of Health Disparities*, 1(1), 93–108.

Statista. (2021). *Estimated share of African slaves who did not survive the Middle Passage to the Americas each year from 1501 to 1866.* https://www.statista.com/statistics/1143458/annual-share-slaves-deaths-during-middle-passage/

Stemen, D. (2017, July). *The prison paradox: More incarceration will not make us safer.* Vera Institute of Justice. https://storage.googleapis.com/vera-web-assets/downloads/Publications/for-the-record-prison-paradox-incarceration-not-safer/legacy_downloads/for-the-record-prison-paradox_02.pdf

Tippett, K. (Host). (2020, June 4). Resmaa Menakem: "Notice the rage; notice the silence" [Audio podcast episode]. *On Being with Krista Tippett.* https://onbeing.org/programs/resmaa-menakem-notice-the-rage-notice-the-silence/

Waterland, R. A., & Jirtle, R. L. (2003). Transposable elements: Targets for early nutritional effects on epigenetic gene regulation. *Molecular and Cellular Biology*, 23(15), 5293–5300. https://doi.org/10.1128/MCB.23.15.5293-5300.2003

2

Antiblackness in the Policies of Policing

Why a Culture of Enslavement Still Matters

Kenneth Davis

Policing Origins and Slavery

The history of policing in America is clouded with political, economic, and social motivations that vary greatly by perspectives. Most traditional scholars focus on the origins of policing from the perspective of non–African Americans descendants of slavery. This is often an incomplete view that ignores the impact of slavery, segregation, discrimination, and antiblackness policies on the evolution of American policing.

Antiblackness illustrates the inability to recognize Black humanity. It allows the depiction of policing as a neutral arbitrator throughout the country's violent and shameful past. Policing in America has evolved from unorganized quasi-police forces to a professional, well-funded, evolving, and highly specialized profession. Initially, policing meant a volunteer force that emphasized community involvement to help catch criminals. The modern law enforcement structure is organized based on jurisdiction and differentiated under the federal, state, or local jurisdictions.

The history of policing in the United States started with England. Beginning around 1285 CE and lasting until the 1800s, law enforcement individuals such as sheriffs or constables were assigned to preserve calm and order in English villages and towns. All men ages 15 to 60 were instructed to help in the apprehension of criminals and help keep order and peace, as well as with other immoral endeavors. This community-based method worked in cities with small populations. But a city such as London could not sustain this code of conduct, and citizen participation forms of law enforcement began to disintegrate in the mid-1700s.

Social unrest was one of the reasons that the system of policing had to be formalized. A magistrate named Henry Fielding founded London's first

Kenneth Davis, *Antiblackness in the Policies of Policing* In: *Antiblackness and the Stories of Authentic Allies*.
Edited by: Norman Kim, Carolyn Coker Ross, Mazella Fuller and Charlynn Small, Oxford University Press.
© Oxford University Press 2024. DOI: 10.1093/oso/9780197642535.003.0003

professional police force in 1749. Another innovator, Patrick Colquhoun, focused on police reform. He believed that the role of the police was to maintain public order, detect and even prevent a criminal act before it happens, and educate the citizenry on bad moral and social habits. Colquhoun believed in proactive policing instead of the usual reactive policing.

Often considered the father of modern policing, an English nobleman named Sir Robert Peel introduced drastic philosophy changes on policing in the 1800s. He proposed concepts such as preventative patrols to stop a crime before it happens, a common clothing standard, and uniformed police similar in structure to the military. He also developed policing principles (Nazemi, 2009).

Large cities in America such as New York, Philadelphia, and Boston had riots about food and earnings frequently and wanted to maintain law and order among the citizens. Boston was the first to incorporate these changes because of successful models in England. In America's southern states, the evolution of policing saw a different route. The beginning of modern policing there was the "slave patrol" (Platt, 1982). Created in the Carolina colonies in 1704 (Reichel, 1992), slave patrols had three principal roles:

(1) to chase down, apprehend, and return to their owners runaway slaves;
(2) to provide a form of organized terror to deter slave revolts; and
(3) to maintain a form of discipline for slave-workers who were subject to summary justice, outside of the law, if they violated any plantation rules (Reichel, 1992).

One version of history offers that political unrest changed how the police operated in northern parts of America. Between the 1830s and 1860s, urbanization due to immigration and industrialization also changed how the police functioned. The voluntary system gave way to a more professional police force, much like what Sir Robert Peel was doing at the same time in England. Peel's reforms paralleled rich slave owners in southern states attempting to maintain the institution of slavery, despite the growing cost to control and prevent slaves from absconding.

According to Schweninger (1999), slave owners argued that the costs of slave hunters, helping pay for patrols (usually assumed by the state), sending overseers in pursuit, lost labor, rewards, and jail fees rose over time, but the comparative costs remained small compared with the price of slaves. They also supported city ordinances and state laws designed to regulate and control the movement of slaves. This was during the time known as the political era. Politics was the dominating force in policing during the 1800s. Politicians were corrupt and at times used the police force for personal gains. The most important interest the police achieved in this century was to follow the commands of the respective political organization or to protect the property of rich landowners. Fighting crime or prevention was an afterthought.

Grow (2012) found that a court ruling in Pennsylvania that prevented northern states' law enforcement or judicial officials from participating in the recapture of slaves caused southerners to become enraged and demand an invigorated Fugitive Slave Law in 1850, which obligated northerners to contribute vigorously to the return of escaped slaves. The law refused slaves many civil rights such as a jury trial, the right to a writ of habeas corpus, and the right to testify on their own behalf. Grow went on to discuss the 1857 Supreme Court decision in Dred Scott, which progressively emboldened slave catchers and the use of the courts system as a tool of oppression. In 1865 Congress ratified the 13th Amendment to the U.S. Constitution, which abolished slavery but allowed punishment for crime to include forced servitude. In consequence, it permitted the criminalization and re-enslavement of African Americans.

Postslavery, Jim Crow, and Civil Rights Oppression

Post–Civil War, vigilante-style organizations grew in contemporary southern police departments. The main goal was controlling freed slaves who were now laborers working in an agricultural caste system and enforcing "Jim Crow" segregation laws, intended to forbid freed slaves equal rights and entry to the political system. Angela Davis (2003) maintains, "In the immediate aftermath of slavery, the southern states hastened to develop a criminal justice system that could legally restrict the possibilities of freedom for newly released slaves" (p. 29). In many ways Black codes served to define criminality in terms of race and shared many commonalities with the prior slave codes. This rearticulation of slave codes into Black codes "tended to racialize penalty and linked it closely with previous regimes of slavery" (Davis, 2003, p. 31).

The expansion of police and their budgets would balloon drastically from the early 1800s to the late 1900s, which ushered in a new way of policing. A historical understanding of the expansion of American policing is broken down into four eras: the political era, the professional era (1890–1910), the reform era (1930–1980), and the community policing era (1980s–present).

The progressive leaders of the time sought to eliminate corruption and professionalize policing as northern and southern states healed from civil war wounds. Tension heightened during the midpoint in the reform era, as police departments across the country began to militarize and mobilize against Black rebellions. As citizens organized in the streets protesting inequities, they were met with a force they've never seen. Canine dogs, water hoses, tear gas, and other people who opposed their movement attacked them viciously.

As protests and demonstrations grew during civil rights movements, police departments and leaders were put in a rather precarious position on how to control Blacks in a postslavery era. Chiefly the protest was to be met with a show of strength and resistance, but as the era shifted toward nonviolent displays of protests, police brutality became more common. The police didn't shift their tactics of brutality despite public outcry and news coverage. The police often were the aggressors, along with White citizens, which led to retaliation and riots by the Black community. Police were seen as a threat and tool of oppression rather than help, and there was a fear in many neighborhoods as the police were allowed to destroy Black communities for no reason and no one would bat an eye. It was a dark time for policing, as cameras started to really depict the life of the inner city.

Crime of course was prevalent, but as the presence of officers grew, a mass incarceration movement was birthed. An age-old, common, and regularly reinforced set of racial narratives about Black people as criminals reinforced public acceptance of the heightened prosecution of Black people and expansion of the prison system (Muhammad, 2011). It wouldn't truly spike until decades later when policy was passed on the premise of "reform." The expansion of the police force was strategic and an evolution that was ongoing, to protect certain groups who felt superior to others.

Civil rights organizations and the leaders in the press fought to place the ongoing problem of police brutality under public scrutiny. Legal complaints against police officers who abused their power were filed. Advocates chronicled police beatings and murder often without justice. State and local prosecutors and juries were rarely willing to punish police and saw them as an extension of themselves. It would take federal intervention to force a breakthrough on police brutality. The social stratification of policing increased, and small cities continued to create police departments as urban populations relocated from large cities to suburban areas.

The community policing era (1980s–present) promoted increased inter-action between police and the citizenry. Local government implemented increased civilian oversight and regional reforms to address biased policing. In response to the nonviolent marches and movements, taskforce policing became significant. The *Du Bois Review* (2018) noted that some prominent American police officials have advocated for greater acknowledgment of the role of law enforcement in historical racial injustice, including violence, in hopes of transforming police–community relations.

While an encouraging development, these calls for transformative jus-tice understate the scope of this historical and contemporary problem, neglecting the often extralegal nature of police-involved violence and injus-tice, its array of spectacular and more subtle forms, and the layered roles of state and nonstate actors in perpetrating and sanctioning White supremacist violence. Dismissals of racist discourse as "personal feelings" or unfortunate but benign aspects of police "canteen culture" (Waddington, 1999, p. 288) must give way to a recognition of its threats to human and civil rights.

Drawing on historical records of racist violence implicating police, researchers who analyze overlapping aspects of White supremacy in policing, including racist ideologies, and political acts of law enforcement officers and officials must conclude that its impact on Blacks in America is devas-tating. This backdrop of normative racist violence—physical, cultural, and structural—must inform a contemporary transformative justice agenda, in-cluding demands for explicit and robust protections from continued abuses.

Costly Expansion of Policing

The community policing era (1980s–present) has seen many reforms and ebbs and flows in policing in America. Antiblackness policing policies in the current era have significantly contributed to the prison system in the United States becoming overcrowded. "American prisons house more than 1.5 mil-lion individuals, an increase of more than 390 percent since 1978" (Mosteller, 2018, para 1).

The increase in incarceration rates in the United States is associated with the war on drugs campaigns and the need for politicians to bring harsher punishments upon those arrested for drug-related charges. When the crim-inal justice system started focusing their efforts on arresting more people for drug-related crimes, it targeted lower socioeconomic urban areas, which were primarily African American neighborhoods. The philosophy of bringing harsher sentences upon those arrested for first-time small drug-related charges was devastating to communities of color.

Federal and state elected leaders used their political power to promote campaign slogans such as "The War on Drugs" and "Tough on Crime." These political agendas played a huge role in convincing taxpaying citizens that there was a need to spend more on prisons. Soon after, prisons were built all over the country and filled with inner-city Blacks (Ahmed et al., 2019). Again, the police force in America was weaponized as a tool that devastated and disproportionately affected Black communities.

At the turn of the 21st century, Blacks in America had overcome many obstacles and were making gains in education and socioeconomics. Instead of providing financial support to enhance this phenomenon, government leaders pushed for spending on the expansion, specialization, and militarization of police agencies. Congress began making Department of Defense equipment generally available to domestic police agencies with the National Defense Authorization Act (NDAA) of 1989 and authorized the direct transfer of equipment to agencies for counterdrug activities with the NDAA of 1990 and 1991 (Bieler, 2016).

Another major support for the expansion of police was the Violent Crime Control and Law Enforcement Act, signed by President Bill Clinton in 1994. The act promised to hire 100,000 police officers by the year 2000 to help decrease crime. The act created the Community Oriented Police Services (COPS) Office, which provided over $8 billion in grants to help police agencies hire the new officers (Call & Cole, 1996). Billions of dollars of taxpayer money is being spent to prioritize specialized units in 21st-century policing. The breakdown of some of these units is listed as follows:

Property Crimes—Resources vary greatly based on the type of crimes being investigated. Bonkiewicz (2016) discussed the division between violent and property crimes and the time and funds needed to investigate each incident type. When police officers respond to violent crimes, they often interact with suspects and victims on scene. They may be able to interview all suspects and witnesses, collect evidence, and make an arrest on scene. When officers respond to burglaries or larcenies, they must dust for fingerprints, swab for DNA, survey a neighborhood for witnesses, and engage in other investigative activities that require hours, days, and even months to solve the case (Bonkiewicz, 2016). Assigned officers are specially trained in these areas.

White-Collar Crimes Units—According to Haugh (2015), corporate and white-collar crime saw the biggest expansion of federal law during the 1970s, 1980s, and early 2000s. These investigations generally include efforts at detecting and arresting people involved in plots and schemes to steal money. The duty to investigate may fall under federal jurisdiction with thefts of federally insured monies; however, this fact alone does not indicate that federal agencies will assume responsibility for the investigation. Many times the monetary value of the loss will play a role in determining who investigates and prosecutes the case. Businesses such as banks and credit card companies are often victims. Theft is often discovered by accident, audit, or anonymous tips. According to Veselak (2015), since its original conceptualization, white-collar crime has been associated with people of upper social status. Officers in this area need skills and education to specifically address white-collar crimes such as forgery, fraud, and embezzlement.

Multijurisdictional Investigative Task Forces—A group of investigators working together to investigate crimes is called a multijurisdictional task force. Multijurisdictional task forces exist for the purpose of addressing specific crime problems that cross multiple jurisdictional boundaries, such as the political boundaries of a city, county, or state. Multijurisdictional task forces are composed of officers/agents from multiple law enforcement agencies to solve the local problem of jurisdiction restrictions.

Special Investigation/Covert Investigation Units—Most drug-connected investigations require an undercover element that plainclothes officers can't provide. Drug enforcement is a top priority in the policing community as it often generates large sums of money through seizures. A crucial part of law enforcement operations is to keep communities free from illegal drug use, as drugs contribute to a variety of social problems and quality-of-life problems across the country. There is a strong correlation between illegal drugs, criminal activity, and acts of violence. Undercover investigations can be tackled in various ways but require complex planning. The nature and seriousness of drug trafficking and the violence related with the subculture involve some supplementary risks. One method of investigation that is often used is infiltrating criminal organizations that deal large amounts of drugs. Another is attacking drug organizations or drug locations by staking out a location and observing drug transactions. Yet another is the buy-then-bust approach, in which an undercover officer purchases drugs and then arrests the dealer. All these types of investigations can be lengthy and expensive and require special skills.

Antiterrorism Investigation Units—Terrorism around the world has a long history. Terrorists share common tactics that have been used frequently by radical and extremist groups to influence public opinion and attempt to force authorities to embrace their agenda. Terrorists have criminal, political, and religious agendas as motives to force change in nonpeaceful ways. Both preemptive and reactive techniques are used to investigate terrorism threats. Preemptive techniques include continued and coordinated planning, intelligence gathering, and investigative activity by numerous agencies. Reactive methods include a quick response to the incident, crime scene processing and analysis, subsequent follow-up investigations, and use of spies and reconnaissance.

Nash (2017) argued that the terrorist attacks on September 11, 2001, are seen by most as the worst terrorist events to occur in the United States, with almost 3,000 deaths, 6,000 injured, and close to $2 trillion in damage. This act of terror pressed U.S. leaders to create the Department of Homeland Security, the agency that oversees most investigations and counterterrorism measures implemented to prevent future terrorist attacks (Nash, 2017). Billions have been spent federally and locally in this area of policing.

Although the federal government has the overarching responsibility of responding to and combating terrorist attacks in America, each act of terrorism is essentially a local problem in the jurisdiction in which it occurs and must be addressed by local authorities also. State and local law enforcement agencies have significantly increased budgets to fight terrorism post-9/11.

Community Policing Units—Community policing is a growing segment of policing budgets and strategies. The concept behind community policing is that the police cannot be the only defense against criminal activities. The community where crime is a problem must play a role in prevention. During the early 1980s, the community policing model emerged and quickly became popular. At the onset many believed that the police and the community would become interconnected in their fight to reduce and prevent crime locally.

One purpose of community-based policing was to change the "us versus the community" mentality that many police departments developed over time. Under President Bill Clinton, Congress enacted the 1994 Violent Crime Control and Law Enforcement Act, which helped communities get funding for community-oriented policing. This funding provided resources and personnel to help reduce crime. Community policing is thought to be a long-term strategy that encompasses all areas of the community to attack crime.

The implementation of this philosophy varies greatly by department. The National Institute of Justice conducted a survey on community-based policing and found that more than 2,000 law enforcement departments that used community-based police tactics for a year or more had a 62% reduction in crime committed against the community. Eighty percent of survey respondents believed that there was less of a threat present in their neighborhoods (Bertus, 1996). However, there can be issues of abuse with community policing. Corruption and favoritism can grow and persist when officers are granted the power to change procedures and fix a specific problem.

Conclusion

So what's next? Political change is usually not accepted in America unless you can reach the masses and convince people that what they're doing is cruel and unconstitutional. Historically policing has been a tool used by the dominant members of society and their antiblackness agenda to capture, arrest, rearrest, suppress, and intimidate the Black community. As America becomes more diverse and less segregated, police—whose primary tools are authority and force—are being tasked with responding to societal problems they are not equipped to handle, from homelessness to mental health to poverty. In recent years, due to advances in technology, police misconduct has been on full display in cases such as Tamir Rice, Eric Gardner, George Floyd, and Breana Taylor. This has led to support for the Black Lives Matter movement and the call for defunding of police budgets and money to be redistributed to community programs. While some states have agreed to examine and possibly defund police budgets, others have stood firm and vowed to increase police budgets.

Based on past injustice, mistrust, and lack of transparency in policing, transformational change is needed going forward. As we progress through the 21st century and the country becomes more diverse, America must find ways to bridge the historical racial gap in police perception through transparency and better outcomes. The goal of safer communities is a common goal citizens overwhelmingly agree on.

The following are recommendations of changes needed to shift the paradigm:

1. **Federal laws requiring states to establish independent regional citizen review boards to investigate all officer and agency complaints.** Citizen review boards would ensure transparency, enhance public confidence and trust, and improve the efficiency of operations through feedback. Citizen involvement would help to bring down the blue wall of silence in police culture.

2. **State laws regulating public access to body cameras within 48 to 72 hours of critical incidents.** This would remove barriers for requests for officer body camera footage in critical incidents. It would also limit an agency's ability to protect bad actors and trigger swift action if needed by citizen review boards.

3. **Local outcomes-based funding that rewards community policing and alternatives to incarceration.** This strategy not only promotes safer communities but also encourages more holistic and rehabilitative methods over traditional incarceration.

These transformational changes will be met with skepticism from internal and external stakeholders; however, changing demographics and the history of policing will eventually require that policing policies evolve.

References

Ahmed, R., Johnson, M., Caudill, C., Diedrich, N., Mains, D., & Key, A. (2019). Cons and pros: Prison education through the eyes of the prison educated. *Review of Communication, 19*(1), 69–76.

Bertus, F. (1996). *The use and effectiveness of community policing in a democracy*. National Institute of Justice.

Bieler, S. (2016). Police militarization in the USA: The state of the field. *Policing, 39*(4), 586–600.

Bonkiewicz, L. (2016). Exploring how an area's crime-to-cop ratios impact patrol officer productivity. *Policing, 39*(1), 19–35.

Call, J. E., & Cole, R. (1996). Assessing the possible impact of the violent crime control act of 1994 on prison and jail overcrowding suits. *Prison Journal, 76*(1), 92–106.

Davis, A. (2003). *Are prisons obsolete?* Seven Stories Press.

Ward, G. (2018). Living histories of white supremacist policing: Towards transformative justice. *Du Bois Review, 15*(1), 167–184.

Grow, M. J. (2012). Fugitive slaves, the higher law, and the coming of the civil war. *Reviews in American History, 40*(1), 68–72.

Haugh, T. (2015). Overcriminalization's new harm paradigm. *Vanderbilt Law Review, 68*(5), 1191–1241.

Mosteller, J. (2018, June 22). *Why prison reform matters in America.* https://www.charleskochinstitute.org/issue-areas/criminal-justice-policing-reform/why-prison-reform-matters/

Muhammad, K. G. (2011). *The condemnation of blackness: Race, crime, and the making of modern urban America.* Harvard University Press.

Nash, R. M. (2017). Predicting the impact of urban area security initiative funding on terrorist incidents in the United States. *Western Criminology Review, 18*(2), 1–20.

Nazemi, S. (2009). *Sir Robert Peel's nine principals of policing.* http://lacp.org/2009-Articles-Main/062609-Peels9Principals-SandyNazemi.htm

Platt, T. (1982). Crime and punishment in the United States: Immediate and long-term reforms from a Marxist perspective. *Crime and Social Justice, 18*, 38–45.

Reichel, P. L. (1992). The misplaced emphasis on urbanization in police development. *Policing and Society, 3*(1), 1–12.

Schweninger, L. (1999). Counting the costs: Southern planters and the problem of runaway slaves, 1790–1860. *Business and Economic History, 28*(2), 267–275.

Veselak, K. M. (2015). The relationship between educational attainment and the type of crime committed by incarcerated offenders. *Journal of Correctional Education, 66*(2), 30–56.

Waddington, P. A. J. (1999). Police (canteen) sub-culture: An appreciation. *British Journal of Criminology, 39*(2), 287–309.

3

The Maniacal Imagination and Moral Ineptitude of the Church

The Construction and Sustainment of White-Skin Supremacy

Kris Watson and Clare Twomey

One essay cannot possibly give a comprehensive account of the church universal's evil and maniacal imagination, and gross moral ineptitude, in creating and implementing the plan that would become White-skinned supremacy. That said, this chapter is specifically crafted as a brief survey into those edicts, attitudes, and events instigated and sustained by the church that are directly responsible for many of the horrors perpetrated in the name of European exceptionalism and White-skinned supremacy. We highlight the ways in which White supremacy manifests itself in the lives of people (specifically ministers) of African descent in the church. We contend that "racism," and the systems it has created, cannot be dismantled without understanding the impact that White Christianity has had on racial injustice in this country.

It is critical that we know our complicated and long distorted history so as not to remain complacent and ignorant to the soul-crushing injustices caused by White-skinned supremacy. One does not have to identify as religious, in any definition of the word, to find this useful and necessary. While the religious implications are profoundly disturbing, the ramifications of what remains are even more unsettling as they continue to ungird this nation's policies—foreign and domestic—as they pertain to the racialized other.

Beginnings: The Early Christian Church

Whatever else the early followers of the Brown-skinned Palestinian Jew Jesus may have been, they were not adherents to the precepts and ethos of

Kris Watson and Clare Twomey, *The Maniacal Imagination and Moral Ineptitude of the Church* In: *Antiblackness and the Stories of Authentic Allies*. Edited by: Norman Kim, Carolyn Coker Ross, Mazella Fuller and Charlynn Small, Oxford University Press. © Oxford University Press 2024. DOI: 10.1093/oso/9780197642535.003.0004 the Roman Empire. When Constantine adopted Christianity as the religion of the Roman Empire in 312 CE, empire Christianity took center stage. This allowed those who had been baptized in peace to now engage in holy and just wars for the expansion of Rome's dominion. This weaponized and codified version of Christianity would be used to syncretize peoples and cultures as the Roman Empire moved through Europe. This strategic move would set the stage for periods of war and oppression, through the Crusades and Inquisitions, that would inevitably make room for the doctrine of discovery.

The trans-Atlantic slave trade began in the 15th century. Pope Nicholas V authored the papal bull *Dum Diversas* in 1452, the blueprint for what would become the doctrine of discovery (Charles & Rah, 2019). Here, the church provided the imperative for King Alphonso of Portugal

to invade, search out, capture, vanquish and subdue all Saracens (Muslims) and pagans whatsoever, and other enemies of Christ whosesoever placed, and the kingdoms, dukedoms, principalities, dominions, possessions, and all moveable goods whatsoever held and possessed by them and to reduce their persons to perpetual slavery and to apply and appropriate to himself and his successors the kingdoms, dukedoms, counties, principalities, dominions, possessions and goods and to convert themto his and their use and profit. (Indigenous Values, 2018, p.1, paragraph 2)

Romanus Pontifex followed, allowing all European Catholic nations to expand their dominion over "discovered lands" (Indigenous Values, 2018a). This pronouncement gave blanket permission to Portugal, and ultimately all other European empires, to capture and enslave anyone who stood in the way of settler colonialism (Dunbar-Ortiz, 2015) in perpetupity.

Completing this death warrant trifecta for Native peoples and enslaved Africans was *Inter Caetera*, issued in 1493. In this edict, Spain and Portugal were given the right to colonize, convert, and enslave the Americas (U.S. National Library of Medicine, n.d.). While the previous two bulls created a blueprint for what was to come, this one codified the doctrine of discovery by declaring "the Catholic faith and the Christian religion be exalted and be everywhere increased and spread, that the health of souls be cared for and that barbarous nations be overthrown and brought to the faith itself" (Indigenous Values, 2018, p. 1, paragraph 2).

This so called "Doctrine of Discovery", codified in 1823 by Chief Justice John Marshall's Supreme Court opinion, became the lawful justification for the appropriation and ownership of indigeouns lands, while also justifying western expansion. (landgrantpatent, p. 1, parapgrah 1–8)

Thus, the church became the architect of systems that would perpetrate the genocide (Dunbar-Ortiz, 2015) of 100 million Indigenous people over the next five centuries and the enslavement of an estimated 12.5 million African people who were kidnapped and removed from their ancestral lands and sold into chattel slavery in the so-called New World (Equal Justice Initiative, 2018). These bulls married the European idea of race superiority with the conclusion that Eurocentric Christianity was *the* word of God. Christians were the new chosen people whose goal it was to ensure the conversion of all peoples by any means necessary. This influenced puritan leader John Winthrop in 1630 to claim that those settling the New World were "a city upon a hill. The eyes of all people are upon us, and even God is watching" (Douglas, 2015, pp. 11–12). This simple reference to God stresses "that to these reformers exodus from England was first and foremost a religious mission" (Douglas, 2015, pp. 11–12) and therefore they had God's blessing. This blessing upon the colonizers and enslavers was also demonstrated by Rev. Dr. Basil Manly, who in 1798 "asserted forcefully an unapologetic theology of white supremacy, arguing that slavery was not an unfortunate necessity but rather a part of the divinely ordained hierarchical order of Christian society" (Douglas, 2015, p. 11).

Throughout the history of the church, the evil myth is the same: God had ordained people of European descent to go forward and vanquish all in their path for their own use and profit. Of course, it helps to have sacred biblical texts to justify these horrors. The texts themselves are not the issue; what is at fault is the White Christian lens through which one interprets the text and the arrogance of thinking that this lens is the only legitimate one. Reading the Bible through the lens of European superiority fortifies the myth of supremacy while offering a panacea for the cognitive dissonance that results when one attempts to justify the murder, torture, and enslavement of human beings. If one believes or trusts in some kind of all-loving deity, one has to do ridiculous, spiritual, and psychological gymnastics to think that genocide and slavery would be sanctioned by that deity. Unfortunately, these calisthenics continue to be performed by Christians and are inaccurately supported by distorted interpretations.

Genesis 9:18–27 (Jones, 2021), the story of the curse of Ham, was a staple in plantation theology. Noah's son Ham walks in on him while he sleeps naked. Noah's other two sons walk into the room backward so as to avoid this indecency. When Noah hears of Ham's indiscretion, he curses Ham for having robbed him of his dignity: "Cursed be Canaan; lowest of slaves shall he be to his brothers . . . and let Canaan be his slave." Ham was "in charge" of Canaan, which was mistakenly thought to represent Africa and everyone on that continent. Cursing him to be a slave to his brothers gave the church biblical authority to craft papal bulls that would set in motion the belief that God had cursed Africa forever.

Additionally, Ephesians 6:5–7 supports enslavement and murder: Slaves obey your masters "with fear and trembling" (Harrelson, 2003, pp. 21–23). The letter of Paul to Philemon assures Philemon that Paul will return his slave to him. The logic goes: If the Bible condoned slavery anywhere, then it must be okay everywhere. Even as some struggled with the possible immorality of owning another human person, the church would quickly provide a corrective. "The rationale went something like this: slavery was a sin, but if a Christian owner held slaves, the Christian was not sinful, because God had ordained slavery in the bible" (Harrelson, 2003, pp. 2149–2150). Also, they reasoned, slavery was a good and necessary thing for barbarous people, who needed their master in order to be saved.

This kind of dysfunctional theology (Butler, 2021) led to the creation of Indian boarding schools in the United States, its territories, and Canada in the early 19th century (Charles & Rah, 2019). The presence of Native peoples caused much vexation within settler colonialism, which sought to find a final solution to the "Indian problem" (Dunbar-Ortiz, 2015). Following years of scorched earth/total war campaigns, which called for the murder of women and children and the destruction of homes and crops, and offered bounties on scalps if there was no immediate surrender in the attempt to eradicate Indigenous people, the church implemented another approach: Indian boarding schools run by Christian missionaries. Children kidnapped from their families and placed in these schools were stripped of their given names and cultural and spiritual identities, forbidden from speaking their native language or wearing native clothing, and beaten and raped without provocation—all of this to "kill the Indian to save the man" (Dunbar-Ortiz, 2015, p. 151). New discoveries continue to be unearthed in both countries that show the extent to which these horrors existed.

Theology as Terrorism

> The theologically backed assertion of the superiority of both "the
> white race" and Protestant Christianity undergirded a century of re-
> ligiously sanctioned terrorism in the form of ritualized lynching and
> other forms of public violence and intimidation.
>
> —Robert P. Jones (2021, p. 5)

Christianity and White supremacist values were inextricably bound together before and after the Civil War. This is demonstrated in the Lost Cause
myth—a pseudo-reframe of both the cause and outcome of the war. While
there are numerous reasons this ideology was embraced by those in the de-
feated South,

> the future implication is clear: just as Jesus was resurrected from the dead
> and will ultimately come again to rule the earth in righteousness, there will
> yes be a time when the noble ideas of the confederacy, even if not the prac-
> tice of chattel slavery itself, will rise again. (Jones, 2021, p. 57)

The values of virginal innocence and purity projected onto White women
and of chivalry and protection projected onto White men were wedded
to so-called Christian values. African men were (and are) demonized and
punished. African women were lusted after while simultaneously reviled.
Africans, not thought to be human, were systematically used and discarded.

We cannot examine the horrors of enslavement and lynching of Black and
Brown bodies without also implicating the church in these egregious acts.
And while these acts of violence may not have been as obvious in the so-called
more progressive North, White supremacist ideology undergirded these acts
and have persisted to this day: "The link between political leaders and prominent white churches was not just incidental; these religious connections
served as the moral underpinning for the entire project of protecting the
dominant social and political standing of whites" (Jones, 2021, p. 30).

The 20th century witnessed a kind of distorted evolution of White supremacist ideology in Christianity. Religion, politics, and patriotism had been
circling one another for decades. With the emergence of what was called
"new evangelicalism" (Jones, 2021, p. 5), Billy Graham crafted a theology of
personal salvation and piety that requires one to be born again to be saved.
This is the cornerstone of evangelical Christianity. Robert Jones offers that

one is more likely to be racist if one attends a Christian church, particularly an evangelical church (Jones, 2021). This emphasis on the individual, besides fitting in beautifully with the rugged individualism upon which America is founded, dismisses the need for the church to confront the corporate sin of systemic racism and White supremacy. Graham's response to Rev. Martin Luther King's "I Have a Dream" speech was: "Only when Christ comes again will little white children of Alabama walk hand in hand with little black children" (Alliance of Baptists, 2021). His goal was to dismiss and demonize any civil action intended to fight for racial equality and civil rights. By equating civil rights with communism, Graham established the religious basis of the ongoing legacy of political and systemic opposition to the quest for equality and reparations. As Anthea Butler (2021) notes:

> As evangelicals formed themselves in political activity, entering into the print and television world, their grip on the cultural and social visions they wanted to promote was pointedly circumscribed not by racial inclusivity, but by racial exclusivity. The exclusivity, which translated to the outside world as a form of belief, was about high boundaries and conformity. American Christians were encouraged by the new evangelicalism to adhere to particular political and social beliefs. With Graham's ascension and the organizing of evangelical universities, seminaries and parachurch groups, the political action they engaged in set them up to claim new power while also placing them in opposition to the movement for civil and social rights. (p. 34)

The evangelical voices in opposition to the full humanity of people of non-European descent included those of Charles Fuller, Norman Vincent Peale, Jerry Falwell, the Bakkers, Pat Robertson, the Osteens, and Jim Dobson. "Renowned" institutions formed for the purpose of this opposition include Fuller Seminary, Youth for Christ, Bob Jones University, the National Association of Evangelicals, the Moral Majority, the Christian Coalition, the Family Research Council, and the Heritage Foundation (Butler, 2021, p. 36). Butler (2021) states:

> Evangelicalism is an American Christianity born in the context of white Christian slaveholders. It sanctified and justified segregation, violence and racial proscription. It is not simply a religious group at all. Rather it is a nationalistic political movement whose purpose is to support the hegemony of white Christian men over and against the flourishing of other. (p. 33)

Writing as a woman of European descent who identifies as a progressive minister, I must extend Butler's statement to include all Christians, not just evangelicals, lest those of us who believe we are immune from our own internalized bias and racism think we get a pass. Our particular corporate sin is to assume that we have somehow bypassed the necessity to do our own antiracism work because we are "progressive."

We tend to be more passive-aggressive or even clueless in our aggressions. This makes us very dangerous do-gooders, projecting an air of compassionate superiority when we are really just as patronizing and racist as our conservative siblings. We can become immensely defensive when confronted with the notion that we remain culpable for the harm that continues to be perpetrated upon people of non-European descent. This level of "denial" suggests that we are so disconnected from the reality of racism that we fail to recognize that we all participate in this mythology. **None of us is immune.**

And So, It Continues . . .

The legacy of the doctrine of discovery, manifest destiny, enslavement, Jim Crow, and thousands of years of White supremacist philosophy, psychology, bad science, law, and theology is openly displayed daily in the church, including many of our Black churches. People of African descent who worship and serve in the mainline Protestant denominations are subjected to the ongoing manifestation of White supremacist ideology that has been embedded in the church.

We have just presented a very brief thumbnail sketch of the development of racist theology and ideology by the church. People of European descent *will never* directly experience how this plays out in the lives of people of color within the church.

Writing as Rev. Dr. Kris Watson, I was educated, baptized, and confirmed in the Episcopalian church. In these educational and religious settings, I was not taught the truth about the real history of the country or the church and its complicity as architects and perpetrators of White supremacist ideology. There was no mention that Africans knew Jesus and the Christ event well before murderous missionaries invaded, pillaged, and kidnapped my ancestors. There was substantial intellectual discourse, liturgies, and hymns in Latin, and significant embedding of White supremacist ideology.

Firmly entrenched in the ways of White supremacist ideology, I entered into my secondary and postsecondary education unwittingly embracing this ideology, which resulted in a deep sense of internal division. There is danger in trying to fit into both worlds and belonging to neither entirely.

I did not discover the Black church until later in life. Historically the Black church has been one of the main sources of hope and inspiration, political action, and faith rooted in organizing the fight against systemic racism. It is a space of solace and comfort, a place to be in community. But it is not without its own set of issues. There are intersectional inequities including misogyny, ageism, and homophobia that demonstrate the deeply embedded "isms" practiced in the church. The impact of colonization and White supremacist ideology does not elude the Black church.

Racism in the Black church goes beyond the continued use of inaccurate depictions of Jesus. It extends to the theology not of liberation but of prosperity, to the repressive and death-dealing language in the hymns, to a theology that emphasizes personal over systemic evil and preaches against homosexuality and women in the pulpit. Many Black churches embrace very conservative theological positions, including being against a woman's right to choose, in favor of the Second Amendment as though it is the Second Commandment, against marriage equality, and more. Often there is a failure to properly contextualize the biblical text and interpret it from the margins. These failures discourage thoughtful engagement and further oppress rather than liberate members. There are many instances of theological malpractice demonstrated by the failure to teach the liberative gospel of the carpenter.

The Black church often encourages a cult of personality, creating a cesspool of slavish adoration and service to pastors who abuse power and profit from pain. Many will encourage their congregants to strive for the values of the world so that they can and will support the financial health of the church, not the people. This is empire Christianity in blackface.

Ultimately, I was ordained in the United Church of Christ (UCC), a denomination that credibly touts a pioneering reputation. As with most predominantly European descendent institutions, it reflects deeply embedded White supremacist ideology, at the institutional level, at the middle judicatory level, and even at the level of the local church. With a governance structure that supports local church autonomy, despite urging from national leaders, most churches in the UCC refuse to examine or begin the journey toward antiracism. There is no consequence for maintaining the White supremacist status quo in its churches or even in the middle judicatory levels.

For example, despite a requirement for a psychological examination to be ordained in the UCC, there is no assurance that psychological evaluators will be culturally competent. Testing is normative for White people. The standard by which ministers of color are evaluated is whiteness. People of African descent are poorly represented in the middle judicatory level, the level that navigates and provides resources to ministers and local churches.

Pastoring in a White Church

Despite experiencing a profound call to serve, those of us of African descent are not prepared to encounter the systemic and personal racism in and of the church. Disillusionment and disappointment are experienced in settings we had hoped would be guided by justice, love, and compassion. There is an ongoing racialized trauma even at the hands of so-called progressive Christians. To be an African descendent minister in a predominantly White denomination is to enter the unsafe world of empire Christianity.

Racism persists and thrives in the church universal because the church is the architect of it. Christianity co-opted by empire under Constantine has little interest in the communal and transformative nature of the teachings of a Brown-skinned Afro-Asiatic Jew. The church remains a bastion of empire, ever enacting new forms of colonization. Many who profess Christianity continue to perpetuate the myth of race, maintaining the notion of a hierarchy of human value. The Bible is wrapped in the American flag and selectively used to perpetuate White supremacist and racist ideas.

Empire Christianity is more beholden to the rugged individualism of American empire than to Jesus, whose state-sanctioned execution is easily comparative to the ongoing lynching of Black and Brown bodies in this country. Despite the moral imperative to do so, many ministers, irrespective of skin color, refuse to challenge this empire system because they have embraced the status quo and will forever protect it.

Is There Hope?

Dismantling racism and decentering whiteness is an exercise of confronting fear and loathing that is fueled by miseducation. It requires profound self-awareness and a level of spiritual maturity. It requires the full embrace of

Jesus, the Brown-skinned radical revolutionary who walked the "ghettos" of his time and preached a message of hope and empowerment to the poorest of the poor.

Our work as facilitators of sacred and courageous conversations to end racism was formed in the crucible of crisis. COVID-19 had the world on lockdown. George Floyd was murdered in an act of state-sanctioned violence. Risking COVID infection, huge numbers of well-meaning people took to the streets in the Black Lives Matter movement. Churches were starting to wake up to their deeply embedded White supremacist ideology and how it impacted the world. There was renewed interest in the church and society to begin again the hard work of dismantling White-skinned supremacy by learning the truth. The COVID virus provided a painfully rich opportunity to reassess our values and rethink what it means to value the human flourishing of all.

There is little hope for those who embrace a dehumanizing theology. Given the current political climate and the obvious push to roll back any racial progress in America, *now is the time for the people in the pews to demand the truth and engage in action.*

Collective lament and awakening can result in a profound bond of human spirit, inspiring a vow to develop the courage to dismantle White supremacist ideology irrespective of the cost. For hope to flourish, there must be a long-term, unrelenting commitment to decenter whiteness. Only then will we see and experience the Divine Spirit within all of humanity.

References

Alliance of Baptists. (2021, July 19). *Engaging whiteness in your congregation: A conversation with Robert P. Jones.* YouTube. https:/www.youtube.com/watch?v=cp1myuihf9Q

Butler, A. (2021). *White evangelical racism: The politics of morality in America.* University of North Carolina Press.

Charles, M., & Rah, S-C. (2019). *Unsettling truths: The ongoing dehumanizing legacy of the doctrine of discovery.* InterVarsity Press.

Douglas, K. B. (2015). *Stand your ground: Black bodies and the justice of God.* Orbis Books.

Dunbar-Ortiz, R. (2015). *An Indigenous peoples' history of the United States.* Beacon Press.

Equal Justice Initiative. (2018). *Slavery in America: The Montgomery slave trade.* https://eji.org/reports/slavery-in-america

Harrelson, W. (2003). *The new interpreters study Bible: New revised standard version with apocrypha.* Abington Press.

Indigenous Values. (2018a). *Dum diversas.* Doctrine of Discovery. https://doctrineofdiscovery.org/dum-diversas/

Indigenous Values. (2018b). *Inter caetera*. Doctrine of Discovery. https://doctrineofdi scovery.org/dum-diversas/

Jones, R. P. (2021). *White too long*. Simon and Schuster.

Land Grant Patent. (2009). *Chief Justice John Marshall Explains the Discovery Doctrine Johnson & Graham v. M'Intosh Opinion of the U.S. Supreme Court Feb. 28, 1823*. Johnson versus MIntosh (landgrantpatent.org)

U.S. National Library of Medicine. (n.d.). AD 1493: The pope asserts rights to colonize, convert, and enslave. *Native Voices*. https://nlm.nih.gov/nativevoices/timeline/171.html

4

Before Race. After Race. Post Racial.

Nerine Tatham

The truth is like lava. No matter how deeply in the earth's core it is buried, it's always searching for a path to bubble up. It makes its own path, and when it does it scorches everything in its way. Truth is hot. And yet, it can also be very cold and slow moving, like a glacier. But either way, it reshapes everything in its way.

It is very difficult to understand the present without knowledge and understanding of the truths, circumstances, and actions that put in place the contemporary status quo. This is true for any aspect of human anthropological experience you care to examine. For example, while you don't have to know anything about the history of instruments to listen to digitally downloaded music, most listeners intuitively understand that there has been a historical evolution of music. It's the same with fashion, technology, education, gender, gender roles—pick any human topic.

Take race, for example. There is a history and evolution to it. Even within the past year, so many events have been added to the racial timeline that will impact the future. Consider that each event was preceded by a connecting, influential event. Because of the interconnectedness of events from which our human historical reality emerges, to understand the present of a thing, you must understand its past.

> Don't start nothing, won't be nothing.
>
> —African American adage

This multifaceted saying can be interpreted in several ways. A most common interpretation and certainly the way I've usually interpreted it is this: If you do not do things to create a problem, there will not be a problem. Another perspective is: If you never initiate a plan, you will never achieve your goals. When it comes to White supremacy racism and a path to an anti-racist, just, and equitable world, both interpretations apply.

Nerine Tatham, *Before Race. After Race. Post Racial.* In: *Antiblackness and the Stories of Authentic Allies.*
Edited by: Norman Kim, Carolyn Coker Ross, Mazella Fuller and Charlynn Small, Oxford University Press.
© Oxford University Press 2024. DOI: 10.1093/oso/9780197642535.003.0005

By now, it is well documented by scholars of sociology, anthropology, political science, and history that race is a made-up construct designed to create systems of advantage for one group while disadvantaging all other groups in a tiered fashion based on skin color, with people designated as Black skinned at the bottom of the hierarchy. The invention of race was "starting something."

In her master work *Caste*, Isabel Wilkerson (2020) brilliantly and thoroughly interrogates the construct of race and the de facto caste system it institutionalizes. Many others have painstakingly detailed the who, what, when, and where of race, and I refer you to their already comprehensive, factual, carefully researched, and thought-out works that are the must-read bibliography for those truly interested in the canon of social justice.

I invite us to reflect on the "why": Why start the race system?

Europeans have proudly recorded a history of "discovering" other people's stuff and claiming it as their own. At the behest of Ferdinand and Isabella, the *Nina*, *Pinta*, and *Santa Maria* crews were off to find India, got lost, accidentally discovered inhabited land, renamed it "The West Indies" (Markham, 2010), and promptly decimated the land owners who rescued them, in a genocide of the western band of the Arawak-speaking Taino people.

From Columbus's own diaries we know the playbook (Markham, 2010). The "explorers" washed ashore battered and decrepit, ailing with what we now know to be scurvy. The gracious Taino welcomed and nursed the sorry lot back to health. For their hospitality they got beta tested with the precursor to White supremacy racism: European supremacy. First came the softening up with religious propaganda, then the almost simultaneous hypocritical enslavement by brute force completed by the relentless cruelty to the point of genocide. In short order, by the early 1600s, the gracious Taino hosts were reduced to slaves and then corpses in their own home.

This discovering of people, places, and things that already exist I call "columbusing." So began the tragic tale of Anti-Indigenous European supremacy and columbusing that has evolved intentionally into a global Anti-Indigenous Anti-Black White supremacy racism (AIABWSR).

Imagine men showing up at your home looking forlorn, claiming to be travelers from faraway with a sob story about how they got lost and their vehicle broke down after running out of fuel. And out of the goodness of your heart you invite them in, feed them, and give them a chance to rest, repair, and refuel their vehicle. You provide them with supplies to make the return journey back to where they came from. You go on about your life feeling quite pleased about the good deed you've done and the hospitality you've shown.

A year or two passes and, suddenly, the strangers reappear. This time they are heavily armed, with a serious attitude claiming God told them they have the right to come back and take over your place and all your stuff and enslave you—and that's just how it's going to be from now on. You can either cooperate or they'll make you. Columbusing in action.

Before something happens, it is unimaginable. Once it happens, it's a precedent. Thus, the precedent of the cry, charm, co-opt, kill, and cosplay strategy was set.

CRY: *Our ships got lost, now we have scurvy, please help us!*

CHARM: *Your folkways have saved our lives, you are amazing, show us all your secrets.*

CO-OPT: *Join us as we work together in this fantastic new world and let us make lots of money with your stuff.*

KILL: *Now that we are in, why should we share with you primitives?*

COSPLAY: *Let's pretend we are great saviors and inventors until everyone forgets how this started* (takes about 40 years, as we've learned from religious cosplay), *then we can just pretend forever once all institutional memory is gone.*

At the heart of AIABWSR is a stinginess that springs out of the ungenerousness of spirit that is at the heart of any supremacist ideology.

Based on an examination of the behavior and its outcomes, whatever God those Europeans were claiming to believe in via a religion they also hijacked (see Constantine history conversion from paganism to monotheism; Swain & Edwards, 2008) and claimed to be proselytizing for, this belief did not translate into a practical application of human decency in behavior toward other living beings. In fact, it led to advancing the propaganda that *these people aren't really human anyway, so of course we can take their stuff and enslave them*. Hypocrisy.

Once the Portuguese/Spanish established that Old World precedent in the so-called New World, it did not take long for this inhumane, antisocial behavior to go viral with the French. The British followed suit in the Americas, and the rest of the European colonial wannabes traipsed across Africa in a looting spree that has continued under evolving guises to date.

With the columbusing of the continent renamed "Africa," the tragic cry, charm, co-opt, kill, cosplay tale continued. The triangular trade route and its brutal and inhumane treatment of human cargo—legalized trafficking for profit of Africans between 1525 and 1826—have been well described in the historical canon. The ongoing resistance by the enslaved peoples and subsequent joining by first allies in the abolition struggles have been less well detailed despite their tremendous importance.

In 1884–1885, 13 European countries, spearheaded by Britain, France, Germany, Italy, Spain, and Portugal, and the United States met at what is now known as the Berlin Conference to literally divvy up African lands among themselves ("Berlin Conference," 2010). By the late 20th and 21st centuries, Asia, after millennia of respectful trading partnership, has jumped on the bandwagon of toeing that shifting goalpost/hypocrisy line of exploitation for profit.

So, from 1492 to today, European Anti-Indigenous, Anti-African, anti-Black White supremacy racism has become so entrenched as the global default that it's unquestioned acceptance has become just how things are. Forever.

Wilkerson (2020) eloquently describes the de facto impacts designed to run as a perpetual human system machine. However, enough Black people of African descent have continued to resist the tragic genocidal outcome of discovery and renaming that has befallen too many others (Tainos, First Nations, Aborigines, African Tribal peoples). Of the survivors, a critical Anglophone mass out of America has dared to speak the phrase now heard, translated, and resonating in every language across the globe: "Black lives matter."

White supremacy has been about erasing the original identities of humanity and replacing them with an inauthentic, homogenized pseudoreality. It was created to serve the base purpose of excessive materialism of a few at the expense of basic living standards and human and civil rights for the majority. It is a pyramid scheme. Black Lives Matter is a call to reverse the erasure, upend this terminal scheme, and return or create a humane, authentic reality for all persons.

To maintain the pretense of superiority, you can't appear to be acting amorally. So psychological techniques to project unsavory characteristics onto those who are the target of exploitation is a key tactic. For example, women are sexual temptresses, gay people are here to abuse your children, non-Christians are here to terrorize, and dark-skinned people are violent.

It is a splitting technique employed on a macrosocietal scale with all the devastating results for those on the receiving end and a projective iden-tification handwashing—*see I told you "they" were the problem*—on the giving end.

After pulling off the genocide and takeover of four continents (North, Central, and South America and Australia), Europeans decided that the real golden goose was continent number 5: Africa. While genocide on the scale done to Aboriginal, Taino, and other First Nations peoples has remained elu-sive, a globalized systemic White supremacy racism has facilitated the on-going de facto takeover and control of African resources by non-African peoples.

Fast-forward to the 21st century: Now every Tom, Dick, and Harry, not limited to European/Americans, still seem to believe they can buy, bribe, or con their way into a stake in Africa. While what's theirs and their continents' are theirs only, what's Africa's is apparently for everybody, with Africans getting the least benefit from their own stuff. With a Borg-like singlemindedness, AIABWSR has been on a 400-year "resistance is futile" reign of terror. With "manifest destiny" as the rallying cry, Europeans have endeavored to suck every continent dry of its natural resources to the point where we are in danger of becoming a hollowed-out sphere floating in space where Earth used to be.

Systemic racism is like being in an abusive relationship. It is about power, control, and the ability to induce suffering with written and unwritten rules to keep the victims of abuse aware of the power differential should they ever get relaxed and forget. Abusers like to control the bodies of others and, when-ever possible, the resources they have access to. It is the same with systemic racism. People find themselves emboldened to do things as a group that most would never do individually. Similarly, armed persons are a lot more over-confident and rash than the un- or underarmed.

These are the underlying "principles" animating most exploitative groups: Let us band together and be very powerful and use that unified front and force to take what we want. Since unity and force are the essential mechanisms of our existence, let us also disunify and disempower the target group at every opportunity to perpetuate our own position and find increas-ingly sophisticated ways to make it an unconscious, automatic, almost invis-ible, perpetual machine. Furthermore, let us position ourselves as good and admirable, the standard to be strived for no matter how destructive we are in reality.

Make no mistake about it, AIABWSR is a global pandemic for which the only vaccination is a hybrid of historical knowledge, contemporary awareness, and human decency.

Hate never goes away, it only hides.

—Joseph R. Biden

One of the functionalities of our brain is to protect us from unpleasant experiences using a variety of techniques. The most primitive protective brain mechanism is the creation of the sensation experienced as anxiety. It's the feeling you get as a warning that something might be dangerous.

To protect us from the unpleasantness of real danger, our body generates a nondangerous unpleasantness. What's considered dangerous is purely subjective from human to human. Each of us can likely situate ourselves on an anxiety continuum, from nothing is dangerous to everything is dangerous. What makes us anxious is probably one of the key defining factors of who we are as a person, influenced partly by temperament and partly by environment. That interplay of nature and experience then leads to the tremendous variability, and at times unpredictability, present among humanity. Every good or bad idea starts from one's anxiety. It seems to be a key, if not *the key*, motivating factor in decision-making. From the absence of it to the presence and intensity of it, anxiety runs the show.

We are designed to use our higher brain centers to think critically to analyze and distinguish the false from the real. The primitive anxiety mechanisms are the same in the human brains of the 21st century as they were in the 1400s, the 1600s, or the year 1. The only things that change over millennia seem to be things to be anxious about. *Am I tall, short, thin, muscular, smart, prepared, respected, admired, loved, physically, financially secure, enough?* The possibilities are myriad.

At the heart of all "isms," supremacy or oppression is the notion that one person's or group's anxieties are more important than another person's or group's rights. It has been heartbreakingly fascinating to observe the impact of White supremacy, as most cultures subsume their own cultures into a sycophantic Eurocentrism in a tragic identification with the aggressor.

A big-time source of anxiety for many remains the dissonance that occurs when we act outside of our values. Now we are at the intersection of our collective human history, our individual and collective anxieties, and our values. The lava has reached the surface.

In his 1762 work, Rousseau outlines the philosophy of the social compact. To paraphrase: It is in the interest of the individual to care about the welfare of others, but no one is obligated to do so if they feel it goes against their own self-interest. Rousseau is certainly not the first to "discover" this notion. Ideas regarding the individual's obligation to oneself and relation to others have been a through thread since the recording of human history. First religions tried to advance what, on examination, are philosophies of the "social compact." Modern political constructs have sought to remove the religious and evolve a secular philosophy of why we should care about each other. However, like a matter-destroying wormhole, White supremacy has sought to obliterate all moral underpinnings of a social contract using whatever means necessary to perpetuate itself.

Whether God and religions, guns and murder, or unjust laws and political machinations, White supremacy is a firm middle finger to the social compact and values regarding humans' responsibilities toward each other. It centers self-interest of the relative few at the top of the pyramid scheme as it's raison d'être. White-identified people have been given many chronological off-ramps from White supremacy, but at each opportunity they balk and double down (e.g., Civil War, Antebellum, Reconstruction, Jim Crow, civil rights movement, COINTELPRO). There is always a pushback against social progress.

We are now living through such an era when, instead of choosing the off-ramp of social justice and equity, we are seeing insurrection, antiwokeness, and a movement to change the textbooks and pretend any factual history we don't like never happened. It is a pushback against justice, truth, facts, and reality. The desire to try and bury unflattering historical facts is what legal philosophy might dub "consciousness of guilt": the preemptive denial suspects make to try and throw people off the trail that can only inevitably lead to them based on the facts.

> "In one word, if public principles and motives, and arguments were alone to determine this dispute between the two countries, it might be settled forever in a few hours; but the everlasting clamors of predjudice, passion and private interest drown every consideration of that sort, and are precipitating us into a civil war.
>
> —John Adams (1819)

The second president of the United States left behind a treasure trove of wisdom in his writings. I take the above quote from another context, but if you substitute "the races" for "the two countries," this Adams quote remains eerily relevant to our times. He further said in the same essay: "an empire is a despotism, and an emperor a despot, bound by no law or limitation but his own will; it is a stretch of tyranny beyond absolute monarchy" (Adams & Sewall, 1819). White supremacy is both the despot and the despotism.

As a woman of African descent born in the Caribbean and living in early 21st-century America, I would hope that the history of anti-Black, anti-African, anti-Indigenous White supremacy racism would be as remote as gladiators at the Coliseum or Pharoah Tutankhamen. However, while the former no longer exist outside of history books and museums, AIABWSR is alive and well right here, right now. It remains a horrific anachronism that keeps getting re-energized from generation to generation.

Allyship cannot therefore be an end goal. It is an ever necessary and relevant dynamic principle to combat the strategies of disunification and over-whelming force, the necessary counter to the energy invested in perpetuating AIABWSR.

Plato's allegory of the cave, in summary, describes the experience of a group of people who have lived their entire lives chained up inside with their backs to the opening of a cave and a fire between them and the opening. So, everything that passes by outside is seen as a reflection.

These chained-up people have never seen what anything actually looks like. One day one of the chained-up guys gets free, goes outside, and sees what things actually look like. He excitedly comes back and tries to describe "reality" to the cave people. They think he's nuts and prefer to believe the reflections they have seen all their lives are the "real reality."

All that to is say, people tend to believe what they are raised to believe. Unless some random event happens to move us out of our cave, many won't spend time questioning their reality. That is why to be an ally, you must turn your head. This is one of the most significant things you can do—to imagine that the reality you have experienced isn't the only version. That can open up intellectual curiosity about how others are living and further lead to empathy for and connectedness to other people. Understanding that others may have different experiences than you but are still and fully human expands the possibilities for shared reality and coexistence.

We are separated as individuals by our values. We also come together based on shared values, a sense "that something in common" makes the key difference. Ignorance is not bliss for humanity. We keep making the same deadly mistakes every generation or so. A seemingly intentional part of White supremacy is a disruption of the "collective unconscious" as well as a "collective consciousness" that humans need to learn from and overcome our societal mistakes.

We are born into this world "a blank slate," so it is difficult to understand how much you don't know. Each individual tabula rasa, however, emerges and is then integrated into an ongoing human story. Depending on your belief system, this story has been unfolding for between 5,000 and millions of years. Regardless of what you believe, that's a lot of generations of humans. Each generation of individuals, families, and societies has contributed to the overarching story of humanity, just as those of us alive are contributing right now. Many enjoy the blankness. There is an absolution of responsibility to both the present and the future in not knowing history.

White supremacists have unhesitatingly set precedents of slavery, genocide, interring people in concentration camps, and creating unjust laws in the New World. Then they brazenly want to pretend that history never occurred the way it did. That consciousness of guilt leads to the desire to cover up unflattering facts, which at least indicates some vestigial conscience. But the cover-up is just an attempt to perpetuate the scheme; White supremacy uses every psychological technique in the book to influence public opinion and discourse and to keep intergroup tension present, high, and ready to harness for action.

Humanity needs to make the crucial psychological breakthroughs that allow us to learn from history and not ignore it in ways that leave us vulnerable to repeating atrocities. White supremacists know that the lessons of history are so powerful that to keep the status quo, the teaching of the fullest recounting of history must be suppressed at any cost.

For example, White supremacists have suddenly become sensitive to notions of "replacement" simply because it's one of the wacky theories they made up and used to remove Native and Aboriginal peoples from their land. It's simply a projection. Projection is a staple of White supremacist thought. It always precedes justifying some horrific action—for example, "they are savages who scalp people so we can kill them," even though De Tocqueville in his book *Democracy in America* (1835) reported that scalping was a technique introduced by the French. This allows for "ignorance in the service of deniability": Claiming not to know basic historical and contemporary facts is a huge shield from psychological discomfort in the face of atrocities.

This is a perennial human struggle. That is how Columbus and company can go from "Wow, these people nursed our scurvy-ridden bodies back from the brink of death" to "These people have something we want, so let us dub them savages and take it."

Any system or society can only ever be as good as the foundational values it is built on. If we get over the false notion that evil actions happened in some remote "then" and only good actions are undertaken "now," it can help us to make more sense of what at times feels like an inconsistent and paradoxical experience.

Today, many of us are coming from a sincere place looking for answers. We must unify around higher principles and values and harness the overwhelming force of love, lovingkindness, and nonharming to create a safe, just, equitable world (King Jr., 1967). Love and community are the automatic, perpetual machine we can and must set in motion.

If you can't help, don't hinder.

References

Adams, J., & Sewall, J. (1819). *Novanglus, and Massachusettensis; or Political essays, published in the years 1774 and 1775, on the principal points of controversy, between Great Britain and her colonies.* Essay no. 7. Hew and Goss.

Berlin Conference. (2010). In H. L. Gates Jr. & K. A. Appiah (Eds.), *Encyclopedia of Africa.* Oxford University Press.

de Tocqueville, A. (1835). *Democracy in America.* Saunders and Otlley.

King, M. L., Jr. (1967). *Where do we go from here: Chaos or community.* (Josiah Royce, Ed.). Beacon Press.

Markham, C. R. (Ed.). (2010). *The journal of Christopher Columbus (during his first voyage, 1492–93): And documents relating to the voyages of John Cabot and Gaspar Corte Real.* Hakluyt Society. https://doi.org/10.4324/9781315556482

Rousseau, J-J. (1762). *The social contract.*

Swain, S., & Edwards, M. (2008). Approaching late antiquity: The transformation from early to late empire. In *Pagan and Christian monotheism in the age of Constantine.* Oxford University Press.

Wilkerson, I. (2020). *Caste: The origins of our discontents.* Random House.

PART II
ANTIBLACKNESS AND THE WORKPLACE

5

Do You See Me or Am I Invisible?

An African American Female Physician Working in a White Male–Dominant Profession

Colleen P. Ramsey

It seems like only yesterday that my journey into medicine began, with the planting of the seed in middle school. Back then, I was naive and believed that race relations had progressed further than they actually had. It was not until I was hit and bruised by reality that I realized things I had been led to believe were not true.

It was in 1954 when Brown V. Board of education was the landmark decision that segregation of schools was deemed unconstitutional. Both the Civil Rights Act of 1964 and the Higher Education Act of 1965 made it possible for Blacks to have better access to further their education. "Through desegregation of higher education and the removal of structural barriers into the medical field," wrote Onyinyechi and colleagues (2017), "one would assume more significant representation of African American women in this field. However, this change has only produced small gains as evidenced by under-representation of Black women in medicine" (p. 5). The *New York Times* reported, "Shockingly, only 5% of American physicians in the workforce are African American and about 2% are Black Women" (Goldberg, 2020).

Looking back, it has been almost 30 years since I joined the profession, and I wonder where the time has gone. Have I truly made inroads navigating the roadblocks, potholes, and diversions that might help others coming after me? Or am I delusional and things are about the same—and if so, how sad is that?

Colleen P. Ramsey, *Do You See Me or Am I Invisible?* In: *Antiblackness and the Stories of Authentic Allies.*
Edited by: Norman Kim, Carolyn Coker Ross, Mazella Fuller and Charlynn Small, Oxford University Press.
© Oxford University Press 2024. DOI: 10.1093/oso/9780197642535.003.0006

Bias and Bigotry

In 1995, I attended a birthday gathering for a colleague. As per usual I was the only person of color in attendance. A Caucasian female approached and commenced to inform me of how familiar I looked. I told her that I worked in the office with the man of the hour. Immediately, she began to fire off a series of questions: "Are you a nurse? Do you work in the lab, or is it the front desk?"

Mind you, I wore a white doctor's coat along with a stethoscope back then. She walked by me every time she saw her primary care provider, and that was frequently. So I informed her that I worked in none of these positions, nor did I clean the bathrooms or sweep the floors! My colleague came rushing over to diffuse the situation by introducing me as his partner. Sadly, this was not the first nor would it be the last encounter of discrimination, racism, and gender bias I experienced during my career.

During my early years in practice, I worked in an urgent care center. While in the lab, I asked the technician a question and she responded by addressing me as Dr. Ramsey. In the chair getting blood drawn was an elderly White female.

When she thought I had left the room she asked, "When did you all start hiring their kind?"

I turned around and asked her, "What kind would that be?"

I was so angry at the time.

What made it worse was that people were always refusing to acknowledge the presence or position of myself or people who looked like me in this profession. We were—and still are—often questioned: "Where do you come from? Where did you attend school? How did you land at this prestigious university?"

Recently, a patient I have managed for at least 10 years presented for a follow-up. This time, she was accompanied by her husband. It was obvious upon entering the exam room that he was surprised that I was African American. Mind you, I have never met this gentleman in person and have only spoken to him on the telephone. During the visit, he questioned everything I said or suggested.

I finally asked him, "Is there a problem?"

I followed up by asking him why he was interrogating me and challenging my competency. His wife finally interjected, stating that she did not like his tone or what he was implying. She informed him that she had been a patient of mine for many years and had a wonderful working relationship with her primary care physician and that together we had successfully managed her complicated health issues.

I clearly understood why he behaved as he did. And I was also certain that he was used to talking to people any way he chose. As a Black woman who is also a physician, this was not new or different for me. However, I no longer allowed it to derail me from the task at hand, which was providing excellent care to my patients. Bigots are everywhere, come from different walks of life, and present in various ways, though they think they are disguised and therefore not seen as such. No longer am I naive or wearing rose-colored glasses. On the contrary, my vision is clear and I am extremely aware of the climate that surrounds me and that permeates our country.

For quite a while I thought I was alone on an island with my feelings, often feeling isolated and unaware of whom to talk to or trust. But after conversing with colleagues across different specialties, I have heard familiar stories. Who would think that in this day and time, we still would be dealing with such challenges in our work environment and the climate at times would be so difficult? A common story is one of the health care provider walking into an exam or hospital room and introducing herself, only to be asked, "When is the doctor coming in?"

Once I saw a gentleman who was adamant about addressing me by my first name. I informed him he could call me Dr. Ramsey. He then commenced to tell me that my badge displayed my full name as Colleen Ramsey. I informed him that this was correct; however, I was not his provider, nor did he know me, nor had I given him permission to call me Colleen. I explained firmly that if he felt he could not address me appropriately and respectfully, he could see someone else in the practice.

His wife, who also was present during the exchange, questioned him on why he was behaving in this manner. I responded to her by saying flatly, "Because he thinks he can. He also assumes that I must accept it, but his assumption is wrong. No, I don't have to allow him or anyone to treat me with such disrespect."

He subsequently apologized and the visit went forward. As Onyinyechi and colleagues (2021) reported, "The burden for African American female physicians of having to constantly prove themselves in the face of covert and overt racism is exhausting and can take both physiological and psychological tolls" (p. 6).

Lack of Allyship

How do you know if you matter if on a regular basis you are dodging landmines, microaggressions, racial undertones, and defiance of recognition? "The term microaggressions was coined in the 1970's by a psychiatrist named Dr. Chester Pierce. It describes subtle, stunning and often automatic, and nonverbal exchanges which are meant as 'put downs' of Black people and members or other minority groups" (Goldberg, 2020, p. 1). I live in reality, but it is disheartening when you are in a meeting with colleagues and raise a concern or issue and they shoot it down or dismiss it, and not until a White counterpart chimes in with support does this issue then become validated. This is a frequent occurrence and often stymies participation by those who have experienced this type of treatment.

There was one incident that I had with a male provider concerning holiday vacation. He had been off the two previous Christmas holidays and I was requesting to be off that year. But for that to occur, he would have to work. The conversation deteriorated with him raising his voice, yelling at me, and being disrespectful in what he said. I was really shocked, saddened, and overwhelmed by his response, not to mention his behavior.

As Black women, we are always juggling monitoring our tone, volume of speech, and word choices so as not to be considered "threatening" or labeled as an "angry Black woman." I told the group of mostly White males and two White females that I was disappointed with the lack of support, especially since what I was requesting was what the group had always agreed on until it involved me. Later that day, several of them sheepishly came by my office to say he was wrong in how he had behaved and to apologize for not speaking up in support of my cause.

I asked them why they had not said anything during the meeting. There was no real response, just them glancing at the floor. "The experiences of female physicians are much different on average than their male counterparts and not always in good ways. They tend to get paid less for doing the same work and yet may experience more negative psychological states and burnout then their male colleagues" (Hoff, 2019, p. 1).

Finding Balance in Spite of Unfairness

It is humbling to be a physician and to take care of patients who entrust their lives to you. It brings me joy to know that I am making a difference even in some small way. We must learn to take our wins regardless of the size and be appreciative, for this is a wonderful profession that I love but that carries significant responsibilities and stress. I think that far too often we are seen and identified by what we do and not by who we are—we are people, just like our patients. Sometimes I tell patients, "If you cut me I bleed; if you hurt me I cry. I too have feelings."

Because of the intense daily mental and sometimes physical requirements of this profession, it is of the utmost importance that as medical professionals we have balance in our lives. I believe you need to be surrounded by people who love, care about, and support you and understand the rigorous demands of your daily life. Having friends and acquaintances from different walks of life also decreases the chances of conversations deteriorating into a continuation of work speak.

It is also important to find something that grounds you and moves you, something you can carry with you. For me, music is my calming and steadying thread. I am a lover of all genres of music and am often humming or singing a tune as I go through my day. "Through It All" is a gospel hymn that calms my spirit and gives me perspective into what is important.

I also find equilibrium in helping others. Frequently I am asked to mentor minority undergraduate students who are interested in the medical field. This is extremely satisfying and important because they get to interact with someone who truly understands their unique struggle and can guide them to where they want to go. Creating safer spaces for anyone who might be struggling is incredibly rewarding. It is very easy to get lost in the hoopla of this exciting profession. You cannot allow those who want to demean or belittle you to determine your self-worth. Nor can you mentally afford to spend countless hours on others' ignorance and flat-out racism. Only you can control the impact outside influencers have on your destiny and your contribution to the profession you love.

What I have come to realize is that if I keep the patient's best interest first, ensure they get all they need and require, and give them care with compassion, then I have done what I was put here to do!

References

Goldberg, E. (2020, August 11). For Doctors of Color, Microaggressions are all too familiar. *New York Times*.

Hoff, T. (2019, July 9). The challenges of being a female doctor. *Journal of Medical Economics*.

Hurt, J. (2017, April 12). Black female physicians face challenges just doing their jobs. *The Journal of Medical Economics*.

Onyinyechi, E., et al. (2021). Black women in medicine-rising above invisibility. *The Lancet, 397*(10274), 573–574.

6

Black American Women in Academia and Clinical Settings

Challenges and a Way Forward

Jacqueline A. Conley, Kisha B. Holden, Maisha Standifer, and Courtney E. Randolph

Black women in the United States have unique experiences that have affected their career trajectories and their mental and physical well-being. In this chapter, we share two fictional characters whose experiences reflect that of the lived experiences of many Black women in psychology. We also present research on gendered and racial microaggressions and structured racism and discrimination (SRD) and their impact on Black, Indigenous, and people of color (BIPOC), specifically Black women. It is imperative that positive ecosystems and practices are cultivated that support BIPOC women professionals.

Compilation of African American BIPOC Women Experiences

Dr. Brown's Story

Dr. Candice Brown is a Black woman who holds a PhD in Psychology from a historically Black college and university (HBCU); she trained under a scientist-practitioner model. She was mentored by faculty members during her doctoral program. Her professors engaged in research activities like presenting at conferences and publishing in peer-reviewed journals; however, their research was not fundable through federal grants. Dr. Brown's professors carried large teaching loads compared to faculty members

Jacqueline A. Conley, Kisha B. Holden, Maisha Standifer, and Courtney E. Randolph, *Black American Women in Academia and Clinical Settings* In: *Antiblackness and the Stories of Authentic Allies*. Edited by: Norman Kim, Carolyn Coker Ross, Mazella Fuller and Charlynn Small, Oxford University Press. © Oxford University Press 2024.
DOI: 10.1093/oso/9780197642535.003.0007

at predominantly White institutions (PWIs). Dr. Brown's HBCU was underfunded, contributing to other systemic issues inherent and salient to underfunded institutions. Outside of her dissertation, she had limited exposure to engaging in research.

Dr. Brown applied for several teaching positions in academia; however, she was informed that because she did not have a strong research agenda, she was not offered jobs at competitive teaching/research institutions. Dr. Brown was offered a tenure-track position at a small state-funded university, and she gladly accepted the opportunity. She was given a large teaching load and found it difficult to embark on a research agenda. In addition, most of her colleagues did not have a research agenda or were already engaged in research, and thus she could not collaborate with them. Similar to her faculty members in graduate school, Dr. Brown engaged in nonfundable research; however, she was able to publish several articles in peer-reviewed journals.

Despite the lack of opportunities to build a research agenda, Dr. Brown was an enthusiastic mentor and caring professor and served as her students' surrogate mother. After 7 years at the state-funded institution, Dr. Brown earned tenure; however, she decided to look for jobs at both HBCUs and PWIs that were more lucrative and where she could build a research agenda and collaborate with colleagues on research. Repeatedly, Dr. Brown was told, "You do not have a strong research agenda" or "You do not have enough publications." It was a disheartening, revolving story.

Currently, Dr. Brown also works part time as a clinician in a local clinic. She works with clients who do not respect her credentials, which she believes is predicated by her race. Her supervisor, a Caucasian male, tries to ally but dismisses most of her concerns, and her colleagues concur with her supervisor. Dr. Brown feels invisible.

Dr. DeVaughn's Story

Dr. Tamika DeVaughn is a Black woman who holds a PhD in Psychology from a PWI; her training is as a scientist-practitioner. During Dr. DeVaughn's doctoral program, she had opportunities to participate in federally and privately sponsored grant-funded research with her tenured faculty members, published with her faculty professors in tier 1 peer-reviewed journals, and attended and presented at professional conferences. Upon completion of her doctoral training, Dr. DeVaughn had 10 publications, plus her dissertation, a strong research agenda, and a strong faculty-mentored relationship.

Dr. DeVaughn was offered a job at a PWI where she taught two classes per semester, had teaching and research assistants, secured several large federal research grants, and earned the rank of a tenured professor. Despite her accomplishments, Dr. DeVaughn felt lonely and isolated and worked twice as hard as her peers.

Currently, Dr. DeVaughn also works part time in a group private practice, where she experiences racial epithets from White clients and receives negative and insensitive comments from White colleagues about her dreadlocks, and is given a larger client caseload compared to White colleagues, which primarily consists of Black clients. In this setting, Dr. DeVaughn feels disrespected, underappreciated, and stressed.

What Does the Workforce Look Like, in General, in Academia and Psychology for Black Women?

We must unveil the systemic structures that are inherent in the racialized, patriarchal structures in Western academic settings. Systematic barriers in the HBCU institutional networks have historically been underfunded, underperforming, and lowly respected. Having no external academic validity in the system, and always proving that "Black education" is worthy, is taxing. This weighs on professors and students attending HBCUs.

For a graduate student being trained within an overtaxing setting, it is extremely difficult to cultivate knowledge for securing a successful academic career for all the reasons displayed in Dr. Brown's setting. While Dr. DeVaughn had a much "easier" roadmap for her distinguished journey into the proverbial academic marathon, both women were victims of the stigmatized societal gaze of being a Black female in unsatisfying conditions in higher education in the clinical profession.

In 2020, Black women represented approximately 58% of Black workers in the labor force (U.S. Bureau of Labor Statistics, 2021). The National Center for Education Statistics (2018) reported that all full-time faculty in degree-granting postsecondary institutions were 40% White males, 35% White females, 7% Asian/Pacific Islander males, 5% Asian/Pacific Islander females, and 3% each of Black males and females and Hispanic males and females. According to the American Association of Academic and University

Table 6.1. Psychologists in the Workforce

	Asian	Black	Hispanic	White	Other
U.S. psychology workforce	5%	13%	6%	86%	1%
Health service psychologists	3%	3%	4%	88%	3%
Psychologists in academia	6%	6%	5%	81%	2%
Early-career psychologists	4%	11%	17%	66%	22%
Psychology doctorates awarded in 2016	6%	10%	13%	68%	2%
U.S. doctorate holders	13%	5%	6%	73%	2%
U.S. population	5%	12%	18%	62%	3%

Professors (2018), only 6% of faculty at private and public institutions were Black, less than half were tenured, and 2% were tenured Black women. The American Psychological Association (APA) published workforce findings in psychology and the U.S. population, shown in Table 6.1 (Lin et al., 2018).

The Center for Workforce Studies (2019) reported a projected increase in the number of Black people in demand in the psychology workforce by 2030: 11,870 full-time employee licensed doctoral-level Black psychologists, of which approximately 6,360 are women and 5,510 are men. Despite the projected increase of Black people in the profession, structural barriers need to be addressed due to the potential impact on the trajectories of BIPOC professionals.

The APA Committee on Women in Psychology (2017) reported that women in the field experience a variety of equity gaps compared to men. Specifically, women are underrepresented in leadership positions including full professorship, are paid 78% less than men, and only represent 18% of journal editorships. These statistics highlight the workforce inequities that Black women experience.

Barriers to Success

Research on Black women is often combined and generalized with research on women in general (Stanley, 2009). This contributes to the lack of understanding about unique racial microaggressions that many Black professional women experience compared to other racial groups. Black women experience double oppression (Thomas et al., 2008) based on the intersection of their race and gender (Lewis & Neville, 2015).

The DeCuir-Gunby et al. (2019) study on Black professionals in higher education reported that Black professors and administrators experienced undue health complications due to prevalent and persistent racial microaggressions. In addition, such racial microaggressions have led academic professionals to avoid interactions with colleagues, lose faith in peers and administration (Louis et al., 2016), and invoke coping methods to deal with the psychological stress (Holder et al., 2015).

Researchers have reported on the influences of racial microaggressions among Black employees, noting effects on mental health and well-being across different fields in the workforce (DeCuir-Gunby & Gunby, 2016; Louis et al., 2016). Black women who experienced more gendered racial microaggressions had significantly more negative mental health outcomes, poorer mental and physical health, and more psychological distress (Chadwick & DeBlaere, 2019; Lewis et al., 2017; Williams, 2018).

Career Trajectories in Academia

Davis and Maldonado (2015) explored professional development among Black women academics and reported five themes that emerged from the impact of microaggressions on their experiences:

1. Predestined for success: Black women come from a tradition where family is valued and provides support that contributes to their development as leaders.
2. Sponsorship from the unexpected: This significantly contributed to leadership roles.
3. Double jeopardy of race and gender: This intersection hindered Black women's potential to ascend to senior-level positions.
4. Learn how to play the game: Black women must know and understand the rules in their workplace to overcome barriers and leverage themselves for success.
5. Pay it forward: Giving back and mentoring other Black women contributes to the growth and success of future leaders.

Moreover, quantifiable evidence and personal stories note that the obstacles in academia are higher for women of color than for White academics in ways that can be hard to imagine for those on the outside (Fossett, 2021). One sentiment echoed by many women of color and illustrated by the experience of Hannah-Jones (a Pulitzer Prize–winning scholar from the University of North Carolina-Chapel Hill who was denied tenure) is the notion that you could be excellent, the best in the field, and still be discarded and disrespected by people who do not have the capacity to judge you. This speaks to the larger disconnect present between the diversity of university boards responsible for awarding tenure and those BIPOC women pursuing tenure.

BIPOC women in academia who are described as talented and ambitious report that they either burn out or are essentially forced out of the academy as a result of having to bear the weight of the lack of diversity at institutions. These exits are often predicated by an inconsistency in receiving support. Thus, BIPOC women rarely progress to a place where they can be eligible for and awarded tenure and promotion (Fossett, 2021).

Overall, microaggressions and SRD are supported by the power structures that exist societally, institutionally, and individually and are most likely to influence the career trajectories and health outcomes of the BIPOC professional. Black women are still experiencing racial microaggressions and SRD in the workplace, preventing them from advancing in their careers (DuMonthier et al., 2017).

Career Trajectories in Clinical Settings

BIPOC psychologists and mental health professionals are trained to provide a therapeutic milieu that fosters a better quality of life for others. As trained professionals who are culturally sensitive and responsive to clients, the BIPOC psychologist is most likely to experience racism and discrimination from three groups of people who perpetuate SRD against them in clinical settings (i.e., clinics, private practice, and hospitals): (a) clients/families, (b) coworkers and supervisees, and (c) supervisors/managers.

Pedrotti and Burnes (2016) identified several challenges experienced by BIPOC professionals in clinical settings:

1. difficulty finding mentors and supports within work settings

2. credentials being dismissed by clients and coworkers, thereby causing BIPOC professionals to insist on being addressed formally by the title "Dr."

3. anxiety about self-efficacy in performing duties related to discrimination and racism from clients, supervisees, and coworkers

Cencirulo et al. (2020) reported that trainees at a Veterans Affairs health care facility experienced racism, sexism, heterosexism, and ableism ("isms"). Sixty-nine percent of the respondents reported experiencing moderately to extremely stressful, upsetting, or bothersome isms. One Black woman respondent stated, "I often struggle with balancing asserting my needs with not wanting to be seen as the 'angry Black woman.' I believe in the moment [of the isms], I wanted to assert myself but was balancing expectations from others while in the professional role" (p. 245).

In addition, BIPOC psychologists may feel responsible for representing minorities in a socially acceptable manner—for example, feeling pressured to match White colleagues' grammatical accuracy, enunciation, dialect, "socially acceptable" hair, facial expressions, and dress attire. Dickens and Chavez (2018) posited that Black women professionals often succumb to identity shifting, which is altering one's behavior, language, and appearance to conform to cultural norms within a given environment, because they are often ill-typified in mainstream media as angry, sexually focused, and unladylike; therefore, they work hard to change this stereotype.

Challenges to Psychosocial, Physical, and Mental Well-Being

The various challenges faced by BIPOC professionals have contributed to negative physical and mental health outcomes such as increased rates of depression, heart disease, diabetes, hypertension, anxiety, and substance abuse (Al-Mateen, 2016). BIPOC professionals are at a greater risk of developing depression because of the various disparities they experience throughout life. Abrams et al. (2019) posited that Black women suffer from depression, anxiety, and psychological distress owing to racial microaggressions: "Depression among U.S. Black women has significant implications for the social and psychological well-being of the Black community" (p. 518). The psychological toll of racism is unwarranted, inappropriate, and avoidable.

Additionally, research has indicated, BIPOC individuals are not always given full proper medical care (Philbert, 2014); more specifically, Black women have been tagged as "superwomen" because of their resilience. Although it is true that they have strength and resilience, a large sum of these attributes manifested from mastering the art of representing strength through masking trauma (Abrams et al., 2019). The balancing act of their strength, though most times understood as a positive trait, was not acquired by choice but by obligation.

A Way Forward

With growing diversity concerning various ethnicities and nationalities, we must delineate strategic efforts that encourage system-level recommendations and suggestions that are action oriented relative to education, training, and work environment that may be an impetus for transformation and can provide support for BIPOC professionals in general and Black women in particular.

Research by Alston (2012) indicated that Black women's leadership experiences and "herstories" are absent from leadership positions in the United States. In the context of preparation, practice, and research, a few cornerstones of leadership (power, control, authority, and influence) have historically been used negatively to marginalize, silence, and erase the accomplishments of historically underrepresented groups (i.e., Black women). Power, privilege, and inequities are quite prevalent in various professional settings and do not endorse a trajectory for successful outcomes (White, 2008).

General Systemic Support for BIPOC Professionals

Some of the general system-level suggestions for support of Black professionals seeking success include the following:

- leadership
- education and training
- mentorship

- allyship
- mental and physical well-being

Leadership

Under leadership, we suggest that three main areas be considered to promote successful career paths and trajectories among BIPOC African American women:

- *Black scholars in leadership positions*
  It is critically important that Black scholars are elected and/or appointed to key leadership positions. This will support diversity and the use of experiences to bolster the possibility of enhanced decision-making.
- *Promote collaboration and partnership*
  It is imperative to promote collaborations and partnerships with organizations and agencies that recognize the significance of scholarship and advancement among Black professionals. This may require engagement with nontraditional entities that may offer varied perspectives.
- *Enact policies that positively impact Black communities*
  It is critical that federal, state, and local policies be enacted that value and enrich Black communities. This is particularly important since the Black community is the breeding ground and impetus for a pipeline for education, employment, and achievement to exist.

Education and Training

Education and training is another major area where general systemic support is needed. Under this section, we have identified three main areas:

- *Include equity-focused material in curriculum and educational modules*
  Learning opportunities exist for diverse individuals who adopt the use of equity-focused materials. Specifically, educational tools that recognize that inequities exist can serve as a platform for further scholarship (e.g., publications, professional presentations, etc.) to occur that may include Black professionals.

- *Expand the number of Black professors/teachers/intellectuals*
  There must be an increase in the number of Black intellectuals at various levels of education, from prekindergarten to postdoctoral training. This is important because Black children, teens, and adults must visualize successful Black individuals to help motivate their psychosocial reality of productivity.
- *Increase funding for Black institutions of higher learning*
  Although Dr. Brown, whom we met at the beginning of this chapter, attended an HBCU that provided excellent academic training, the limitations at her institution contributed to her career trajectory. Thus, financial support through federal grants, private foundations, and philanthropic donors is essential for the survival of HBCUs, which are the number one producers of Black professionals.

Mentoring

Dr. Brown received limited to no mentorship from her professors due to their teaching load and other duties required of faculty at HBCUs. On the other hand, Dr. DeVaughn received mentorship around research, publications, and grant writing. However, she did not receive the level of mentorship that made her feel like she belonged in the academic and professional arena despite her successes.

Thus, mentoring plays a key role in whether a professional reaches the highest echelons of corporate rank and authority (McGlowen-Fellows, 2004). For Black scholars, participation in a mentoring program and/or the establishment of a mentoring team has a significant role in nurturing professional networks, a sense of belonging, and coaching for a promising career path.

Allyship

Professionals should examine their role as an ally to BIPOC professionals and read the chapters in this book on allyship. Additional readings that can be valuable are works on White allyship (Spanierman & Smith, 2017; Sue, 2017), antiracist advocacy (Hargons et al., 2017), and radical healing for BIPOC individuals (French et al., 2019) to develop a better understanding of how social injustices, inequity, microaggression, and SRD have impacted BIPOC professionals.

Mental and Physical Well-Being

Stress management and burnout prevention can promote mental and physical well-being of BIPOC professionals, and these strategies should be action oriented. In addition, a strategic framework is provided that institutions, allies, and others can utilize to decrease microaggressions. Personal steps that BIPOC professionals can implement include developing action-oriented plans, reducing individual vulnerabilities, building resistance, and reducing stress reactions.

Moreover, use of a strategic framework that includes concrete action steps that targets, allies, and bystanders can perform (i.e., microinterventions) may be promising. Sue et al. (2019) developed a list of useful and concrete microinterventions:

- Stop, diminish, deflect, or put an end to the harmful act.
- Educate the perpetrator.
- Validate and support the targets.
- Act as an ally.
- Enlist outside authority or institutional interventions.
- Achieve any combination of these microinterventions.

Final Thoughts

Research has shown that there are inequities and racial disparities experienced by BIPOC professionals, specifically Black women. The personal and collective negative experiences of BIPOC professionals are countless, but the unfair treatment does not have to continue.

The first step toward a more equitable future is to inform society of these occurrences, which is the premise of this chapter. Second, accept that there are racial disparities that prohibit BIPOC professionals from equity. Third, enact the necessary changes to improve the experience of BIPOC professionals that will avail opportunities for advancement for all.

It is imperative that multidisciplinary professionals in leadership roles acknowledge and elucidate strategies to help ameliorate the nexus of psychosocial, sociocultural, and environmental issues that concern Black women scholars and clinicians. It is critical that an examination of the key factors that create, perpetuate, and exacerbate inequities be prioritized. Action-oriented steps that serve as an impetus for transformation must occur to support the creation of a more equitable discourse for Black women not only in psychology and their career trajectory but also, more importantly, in their daily lives.

References

Abrams, J. A., Hill, A., & Morgan, M. (2019). Underneath the mask of the strong black woman schema: Disentangling influences of strength and self-silencing on depressive symptoms among U.S. black women. *Sex Roles, 80*(9–10), 517–526. http://dx.doi.org.ewc.idm.oclc.org/10.1007/s11199-018-0956-y

Al-Mateen, C. (2016). Unconscious bias, microaggressions, and health. *Journal of the American Academy of Child and Adolescent Psychiatry, 55*(10), s47–s48. http://dx.doi.org.ewc.idm.oclc.org/10.1016/j.jaac.2016.07.623

Alston, J. (2012). Standing on the promises: A new generation of black women scholars in educational leadership and beyond. *International Journal of Qualitative Studies in Education, 25*(1), 127–129. https://doi.org/10.1080/09518398.2011.647725

American Association of Academic and University Professors. (2018). *Data snapshot: Full-time women faculty and faculty of color.* https://www.aaup.org/news/data-snapshot-full-time-women-faculty-and-faculty-color#.YTATTo5KiUk

American Psychological Association Committee on Women in Psychology. (2017). *The challenges gender composition of psychology.* American Psychological Association.

Cencirulo, J., McDougall, T., Sorenson, C., Crosby, S., & Hauser, P. (2020). Trainee experiences of racism, sexism, heterosexism, and ableism (the "ISMs") at a Department of Veterans Affairs (VA) healthcare facility. *Training and Education in Professional Psychology, 15*(3), 242–249. https://doi.org/10.1037/tep0000312

Center for Workforce Studies. (2019). *Demographics of the U.S. psychology workforce.* American Psychological Association. https://www.apa.org/workforce/data-tools/demographics

Chadwick, C. N., & DeBlaere, C. (2019). The power of sisterhood: The moderating role of womanism in the discrimination-distress link among women of color in the United States. *Sex Roles,* 5–6, 326–337.

Davis, D. R., & Maldonado, C. (2015). Shattering the glass ceiling: The leadership development of African American women in higher education. *Advancing Women in Leadership, 35,* 48–64.

DeCuir-Gunby, J. T., & Gunby, N. W., Jr. (2016). Racial microaggressions in the workplace. *Urban Education, 51,* 390–414. https://doi.org/10.1177/0042085916628610

DeCuir-Gunby, J. T., Johnson, O. T., Edwards, C. W., McCoy, W. N., & White, A. M. (2019). African American professionals in higher education: Experiencing and coping with racial microaggressions. *Race Ethnicity and Education*, *23*(4), 492–508. https://doi.org/10.1080/13613324.2019.1579706

Dickens, D. D., & Chavez, E. L. (2018). Navigating the workplace: The costs and benefits of shifting identities at work among early career U.S. black women. *Sex Roles*, *78*, 760–774. https://doi.org/10.1007/s11199-017-0844-x

DuMonthier, A., Childers, C., & Milli, J. (2017). *The status of Black women in the United States*. Institute for Women's Policy Research.

Fossett, K. (2021, July 9). *Burnout, racism, and extra diversity-related work: Black women in academia share their experiences*. Politico. https://www.politico.com/newsletters/women-rule/2021/07/09/nikole-hannah-jones-black-women-academia-493523

French, B. H., Lewis, J. A., Mosley, D. V., Adames, H. Y., Chavez-Dueñas, N. Y., Chen, G. A., & Neville, H. A. (2019). Toward a psychological framework of radical healing in communities of color. *The Counseling Psychologist*, *48*(1), 4–46. https://doi.org/10.1177/0011000019843506

Hargons, C., Mosley, D., Falconer, J., Faloughi, R., Singh, A., Stevens-Watkins, D., & Cokley, K. (2017). Black lives matter: A call to action for counseling psychology leaders. *The Counseling Psychologist*, *45*(6), 873–901. https://doi.org/10.1177/0011000017733048

Holder, A. B., Jackson, M. A., & Ponterotto, J. G. (2015). Racial microaggression experiences and coping strategies of Black women in corporate leadership. *Qualitative Psychology*, *2*(2), 164–180.

Lewis, J. A., & Neville, H. A. (2015). Construction and initial validation of the gendered racial microaggressions scale for Black women. *Journal of Counseling Psychology*, *62*(2), 289.

Lewis, J. A., Williams, M. G., Peppers, E. J., & Gadson, C. A. (2017). Applying intersectionality to explore the relations between gendered racism and health among Black women. *Journal of Counseling Psychology*, *64*(5), 475–486. https://doi.org/10.1037/cou0000231302

Lin, L., Stamm, K., & Christidis, P. (2018, February). How diverse is the psychology workforce? *Monitor on Psychology*, *49*(2), 19. ttp://www.apa.org/monitor/2018/02/datapoint

Louis, D. A., Rawls, G. J., Jackson-Smith, D., Chambers, G. A., Phillips, L. L., & Louis, S. L. (2016). Listening to our voices: Experiences of black faculty at predominantly white research universities with microaggression. *Journal of Black Studies*, *47*(5), 454–474. https://doi.org/10.1177/0021934716632983

McGlowen-Fellows, B. (2004). Changing roles: Corporate mentoring of black women: A review with implications for practitioners of mental health. *International Journal of Mental Health*, *33*(4), 3–18. https://doi.org/10.1080/00207411.2004.11043387

National Center for Education Statistics (NCES). (2018). *Fast facts: Race/ethnicity of college faculty*. https://nces.ed.gov/FastFacts/display.asp?id=61

Pedrotti, J. T., & Burnes, T. R. (2016). The new face of the field: Dilemmas for diverse early-career psychologists. *Training and Education in Professional Psychology*, *10*(3), 141–148. https://doi.org/10.1037/tep0000120

Philbert, R. (2014). *An exploratory study: The relationship between the stress of racial microaggressions and low-birth weight, pre-term labor and infant mortality on the children of college educated African American women*. https://www-proquest-com.ewc.

idm.oclc.org/dissertations-theses/exploratory-study-relationship-between-stress/docview/1646788395/se-2?accountid=34905

Spanierman, L. B., & Smith, L. (2017). Roles and responsibilities of White allies: Implications for research, teaching, and practice. *The Counseling Psychologist, 45,* 606–617. https://doi.org/10.1177/0011000017717712

Stanley, C. A. (2009). Giving voice from the perspectives of African American women leaders. *Advances in Developing Human Resources, 11*(5), 551–561.

Sue, D. W. (2017). The challenges of becoming a white ally. *The Counseling Psychologist, 45*(5), 706–716. https://doi.org/10.1177/0011000017719323

Sue, D. W., Alsaidi, S., Awad, M. N., Glaeser, E., Calle, C. Z., & Mendez, N. (2019). Disarming racial microaggressions: Micro intervention strategies for targets, White allies, and bystanders. *American Psychologist, 74*(1), 128–142. http://dx.doi.org/10.1037/amp0000296

Thomas, A. J., Witherspoon, K. M., & Speight, S. L. (2008). Gendered racism, psychological distress, and coping styles of African American women. *Cultural Diversity and Ethnic Minority Psychology, 14,* 307–314.

U.S. Bureau of Labor Statistics. (2021). *Blacks in the labor force.* U.S. Bureau of Labor Statistics. https://blog.dol.gov/2021/08/03/5-facts-about-black-women-in-the-labor-force#:~:text=For%20instance%2C%20in%202019%2C%20Black%20women%27s%20labor%20force,unemployment%2C%20especially%20in%20the%20wake%20of%20the%20pandemic

White, P. (2008). The hot seat: Black scholars perception of the chilly climate. In A. Wagner., S. Acker, & K. Mayzumi (Eds.), *Whose university is it, anyway? Power and privilege on gendered terrain. 231pp.* Sumach Publishing.

Williams, D. R. (2018). Stress and the mental health of populations of color: Advancing our understanding of race-related stressors. *Journal of Health and Social Behavior, 59*(4), 466–485. https://doi.org/10.1177/0022146518814251

7

Camouflaged Microaggressions

Thank You for Your Service

Cy'Tique T. Davis

When Cheering Is a Disturbance

The desert heat reached a scorching 116 degrees, and there was nothing to look forward to in Taji, Iraq, except incoming mortar rounds, improvised explosive device blasts, chow (eating), and the pallets of drinking water that were delivered every so often via military aircraft, since drinking water was a hot commodity. My days on this 15-month deployment were, at this point, routine and without variation or spontaneity.

However, on this particular day in November 2008, even the presence of mortar rounds could not deprive one African American female Soldier of the right of running through the container housing units celebrating the election of Barack Obama as the 44th president of the United States. Her squeal was loud, as if it came from the very bottom of her stomach and had been waiting for the past 400-plus years to be let out. Nothing stopped her squeals, not even the crowd of visibly confused and fearful onlookers, who likely were wondering if we were being mortared again or if there was a roadside bomb that had claimed the lives of more of our battle buddies—because surely that would be the only logical reason someone would yell and cry as frantically as she was in the middle of a war zone. It was not until she lapped the pod again, screaming, "My commander in chief is Black!," faced covered in tears, that we knew what was going on.

No one stopped her, and no other African American officer or senior-enlisted Soldier joined her. There was a great sense of apprehension and a slight feeling of offense in the air that the celebration of the first African American president of the United States would somehow infringe on some of the onlookers' White fragility, or maybe it was the perception that her celebratory screams and tears would create a wedge between the bonds of

Cy'Tique T. Davis, *Camouflaged Microaggressions* In: *Antiblackness and the Stories of Authentic Allies.*
Edited by: Norman Kim, Carolyn Coker Ross, Mazella Fuller and Charlynn Small, Oxford University Press.
© Oxford University Press 2024. DOI: 10.1093/oso/9780197642535.003.0008

majority and minority that had been otherwise formed in a war zone where all we had was one another.

The apprehension and fear would serve as the first time I was introduced to microaggressions and racial anxiety. As time went on, the rumor mill had it that the Soldier received a negative counseling statement for disturbing the peace as clearly we were in the middle of a warzone. This notice, coupled with the statements allegedly made by both White and African American service members—such as "This is why they cannot have anything" or, the one I thought was most offensive, "She's too articulate to carry on in such a manner"—struck a nerve within me that I carry to this day.

I could not fathom how her celebration had any bearing on her ability to be articulate, educated, or a great Soldier. I was utterly shocked at how her ability to articulate herself and how far she had come somehow meant that she was not supposed to have this Black experience, one that I imagined even our ancestors celebrated, and now all of what she had worked so hard to obtain was under scrutiny. All this scrutiny and hypocrisy, coupled with the newfound revelation that cheering was considered a disturbance—the same cheering as is done in February, in the same manner, during the Superbowl by ecstatic fans—was now considered a public disturbance; imagine that. Or maybe it was the unspoken resentment of the achievement that made the offense that much more egregious.

I often look back on her celebration and am filled with great conviction, wondering why I never chimed in or became a part of the change that Gandhi encouraged in the world. I could have raised my fist or given a high five, even a slight grin, or stood up for her when I heard those statements of offense and ignorance. *Why was I afraid to celebrate even though I felt it rising within me?* I did not even smile with my eyes, offer a slight grin, or suggest another way to celebrate, as maybe running through the container housing units in a warzone was too much, even though this celebration was necessary after years of oppression.

What I did do was cowardly walk back into my container housing unit and cry, as I was honestly afraid to celebrate this occasion publicly. I was afraid to code switch. I didn't want to undo all I had accomplished in earning a name for myself or be considered less than my fellow Soldiers who lacked melanin or were not built like me anatomically? I wasn't sure if cheering for the progress of my people and celebrating would have discredited my relationship with my superiors. I even wondered and feared that it could impact my advancement in the military, and at that moment, everything—and I do mean everything—was about advancing, even if advancing and making a name for myself robbed me of this moment in history, or maybe this feeling that I desperately wanted to deny was just implicit bias.

Or perhaps this uncertainty on which stance to take was because I foolishly chased the American dream. I sometimes wondered whether the American dream was meant for me at all: *Was I American enough for this dream?* I wondered where these thoughts were coming from and why now. I began to wonder if this fictitious sense of being at the table was all in my head. I started to recall the times I had been referred to as the bulldog (superhuman) but also all the times I and others were treated as subhuman.

Unknowingly, this uncertainty was because the microaggressions I heard and witnessed personally over time had caused damage to my self-identity, and I shamefully didn't feel that belonging or associating would have been appropriate even in the most subtle form.

I was happy to be a part of the United States Army. I did not question the rules, regulations, policies, or procedures, nor did I ever look into its history beyond what was required for my benefit or personal gain. To be clear: The military is not all bad; there were just bad moments, some bad people, and instances of blatant racial injustice.

The experiences, benefits, education, and camaraderie of the Army lend to my ability to write this simple but honest essay. This feeling of belonging would later be diminished once cultural appropriation made it apparent that the Army's body composition, military justice, and officer promotion standards were extremely biased against and detrimental to the careers of minorities. The rules associated with these standards were not necessarily made to protect me or to maintain equality; instead, I believe they were made to keep me in my place and confined to a standard I would struggle to maintain because of how God made me, which conflicts with how the Army directed I be.

For the sake of transparency, I progressed in the military because I became the bulldog. I barked loudly and oftentimes without reason or fact. I had superlative technical competency, and my physical abilities were unmatched; it was as if I exceeded standard human capabilities. Belonging to something that saw you as superhuman while the rest of the world saw you as subhuman had a way of making you feel great, even if it was as a mule.

The history and lineage of this organization, along with my slumbered mind, told me I was safe from systemic racism. You can attribute this lack of knowledge to my temporary blindness as a result of shiny backhanded compliments such as "Not too bad for a little black girl," when I would do something really well in a male-dominant organization, and "you speak very well." Or maybe my blindness to the microaggression was the result of the early advancements within my career. Either way, my slanted perspective would change the minute I was awoken with the dire need to know my role and duty as an orator and speak up against the blatant racism in the military, which seemed to decrease with the enforcement of its equal opportunity program, although camouflaged microaggressions remained, including African American females' hair being referred to as unkempt and matted.

Microaggressions in the Military

In the United States, racial microaggressions have become the norm. Racism has evolved from the "old-fashioned" overt form to something more subtle but just as potent. People of color experience hostile insults and unfriendly racial slights daily. Mostly these microaggressions happen as either microinvalidations, microassaults, and microinsults. African Americans face racial microaggressions in almost every public context. For instance, during a time when I took the public transit, I observed African American travelers be ignored while using or operating trains and buses by White commuters. Meanwhile on the same transit system, the White travelers socialized more with White bus drivers by saying hi to them and appreciating their service more than African American drivers.

Biases in the Military Judicial System

In the military context, African American service members are believed to have an equal opportunity to make it to the top based on merit, but this is not the case. The military's judicial system primarily lacks an explicit class for hate crimes, making it impossible to quantify microaggressions driven by prejudice. In addition, the Uniform Code of Military Justice fails to prevent discriminatory occurrences. And rank-and-file African American people often become subject to court-martial panels composed of all-White service members (Smither & Houston, 1991). This unbalanced composition of the panel contributes to harsher and more frequent punishments for African American service members (Solórzano & Huber, 2020). African Americans and Hispanics are more likely than Whites to face trials in a court-martial proceeding in all military services. The military service has failed to record information on race and ethnicity; thus, it becomes challenging to track disparities within the service.

According to Burk and Espinoza (2012), the Marine Corps faces racial issues, mainly in situations where severe fines are likely. On an annual average, African American Marines are 2.6 times more likely than White Marines to be subjected to an offense finding at a general court-martial, the military justice trial for various adverse crimes. The study also found that African American Airmen were 71% more likely than White Airmen within the Air Force to experience court-martial or nonjustice penalties, discipline dispensed for minor crimes (Knouse, 1991). Likewise, the Army and Navy have similar instances of disparities: African American service members are 61% more likely to become subject to court-martial than their White counterparts in the Army (Knouse, 1991), and African American sailors are 40% more likely than Whites in the Navy to be court-martialed (Burk & Espinoza, 2012).

Cooper (2020) revealed that 43% of the 1.3 million active service members in the U.S. military are people of color. Owing to the racial disparities prevalent in the composition of the military, the manifestation of microaggressions is not merely a contemporary blemish. Implicit biases and stereotypes significantly influence the rates of arrest, prosecution, and the granting of plea deals, thereby underscoring the pervasiveness of racial bias within the criminal justice system. Consequently, racial bias emerges as a salient societal concern, reflective of broader issues currently facing America. African American service members indicate that they lack room for error and that incidents with minimal or zero consequences for their White counterparts ended their careers.

White Supremacy in the Highest Ranks

African Americans are primarily within the military composition but invisible at the high ranks. Over 75 years of integration, the top tiers of the U.S. military have remained the domain of the White race. According to the *New York Times*, an October 2020 photograph showing President Trump with the highly ranked white-star generals and admirals angered many Americans because it depicted the high level of racism within the military

(Cooper, 2020). Lt. Col. Walter J. Smiley, an African American officer who participated in both the Afghanistan and Iraq Wars, said one could think the photograph was taken in the 1950s, when racial disparities within the military were rampant (Cooper, 2020). Another African American retired major general, Dana Pittard, stated that the pictures did not reflect the American value of equality among all its races.

Whites predominantly occupy the elite Special Operations forces at their top military ranks. The forces constitute the Navy SEALs, Army Green Berets, Rangers, and Delta Force commandos. General Michael Garret (retired), an infantry officer and then the Army's only Black four-star general, reveals that the absence of minority leadership at the top positions is a threat to the unity of the military. Primarily, African American service members should abandon support areas and take combat roles and responsibilities.

In interviews with African American, Asian, and Hispanic personnel and enlisted service members, they describe feeling constantly challenged over their right to become members of the U.S. elite units. African Americans experience limited chances for advancement in the military promotion system, unlike Whites (Finlan, 2019).

The detailed history of racism within the miliary explains why few African Americans are occupying top military positions. A 1925 directive for Army personnel noted that African American service members came from a class that produced few competent military leaders. Even after World War II, the U.S. defense forces did not fully integrate.

However, the elite service training colleges feeding the officer class—the U.S. Military Academy at West Point; the Naval Academy in Annapolis, Maryland; and the Air Force Academy in Colorado Springs—have boosted recruits from minority groups, but the recruitment panel remains primarily White dominated. African Americans who luckily become officers are mostly steered to deal with logistics, human resources and transportation duties instead of the marquee combat arms specialties leading to the high positions or jobs. As a result of this racial composition, African American and Hispanic service members portray a system with cementlike limits for Americans from marginalized groups (Cooper, 2020). During Trump's presidency, African American service members revealed that this regime only enlarged the logic of isolation evident within a stratified system.

Embedded White Ideologies

Military racism is significantly increasing and taking a vibrant course. According to Cooper (2020), research involving 1,630 active personnel consumers of *Military Times* revealed that 36% of those surveyed and 53% of service members from marginalized groups stated that they had witnessed various instances of White patriotism or ideology influenced by racist colleagues. Cooper (2020) reveals that these numbers rose over time, as the same survey carried out in 2018 noted that 22% of all participants revealed White nationalism within the service.

In recent years the Pentagon has received intensified reproval for multiple racist incidents. A case presented before a federal court in February 2020 by a Navy fighter pilot alleged that Air Force leaders and personnel at the Naval Air Station Oceana in Virginia Beach have always tried to hide the existing racism against African American aviators (Cooper, 2020). In the lawsuit, this Navy fighter pilot stated that institutional racism has contributed to the wrongful removal and exclusion of African Americans from pilot training programs. Cooper (2020) reveals that in an interview, the pilot's lawyer noted that African American airmen at the base were subjected to racially belittling call signs such as "8-Ball" and "eggplants" in group conversations on platforms such as Facebook, Instagram, WhatsApp, and Twitter.

In December 2020, West Point announced the discontinuation of its African American Knights football team from participation in the "God Forgives, Brothers Don't" flag (Cooper, 2020). This removal came after learning that the slogan demands allegiance to the Aryan Brotherhood of Texas, a White-based supremacy jail group. Cooper (2020) shows that despite the swift actions of Marine Corps leadership to ban the slogan after a picture with an S.S. flag emerged in Afghanistan in 2012, it continues to persist, like an underlying handshake.

Equally critical is where a person comes from. Cooper (2020) states that West Point, Annapolis, and Colorado Springs graduates are entitled to the military top ranks. Still, graduates of iconic African American colleges do not have the opportunity to obtain these leadership positions. Graduates from African American military training institutions who succeeded in their military profession specialize in transportation and logistics, including moving supplies or driving military transit trucks, rather than taking part in combat arms departments such as infantry. The logistical and transportation facets prominently feature the segregation within the military, particularly given that a majority of African American service members serve as quarter-masters and drivers for military vehicles (Cooper, 2020). But it is the combat positions, mainly during the last two years of the Wars in Afghanistan and Iraq, that result in top leadership jobs.

Racist Appearance Standards

In February of 2021, both the Army and Navy announced updates to their appearance standards. For a long time, the Navy and Army had banned hairstyles that were matted or unkempt and even referred to them as dread-locks. To reference this hairstyle, which speaks to the soul of a race of people, as dreaded is a microaggression in and of itself, as there is nothing dreaded about it. This is why the Air Force now calls them locs. Banning these hairstyles alluded to an assumption that individuals wearing these styles could not maintain or project a sense of professionalism that meets the standards of the branches of service. This notion was indicative of a lack of the cultural sensitivity necessary to create an environment inviting to minorities.

While the military body composition standards may be a good predictor of the total body fat in a population that is ethnically diverse, it fails to ad-dress the difficulties in evaluating body fat estimated by hydrostatic weighing as it is influenced tremendously by variations in bone density (Institute of Medicine Committee on Military Nutrition Research, 1990). This is prob-lematic as African Americans have greater bone mineral density than any other race (Hochberg, 2007).

Conclusion

The recent military experiences of racial microaggressions result from the perceptions of workplace discrimination and service members' poor mental health outcomes. As a result of these experiences, African American service members are seperated at rates disproportionate to those of their White counterparts. The military-based microaggressions have been primarily via avoidance, discrimination, and invalidation through denial and exclusion (Smither & Houston, 1991). These aspects relate to service members' ethnic heritage. Since the U.S. military has turned out to be a predominantly White organization, African American service members face different worlds and different regulations and assumptions of inferiority, undermining their capacity to depict good performance (Ray, 2019).

Conclusively, the microaggressions that African American service members experience are like the uniforms they wear—camouflaged. The top military ranks have failed to enforce equal standards for officers' promotions and the administration of military justice. Thus, there is no significant difference in terms of microaggressions experienced by African American civilians and African American service members. All people of color, irrespective of their position, are vulnerable to racism, as evidenced in the U.S. military. Therefore, the idea that African American service members get exempted from the microaggressions that their civilian counterparts experience daily is misleading and untrue. As an African American female officer who served this country without blemish or mistake and who was often considered a unicorn, I cannot guarantee an exemption from the world's rugged nature, even within professional fields.

Oh, and I joined in on the celebration this time around when a double minority, Kamala Harris, became the vice president of the United States and Lloyd J. Austin III, an African American man, became the secretary of defense for the first time since 1775. To that I say, "HOOAH!"

References

Burk, J., & Espinoza, E. (2012). Race relations within the U.S. military. *Annual Review of Sociology, 38*(1), 401–422. https://doi.org/10.1146/annurev-soc-071811-145501

Cooper, H. (2020, June 9). African-Americans are highly visible in the military, but almost invisible at the top. *New York Times*. https://www.nytimes.com/2020/05/25/us/politics/military-minorities-leadership.html

Finlan, A. (2019). A dangerous pathway? Toward a theory of special forces. *Comparative Strategy, 38*(4), 255–275.

Hochberg, M. C. (2007). Racial differences in bone strength. *Transactions of the American Clinical and Climatological Association, 118*, 305–315.

Institute of Medicine Committee on Military Nutrition Research. (1990). Body composition and military performance: Origins of the army standards. In B. M. Marriott & J. Grumstrup-Scott (Eds.), *Body composition and physical performance: Applications for the military services* (p. 3). National Academies Press. https://www.ncbi.nlm.nih.gov/books/NBK235960/

Knouse, S. B. (1991). Introduction to racial, ethnic, and gender issues in the military: The decade of the 1990s and beyond. *International Journal of Intercultural Relations, 15*(4), 385–388.

Ray, V. (2019). A theory of racialized organizations. *American Sociological Review*, *84*(1), 26–53.

Smither, R. D., & Houston, M. R. (1991). Racial discrimination and form of redress in the military. *International Journal of Intercultural Relations, 15*, 459–468.

Solórzano, D. G., & Huber, P. L. (2020). *Racial microaggressions: Using critical race theory to respond to everyday racism.* Teachers College Press.

8

The Right to Be Here but Still Marginalized

Renée Evans

Soleas (2021) states:

> The best you can hope for is to be aware of how you are biased and mitigate
> its impact. Our perspective on something as simple as a hockey hit or as
> complex as thoughts that spur discussion of histories that could demand a
> shift in worldview, are influenced by our past experience. (p. 3)

I attempted to write this chapter multiple times. However, in the mix of
reading about the happenings of Dr. Nikole Hannah-Jones (Dennie, 2021),
heightened current events around social unrest, the impact of COVID-19,
and experience in working with employees and supervisors around the integration of diversity and inclusion efforts, I've experienced mixed emotions
about the impact of it all. I've considered challenges around the above as
well as my own experiences around the "isms," diversity, and inclusion. The
isms are my own way of referencing my personal journey with experiencing
ageism, racism, and sexism.

Present Because I Qualify

As I'm a proud mental health professional who has worked hard for everything I've ever accomplished, I've found that to some in the workplace
my presence is still questioned (although I've met significantly more than
the minimum requirements for the job). The questions do not verbally
present themselves as inquiries or statements such as "Are you supposed to
be here?" or "You are not wanted here." Instead, these isms present themselves in the forms of statements of shock that I am capable of meeting professional milestones. Additionally, presentations of the isms come as private

Renée Evans, *The Right to Be Here but Still Marginalized* In: *Antiblackness and the Stories of Authentic Allies*.
Edited by: Norman Kim, Carolyn Coker Ross, Mazella Fuller and Charlynn Small, Oxford University Press.
© Oxford University Press 2024. DOI: 10.1093/oso/9780197642535.003.0009

and individual verbal acknowledgements of my accomplishments but a lack of acknowledgement and observable distance when it is time to recognize accomplishments to a larger professional group.

Rucks-Ahidiana (2021) notes that oftentimes Black women are perceived as being present in their work setting as a result of affirmative action or other efforts to hire minority employees. Adams (2006) recounts her experience as the only Black female faculty member in her department of a higher education institution. She reflects on being met with resistance in welcoming her to the department, having a lack of support from colleagues during the tenure process, and being dismissed by her mentor because she was smart. Adams (2006) further explains that she always felt the need to excel beyond the norm. Specifically, "many faculty of color have been instructed to always do their best and be better than the rest. While excellence is demanded of you, mediocrity is accepted of others" (Adams, 2006, p. 39).

This thought process and desire to excel beyond the norm stayed with me as I developed professionally. Therefore, to be questioned or discounted as not being capable of performing at the same level as my colleagues was a disheartening experience. However, I'm sad to share that it was not a surprise and I always knew it might occur.

Presentation of the isms appeared when I, along with colleagues, observed bold and direct disrespect toward me as a woman in comparison to male colleagues in the room. Presentations of the isms arose when there was an opportunity to show support for my professional advancement but instead, there was a clear lack of inclusion and acknowledgement of competencies from those in a position to show support. Presentation of the isms occurred when the individual expected to support me failed to do so during a time when I was being misrepresented.

Some may argue that the presentation of what I call the isms can be explained as harmless or without the intent to offend or maybe was just based on one's personality or their everyday way of being. Some may even say that these experiences have nothing to do with race, sex, or age and that I may have been too sensitive and was merely incorrect in my perceptions. Others would describe my experience as valid and understood due to *implicit bias*. FitzGerald and Hurst (2017) describe implicit bias as a lack of conscious awareness that negatively impacts one's evaluation of a person.

Recognizing Implicit Bias for What It Is and Its Impact

Implicit bias is the process by which one unconsciously allows their assumptions or stereotypes towards a group of people to guide the way they perceive or receive those individuals and thus impacts the way in which they treat those same individuals (FitzGerald & Hurt, 2017; FitzGerald et al., 2019; Pritlove et al., 2019). When experienced, it should not be explained as an excuse and then given a pass. It should be addressed, then received with an effort to gain awareness first, be understood second, and eliminated as best as possible in future interactions third.

Further, it is necessary for those who exhibit implicit or explicit bias to understand that everyone has a right to be treated as human beings with individual dignities. It is equally important to consider the impact of those biases on others at work. Soleas(2021) expresses that "Our biases remain innocuous until our assumptions impact our behaviors toward other people. By acknowledging our biases we can find ways to mitigate their impact on our decision making" (p. 1).

Additionally, the level of employee engagement may decrease due to lack of belonging in the workplace. The psychological impact, which includes one's ability to focus while at work, may also be eroded due to unfair implicit biases. Hofhuis et al. (2016) suggest that a company's ability to promote openness towards individual differences in the workplace may increase *psychological safety* among employees. Psychological safety is described as being similar to trust in the workplace. When there is intention to address implicit biases in the workplace, employees feel a sense of belonging and value. Ultimately, a feeling of psychological safety says employees have a right to be there, are accepted, and are respected in their roles.

Morrison (2013) shares her experience as a White person trying to manage her own realities of dealing with racism when trying to be a trustworthy ally for someone being discriminated against. She states that "as white people, we have inherited an intergenerational legacy of silence, looking away, pretending not to notice, and numbness to pain. As Robert Terry said, 'To be white in America is not to have to think about it'" (Morrison, 2013, p. 2). This is powerful as she works through her own implicit biases that might negatively impact others.

It is essential for employees and supervisors to become aware of how they have been influenced from childhood to the present day. This allows them to better understand themselves. Morrison (2013) further explains that it is necessary for individuals of privilege to make their privilege visible, which in turn allows them to be more vigilant:

> Without that vigilance, we are indeed dangerous because we behave like dinosaurs that drag a large tail behind us. Unable to see the tail, and convinced of our good intentions, we are oblivious to the havoc we wreak as we move through the world, knocking people over and flattening things in our path. (p. 3)

Executive leadership and members of management in the workplace have an obligation to ensure that the workplace climate is inclusive and welcoming of individuals from diverse backgrounds, perspectives, experiences, etc.

Diversity and Inclusion

Oftentimes when we consider *diversity* and *inclusion* work, individuals will combine the two terms. However, diversity is the visible representation of differences such as hiring members of diverse races. Inclusion is the intentionality of having diverse teams represented when effecting systemic change. This process includes a representation of diverse voices, perspectives, and ability to influence policy and other major decision-making processes.

Sharma (2021) describes diversity and inclusion in the workplace as

> "the set of strategies, policies, and missions adopted by a company to create and encourage an inclusive workplace that attracts a diverse pool of talent from various cultural backgrounds". . . Diversity in the workplace refers to an organization's workforce comprising people from different genders, sexual orientations, religions, races, ethnicities, ages, etc. . . Inclusion in the workplace means ensuring that every employee feels included and a part of the team. An inclusive workforce will feel valued, seen, heard, and respected. Consequently, you will notice a boom in innovation, higher cooperation, and increased employee engagement. (pp. 2, 8)

Sharma (2021) discusses the importance of companies being intentional about integrating both diversity and inclusion into the work setting. It is believed that while diversity may show a variety of people, perspectives, etc., it does not automatically mean that there is a practice of inclusion in that company, thus the need to be intentional around enhancing diversity, and ensuring employees have a seat at the table in effecting systemic change.

Inclusive Leadership

"Inclusive leadership is needed to support an inclusive climate in which different team members are valued for what they bring to work practices. Inclusive leadership is crucial for fostering inclusiveness in diverse teams" (Ashikali et al., 2020, p. 1). Ashikali et al. (2020) explains that inclusive leadership is necessary when promoting a sense of belonging and community among employees. The following are key tenets for observable inclusive leadership efforts:

1. supports diversity of team members and perspectives
2. encourages cooperation among diverse team members
3. recognizes uniqueness among team members while identifying positive and negative team outcomes
4. promotes a safe workplace climate in which diverse employees feel welcomed
5. promotes workplace climate that is open to differences to a point that employees are able to discuss their distinct differences as well as diverse views

Dennie (2021) further explains the importance of supportive leadership in the workplace, specifically in higher education:

> There can be no academic freedom where boards of trustees cultivate an atmosphere of disdain for antiracist work. There can be no academic freedom without the freedom to study race and racism. Faculty of color, in particular, require the security to do their jobs without the threat of being fired or denied tenure simply for interrogating systems of oppression. (p. 3)

Leaders who are intentional about diversity and inclusive practices must be willing to address issues of implicit and explicit bias (as it relates to all isms), have hard conversations about the impact on employees/leadership, and be willing to stand alone, if needed, when their efforts may seem different or outside the norm. Soleas (2021) asserts that when we don't address biases, this contributes to difficulty in encouraging conversations among members of one's work setting. Soleas (2021) also shares that this feeds one's desire to consider biases as truth and supports the thought that others' concerns around biases are invalid.

Inclusive leaders also understand the importance of developing their minority staff and ensuring they have the same options as their majority-demographic coworkers. Specifically, recognizing minority employees for leadership development programs and other professional development training is key to exhibiting a commitment to support diverse staff.

Part of this training includes the subject of diversity, inclusion, biases, and cultural awareness. Pritlove et al. (2019) explain

> that implicit bias training can make individuals aware of their unintentional involvement in the perpetuation of discrimination and inequity as well as the unrecognised advantages they enjoy based on group membership. Such training encourages individuals to confront their own biases and unearned privileges and to learn strategies aimed at reducing discriminatory thoughts and practices. Additionally, as the concept of implicit bias has gained popularity, it has enriched public consciousness and discourse on gender inequity. (p. 1)

Sharma (2021) describes steps to promote diverse and inclusive work settings:

1. Educate leadership. It is the responsibility of human resources and executive leadership to ensure managerial staff are trained on diversity and inclusion policies. Leadership should be trained at all levels of diversity and inclusion, as should all employees.
2. Develop an employee council. This may include employees who represent the demographic makeup of all employees.
3. Hire diverse employees. Intentionality during the recruitment, hiring, and retention process is essential. Human resources may include minority resource groups to assist in the hiring process.
   Additionally, there has to be a commitment to implement equitable opportunities for minority candidates (Ashikali et al., 2020). Dennie (2021) explains that the University of North Carolina's Department of Chemistry wrote a letter to their chancellor expressing concern

about the university's hiring practices around the treatment of Nikole Hannah-Jones (regarding their lack of offering her tenure initially as a Knight Chair). Specifically, they expressed concern around this experience hurting their ability to recruit minority faculty. Executive leadership and managers should be mindful of whether others are directly and negatively impacted by their decisions. It could also contradict the desire to be intentional about diversity and inclusion (Rucks-Ahidiana, 2021).

4. Focus on a "culture add" versus a "culture fit" approach.

   A Culture Fit approach focuses on familiarity. It encourages more of what is already working. On the other hand, a Culture Add approach focuses on welcoming new voices and talents that will positively impact the company culture. The Culture Fit approach limits or somewhat lacks diversity. It prohibits a company from welcoming new talent. With the Culture Add mindset, both employers and employees can address their own unintended and unconscious biases that come into play while making decisions." (Sharma, 2021, p. 14)

5. Stay connected through communication with employees. The ability to build solid working relationships with employees, from a genuine space, is a gift that does not naturally happen for all managers. Employees should know they have access to their managers and have open and consistent communication. A lack of communication leads to ambiguity and allows employees to create their own narratives about workplace happenings. This could cause a breakdown in the sense of community among employees.

6. Provide diversity and inclusion training. It is pivotal that all staff, managers, and employees are trained. This is ongoing work and requires progress over time. However, it is a must-do.

7. Promote creativity and innovation. Employees' comfort in sharing unique ideas is essential. Managers become key systemic game changers when they commit to diversity and inclusion. This includes developing and recognizing creative skillsets and viewpoints from employees. Ultimately, this says to employees that they are valued and that their opinions count.

8. Be accountable. Executive leadership must measure the effectiveness of integrating diversity and inclusive efforts:

"The best way to measure if a company's D&I strategies are effective is by measuring metrics like employee productivity, employee morale, and employee engagement. These metrics should give a clear picture of how accepted, appreciated, and welcome employees feel in their organizations." (Sharma, 2021, p. 16)

These steps are necessary for leaders who are committed to inclusivity and contributing to the systemic process of the company.

Watching Fellow Employees Watch You Being Marginalized

Workplace performance suffers when there is consistency of mistreatment due to biases, whether departmental or systemic (FitzGerald & Hurst, 2017; Hofhuis et al., 2020; Perry & Li, 2019). Regardless of the level from which the treatment comes, it is always interesting to watch those who provide support to those who are suffering. Sometimes a supportive individual has had the same experiences and, therefore; directly understands. Sometimes people respond by way of silent advocacy: They may advocate, but privately with a manager or fellow coworker.

On the other hand, some people are in positions of influence merely by belonging to the majority group or to the leadership group (Morrison, 2013; Spanierman & Smith, 2017). When it is time to effect change that may challenge the historical way of being, these individuals will not participate (Morrison, 2013). It is always interesting to watch these employees watch other employees being mistreated yet choose to not positively effect change.

When approached to respond to or advocate against the mistreatment, these individuals may choose to avoid direct involvement; however, in a one-on-one exchange, they present themselves as supportive of the individual being mistreated and in disagreement with the mistreatment. These same individuals may also distance themselves from the employee being mistreated even though they have observed the mistreatment happening. This is one of the most puzzling aspects of experiencing intentional bias in the workplace.

There is a dearth of literature around fellow employees watching coworkers being marginalized. The closest may be related to information about White allies or allies (Morrison, 2013; Soleas, 2021; Spanierman

& Smith, 2017), but that is typically about their intention to help the marginalized person. Because of this lack of information, I hope to evoke conversation and interest in research around the subject area. Here are a few points to ponder about employees who watch other employees being marginalized:

1. Is the person witnessing you being marginalized a coworker or leader who is in a position of influence to reverse the mistreatment?
2. Is the person witnessing you being marginalized in a position to change/develop policy to address the mistreatment?
3. Is the person witnessing you being marginalized a bystander who is encouraging the mistreatment, enjoys watching, or feels superior to you because they view you as a target for the mistreatment?
4. Should the person witnessing you being marginalized automatically be expected (or be perceived as obligated) to influence change by addressing the mistreatment? Is this fair to them? Is this an issue they should take on?
5. Should there be consideration for potential job loss/retaliation if the person witnessing you being marginalized chooses to assist you?
6. Should there be consideration that the person witnessing you being marginalized may not have enough confidence to advocate for you?
7. Should there be consideration for the person witnessing you being marginalized if that person believes they may cause more harm if they assist you?
8. Is the person witnessing you being marginalized benefiting or losing in any way by you being marginalized?

Although one may be experiencing bias in the workplace and need support, it is necessary for that person to identify those who are in the best position to assist them. It should be a trusted person who can be a resource and help the employee identify the best ways to navigate the situation.

White Allies

Spanierman and Smith (2017) describes a *White ally* as a White person who recognizes their privilege and is comfortable using it to advocate for change. This change may be at an individual, departmental, or company/systemic level. Although historically many minority groups have had the support of allies, there have been roadblocks in ally work. Morrison (2013) states:

> "To understand what it means to be white in America and break the silences that surround it requires arduous, persistent, and soul stretching work. Sadly, too many of us stop short of the deep work. We assume that our good intentions and eagerness to help are enough." (p. 1)

Spanierman and Smith (2017) identify treating employees in a paternalistic way as one roadblock. As a result, employees may perceive a hierarchical stance in the relationship and thus feel like a subordinate to the ally. This may also make the employee feel like they are seen as a charity case to the ally.

Another roadblock is the assumption that one's oppression may be comparable to another's experience of oppression. Although the ally may be able to show empathy toward another employee about a discriminatory experience, the ally must be careful not to minimize the coworker's experience. Sometimes this is viewed as not taking them seriously.

A third roadblock is overemphasis of White racial identity development in a way that comes across as undermining the actual racial issues and their impact on minorities. Although it is necessary to note these roadblocks, the work of allies has always been acknowledged and appreciated. Therefore, those who are allies are encouraged to not give up on their work but to also try to understand the impact of these roadblocks with intentionality so as not to mimic them.

Conclusion

Employees from underrepresented groups often encounter unique and unfair experiences that are specific to them. This comes in the form of biases, discrimination, and other unfair treatment. Oftentimes an employee's right to belong in the workplace is questioned.

There is necessity to ensure that leaders are intentionally inclusive in their daily workplace practices and considerations for those leaders as they move towards this intentionality is paramount. The impact of fellow employees watching another employee being marginalized and its intent is a topic that would benefit from further research. Finally, the importance of White allies and considerations for those allies has a significant impact in the workplace.

One purpose of the author's recounting of experiences and discussion of the subject area is to speak truth and give validation and affirmation to someone else's experience. Another is to ensure that others are not alone and are supported in what they know their experience to be/has been. A third is to confirm for many that it is understood that these experiences are not new and are recognized as taxing to an employee in the workplace.

It is encouraged for employees with similar experiences to remember that the goal is to remember your skillset, worth, and commitment to being about the business of good work. When necessary, remove yourself from toxic settings. Always address issues as you are able and as necessary in a professionally appropriate manner. Remember to thank those who see, hear, and support you. Pull from your strength source to allow you to continue to manage daily. When you do good work without biased or selfish agendas, the universe will use it for your good.

This chapter also aims to motivate executives and managers to be intentional about their awareness of who they are personally and its impact as they support diverse employees. The goal is to challenge leadership to determine ways in which their systemic process supports or discourages inclusivity of employees. The hope is that underrepresented team members will be seen/heard as competent beings and supported in workplace advancement and career development.

Soleas (2021) states that our biased perceptions and experiences affect how we interact in our environments. Morrison (2013) shared the following quote about White allies. I believe it is true for all in the workplace:

"I believe it is possible to become trustworthy white allies if we are willing to move out of our comfort zones, risk having our assumptions challenged, our lives disrupted, and our way of viewing the world transformed. Most important is the commitment to stay on the journey." (Morrison, 2013, p. 5)

The ultimate goal is for managers and executives to always measure and improve upon their efforts with the hope that they will be better and do better in supporting all employees.

References

Adams, S. G. (2006). Succeeding in the face of doubt. In C. A. Stanley (Ed.), *Faculty of color* (pp. 36–40). Anker Publishing Company.

Ashikali, T., Groeneveld, S., & Kuipers, B. (2020). The role of inclusive leadership in supporting an inclusive climate in diverse public sector teams. *Sage Publishing, 41*(3), 498–519. https://journals.sagepub.com/doi/pdf/10.1177/0734371X19899722

Dennie, N. D. (2021). The assault on black academics. *The Review*. https://www.chronicle. com/article/the -assault-on-black-academics

FitzGerald, C., & Hurst, S. (2017). Implicit bias in healthcare professionals: A systemic review. *BMC Medical Ethics, 18*(19), 1–18. https://doi.org/10.1186/s40359-019-0299-7

FitzGerald, C., Martin, A., Berner, D., & Hurst, S. (2019). Interventions designed to re-duce implicit prejudices and implicit stereotypes in real world contexts: A systematic review. *BMC Psychology, 7*(29), 1–12. https://doi.org/10.1186/s40359-019-0299-7

Hofhuis, J., van der Rijt, P. G. A., & Vlug, M. (2016). Diversity climate enhances work outcomes through trust and openness in workgroup communication. *Springerplus, 5*(1), 714. DOI 10.1186/s40064-016-2499-4

Morrison, M. S. (2013, Spring). Becoming trustworthy white allies. *Reflections*. https://refl ections.yale.edu/article/funny-race/becoming-trustworthy-white-allies

Perry, E. L., & Li, A. (2019). Diversity climate in organizations. https://doi.org/10.1093/ acrefore/9780190224851.013.45

Pritlove, C., Juando-Prats, C., Ala-leppilampi, K., & Parsons, J. (2019). The good, bad, and the ugly of implicit bias. *The Lancet, 393*, 502–504. https://www.thelancet.com/action/ showPdf?pii=S0140-6736%2818%2932267-0

Rucks-Ahidiana, Z. (2021). *The systemic scarcity of tenured black women*. https://www. insidehighered.com/advice/2021/07/16/black-women-face-many-obstacles-their-effo rts-win-tenure-opinion

Sharma, P. (2021). Diversity and inclusion in the workplace: A complete guide. *Vantage Circle*. https://blog.vantagecircle.com/diversity-and-inclusion/

Soleas, E. (2021). Bias is natural: How you manage it defines your ability to be just. *The Conversation*, 1–5. https://theconversation.com/bias-is-natural-how-you-manage-it-defines-your-ability-to-be-just-161874

Spanierman, L. B., & Smith, L. (2017). Roles and responsibilities of white allies: Implications for Research, teaching, and practice. *Sage Journals, 45*(5), 606–617. https://doi.org/10.1177/0011000004269058

PART III
ANTIBLACKNESS AND INTERSECTIONALITY

9

How to Be an Anti-Ableist Clinician

Addressing Intersectionality of Race and Ability in Mental Health Care

Janelle A. Johnson

Introduction: A Tale of Two Women

Imagine this scene and setting: It is late spring, and you have been invited to a prestigious award dinner. When you arrive early, you sit at your assigned table and find yourself alone with one other person. She seems to be a kind and determined Black woman in her mid-30s; you sense this because her serious look is occasionally interrupted by a broad and inviting smile. As you engage in small talk, you learn that she is an accomplished clinician who owns a group practice and has recently been elected as president of her state professional board.

Her passion is using systemic therapies to treat trauma, particularly in historically marginalized families, and she is well known and respected in her community. When you ask what brings her to the dinner tonight, she says, "I was nominated for the prestigious award. I'm not sure how it's going to go, so wish me luck!" You do so with sincerity before drifting to another conversation at a table nearby.

Not long after, you excuse yourself to visit the restroom. Along the way, you happen across another Black woman who seems in distress. She is staring at a wall, taking deep breaths, and mumbling to herself. When you stop to ask if everything is all right, you learn that she is in her mid-30s, and for her whole life she has struggled with parties and social gatherings.

"I'm neurodivergent," she sighs, then goes on to explain how taking deep breaths and finding a calm, quiet space helps her manage the overwhelm. She briefly mentions a history of trauma, depression, and several chronic illnesses.

Janelle A. Johnson, *How to Be an Anti-ableist Clinician* In: *Antiblackness and the Stories of Authentic Allies.*
Edited by: Norman Kim, Carolyn Coker Ross, Mazella Fuller and Charlynn Small, Oxford University Press.
© Oxford University Press 2024. DOI: 10.1093/oso/9780197642535.003.0010

"I haven't attended anything like this since being diagnosed; it's been over 2 years!" she exclaims.

When you commend her for coming anyway, she says: "But I had to. I was nominated for the prestigious award tonight, I refused to miss it." She thanks you for checking on her and heads into the ballroom, leaving you to process what just happened.

Processing your thoughts regarding each woman is a good start to exploring your understanding of intersectionality—the interconnected nature of social categorizations, regarded as creating overlapping interdependent systems of discrimination or disadvantage (Rogers et al., 2013). If you are like most people, you may have taken note that the first woman was Black and received a nomination, while experiencing a feeling like surprise that the second Black woman also received a nomination. Perhaps even more surprising is that both women are different descriptions of just one person: me.

As a disabled Black mental health leader, educator, and business owner, the version of me that you will experience depends on myriad factors. Yet disability is part of my identity no matter how "normal" or "productive" I am perceived to be.

Because disability often manifests in multifaceted ways like this, most disabled people need accessibility at work, school, and community designed using a both/and paradigm and a society that embraces both our unique contributions and our necessary accommodations. Unfortunately, the opposite tends to happen, and discrimination abounds, with too few spaces where such holistic support can be found.

Finding examples of discrimination against disabled people in our day-to-day lives can be difficult not because it is rare, but precisely because it is so common, so deftly woven intothe fabric of society for millennia. This form of social and systemic oppression can make embracing one's Blackness and disability together uniquely difficult, since, much like multiracial people, neither Black culture nor disability culture has fully accepted the other.

As such, Black clients are seeking trauma-sensitive, culturally humble, empowering clinicians to collaboratively support them as they manage ongoing trauma and life stressors. In this chapter, we will explore ability, disability, and critical disability theory in the context of the Black experience. This will serve as the foundation for a simple yet profound anti-ableist framework clinicians and counselor educators can utilize with Black and Brown disabled people, in and out of the therapy room.

Importance of Anti-Ableism

Before we begin, you may notice my use of the word "disabled" as a pronoun. This is purposeful, due to the majority of people in disability culture self-identifying in this manner and preferring to be referred to as such. There may be times in this chapter where I also use a more popular term in academia, "person(s) with disabilities," or PWD. Be mindful that best practice is to ask someone how they identify—a person may or may not hold their disability as part of their identity.

Now, to understand how to become an anti-ableist clinician, one must understand *ableism*—the systemic discrimination against those who are disabled. Much like racism, it is a system that places value on bodies and minds based on faulty social constructs like "normalcy," "intelligence," "productivity," and more (Lewis, 2022). In fact, racism and ableism are the wonder twins of systemic oppression; ableism in its ancient familiarity was used as a tool to commit heinous crimes against Blackand Native Americans. Genocide, enslavement, theft of land, eugenics, segregation, and more were all made acceptable because according to the scientists of the day, these people were mentally inferior, had a low IQ, were underdeveloped, and the like.

To be anti-ableist is to purposefully choose to grow in one's knowledge, advocacy, and empowerment of disabled people. Though we know better than our ancestors, the existence of ableism is not well known like racism and is lost on much of society, even among mental health practitioners and educators.

For Black people, this is particularly challenging for many reasons, all of which contribute to higher rates of disability (Courtney-Long et al., 2016). 25% of Black individuals in America are disabled, with only Native Americans having a higher rate at 30%(2016). In addition, the rates at which Black people receive mental health care is significantly lower than White counterparts (Primm et al., 2010). This coupled with the underrepresentation of Black clinicians and barriers to access lends itself to a recipe for disaster, evidenced by Black people with mental disabilities being overrepresented in the criminal justice system (Hawthorne et al., 2012).

When a person is more likely to be disabled and more likely to be underdiagnosed, overdiagnosed, or overlooked entirely, they are often left feeling disempowered. When they also have less access to care and increased likelihood of punitive or deadly actions against them for having a mental health concern, that person is existing between a proverbial rock and a hard place. This is where many of the Black clients at our practice find themselves, one of whom I will introduce to you later in this chapter. Yet we succeed in our work with them in part because do we define ourselves as not only therapists but also disability advocates—and we encourage all other clinicians to do the same.

Legal, Ethical, and Moral Considerations

How can I say with such certainty that all mental health professionals are also supposed to be disability advocates? In 1990 the landmark ruling was finalized for the Americans With Disabilities Act (ADA). This was the culmination of over 25 years of advocacy and activism by the disabled community and their allies; it included mental health disorders. This was key, as approximately 20% of Americans have a mental health disorder, making psychiatric disability the leading cause of disability in the workplace.

However, many Black people with mental impairment are not aware of their inclusion in this law and subsequent rights and protections provided by it. Because of the challenges with diagnosis coupled with other systemic issues like racism, Black people often find themselves denied rights when they advocate for them. Why would this matter to us as mental health professionals? For two reasons: first, our ethical guidelines hold us to a standard of anti-ableism and antiracism, so it is required of us. Second, we entered this field to help people improve their mental health, and to do that, anti-ableist advocacy is necessary.

The mental health professions have not always included standards regarding discrimination, equity, and advocacy in their guidelines. In fact, much harm has been done to the Black community because of the mental health system, starting with the creation of diagnoses like *drapetomania*—a supposed mental illness meant to explain why enslaved Africans attempted to run away. As such, all mental health professional organizations have begun to address this oversight, and subsequent harm, in more recent iterations of their codes and guidelines. One of the clearest examples is the American Psychological Association (APA), which issued the following declaration (emphasis added):

Whereas it is essential for psychologists to understand how stereotypical and stigmatizing language, attitudes, and behaviors can demean and devalue people with disabilities and have an adverse impact on self concept, self esteem, self efficacy, and relationships with others; . . . Whereas the American Psychological Association (APA) has endorsed a set of Ethical Principles for Psychologists that recognize the dignity and worth of all people, including their right to self-determination, and the duty of psychologists to safeguard the welfare and rights of those with whom they interact professionally and other affected persons; . . . *Whereas some persons with disability also experience oppression due to their racial/ethnic identity, gender identity, sexual orientation, and/or gender expression (transgender, transsexual);* . . . Therefore be it resolved that The American Psychological Association (APA) reaffirms its opposition to discrimination based on disability status, and promotes full implementation of the ADA; The APA vigilantly seeks to ameliorate adverse mental health effects of discrimination against people with visible and invisible disabilities. (APA, 2009, para. 8–22)

It is clear that the APA supports anti-ableism while acknowledging the unique challenges that intersectionality of race and ability often presents. Another example includes Code C5 in the American Counseling Association Code of Ethics, which states:

Nondiscrimination—Counselors *do not condone or engage* in discrimination against prospective or current clients, students, employees, supervisees, or research participants based on age, culture, *disability*, ethnicity, race, religion,/spirituality, gender, gender identity, sexual orientation, marital/partnership status, language preference, socioeconomic status, immigration status, or any basis *proscribed by law*. (American Counseling Association, 2014, p. 9, emphasis added)

Every professional code of ethics, as well as supporting guidelines and statements regarding those ethics, has strong and clear direction regarding the expectation of anti-ableist values clinicians are to hold. If you need further proof, look no further than the *Diagnostic and Statistical Manual of Mental Disorders* (DSM), where virtually every diagnosis is contingent upon symptoms causing impairment in daily functioning at home, work, school, or the community. This is in full alignment with the definition of disability in the ADA.

All of this is to say, as mental health professionals, we are key figures in protecting, upholding, and advocating for the disability rights of our clients. Doing this work necessarily includes the requirement of anti-racism, as ableism and racism are more tightly intertwined than any other systemic oppressions. Considering these things, what accommodations are we allowing space for in session and advocating for on behalf of all our clients, particularly Black, Indigenous, and people of color (BIPOC) facing intersectionality challenges? The commitment to addressing this question and revisiting it consistently is the growth process for anti-ableist clinicians. Welcome to the fight for equity, accessibility, and social justice for all.

A Disability Paradigm Shift

Let us return to the DSM again, to note another thing—every section begins with a lengthy description of methods for differential diagnosis as well as common comorbidities. The symptoms are a combination of physical, mental, and emotional experiences that cause distress that manifests differently for every person. This is an attempt to capture and codify the complexity of the human experience. To take this information and then define *psychiatric disability* as a straightforward either/or descriptor is flawed. An excellent demonstration of this lies in legal history. Annamma et al. (2013) describe this phenomenon well in this example:

> The definition (and even the terminology) of intellectual dis/ability has been revised continually, most notably when the AAMD (American Association of Mental Deficiency) revised the definition of mental retardation in 1973 from those with a measured IQ score of 85 to an IQ score of 70. In the stroke of a policy change, many people who had been labeled as mentally retarded were essentially "cured" of their condition. This monumental change was largely the result of special education coming under fire for the over-representation of students of color in programs for students with intellectual dis/abilities.

In fact, ability and disability exist on a multidimensional continuum, where one may be disabled in one way but excel in another. The academic and medical discourse regarding disability is also shifting, from a medical model to a social model—one that understands the sociopolitical context in which disability is defined and experienced.

People with disabilities have come together in social media groups, community gatherings, and universities to define and establish disability as a culture, further cementing this idea. This culture is based on common experiences of marginalization, lack of accessibility, reclaiming disability as an identity, and celebrating the unique contributions PWD make to society. Even Black PWD are learning about our ancestors whose disability identity was erased from history, like Harriet Tubman, who experienced seizures, chronic pain, and narcolepsy and whose work as a freedom fighter was coupled with equally radical disability activism.

In recent events, February 2022 found disabled students at Yale advocating for a long overdue cultural center for people with disabilities, much like centers that already exist at Syracuse and the University of California, Berkeley (Ndubisi, 2022). But what cultural center will embrace BIPOC disabled students best? The many dimensions that define and coincide with disability are often themselves various continuums, like race and gender expression, all connecting at countless points to form a complex network of intersectionality.

Critical Disability Theory and DisCrit

When analyzing intersectionality, some scholars found various frameworks like critical race theory lacking. Out of this came *critical disability theory*, which Devlin and Pothier (2006) found necessary because "disability is not fundamentally a question of medicine or health, nor is it just an issue of sensitivity and compassion; rather, it is a question of politics and power(lessness), power over, and power to" (p. 2). Critical disability is based on several facets, namely:

- Disability is strongly tied to sexism, racism, and classism.
- Disabled voices are centered.
- Critique is focused on the systems, not the disabled.
- Critical disability is built on the social model of disability.

Some years later, education researchers developed a theory of analysis to center the BIPOC disability experience called dis/ability critical race studies, or DisCrit. It is the first theory, critical or otherwise, to speak to disability intersectionality, and its usefulness is described in seven tenets. However, for the purposes of this essay, we will only focus on three: (a) "DisCrit emphasizes the social constructions of race and ability and yet recognizes the material and psychological impacts of being labeled as raced or dis/abled, which sets one outside of the western cultural norms"; (b) "DisCrit privileges voices of marginalized populations, traditionally not acknowledged within research"; and (c) "DisCrit requires activism and supports all forms of resistance" (Annamma et al., 2013, p. 11). These theories lay the foundation for a multisystemic framework I created for our practice. This simple yet detailed framework serves as a guide to clinicians and the faculty who educate them as we grow in anti-ableist practice both personally and professionally.

3A Systemic Framework for Intercultural Connection

The 3A framework is used at Bridges Family Life Center to facilitate growth, healing, and empowerment for historically marginalized leaders and their families. Over half of our primary clients are Black and Brown people, and over 70% are female identifying. One or more of the family members live at the intersections of psychiatric disability and race and/or gender identity.

We also began doing diversity, equity, and inclusion (DEI) consulting after our first 2 years, when we realized we were hearing the same stories— stories of discrimination, ableism, racism, and the like—many of which were internalized with lasting impact on the mental health of the clients. Though we began building the 3A framework for families, we found it was equally effective with organizations across sectors and locations in our DEI work. Based on tenets of critical disability theory and more specifically DisCrit, this framework addresses complex social issues that manifest psychologically.

The framework is called 3A, and we often refer to it as a "social emergency toolkit," since in its most simple form it can be used to de-escalate difficult conversations gone awry. These incidences are relational ruptures— communication challenges that are bound to happen when discussing difficult topics, across cultures and within them.

The 3A stands for acknowledge, ask, and act; these each serve as a simple step-by-step guide through troubled social waters. There are also three dimensions to 3A (Table 9.1). The framework (1) has already been described, and it is built upon a foundation (2) that must be identified based on the

Table 9.1 3A Systemic Framework

1. Framework (use all three)	2. Foundation (choose one)	3. Function (choose one)
Acknowledge	Intrapersonal development: self, parts of self, childhood self, cultural identities of self	Offender(s): due to social context, privilege, or microaggression/oppressive behavior or policy
Ask	Interdependent development: family, partner or spouse, friendship, close professional relationships	Offended: due to social location, intersectionality, or the experience of race- or ability-based trauma/oppression
Act	Inclusive development: group, organization, school, team, community, government	Outside witness(es): friend, loved one, colleague, bystander, human resources, public eye, government; also can be passerby who observed or is aware of the oppression

purpose of the interaction. Last, the function (3) of the user of the framework is selected to guide the manner in which the framework is utilized.

For the remainder of this essay, we will use 3A in its simplest form by focusing on the framework (1), using it to guide an interdependent relationship between client and therapist with the focus on the therapist. The following is an overview of each step for a clinician who may have offended their BIPOC disabled client.

1. **Acknowledge** how one's thoughts, behaviors, silence, words, and the like can cause harm, without excusing that harm because of intent. A clinician may also need to apologize and empathize, all to decenter themselves and privilege the voice of the offended client. This aligns with DisCrit tenet labeled (a), in that we recognize there are many social factors that contribute to the mental state of a person that are outside of our control, like race and ability. What we can commit to is growing toward antiableism and antiracism.

2. **Ask** is the step that clinicians tend to skip, and this is often a matter of power and privilege. It is empowering to ask a client what they want or need you to do next, especially when you have offended them. Even if they do not have answers, you can provide suggestions later, but not until they welcome them. This aligns with tenet label (b), honoring and celebrating the power of the marginalized voice.

3. **Act** is a continuation of the empowerment. If your client asks you to do something to repair the mutual trust of the therapeutic relationship and it is a reasonable request in light of your ethical guidelines, it is imperative that your follow-through occurs. A clinician may also commit to action of their own accord, such as reading a book or getting additional training and supervision. In either case, if follow-through does not occur, the framework falls apart and fails to repair the relational rupture. More than that, it can cause such irreparable harm as to prevent the client from seeking mental health care altogether, as has already occurred with countless Black disabled people. Tenet label (c) encourages activism of all forms—activism in professional practice, like academic activism, is a key part of practicing anti-ableist ideals as a clinician.

3A Framework in Practice

Rhonda[1] was a well-educated Black woman who escaped an abusive relationship a few years ago. She also experienced a sexual assault at her job more than a decade prior and never reported it for fear of losing the job. When I asked her what brought her in for therapy, she said, "I don't know what to do. I can't go back. But my boss doesn't understand why I'm making such a big deal." She went on to describe an incident at work where she was assaulted by a subordinate. "Maybe I should just go back," she said, then paused.

The pause is one with which I am all too familiar. So many questions were in that pause, and so many emotions—questions like *Am I crazy? Even though you're Black, will you dismiss my concerns because I'm a Black woman with issues? Can I just say how I really feel, with all the pain, rage, fear, and colorful language?* In that pause I heard all the unspoken things, and as an antioppression clinician, I decided to utilize the 3A framework.

After sitting in the silence for a short moment, I said, "Rhonda, I hear you and see you. I can't imagine what it is like to be living in your situation right now, but I can imagine what it's like to be belittled, ignored, and dismissed at work. I recognize professionally and personally, being a Black woman in the corporate world has unique challenges. I invite you to bring as much of you

---

[1] Names and some details were changed or omitted to protect confidentiality.

as you would like to this space and we can sort through things together. How does that sound?"

Rhonda breathed a sigh of relief. "That sounds so great. I can't even tell you what a relief that is. I didn't know which way this was gonna go." Rhonda relaxed her posture, stopped code-switching in her language, and asked me to do the same because "you being all formal makes me feel like I need to be formal too." I obliged, and we went on to do great work together.

Several months later, Rhonda said she was going to refuse to return to work due to continued harassment during medical leave for posttraumatic stress disorder (which we collaboratively advocated for a few months prior) and also sue her company for discrimination. I was proud to see her grow from the timid woman considering returning to an abusive work environment to the person sitting in front of me, and encouraged her to do what she needed to channel the anger she felt.

After a grueling 2-year legal battle with a federal corporation, she won her case. Utilizing the 3A framework with Rhonda was central to her healing. The work was both preemptive and responsive, as there were times when I questioned Rhonda's choice to use her voice during our work together and an apology was required. This is just one example of the many ways in which this framework, informed by critical disability theory and DisCrit, can be utilized in the conceptualization, treatment methods, and systemic change for Black clients.

The Future of Anti-ableist Clinical Practice

Using the 3A systemic framework is only one of many ways that clinicians can begin to dismantle ableism and racism. To address change on a systemic level, our practice chose to adopt our framework into a consulting methodology for health care, education, and nonprofit organizations called Collective Conversation™. The possibilities are endless not just with 3A, but with many other methodologies like multicultural therapies, racial trauma therapy, chronic illness counseling, universal design for learning, and more.

People like Rhonda and myself are a dime a dozen, particularly given the current political and social climate. No longer are Black disabled clients willing to settle for antiblackness and ableist microaggressions, either in the therapy room or outside of it. We are seeking antioppression clinicians equipped with knowledge regarding disability history, the ADA, and even DisCrit. Clinicians must be equipped with treatment methods and frameworks like 3A that guide them in acknowledging disability as a social construct with real implications, asking Black clients what they want from therapy and how they want to show up in it, and acting on their wishes to encourage activism while empowering them in all their intersectionality.

The future of anti-ableist clinical practice lies in Black and Brown disabled practitioners and their allies collaborating to educate colleagues and clinicians in training. These disability advocates can fight for policy changes in communities, universities, and government that enable Black people with disabilities to have equitable access to accommodations needed for healthy, interdependent, and fulfilling lives.

References

American Counseling Association. (2014). *ACA code of ethics.* https://www.counseling.org/resources/aca-code-of-ethics.pdf

American Psychological Association. (2008). *Resolution on the Americans with Disabilities Act.* https://www.apa.org/about/policy/disabilities-act

Americans with Disabilities Act, 42 U.S.C. § 12101 et seq. (1990).

Annamma, S. A., Connor, D., & Ferri, B. (2013). Dis/ability critical race studies (DisCrit): Theorizing at the intersections of race and dis/ability. *Race Ethnicity and Education, 16*(1), 1–31. https://doi.org/10.1080/13613324.2012.730511

Courtney-Long, E. A., Romano, S. D., Carroll, D. D., & Fox, M. H. (2016). Socioeconomic factors at the intersection of race and ethnicity influencing health risks for people with disabilities. *Journal of Racial and Ethnic Health Disparities, 4*(2), 213–222.

Devlin, R. F., & Pothier, D. (2006). *Critical disability theory: Essays in philosophy, politics, policy, and law.* UBC Press.

Hawthorne, W. B., Folsom, D. P., Sommerfeld, D. H., Lanouette, N. M., Lewis, M., Aarons, G. A., Conklin, R. M., Solorzano, E., Lindamer, L. A., & Jeste, D. V. (2012). Incarceration among adults who are in the public mental health system: Rates, risk factors, and short-term outcomes. *Psychiatric services (Washington, D.C.), 63*(1), 26–32. https://doi.org/10.1176/appi.ps.201000505

Lewis, T. A. (2022, January). *A working definition of ableism—January 2022 update.* https://www.talilalewis.com/blog/archives/01-2022

Ndubisi, M. (2022, February 18). Students push for Persons with Disabilities Cultural Center. *Yale Daily News.* https://yaledailynews.com/blog/2022/02/15/students-push-for-persons-with-disabilities-cultural-center/

Primm, A. B., Vasquez, M. J., Mays, R. A., Sammons-Posey, D., McKnight-Eily, L. R., Presley-Cantrell, L. R., McGuire, L. C., Chapman, D. P., & Perry, G. S. (2010). The role of public health in addressing racial and ethnic disparities in mental health and mental illness. *Preventing Chronic Disease, 7*(1), A20.

Rogers, A., Castree, N., & Kitchin, R. (2013). *A dictionary of human geography (Oxford Quick Reference).* Oxford University Press.

10

Antiblackness in Latinx Communities

Stiving to Become Antiracist

Meyleen M. Velasquez

Introduction

Communities that have been displaced through enslavement and colonization carry trauma deeply embedded in their nervous systems, affecting generation after generation (Geronimus et al., 2011; Yellow Horse Brave Heart et al., 2011). To provide equitable care, one must understand the barriers created by systems of oppression and how they work. When examining systemic problems, it is vital to know the histories of the different groups represented. Failure to look at historical trauma can lead to ineffective strategies that create and perpetuate harm (Stroh, 2015).

Latinx, *Latine*, *Latino*, and *Hispanic* are terms used to refer to people from Latin America and the Caribbean living in the United States. The words *Latinx* and *Latine* provide a gender-neutral way to identify (Macedo, 2021; Pew Research Center, 2020). However, individuals from Latin America do not have a consensus on an ethnicity label, and each person might describe themselves differently. This essay uses the word *Latinx* to refer to people residing in the United States with roots in Latin America and the Caribbean.

Examining the history of our cultures is a challenging feat. For Latinx individuals, our history contains the best and worst that humanity can offer. On one side, we have our drive to survive and enjoy life even in the face of fascist governments, dictatorships, civil unrest, the constant threat of kidnappings, gang violence, and lack of essential resources, among others. At the other end, our foundations contain the violence, torture, and erasure of Black and Indigenous communities (Chavez-Dueñas et al., 2014). We might celebrate "leaders" who committed genocide in our countries of origin, and many of us unintentionally or intentionally continue to perpetuate a racist and segregated system. To understand antiblackness in Latinx communities,

Meyleen M. Velasquez, *Antiblackness in Latinx Communities* In: *Antiblackness and the Stories of Authentic Allies.*
Edited by: Norman Kim, Carolyn Coker Ross, Mazella Fuller and Charlynn Small, Oxford University Press.
© Oxford University Press 2024. DOI: 10.1093/oso/9780197642535.003.0011

we must examine how conquest and colonization affect current discourses and dynamics among diverse groups.

Foundations of Antiblackness in Latin America

Colorism refers to discrimination imposed by members of the same ethnic group where being light-skinned is perceived as favorable (Chavez-Dueñas et al., 2014). The roots of inequality in Latin America begin with the Spaniard conquest, which led to the mass killing of Indigenous peoples throughout the Americas. As conquistadors met Indigenous peoples, a white supremacist perspective framed the relationship. Conquistadors believed that Indigenous communities were uncivilized because they did not show Eurocentric values. The colonizers believed that they were doing good as they erased Indigenous cultures and traditions and forced European values (Chavez-Dueñas et al., 2014).

Cognitive dissonance occurs when actions do not align with value systems (Harmon-Jones & Mills, 2019). To justify killing, torture, and rape, colonizers began to think of non-European communities as less than human. As the Indigenous population declined during colonization, Spaniards kidnapped, enslaved, and transplanted African people to work in fields and mines (Adames et al., 2021). Colonizers adopted a social stratification system to divide people based on phenotype and skin color. That system placed the Spaniards and their White offspring at the top, ensuring continued access to power and resources as mixed-race Latin Americans were born.

Mestizaje is the racial mixing of Indigenous, Black, and White communities following colonization (Adames et al., 2016). The term served as a way to deny the social stratification system that advantaged whiteness (Adames et al., 2016; Chavez-Dueñas et al., 2014). Discourses around mestizaje propagated the message that all Latin Americans are mixed race or mestizos. This belief system is the foundation of color-blind ideology for Latinx folk. Policies and dogma around mestizaje led to Indigenous and African people's erasure (Adames et al., 2016).

Governments around the Americas implemented whitening policies that encouraged European migration and sent White sex workers to areas with a high concentration of Indigenous and African communities to decrease non-White phenotypes and skin colors (Chavez-Dueñas et al., 2014). Although interracial marriage became fully legal across all of the United

States in 1967, it was encouraged by the Spanish colonizers who desired to whiten the population (Chavez-Dueñas et al., 2014; Pew Research Center, 2017). The remnants of this period are present in Latinx communities, with anti-Black statements such as *mejorar la raza* (bettering the race) referring to having children with a White person.

Impact

Spaniards colonizing the Americas invented race to justify dehumanizing one group of people while securing access to power and resources for themselves (Chaves-Dueñas et al., 2014). British colonizers continued and solidified the early concepts of race as they conquered North America and upheld slavery. The legacy of colonization and the transatlantic slave trade is visible in present-day society.

Racial disparities in the United States marginalize Black communities across preconception, birth, and old age (Cuevas et al., 2016). Maternal mortality rates are up to five times higher for Black and Indigenous birthing people than for their White counterparts (Centers for Disease Control and Prevention, 2020). Black babies in the United States are twice as likely to die than White babies, with a study finding that Black babies cared for by a White doctor were three times more likely to die than those cared for by a Black provider (Picheta, 2020). Horbar (2019) found that infants experience segregation and inequality in neonatal intensive care units, where Black infants experienced lower-quality care and White infants were concentrated in higher-quality ones.

As Black children age, they face barriers navigating a racist system where they are constantly perceived as a threat and experience situations such as getting kicked out of daycares at higher rates and ongoing police brutality (Hardy & Robbins, 2020). As Latinxs migrate and build families in the United States, they encounter a system, similar to our countries of origin, that continuously harms Black communities.

In the United States, Latin Americans are seen as people of color. For many lighter-skinned Latinx individuals, arrival to the United States might be their first experience with discrimination or prejudice (Adames et al., 2021). Although we can recognize the impact of xenophobia and racism on the Latinx community living in the United States, we must acknowledge the reality that one can be a member of a historically marginalized community while benefiting from systemic racism and White privilege. This reality is especially true among those of us holding *Latinidad* (Latinx identity) as our histories bear the erasure of Black and Indigenous communities.

The Pew Research Center (2012) reported that over 50% of Hispanics do not identify with the standard racial category system used in the United States. Latinx communities are more likely to identify by their countries of origin than their racial background. These results might suggest an implicit connection with ideals of mestizaje, conflict with self-identification, and an internalized desire for whiteness (Quiroz & Dawson, 2013). Closer proximity to whiteness brings societal and economic benefits for phenotypically White and light-skinned Latinxs while contributing to adverse outcomes for darker-skinned Latinxs (Quiros & Dawson, 2013). Thus, using *Latinidad* as a substitute for race is a dangerous discourse that propagates harm as people with darker skin tones navigate the world differently than their lighter-skin counterparts and face significant systemic barriers.

Becoming Antiracist

To become antiracist in practice, we begin by examining where we are in our racial equity journey. The *transtheoretical model* (TTM) might offer a way to identify how ready we might be to take steps toward dismantling white supremacy in our lives (A. Harter, personal communication, 2018). TTM is a model used in psychotherapy to determine how ready an individual is to make changes in their lives (LaMorte, 2019). The model has six stages: precontemplation, contemplation, preparation, action, maintenance, and termination.

In the *precontemplation* stage of change, people are not aware of their problematic behaviors or negative consequences. An example of this is an individual who denies that racism still exists in the United States or believes that there is no such thing as White privilege. Individuals in *contemplation* might intend to begin their racial equity work sometime in the future and are starting to believe that they might also benefit from antiblackness. LaMorte (2019) explained that "people [in contemplation] may still feel ambivalent toward changing their behavior" (para. 3). Someone in this stage might think, "Yeah, I might have privilege, but what can I do about it?"

As individuals move past ambivalence and enter *preparation*, they might take small steps to recognize and shift patterns of racism in their lives, maybe working through a reflective workbook or getting ready to engage in some antiracism inner work with a professional. In the *action* stage, individuals actively engage in antiracism in their daily lives, examine their biases, take ownership for dismantling antiblackness, and are ready to continue learning and growing.

Being an antiracist requires a lifelong commitment. As education and reflection take place, individuals begin to enter the *maintenance* stage. In maintenance, we have sustained internal and behavioral changes for over 6 months, and we are committed to preventing going back into any of the earlier stages (LaMorte, 2019). The *termination* stage in this context would reflect a time when individuals have completely dismantled racism in their lives. However, being antiracist means being aware of harmful values and actively dismantling racial inequity in our lives (National Museum of African American History & Culture, n.d.). As such, it's proposed that those of us who live in a white supremacist system must continuously work to increase awareness of our implicit biases and the ways we benefit from and uphold antiblackness.

Moving through the stages means recognizing the vast racial experience of Latinx people. Kendi (2019) explained that being antiracist entails recognizing the difference between individual behavior and culture. When we look at a group of people, we have to acknowledge the discourses, history, and normalization of stereotypes. Lumping Latinx people into one homogenous group is a dangerous practice stemming from colonization that erases the history and experience of Black and Indigenous folk (Quiros & Dawson, 2013). The following section offers a framework to help us move through the stages of change.

Framework for the Work

As Latinx, White, or light-skinned individuals, we each carry different internal biases, messages learned directly and indirectly while growing up, and our privilege. As much as we might consciously reject those messages, they still affect how we interact with the world. King (2018) stated, "Like it or not, the ways of our parents and ancestors are with us, even when we don't know them, don't like them, or don't remember them" (p. 34). Although there is no set of preplanned steps that humans can take to become antiracist, the guidelines below present a way to strengthen our work.

Didactic Learning

White supremacy aims to erase the history of marginalized communities. We see this phenomenon when our school systems portray the conquest of the Americas as a peaceful time rather than a massacre (Chavez-Dueñas et al., 2014). In 2020, different school systems in conservative states began a movement to eradicate *critical race theory* (CRT) from curriculums (Fortin, 2021). Although CRT is an advanced theory that helps us understand how race and racial inequalities operate, opposers argue that teaching students about racism is racist. As we strive to become antiracist, individuals from racial and ethnic backgrounds that hold privilege must make an effort to learn the impact of attempts at systemic erasure. In doing so, we can take a step toward breaking away from discourses that place the responsibility of educating the community on historically oppressed groups.

An antiracist lens calls us to read, learn, and question information through a critical lens. Black and Indigenous communities continue to experience racism, discrimination, and oppression across many Latin American countries and in the United States (Adames et al., 2016). However, policies, societal discourses, research, and scholarship silenced their stories by perpetuating the false message that Latinx communities do not experience racial differences. Another equally dangerous narrative is that all Black, Indigenous, and people of color (BIPOC) communities share the same barriers.

Accurate knowledge is vital to breaking away from false information. We must take the step to find opportunities to learn about the history of marginalized communities, including both the struggle and the strength. This subject needs more attention, research, and public awareness. Our duty as people who want to stop antiblackness is to read, train, and believe the experiential reality of Black and Indigenous communities. The invitation here for the reader is to engage in paid learning opportunities directly from Black and Indigenous Latinx individuals.

Critical Reflection

As we continue our antiracist journey, we must reflect on the history of colonization and enslavement. Denial of racism and racist views is common practice in a white supremacist system (Kendi, 2019). However, reflection must move beyond remembering history to acknowledging how our up-bringing and present-day actions intersect with white supremacy. One way to move into a space of acknowledgment is through *critical reflection* (CR).

CR is a practice that helps individuals to question their beliefs, their experiences, and the meaning of their perspectives (Taylor, 2017). CR is a self-analysis vital to racial equity. As humans gain awareness of their thought process, their capacity to reflect on deep-seated belief systems about skin color, hair type, and other phenotypes transforms.

Examining our belief system and how we have intentionally and unin-tentionally aligned with racism is painful. People struggle with distressing emotions and evade reflection to soothe discomfort without analyzing its impact on Black and Brown communities. Our lack of questioning and need to be seen as good individuals lead Latinx people to continue to advance sys-tems of power that harm Black communities (Adames et al., 2021; Rosen et al., 2017).

As humans, we want others to perceive us as good and well intentioned. Yet, the need to be good or righteous stems from white supremacy. Through CR, individuals move away from ideals of goodness and into examining harmful aspects of ourselves.

How to Practice Critical Reflection

These questions offer a starting point to creating a critically reflective practice:

- What were the values and beliefs that I learned about Black and Indigenous races from my family of origin growing up?
- Did my value system and beliefs regarding blackness change as I transitioned through adulthood?
- If so, in what ways?
- If there was a change, what were the catalysts for it?
- How do these early messages inform my present-day value system?
- If I am a non-Black Latinx person, how aware am I of my proximity to whiteness? What do I think about my privilege?
- How has my proximity to whiteness shaped my experience?
- Which areas in my personal and professional life are still informed by antiblackness?
- How much consideration have I given to the intersection of race and ethnicity for Latinxs?

Relational

Relationships provide us with space to reflect and practice the skills we are learning. A healthy, antiracist relationship can enhance growth and awareness of blind spots. Relationships with people who are not reflective of privilege bring us face to face with where we are in our antiracist journey. For example, recognizing when another person makes an anti-Black comment and choosing to ignore it collaborates with racism.

Singh (2019) proposed that advancing racial healing and equity involves building and examining our communities. Systemic racism divided people into different areas based on racial makeup, both in the United States and Latin America (Adames et al., 2021; Chavez-Dueñas et al., 2014). It also cemented the belief that White culture is preferable and more advanced than Black and Brown. If we are not mindful, white supremacy will continue to limit our exposure to individuals with identities different from ours. When we examine our personal and professional relationships, we need to think about who is in those groups, who is missing, and what changes we want to make.

How to Build Authentic Relationships With Black and Indigenous Latinxs
Here are some reflective questions to explore authenticity within relationships:

- Why am I in (or seeking) this relationship?
- What am I receiving from this relationship?
- What am I giving to this relationship?
- How does it feel to be in this relationship?
- Am I able to be vulnerable in this relationship? What makes it possible for me to be or not be vulnerable?
- How invested am I?
- How much space do I take up in this relationship?
- How does this person experience our relationship? How do I know?

Actionable

Education, reflection, and relationships help to set a foundation for *authentic allyship*. The Anti-Oppressive Network (n.d.) posited that allyship involves intentionally reassessing our values and taking responsibility for increasing equity in our communities. As we move to break patterns that create harm, we stop centering ourselves and our needs. If we hold light-skinned privilege, we evaluate our self-centering by looking at how we advance narratives and tactics that meet our needs. For example, a systemic lens asks, "What does the community need, and how do I work on building a relationship with them to support their needs?" The answer to this will depend on our time and resources.

However, what's truly important is placing historically marginalized communities as the experts, not ourselves. For some of us, the work might be engaging in large-scale collaboration with organizations. For others, it might be looking at everyday actions that create harm, such as acknowledging admiration for European beauty standards and phrases like *pelo malo* (bad hair, referring to nonstraight hair) and *mejorar la raza*, or praising a newborn for their light skin.

When we jump in to rescue communities that we are not a part of, we risk centering and setting ourselves up as heroes or saviors (Saad, 2020). Acting on behalf of a community without consulting with its members plays into the racist idea that Black and Indigenous people are uncivilized, do not know what they need, and require outside support. With this in mind, as you seek to take action against antiblackness, engage in researching, reflecting, and connecting with the resources that might already be in place.

How to Be Intentional

Here are some questions that might be helpful when reflecting on the meaning and impact of your actions:

- What steps are you taking or would you like to take next?
- Are you centering your needs?
- Are you acting based on guilt or shame?
- Are you seeking to create an impact to advance your personal or professional agenda?
- Have you consulted with individuals or organizations who are supporting Black and Indigenous Latinxs?
- How do you react when antiblackness presents in a professional setting? What about a personal one?

Personal Reflection

Action without introspection can lead to upholding antiblackness. For example, as a non-Black Latinx person living with advanced vitiligo, I must acknowledge the racism I grew up with and my intentions in learning and writing about colorism. Failure to take on this internal reflection can lead me to place myself as an expert in antiblackness to advance my personal and professional goals, thereby contributing to performative allyship, racism, and oppression. I hope to increase awareness of colorism, antiblackness, and racism across fields because I constantly see these narratives in my community. I also desire for Latinx communities to take ownership of the harm we've perpetrated on Black and Indigenous folk.

When we start to take ownership, we can begin on the road to equity and equitable treatment. The invitation here is to think about your reflection. *What is your reason for leaning into this work?*

Summary

We are never going to have a complete awareness of implicit biases. But when we are in a space to listen and process feedback, we can grow. Stepping away from white supremacy entails accepting that we make mistakes, hold harmful belief systems, and benefit from antiblackness. This statement is true whether we were born in the United States or Latin America, as both areas contain strong racist roots. It is impossible to grow up in an anti-Black society and not hold anti-Black views. Color-blindness and mestizaje are anti-Black.

To move into an antiracist space means that we have to look at the parts of ourselves that uphold and benefit from oppressive systems. Only then can we step into space where we can learn and reflect on history and our experiences, build authentic relationships, and take action to dismantle racism. White supremacy is not our fault, but we have a collective responsibility to eradicate it from our lives and not ignore it when we see it in others. As you continue the work, remember, "The road toward liberation for all Latinxs begins by acknowledging anti-Blackness, celebrating the greatness of Black Latinx roots, and honoring the role of Blackness within Latinidad" (Adames et al., 2021, p. 29).

References

Adames, H. Y., Chavez-Dueñas, N. Y., & Jernigan, M. (2021). The fallacy of a raceless Latinidad: Action guidelines for centering Blackness in Latinx psychology. *Journal of Latinx Psychology*, 9(1), 26–44. https://doi.org/10.1037/lat0000179

Adames, H. Y., Chavez-Dueñas, N. Y., & Organista, K. C. (2016). Skin color matters in Latino/a communities: Identifying, understanding, and addressing Mestizaje racial ideologies in clinical practice. *Professional Psychology: Research and Practice, 47*(1), 46–55. https://doi.org/10.1037/pro0000062

Anti-Oppressive Network. (n.d.). *Allyship.* https://theantioppressionnetwork.com/allyship/

Centers for Disease Control and Prevention. (2020). *Infographic: Racial/ethnic disparities in pregnancy-related deaths—United States, 2007–2016.* https://www.cdc.gov/reproductivehealth/maternal-mortality/disparities-pregnancy-related-deaths/infographic.html

Chavez-Dueñas, N. Y., Adames, H. Y., & Organista, K. O. (2014). Skin-color prejudice and within-group racial discrimination: Historical and current impact on Latino/a populations. *Hispanic Journal of Behavioral Sciences, 36*(1), 3–25. https://doi.org/10.1177/0739986313511306

Cuevas, A. G., Dawson, B. A., & Williams, D. R. (2016). Race and skin color in Latino health: An analytic review. *American Journal of Public Health, 106*(12), 2131–2163. https://doi.org/10.2105/AJPH.2016.303452

Fortin, J. (2021, July 27). Critical race theory: A brief history. *New York Times.* https://www.nytimes.com/article/what-is-critical-race-theory.html

Geronimus, A. T., Hicken, M., Keene, D., & Bound, J. (2011). "Weathering" and age patterns of allostatic load scores among Blacks and Whites in the United States. *American Journal of Public Health, 96*(5), 826–833. https://doi.org/10.2105/AJPH.2004.060749

Hardy, A., & Robbins, K. G. (2020, June 23). *Standing with Black communities against white supremacy in child care and early education spaces.* https://www.clasp.org/blog/standing-black-communities-standing-against-white-supremacy-child-care-and-early-education

Harmon-Jones, E., & Mills, J. (2019). An introduction to cognitive dissonance theory and overview of current perspective on the theory. In E. Harmon-Jones (Ed.), *Cognitive dissonance: Reexamining a pivotal theory in psychology* (2nd ed., pp. 3–24). American Psychological Association. http://dx.doi.org/10.1037/0000135-001

Horbar, J. D., Edwards, E. M., Greenberg, L. T., Profit, J., Draper, D., Helkey, D., Lorch, S. A., Lee, H. C., Phibbs, C. S., Rogowski, J., Gould, J. B., & Firebaugh, G. (2019). Racial segregation and inequality in the neonatal intensive care unit for very low-birth-weight and very preterm infants. *JAMA Pediatrics, 173*(5), 455–461. https://doi.org/10.1001/jamapediatrics.2019.0241

Kendi, I. X. (2019). *How to be an antiracist.* Random House Publishing Group.

King, R. (2018). *Mindful of race.* Sounds True.

LaMorte, W. W. (2019). *The transtheoretical model: Stages of change.* Boston University School of Public Health. https://tinyurl.com/ymrm5rat

Macedo, L. (2021, October 13). *Latinx, Latine, Hispanic, Latino/a: What do we call ourselves?* https://hiplatina.com/latinx-latino-latina-terms/

National Museum of African American History & Culture. (n.d.). *Being anti-racist.* https://nmaahc.si.edu/learn/talking-about-race/topics/being-antiracist

Pew Research Center. (2012, April 4). *When labels don't fit: Hispanics and their views of identity.* https://www.pewresearch.org/hispanic/2012/04/04/when-labels-dont-fit-hispanics-and-their-views-of-identity/

Pew Research Center. (2017, May 18). *Intermarriage in the U.S. 50 years after Loving v. Virginia.* https://www.pewresearch.org/social-trends/2017/05/18/intermarriage-in-the-u-s-50-years-after-loving-v-virginia/

Pew Research Center. (2020, August 11). *About one-in-four U.S. Hispanics have heard of Latinx, but just 3% use it.* https://www.pewresearch.org/hispanic/2020/08/11/about-one-in-four-u-s-hispanics-have-heard-of-latinx-but-just-3-use-it/

Picheta, R. (2020, August 20). *Black newborns more likely to die when looked after by White doctors.* https://www.cnn.com/2020/08/18/health/black-babies-mortality-rate-doct ors-study-wellness-scli-intl/index.html

Quiros, L., & Dawson, B. A. (2013). The color paradigm: The impact of colorism on the racial identity and identification of Latinas. *Journal of Human Behavior in the Social Environment, 23*(3), 287–297. https://doi.org/10.1080/10911359.2012.740342

Rosen, D., McCall, J., & Goodkind, S. (2017). Teaching critical self-reflection through the lens of cultural humility: An assignment in a social work diversity course. *Social Work Education, 36*(3), 289–298. https://doi.org/10.1080/02615479.2017.1287260

Saad, L. (2020). *Me and white supremacy: Combat racism, change the world, and become a good ancestor.* Sourcebooks.

Singh, A. A. (2019). *The racial healing handbook: Practical activities to help you challenge privilege, confront systemic racism, & engage in collective healing.* New Harbinger Publications.

Stroh, D. P. (2015). *Systems thinking for social change.* Chelsea Green Publishing.

Taylor, E. W. (2017). Critical reflection and transformative learning: A critical review. *Journal of Lifelong Learning, 26,* 77–95.

Yellow Horse Brave Heart, M., Chase, J., Elkins, J., & Altschul, D. B. (2011). Historical trauma among Indigenous Peoples of the Americas: Concepts, research, and clinical considerations. *Journal of Psychoactive Drugs, 43*(4), 282–290. https://doi.org/10.1080/02791072.2011.628913

11

Interracial Relationships

How Antiblackness Informs Kinship and Therapist Responsibility

Liana Maneese

> What white bodies did to Black bodies they did to white bodies first.
> —Janice Barbee (Menakem, 2017, p. 57)

Fostering Individual Curiosity to Understand and Become Antiracist

When I was younger, maybe in my early 20s, I caught myself saying something I had said often as an adoptee when asked about "*what* I was." The very nature of asking a perceived racially ambiguous person *what* they are is anti-Black rhetoric rooted in the dehumanizing of Black people; "*what*" implies "The Human, the modern human, defines itself in opposition to the Black (alleged) nonbeing" (Jung & Vargas, 2021, p. 5). This is what João H. Costa Vargas, professor of African, African American studies, and anthropology, reminds us is "the very expulsion of Black people from the human family."

I understood that

> racism is based on the concept of whiteness—a powerful fiction enforced by power and violence. Whiteness is a constantly shifting boundary separating those who are entitled to have certain privileges from those whose exploitation and vulnerability to violence is justified by their not being white. (Kivel, 1996, p. 19)

So when asked *what* I was, at some point I would say that I was so lucky because my birth mother was probably a prostitute living in abject poverty who didn't want me.

Liana Maneese, *Interracial Relationships* In: *Antiblackness and the Stories of Authentic Allies*. Edited by: Norman Kim, Carolyn Coker Ross, Mazella Fuller and Charlyn Small, Oxford University Press. © Oxford University Press 2024. DOI: 10.1093/oso/9780197642535.003.0012

But one day, this go-to response felt off; it felt vulgar. I decided to visit my mom and talk about my birth mother again. She looked at me with eyes wide and watery as I told her what I remembered. She was shocked and did not know how on Earth I could have that story in my head. In fact, what had happened was quite the opposite.

As tears rolled down her face, my mom assured me that my version of the story was not the one she had told me "countless times." She said wholeheartedly, "Your birth mother was a house worker, and she was told it was you or her job. She left you with a friend in hopes to pay her to care for you, at least until she could figure something out. However, that friend could not afford to do this either and left you to the state." I later found out that this was only partly true.

"Your mother loved you and did her best," my adoptive mother said to me. I felt faint and couldn't breathe as I sobbed uncontrollably. How did those beliefs get implanted into my head, and why did I choose that story to believe?

Antiblackness combined with transracial adoption has proven to be nothing less than a lifelong journey of becoming through undoing. The undoing of the internalized beliefs still plagues me to this day. I am still fighting those voices now as I write this.

Families are informed through a transfer of worldviews, survival skills, and intergenerational trauma. It is also where we ideally build secure attachment and self-worth. In a world founded on antiblackness, how have we considered the realities of what this culture of whiteness has done to humans collectively? What does this look like in a world where in just a decade or so, even faster than originally predicted, the majority of the United States will no longer be a White majority (Frey, 2015)? How do we prevent White supremacy from still ruling through the hearts and minds of America's future?

The latter has always been the major question for me when I think about anti-Black rhetoric, racist ideas, and how I learned to internalize these violent messages. Internalized antiblackness is hard to recognize without a very clear picture. It is more elusive and pushes back against lumping ethnicities and experiences together; it asks us to be explicit. The word "racism" fails to capture the truth of the harm antiblackness creates and is not a specific enough word to describe what is a very specific experience.

In interracial relationships, we are dealing with layered identities, not just simply White and Black racial differences but the manifestations of antiblackness in each of us pertaining to similarities and differences. Wrote bell hooks (2001, p. 53), "Teaching Black folks to hate dark skin was one way to ensure that whether white oppressors were present or not, the values of white supremacy would rule the day" (p. 53). Everyone is capable of reinforcing the color caste system that has become so pervasive that it is part of our culture, not just for White people or as Americans but worldwide— this is the power of antiblackness. And if it is internalized, then it trickles down and has the potential to be taught generationally.

As a transracially adopted Afro-Brazilian Black American, being raised by White parents in the heart of Pittsburgh, Pennsylvania, above the Mason–Dixon line and home to the Fraternal Order of Police #1 (Hasch, 1991), was painful, to say the least. Connecting with a need to decolonize my mind became, quite frankly, a matter of life or death, both in my community and in my own mind. I had seen therapists since I was a child, which was often recommended for adopted children but rarely for the parents who adopted. I had been diagnosed with many things by professionals, all White women who, even at that age, I knew did not understand the complexity of my existence.

Because racism allows for broad strokes of behavior and multiple examples of systemic violence against all people of the global majority, it becomes easier to dismiss, and thus, the specificity of antiblackness gets ignored. What is particularly scary about antiblackness is that it can be internalized, perceived as normative culture, and in fact carried out by all people, including Black folks.

I grew up with the notion that racism was power plus privilege and that we could not be racist because we were Black. I have spent many years researching and have most recently landed on the idea that Black people can in fact carry out racism and antiblackness. This resonated with me because I had beliefs about Black people that were based in the messages of what I now know to be antiblackness; I believed and internalized these ugly messages about myself.

I did not know how to reconcile this until I learned from Ibram X. Kendi (2019), who teaches us that if we see *racism* as an idea and not simply a behavior, as something that is deeply embedded in our private thoughts, we can see that the ideas are what continue to perpetuate not only racist policies but also spaces where the feeling of superiority or inferiority can fester.

As a Black girl from another country, I had no idea just how much of my life had been infiltrated by anti-Black sentiment. As I write this right now I am triggered by the violence I experienced at every level of education. I was consistently reminded that if there was anything special about me, it was that I was an orphaned Black girl and, compared to where I was from—the slums of Goiânia, Goiás, Brazil—anything was better. All of this is rooted in the notion that "what it means to be human is continually defined against Black people and Blackness" (Walcott, 2014, p. 93).

I am here to say that even though I was raised by the most loving, attentive parents, I was filled with anti-Black messaging that even my parents could not wrap their extremely well-read heads around. "But why?" I wondered. "Why is there always this space between us that seems like it can't be filled?" I always thought it was just because of the adoption, but now I know it to be more complicated.

The engrained colonialism that lives in the bodies of White folks has gone unexamined for so long, individually and communally, that it has become easier for them to self-declare that they are "not racist" than to acknowledge they hold profoundly anti-Black values and beliefs. Being "not racist" allows White people to maintain the delusion that they are not in fact racist because they equate racism with being a bad person, which they do not believe they are. This all-or-nothing rhetoric or black-and-white thinking has become a cultural value rooted in European history and enforced by religious beliefs of good and evil. This is why it was so imperative that Black people were not considered human. Maintaining the goodness of whiteness required that those harmed by racist violence not be considered human at all. These are the ideals embedded in culture today.

When I was younger and in a relationship with a mixed-race Asian man, I attended dinner at his family home. I was sitting across from his mother, a Chinese woman, and next to his father, a White American. His father was a self-defined liberal, also known as a White person who considers themself to be "not racist." The topic of race came up. His father equated race to capitalism and concluded that "we are all niggers." Baffled but somehow not surprised, I simply stood up and left not just the room but the house.

At this point in my life, I was more prepared for these situations. I cried, mostly because I was afraid of what this would mean for my relationship with their son. I knew that White supremacy was at play, not just because it always is, but because of the feelings attached. This man was so entitled; his wife, an Asian woman, just stared at me and did not even flinch as the denigrating word came out of his pursed lips. I felt shame. I knew this was not my shame but the shame embedded and internalized through generations of the harsh realities of interracial love, but mostly power.

This is a power dynamic that gets complicated through kinship and identity. When we leave our identities unexamined under a historical lens, we leave the door open to hold power over others as an automatic crutch. Whether the person who holds the power is doing so consciously or unconsciously is irrelevant. When we returned home after the dinner incident, I received a passive-aggressive note on Facebook Messenger from my date's parents. They were defensive—again, expected but just as heartbreaking, not just for me but for their mixed-race Chinese American son, who had to witness a painful part of his parents' authenticity he had not observed before. The parents' defensiveness not only prevented them from building closeness in our relationship but also, in this case, was used to distract from the emotional damage they inflicted by claiming unconsciousness or playing the devil's advocate consciously. Neither are acceptable excuses.

Kindness is an inadequate response to the violence held in White bodies, and unless adequately and thoroughly critiqued, whiteness continues to be violent even through what we consider *loving relationships*. This is where for myself and so many others I have consulted over the years I have wondered, "Are healthy interracial relationships even possible? Can they exist without antiblackness rearing its head?"

Yes and no. They can exist, but not without allowing the conversations about antiblackness in. A committed practice of allowing yourself to learn to recognize antiblackness and other forms of oppression and then valuing the growth it offers you is crucial for a healthy interracial relationship. Embracing the unlearning necessary to see the truth in the world and in ourselves is our birthright, our humanity.

Racialized Hierarchies in Kinship and Beyond: Dangers of Color-Blindness and Language

Why focus on interracial relationships? Because I am adopted, I recognize that kinship can form in ways that honor all families and relationships, not just biologically. I study interracial relationships because we are informed by our relationships from the time we are born. We are taught how to be in this world, and unless we actively resist what we are taught, we carry it and pass along to the next generation our beliefs and ways of being in this world.

I remember having my first baby. I know people have babies every day and it is magical and terrifying and all of the things, but my Leo is special. You see, she is the first biological relative that I have ever known. She almost died in the hospital because a White nurse did not listen to my requests. One day old and already she was at another intersection of anti-Black institutional memory rooted in historical violence: health care.

My daughter Leo reminds me of the complexity of my identity as a mixed-race Black person. She reminds me of the violence of the past and the resilience of our future. hooks (2001) wrote:

> White supremacist practices of breeding black women by white masters produced mixed-race offspring whose skin color and facial features were often radically different from the black norm. This led to the formation of a color caste aesthetic. While white racists had never deemed black people beautiful before, they had a higher aesthetic regard for racially mixed black folks. When that regard took the form of granting privileges and rewards on the basis of skin color, black people began to internalize similar aesthetic values. (p. 57)

This matters so much in kinship because whiteness tells us to ignore the violence in our homes. "Don't talk about race, religion, or politics at the dinner table," which is code for power through zero accountability within the walls of the home and demanded respect for the familial hierarchy—the familial hierarchy being the patriarchal male in the dominant role, the wife following quietly, and the children obeying. These values have become cultural norms in many homes regardless of the identities within. These values prevent love. Love is defined by bell hooks (2000) in her book *All About Love* as a "mix of various ingredients-care, affection, recognition, respect, commitment, and trust, as well as honest open communication" (p. 5). When we utilize all of the dimensions in hooks's definition of love, we have what she termed a "love ethic." This disconnection between the desire for power and the need for love in the family is the beginning of many issues from self-esteem to attachment problems for children.

Practicing this love ethic means that love is not simply a word, for when we do not attach a clear definition to the word "love" it has the potential to be violent and subjective. When we experience violence from those we think are supposed to love us, it is confusing. Although this dynamic can exist in any racial scenario within a kinship, it shows up even more intensely when layers of intersectionality are considered (Crenshaw, 2016). This is important because you cannot separate race from issues of gender and sexuality. All people deserve a love ethic. And those who are marginalized by White supremacy must know that, no matter what, they are worthy of receiving a love ethic, and when they are able to do so safely, they must demand it from others and practice it for themselves.

Returning back to the abuse of Black bodies, we must consider the role of patriarchy embedded in antiblackness. Because antiblackness is inextricably gendered and sexualized, it lives in every relationship and therefore makes every relationship interracial, transracial, or at the very least racialized in some way. Comments such as who has "good hair" or "a phat booty" or calling a woman "loud" are all examples of racialized body-focused attacks that may seem innocent or even like compliments to the untrained ear.

Navigating a family where no one is biologically related means either assimilating or becoming exceptionally curious. We are told the story that adoption, especially transracial adoption, is a gift. The reality is that it is a trauma that gets ignored so that the White savior complex can be upheld, because part of saviorism is that it must be a public display of a false "goodness" to combat the "badness" of the other (Black) to justify violence against Black people.

Whiteness believes that it is inherently good. My adoption, regardless of my parents' intentions, was rooted in antiblackness. Many parents decide to take this personally and become defensive and unable to apply a love ethic to the broader experience of their children. Regardless of what my adoptive parents taught me or the recognition they had, I believed that my birth mother was a whore and I was lucky to not have been given the same fate because of antiblackness. These are connections far too many people ignore. Racial isolation and racialized trauma were a daily experience for me. Antiblackness, imperialism, racism, saviorism, and White supremacist systemic colonial systems are ignored in favor of a more palatable and supportive lie that demonizes those in poverty, with false narratives/stereotypes of negligent birth parents. My spirit and sense of self were crushed under this lie, and this is what inspired me to investigate the harm of interracial relationships gone unchecked, not just with family but in community.

There is a developmental identity process related to race, and it is different for everyone. To understand antiblackness deeply, I had to move away from just studying racism generally and toward an understanding of whiteness and therefore antiblackness respectively. Many therapists are surprised to learn that there are identity models for whiteness measures and identity development, including the following (Schooley et al., 2019):

- MRAI = Multifactor Racial Attitudes Inventory
- SAS = Situational Attitudes Scale
- BWIS = Black–White Integration Scale
- ATB = Multifactor Measure of Whites' Attitudes Toward Blacks
- MRS = Modern Racism Scale
- CoBRAS = Color-Blind Racial Attitudes Scale
- SR2K = Symbolic Racism 2000 Scale
- WRCDS = White Racial Consciousness Development Scale
- WRIAS = White Racial Identity Attitudes Scale
- ORAS-P = Oklahoma Racial Attitudes Scale—Preliminary
- WICIAT = White Identity Centrality Implicit Association Test
- WRCDS-R = White Racial Consciousness Development Scale—Revised
- WRIS = White Racial Identity Scale
- BWAS/PCRW = Being White in America Scale/Psychosocial Costs of Racism to Whites
- POI = Privilege and Oppression Inventory
- WPAS = White Privilege Attitudes Scale
- RAS-I = Reflexive Antiracism Scale—Indigenous

Understanding the Role of Liberation Psychology

Liberation psychology as defined by Mark Burton of the English Language Liberation Psychology Network as a body of thought and practice centrally concerned with the experience, knowledge, and action of those who have been excluded and marginalized (Comas-Díaz & Torres Rivera, 2020). The effects of dominant power and its structures on the oppressed are explored, together with the lived impacts of poverty, social injustice, censorship, repression, and violence. Liberation psychologists aim to hear, amplify, and incorporate in their theory and practice the voices and knowledge of those "others" most affected by the kinds of oppression identified above.

Liberation psychology is not the end all be all; however, it gives us a firm foundation to build upon as we have seen with feminist liberation, womanist, and *mujerista* psychologies, among others (Comas-Díaz & Torres Rivera, 2020). The bedrock of understanding liberation perspectives is that it is about action. It is not about putting on a performance, and frankly, there is no space for this; it must be felt in the bones. Liberation is about love, justice, freedom, and how our individual health and communal wellness intersect with the violent past of colonialism in the Americas and beyond.

Within the liberation framework, we understand that research is not neutral and, more specifically, that neutrality cannot live with liberation. Research is not even objective because it is historically embedded in the culture of privilege, where privileged groups exert dominance and power over marginalized groups (Comas-Díaz & Torres Rivera, 2020). With this framework, we understand that neutrality is itself oppressive. For me growing up I learned this by recognizing that assimilation hurt me emotionally and physically and that I had to, in essence, pick a side; I could no longer protect whiteness and I had to reconcile that my proximity would never keep me safe, free, or even just.

Memory and lived experience are themes of liberation psychology that are particularly important. Memory, as in the recovery of one's origin, community identity, and personal history, is important and must be acknowledged and deeply understood. Discovering that my understanding of my birth story was completely wrong is an example of why memory is so important to uncover in the practice of liberation psychology. We must keep in mind that liberation psychology is not limited to current trauma but in fact is generational, which makes this practice historical and multidisciplinary.

In regard to interracial relationships and kinship, the identity intersections and the current state of the relationship may be overwhelming. For example, clients coming in with depression and low self-esteem must be examined beyond the immediate symptoms. With a broader understanding of how White supremacy created antiblackness and with it a color caste system, among other degrading and dehumanizing behaviors, that dates back to Aristotle (Kendi, 2017), we see that many of our clients experience racialized violence daily in real time. Whether this client is Black or mixed race, they will have been affected by this violence, and they are often not educated on the manifestations of said racialized violence. This can result in a feeling of insanity with its foundation in the gaslighting of White supremacy, internalized and otherwise.

In personal and professional spaces, we must begin to challenge ourselves and those around us. "White Americans are born into a culture which contains the hatred of blacks as an integral part" (Grier & Cobbs, 1968, p. 27). This is one of many reasons White supremacy is so hard to give up—it's easy to feel empowered because that power is embedded in our culture.

This is why a historical and liberatory lens is necessary when doing work (professional and parental) around identity, anyone's identity—because there is an ugly underbelly. Remember and teach that racism is not slavery; slavery is an institution of racism, much like all systems of oppression.

For me, taking stock of what was real and what was a false memory of something said in passing for more than 30 years is what began to change my life. Getting to the truth and integrating personally and communally should be the very function of psychotherapy. When we can use interracial relationships as a gift to understand how antiblackness is harming humanity as a whole and begin to practice and expect a love ethic in everyday life, we may actually begin to heal.

References

Comas-Díaz, L., & Torres Rivera, E. (Eds.). (2020). *Liberation psychology: Theory, method, practice, and social justice.* American Psychological Association.

Crenshaw, K. (2016). *On intersectionality: Essential writings.* New Press.

Frey, W. H. (2015). *Diversity explosion: How new racial demographics are remaking America.* Brookings Institution Press.

Grier, W. H., & Cobbs, P. M. (1968). *Black rage.* Basic Books.

Hasch, M. (1991, August 11). Brutality, competence questions facing FOP as it convenes here. *Pittsburgh Press,* 6.

hooks, b. (2001). *Salvation: Black people and love.* William Morrow.

Jung, M., & Vargas, J. (2021). *Antiblackness.* New York: Duke University Press.

Kendi, I. X. (2017). *Stamped from the beginning: The definitive history of racist ideas in America.* Nation Press.

Kendi, I. X. (2019). *How to be an antiracist.* One World.

Kivel, P. (1996). *Uprooting racism: How white people can work for racial justice.* New Society Press.

Menakem, R. (2017). *My grandmother's hands.* Central Recovery Press.

Schooley, R. C., Lee, D. L., & Spanierman, L. B. (2019). Measuring whiteness: A systematic review of instruments and call to action. *The Counseling Psychologist, 47*(4), 530–565.

Walcott, R. (2021). *The long emancipation: Moving toward Black freedom.* Duke University Press. https://doi.org/10.1515/9781478021360

12

Mixed Messages

Navigating the Intersections of Identity and Intergenerational Trauma

Tiffany Benford

This is a story of dignity and how oppression, antiblackness, and patriarchy, in particular, have assaulted my own sense of worth. In this essay I explore how messages of oppression get internalized and inherited, passed along from generation to generation, and play a pivotal role in shaping who we are as individuals. My story is told through the lens of a cisgender, multiethnic, queer femme, first-generation Cuban American. Though my story belongs to me and no one else, my experience is not entirely unique among Black and Brown people whose families have migrated to the United States.

I pull from both my personal life and professional experience as a clinician specializing in trauma, while also centering the importance of sociocultural contexts. I explore the ways that systemic forms of domination shape the suffering of the individual. It is my hope that these insights demonstrate how complex it is to unpack these layers and that as complicated as it may be, the only way toward personal and collective liberation is to face our trauma—and the social systems that cause them—head on with courage and authenticity.

If we look around at what is happening in the world today, there is no question that the demand for racial justice is palpable. This essay is a humble contribution to that greater call for action. I hope to inspire and engage you in a practice of self-reflection, to explore the ways in which internalized oppression impacts you and has shaped your own personal narrative and worldview.

White supremacy, patriarchy, and all forms of oppression challenge our ability to live our lives authentically, and when unchecked, consciously or not, we can play a part in upholding the core function of these systems, which is to divide and conquer us.

Tiffany Benford, *Mixed Messages* In: *Antiblackness and the Stories of Authentic Allies*. Edited by: Norman Kim, Carolyn Coker Ross, Mazella Fuller and Charlynn Small, Oxford University Press. © Oxford University Press 2024.
DOI: 10.1093/oso/9780197642535.003.0013

For many people who are multiethnic or multiracial, it can be challenging to discuss identity or find the language to describe oneself to other people in day-to-day settings. In many instances these conversations are set aside due to the various degrees of discomfort they can generate for people who are tired of battling overt racial oppression and ongoing microaggressions. In other words, it can feel like an exhausting and never-ending uphill battle.

As a somatically trained clinician, I invite you to notice what is happening in your body as you continue to read. If there is tightness in your chest, I urge you to take a breath and expand your awareness to the feelings coming up. Stay curious with these emotions, and when ready, slowly exhale and if possible allow them to move through you.

My clients find their way to my office looking for answers. Many of my clients grapple with intersecting identities. These threads somehow begin to unravel, and, in search of support, they end up in therapy. I am often sitting with them in moments of deep grief—grief connected to the trauma of simply living life as themselves. They express feeling lost, hopeless, and chronically misunderstood. The role of a therapist is not to "fix" their clients or even to offer advice but rather to empower them to awaken to the wisdom that lives inside of their body, spirit, and psyche.

While from the outside we may see an individual struggle with addiction, thoughts of suicide, or acts of self-harm, these behaviors are often the outcome of intergenerational trauma impacting the individual, their family of origin, and their chosen family, as well as the broader community.

Tasked with assisting individuals to gain new insight, I listen deeply to their life experiences. I witness my clients process these events and interactions, and my goal is to help them to move from the micro (self-reflective) to the macro (broader context) of their community and sociocultural structures.

For example, one client is a Black female freshman in college who finds it harder to navigate being around her White peers, in a predominantly White institution of higher learning, after witnessing George Floyd be killed on national television.

In this case, the student's (micro) personal insight and recognition of feelings such as rage and fear—which are causing her to sleep more and her heart to race on campus for "no reason"—are not seen by me in a silo. I look at these "symptoms" through a lens that takes the macro, national, or global content into consideration when assessing behavior such as tendency to isolate, skip class, or smoke weed rather than be active in the gym or go to a study group where they might be the only Black student present. I work with them to learn new skills that allow them to navigate the issues that present as interpersonal struggles in their professional and personal spaces.

My near-limitless capacity to hold compassion for others is both a gift and, when I overextend or allow my boundaries to be violated, a real growth edge. It is the place where I need to be constantly vigilant for the purpose of my own healing but also, maybe even more important, where I need to be responsible to those to whom I am of service as a clinician. Personal and intergenerational trauma can be a touchstone of transformational growth birthed from deep pain. I have witnessed it time and time again become the greatest teacher and motivator for my clients.

I first learned to make the connection between systemic oppression and individual trauma as part of my own healing journey. By unpacking the ways that patriarchy and antiblackness had impacted my family, my mother in particular, I was able to understand the pain of my own life with greater clarity.

Internal Borders

My mother spent pivotal years of her childhood development inside a Cuban detention camp for children. She and the rest of her family were imprisoned by the Castro regime after a failed attempt to flee the island. During my youth, my mother didn't speak much about her life in Cuba. No one in the family did.

What little has been shared is that my *abuelo* (Spanish for "grandfather") was a poor farmer who worked as a police officer during the Batista regime—much like many working-class people in the United States join the police or military as one of the few options to support their families and have a career that offers a sense of honor. He was from a rural part of Cuba and descended from a mix of African and Indigenous ancestry.

On one hand, I heard my family embracing our African and Indigenous roots, even holding this ancestry in high regard. On the other hand, there was a constant push to assimilate to American culture, specifically White American culture. My mother only remembers flashes of her life in Cuba, but those memories play out vividly like scenes from a movie set in the midst of a revolution, where my family was on the wrong side of the new order coming to power. She remembers being 7 years old and walking with my grandparents for hours in the dark through thick mountain jungle, clutching a stuffed animal in her hand.

She remembers when the boat that she and her family were sailing in to Key West got caught in a hurricane and capsized in shark-infested waters. She remembers washing up back on the shores of Cuba and being surrounded by members of the military as they pointed guns and shouted. She remembers being separated from her parents in that Cuban detention center. And when reunited with my *abuela* (Spanish for "grandmother"), she remembers not recognizing her own mother, who had been severely beaten and no longer had her teeth.

Years later, when my mother was 15, she and her family were granted passage to the United States. Once here, my abuelo was desperate to ensure the survival of his children. He pushed my mother along the path of assimilation through a combination of overt and subtle messages that were shrouded in White supremacy, sexism, and antiblackness. These messages made up the content of the life lessons he passed on to her. My mother, a seemingly care-free Latina immigrant, learned to hide both her trauma and her naivete as part of her survival.

She in turn, whether knowingly or unknowingly, passed these message on to me. *Look beautiful. Appear unbroken even when you are breaking. And above all, don't ever let anyone see you too closely, for they would surely be turned off by the depth of your suffering.*

Growing up I often heard my mother express pride and gratitude that I was born with "good hair" rather than "kinky bad hair" like her. She told me stories about her mother ironing her hair so she could be presentable and pretty. She never wanted her tan to get "too dark" and risk being unattractive to a White suitor. It was always anticipated that she and my aunt would marry "up and out," that is, find a husband who was White and not poor.

The ways in which this legacy has impacted me directly are reflected in my own personal struggles with identity. My skin tone ranges from brown to olive and back again. I recall always hesitating when it came time to check racial boxes.

"Should I mark 'Hispanic'?" I would ask my mom.

My abuela would laugh and say, "Eres Latina chica" (you're Latina).

I was not Hispanic; I wasn't one of those *Spaniards*. There was a difference. The message I picked up from the family chatter was that the Cubans who called themselves Hispanic were rich and claimed whiteness in a way that darker and poorer or working-class Cubans did not. It was confusing at best and harmful at worst to the development of self-esteem and my sense of belonging as I began to emotionally mature.

Checking All the Boxes

No more compromises. I see past your disguises. Blinding me
through mind control. Stealing my eternal soul, Appealing through
material. To keep me as your slave.

—Lauryn Hill (2002)

When I learned that I didn't fit into the boxes that helped make other people's
lives easier, my very existence began to feel burdensome. I carried with me
an intrinsic apology for taking up space. This is reinforced in the ways we are
socialized and taught to think about ourselves, down to the ways in which we
present who we are.

When I was 18 years old I worked as a server for a major hotel in
Connecticut. On one occasion, the hotel was hosting a conference for a well-
known medical company. The night before I had worked a late bartending
shift at my second job, and like many in the restaurant industry, I had had a
few drinks after closing. Working a 6:00 a.m. breakfast conference was the
last thing I wanted to do hungover.

Over the course of my morning I took delight in hearing the starkly
southern accents and expressions, as the majority of attendees hailed from
South Carolina. Being from South Florida, I wasn't entirely new to the sound,
but there was something different in the drawl of vowels as I heard the words
come out of the mouth of one woman in particular.

After pouring more juice into her glass, I went to turn away but stopped as
her voice called out in a high-pitched southern song. The words tumbled out
of perfectly pink painted lips, with her piercing blue eyes peering up at me
from underneath her Victorian-styled hat covering her platinum blonde hair.

"Excuse me, but my friends and I have been wonderin' all morning, well
with your skin and all, just whatever are you mixed with?"

It was that time of year when summer transitions into fall and my skin was
a darker brown due to long summer days in the sun. My hair was long and
black. When I heard this woman's question I immediately felt transported
to another era in time. She could not possibly be serious. Really? What was
I mixed with?

"Vodka," I responded dryly, walking away with a wry smile that hid the
deep rage welling inside me.

This is just one example of many instances in which I felt the dehumanizing
microaggression of White supremacy. Antiblackness and White privilege have

been passed down through generations of my family and continue to shape and define me, as well as forms of resilience. Growing up, I had learned to feel ashamed and embarrassed of my accent, my mother's accent, and in many ways my Cuban culture. So I learned to lose my accent by freshman year in high school.

Over the course of my life I have navigated microaggressions and overt racism—oftentimes not from outsiders but from my own White family members on my father's side. These included being constantly mocked or asked to say ridiculous things in Spanish for their amusement, only for my child mind to be confused and embarrassed when they erupted in laughter. At first I didn't understand the joke, and then I realized the joke was me and the language I spoke every day at home with my Cuban family. Other times the wounds would cut deeper.

When Nowhere Is Safe

Without realizing it, both my parents created a similar world of uncertainty, recreating what they had suffered through in their own childhoods. This was not their intention. Rarely do parents want their children to suffer. That being said, parents can only give what they know or experience.

My parents had a terrible divorce when I was 3 years old. The majority of my formative years were spent shuffling from home to home, with police presence becoming the norm. My father's struggles with bouts of deep depression and a sense of failure regarding his marriage did not help the shame he navigated, which was heavily induced by his Catholic upbringing by a first-generation Irish mother.

My father's struggles with his mental health led to a severe alcohol, drug, and gambling addiction. Even so, he was better off than my immigrant mother because he was a White male and spoke perfect English. His ability to navigate the court system from a place of privilege won him custody of me; I lived with him full time by the time I was 5 years old. And as much as I felt my father's love and in many ways felt safe in his presence, under his care I was left in the hands of people who would abuse me.

I remember vividly the hypersexualization I experienced from adult White men that were either in the inner family circle or in his broader circle of roommates or friends. I remember him leaving me alone often so that he could chase whatever particular form of escape would assuage his internal turmoil, temporarily quieting his own pain.

From a very young age I was a sensitive child and felt deep empathy for my parents. So despite being harmed often, I lived with an innate desire or need to protect them. So I did, over and over again with my silence.

It would be years before I understood this impact and the depth to which it shaped my own existence. As I grew older I became filled with a deep sense of shame not much different from the shame my parents felt. Though painful, these experiences gave me the rare opportunity to heal some of the deepest wounds experienced in my childhood that resulted from intergenerational traumas passed along from both sides of my family.

Sin Vergüenza (Without Shame)

As a mixed-race child I was constantly looking for ways to make sense of who I was and how I came to be. I experienced compounded feelings of deep shame and self-doubt under the cultural crossfire of my parents' differing cultural beliefs, practices, and norms, as well as the emotional and physical neglect I experienced due to the ways they ignored their own trauma.

As a practitioner who is interested in deepening my knowledge and practice, I have connected to the Center for Healing Shame, a network of clinicians, coaches, and educators dedicated to understanding the impact of shame within personal transformation. One of the clinicians of this international cohort shared a simple yet compelling perspective:

Shame, like trauma, puts the body in a freeze state and lowers the ability to think and act clearly. Shame feels like a fog or cover, something that is external, that makes it hard to function. Usually, it is not a single shock to the system, like an accident or a hospitalization, but a series of more subtle shocks, a slow drip, drip, drip that disrupts normal functioning and creates feelings of isolation and powerlessness. (Lyons & Rubin, 2021)

My parents, who both only had high school educations, came from entirely different worlds and didn't really know how to explore these concepts among themselves, let alone talk to me about the ways they might play out in my life. Even with the best of intentions, they lacked the tools and awareness to deeply question the traumatic ways in which they might be reproducing oppression in their own lives and passing on or acting out these internalized ways of being among each other and to me.

Doing the Work: Healing Family Trauma Bonds

"When you are born into a world where you don't fit in, it's because you were born to help create a new one.

—Anonymous

Love or being loved was not something I often felt or could describe witnessing as a child. Feelings of loneliness riddled me and I found solace in humor, writing, and dance. But I also experienced profound feelings of dissociation and fear. During my adolescence and young adulthood, my childhood coping mechanisms developed into new survival skills, some healthy and others destructive, as I sought to find my place in the world.

The child brain is not fully developed, so the ways that one makes sense of the world are very much informed by the subtle and overt behaviors displayed by the adults in one's everyday environment. Even with a depth of awareness and knowledge, rooted in both personal experience and intentional study of psychology and neuroscience, as a parent I'm challenged with how to help my own son, who is born of two mixed parents, avoid the internalization of White supremacy as his own identity develops. By the age of 5 my son was already noticing different skin tones and seemed to be noticing that our society is organized by these differences.

The opportunities to help our children develop positive self identities often present themselves in unexpected moments. I experienced one of these moments one evening as I helped my child climb out of the bathtub. Giggling, he looked up from under his wet curls that I was toweling off. It was a ritual, one of many we created in the short span of his young life.

"Mommy," he said, looking up at me and gently tracing his tiny fingers against my olive skin.

"Yeah, baby, what's up?"

"Why are there so many color browns?"

"What do you mean, baby?"

"Mommy, there is more than one brown. You're one kind of brown . . . and me too. But our brown is different from Daddy's and Pop-Pop or . . . " He trailed off, getting lost in the circles he was making on my arm while yawning.

My chest tightened immediately. A whisper seemed to get caught in my throat. My heart sank.

What was this feeling? It felt so familiar, but I had never been here before. My mind was racing to make sense of my body's response while also attempting to remain present with my child's question.

I recognized it as that same question I had grappled with my whole life, now reflected back to me in my son's eyes that day in the bathroom. I felt a deep awareness of my child's innocence and how quickly that innocence would be challenged by the world around him. The urge to protect my child by disrupting the chain of trauma passed down to me was primal. I also felt a grave sense of responsibility and fear of how the world would receive (or reject) him. With his green eyes and light skin, my son can pass for White even more easily than I can, and definitely more easily than his father.

As a light-skinned person of color, I have benefited from a system set up to demean and denigrate darker-skinned people. At the same time, that system has hurt me in profound ways, especially as a woman.

For most of my life and even now (though less so) I have lived with a constant anxiety of not being "seen" by one group or the other. What I call the "mixed dilemma" is usually referred to in academic circles as "racial identity invalidation." Franco and O'Brien (2018) describe this as the denial of one's racial identity by others. This denial of identity is a salient racial stressor that does meaningful harm to the mental health and well-being of multiracial people. The mixed dilemma is characterized by not being "Black" or "Brown" enough while also remaining outside of whiteness. It's nearly impossible for mixed people to belong when belonging is defined by rigid racial categories.

The reality is that human beings do not fit cleanly into these categories based on colorism. White supremacy's need for the "one-drop rule" is evidence of how crude the definitions of race are in our society. The need to define whiteness as something that is pure leads to the manufacture and perpetuation of a fear of mixed people and the places in which their various identities intersect.

In the face of intergenerational trauma, raising children can be extremely challenging and overwhelming. Disrupting the cycle of trauma requires a deep awareness and acknowledgment of the pain one has experienced, a desire to not recreate those same experiences, followed by a commitment to implementing new practices. This is a tall order for anyone. When you add factors like poverty, abuse, and inadequate health care or education, that tall order can begin to feel impossible.

It is no wonder that many parents feel ill-equipped, exhausted, and fearful when attempting to prepare their children to face discrimination, prejudice, and other forms of oppression they will inevitably encounter as they develop within an unjust world. Rather than fumble, many of us just avoid, ignore, or minimize the problems away.

Deepening Our Commitment to Liberation

You either walk inside your story and own it, or you stand outside
your story and hustle for your worthiness.

—Brene **Brown** (2010)

My training and education offer me frameworks to understand how the different parts of me and my family inform the way the world views me. I live in a system that uses race and ethnicity to shape how I ought to be treated and ultimately how I relate to myself. White supremacy, as a system in America, functions to create a power structure that asserts whiteness over blackness. We have all been socialized to play our particular roles to keep that structure in place.

In so many ways my and my family's story is like a mosaic, broken shards of colorful glass reflecting the light and hiding the shadows in the distraction of art that is displayed to the world. Like so many people of color, my story is one of resilience and perseverance in the face of a system that was not designed for my success. Throughout the years I have put the pieces together, and through that process I found my calling in life.

This belief is coupled with a deep understanding that trauma is experienced on a collective scale. The simple fact is that if we do not unpack the trauma we have experienced, we will pass it on to the next generation. These structures upholding oppression will only be challenged by a deep commitment to vulnerability for the sake of true liberation. A more just world will require a new generation of clinicians, healers, and educators to become comfortable with leaning into discomfort. It is uncomfortable to explore oppression, but the cost of not doing so will only perpetuate the harm that has already been inflicted upon us.

References

Brown, B. (2010). *The power of vulnerability.* TedX.

DeGruy, J. (2017). *Post traumatic slave syndrome: America's legacy of enduring injury and healing.* Uptone Press.

Franco, M. G., & O'Brien, K. M. (2018). *Racial identity invalidation with multiracial individuals: An instrument development study. Cultural Diversity and Ethnic Minority Psychology, 24*(1), 112–125. https://doi.org/10.1037/cdp0000170

Hill, L. (2002). I get out. *MTV Unplugged No. 2.0.* Columbia Records.

Lyons, B., & Rubin, S. (2021). *Center for Healing Shame.* https://healingshame.com/about

13

How *Not* to Be an Ally

Critical Race Theory, Afro-Pessimism, and White Women Who Pass as Black

Matthew Oware

In 2013, Black Lives Matter began as a hashtag response to the acquittal of George Zimmerman, a Hispanic White male, in the murder of Trayvon Martin, a young Black male. It formalized as an organizing principle during the social protests in Ferguson, Missouri, over the killing of Michael Brown— another young Black male—by the police (Lebron, 2017; Taylor, 2016). Since then, the United States has witnessed the growth and impact of Black Lives Matter protests across the world.

These movements, whose impact rivals previous civil rights organizations, were started by three Black women, Patrisse Cullors, Alicia Garza, and Opal Tometi. These individuals argued that racism and antiblackness permeate the criminal justice system, leading to brutality against Black people. (Taylor, 2016). Closing in on a decade after Trayvon Martin's death, their assertions remain prescient, with the police shootings and deaths of dozens of Black individuals from George Floyd to Breonna Taylor by 2020.

Self-identified Black individuals have put themselves on the frontlines to fight against forms of interpersonal and systemic racism in the United States. Yet, within the last decade, there have been cases of White people masquerading as Black activists and assuming leadership roles in prominent social movements. Why would these White individuals pose as Black and take on these prominent positions?

This chapter explores cases of two White women and one White gender nonconforming individual who "reversed pass" (Beydoun & Wilson, 2017) as Black from the theoretical perspectives of critical race theory and Afro-pessimism. Rachel Dolezal, Satchuel Cole, and Jessica Krug were exposed for having presented themselves as Black. Moreover, Dolezal and Cole were leaders of organizations devoted to addressing racism and police

Matthew Oware, *How Not to Be an Ally* In: *Antiblackness and the Stories of Authentic Allies.* Edited by: Norman Kim, Carolyn Coker Ross, Mazella Fuller and Charlynn Small, Oxford University Press. © Oxford University Press 2024. DOI: 10.1093/oso/9780197642535.003.0014 brutality. Krug masqueraded as an Afro-Latina in academia, challenging White supremacy in her writings and presentations.

One may ask why these individuals did not act as White allies and collaborators with Black leaders and Black groups. Why pretend to be Black and assume leadership roles? Both critical race theory and Afro-pessimism inform and help answer these questions.

Moreover, the intersection of race and gender in these cases highlights another facet of these theories. On an interpersonal level, Dolezal, Cole, and Krug demonstrate the continued importance of race in our society through their appropriation of Blackness, as articulated by *critical race theory*. Critical race theory contends that race is a central axis that overlaps with other identities such as gender and class in understanding the operation and maintenance of the judicial system and other institutions in the United States. However, through the lens of *Afro-pessimism*, these White individuals express antiblackness. Afro-pessimism states that antiblackness is the primary factor for understanding race in the United States and worldwide (Ray et al., 2017). In this regard, they commandeer blackness to meet their wants and desires—achieving leadership roles and financial gain—seemingly in the name of Black liberation. This behavior reveals the ability of Whites to take on and discard a marginalized Black identity at their whim.

Critical Race Theory

Critical race theory began as an in-depth analysis of the American legal system in the mid-1970s. It articulates race as an organizing principle in the United States (Delgado & Stefanic, 2001). The first tenet is that racism is an everyday occurrence for people of color and a driving force of institutions in the United States, what critical race theory scholars refer to as "racial realism." Its second feature argues that there is an "interest convergence," whereby racial progress must satisfy the self-interests of Blacks and Whites. For example, Black advancement in education—equal access to resources— happens only through White approval and benefit.

The third aspect of critical race theory contends that race and racial groups are socially constructed, meaning that racial categories such as Black, White, Asian, Latinx, and so forth are categories created and imbued with meaning in the United States. The identities are not inherent, fixed, or biologically rooted. Indeed, they are malleable and mutable, changing in importance and impact based on the social, political, and economic forces transpiring in a particular moment.

A final component of critical race theory rests on the idea of intersectionality. This is the belief that no individual has a singular, unitary identity; instead, individuals possess multiple identities that interact and intersect with one another across space, time, and place (Delgado & Stefanic, 2001; Ray et al., 2017).

Afro-pessimism

Afro-pessimism diverges from critical race theory. This idea argues that antiblackness—the belief that Blacks are nonhuman—embeds itself at the institutional level and directs interpersonal interactions among and between racialized groups. Afro-pessimism eschews a binary White versus Black systemwide analysis and replaces it with a Black versus non-Black approach for understanding how race operates in the United States. Institutions and organizations immobilize and devalue Blacks and blackness. Moreover, Afro-pessimism asserts that non-Black racialized groups achieve upward mobility through assimilative processes predicated on anti-Black sentiments. For example, Irish and Italian ethnic identities morphed into primarily White identities due to Black antipathy (Takaki, 2008). Hence, in Afro-pessimism, antiblackness moves to the center of racial analysis rather than existing on the periphery (Ray et al., 2017).

Furthermore, Black individuals experience qualitatively different forms of oppression and racism than other marginalized groups such as Asians and Latinx folk for Afro-pessimists. Essential to the theory is the notion that the enslavement of Africans produced an "afterlife" that impacts Blacks and descendants of slaves through gratuitous violence and social dishonor. Police brutality and the killings of Black people are instances of gratuitous violence.

In addition, findings that show how Blacks hold the lowest statuses in health outcomes, educational and wealth attainment, and occupational prestige illustrate the idea of social dishonor (Oliver & Shapiro, 1995; Ray et al., 2017). Thus, both critical race theory and Afro-pessimism can enlighten our understanding of Whites who reverse pass as Black.

Reverse Passing

Scholars have documented cases where Blacks have posed as White (Kennedy, 2003; Larsen, 2013). Many did so to escape anti-Black violence, navigate Jim Crow segregation in the South, undermine White supremacy, or obtain the tangible and intangible privileges tied to whiteness.

Newer research has explored White "reverse passers" (Beydoun & Wilson, 2017). Beydoun and Wilson (2017) identify two types of reverse passing, legal and cultural. *Legal reverse passing* is "the process by which whites disavow their white identity and present themselves as per se non-white on legal and administrative documents" (Beydoun & Wilson, (2017, p. 310), for example, on college and graduate school applications, employment documents, census and state forms, and birth certificates. However, they may not present themselves as non-White in their day-to-day lives.

Cultural reverse passing is "the process by which whites disavow their white identity and present themselves as non-white in cultural spaces" (Beydoun & Wilson, 2017, p. 310). In this case, "passers" identify as non-White in their day-to-day interpersonal interactions with others. Yet, they may or may not claim a non-White identity on legal documents.

In recent years, White male impersonators have received attention (Dreisinger, 2008; Larsen, 2013). For example, Mezz Mezzrow, a Jewish jazz musician in the 1940s, was mistaken for and eventually passed as Black (Dreisinger, 2008). John Howard Griffin, endeavoring to understand the experiences of Black men, darkened his skin and wrote a book, *Black Like Me*, about his experiences in the Deep South in the 1960s (Griffin, 1962). Current work explores White female passers (Brubaker, 2016).

Rachel Dolezal

The most infamous case of a White woman passing as Black is Rachel Dolezal. Her tale has spawned multiple articles and books (Brubaker, 2016; Dolezal & Reback, 2017). Sociologists Brubaker (2016) and Morning (2017) unpacked and explored Dolezal's identity claim as a Black woman, urging readers to reassess and expand our conceptions of racial identity and to fully engage with the idea of comprehending race as a social construct. Indeed, these scholars implicitly anchor their analysis of Dolezal from a critical race theory perspective. Yet, much more is learned by applying Afro-pessimism to this case.

In a live interview on June 10, 2015, reporter Jeff Humphrey asked Dolezal, the president of the Seattle branch of the NAACP chapter, if she identifies as African American. The idea was to force her to openly state her race. Dolezal looked the part of someone engaging in reverse passing: a Brown, caramel-complected, curly-haired woman. She personifies Beydoun and Wilson's

(2017) notion of a cultural reverse passer, changing her physical features to fit those of an African American woman. For example, in various pictures on her Facebook page, she wore her hair in braids and dressed in African garb—presumably performing an Africanized Black identity.

Ruthanne and Lawrence Dolezal are listed as Rachel's biological parents on her birth certificate. Both self-identified as White and asserted that their daughter was the same. In addition to her position as NAACP chapter president, Dolezal served as a member of the Office of Police Ombudsman Commission in Spokane, Washington. On her application for the commission, she identified as White, Black, and Native American—reflecting Beydoun and Wilson's (2017) notion of legal passing. Moreover, Dolezal taught Black feminism in the African American studies program at Eastern Washington University (Dolezal & Reback, 2017). Additionally, from 2008 to 2010, she worked at the Human Rights Education Institute in Coeur d'Alene, Idaho. The organization addressed social justice matters. Hence, Dolezal participated in activist work as the leader or head of multiple organizations focused on addressing inequality.

After the question from the reporter, Dolezal abruptly walked away without answering. Shortly after that incident, Dolezal stepped down from the presidency of the NAACP due to accusations that she misrepresented her race on the police commission application. In a Facebook post, she responded: "It is with complete allegiance to the cause of racial and social justice and the NAACP that I step aside from the presidency."

After the Humphrey interview, she appeared on NBC's *Today* show with Matt Lauer in 2015. Here, she claimed that she "identifies as Black." Moreover, she connected with the Black experience at age 5, "drawing self-portraits with the brown crayon instead of the peach crayon, and Black curly hair . . . that was how I was portraying myself." When Lauer asked her when she started "deceiving people," she replied that newspapers first classified her in Idaho as "transracial," then "biracial," and finally as a "Black woman," during her time as a member of the human rights organization. She stated that she never corrected these characterizations. When asked if she did not clarify her race because it worked to her advantage—securing the presidency of the NAACP's local chapter—she disagreed with that characterization.

To this day, Dolezal continues to identify as Black. Furthermore, she has changed her name to Nkechi Amare Diallo, given to her by a supportive Nigerian man from the Igbo tribe in Africa. As detailed in the "Blackface of White Leadership" section below, Dolezal demonstrates both critical race theory and Afro-pessimism through her performance and exoticization of Black identity. Even more recently, other White individuals have passed as Black.

Satchuel Cole

The second case of reverse passing focuses on Satchuel Cole. Cole self-identified as a biracial Black individual and appears in photos and media programs with a tanned or bronze-colored skin tone, curly hair, and green eyes. Cole, who is gender nonconforming and uses they and them pronouns, was a prominent activist in Indianapolis, Indiana. They led the organizations Indy10 Black Lives Matter and Indy Showing Up for Racial Justice. Also, they were vice president of the activist group Don't Sleep, which advocated for LGBTQ+ rights. In 2018, Cole founded the nonprofit organization No Questions Asked Food Pantry. Finally, Cole acted as the spokesperson for the family of Aaron Bailey, a Black male killed by the Indianapolis Metropolitan Police Department during a traffic stop (Evans & Contreras, 2020).

Due to their activism, Cole made the headlines of numerous local articles and appeared on televised news channels. There was a story in *Freedom Indiana* with Cole pictured with an older, darker-complected Black male. They identified him as their long-lost father—not known to the man in the picture (Evans & Contreras, 2020). In the summer of 2020, Cole's masquerade came undone.

Members of the Indianapolis activist community suggested that Cole impersonated as Black. Specifically, individuals in Black Indy Live thought Cole reversed passed, securing thousands of dollars for their organizations. Black Indy Live revealed Cole's actual background. Cole's original name was Jennifer Benton. John and Rachel Benton were Jennifer's parents; they both identified as White. John moved out when Jennifer was young, and Rachel remarried. Shortly after that, Jennifer's older sister, Melissa, served jail time for killing their mother. Revealing deep family trauma, Jennifer testified in court that the siblings were victims of sexual and physical abuse at the hands of their stepfather (Black Indy Live Staff, 2020).

In 2010, Jennifer legally changed their name to Satchuel Cole. The name was a combination of the Negro League baseball player Leroy Robert "Satchuel" Paige and Jennifer's close friend, Chantelle Owens-Cole. Before this change, Benton was classified as White on legal documents. But, like Dolezal, Cole transformed their race along cultural and legal lines (Beydoun & Wilson, 2017). Benton started identifying as Black and gender nonconforming with the name change, becoming involved in social movements in the Indianapolis area. In essence, their activism solidified their Black identity. Yet, Cole's actions after the death of their friend Chantelle Owens-Cole raised red flags (Black Indy Live Staff, 2020).

In an obituary Cole wrote for Owens-Cole, they claimed Chantelle was their biological sister and that Chantelle's son was Cole's offspring. Moreover, the obituary listed No Questions Asked Food Pantry as Owens-Cole's sole beneficiary, allowing Cole to receive funds donated to the organization. Hence, Cole profited from the death of their friend. Cole was even more problematic as a "slum lord" property manager who misappropriated funds (Black Indy Live Staff, 2020).

As a result of these revelations, Cole wrote a Facebook post stating: "Friends, I need to take accountability for my actions and the harm that I have done. My deception and lies hurt those I care most about. I have taken up space as a Black person while knowing I am white." Further, they wrote, "I have used Blackness when it was not mine to use. . . . I have caused harm to the city, friends, and work that I held so dear" (Summers, 2020) . When examined through a lens of critical race theory, Cole, similarly to Dolezal, uses a Black racial identity to create economic and political gain. More damning, though, is Cole's use of antiblackness to exploit marginalized individuals, as explained in the "Blackface of White Leadership" section below.

Jessica Krug

Jessica Krug, a former associate professor in the history department at George Washington University, apologized for pretending to be Black in her September 2020 post on Medium. Paralleling the language of Dolezal and Cole, Krug wrote, "I have eschewed my lived experience as a white Jewish child in suburban Kansas City under various assumed identities within a Blackness that I had no right to claim: first North African Blackness, then US rooted Blackness, then Caribbean rooted Bronx Blackness" (Krug, 2020).

Before being exposed, in previous venues Krug directed colleagues to pronounce her last name as "Cruz." In public, with a tanned hue, she wore large hoop earrings, dark black hair, and clothing that suggested a Black Latinidad identity. Reportedly, she spoke in stereotypically inflected Puerto Rican

Bronx vernacular. Further adding to her performance, in an article in *Essence* magazine, she asserted, "I am boricua, just so you know"—a proclamation of Puerto Rican pride (Jackson, 2020). She passed as Afro-Latina, conveying an image and dialect that she considered Latinized blackness.

Like Dolezal and Cole, she reverse passed along cultural and legal lines (Beydoun & Wilson, 2017). However, some scholars of color suspected a fraudulent identity. Researching Krug's background, Yamaira Figueroa-Vasquez and Yarimar Bonilla, Afro-Latina professors, contacted people who knew Krug. They found gaps and contradictions in Krug's personal stories. Writing for the *Guardian*, they asserted that "over the course of her life, Krug built an identity based on the worst stereotypes, beliefs and supposed dysfunctions of Black and Latinx people" (Figueroa-Vasquez & Bonilla, 2020). Krug claimed that she was the daughter of drug addicts and grew up in the barrio. The story was made up, conveying caricatured and stereotypical Latina and Black backgrounds.

The name on Krug's birth certificate is Jessica Anne Krug. She grew up in Kansas City, Missouri, and attended a Jewish elementary school, going on to attend a college preparatory high school. Krug graduated from Portland State University and obtained her doctorate in history from the University of Wisconsin-Madison in 2012. Francisco Scarano, a member of her dissertation committee, stated that Krug was "passionate about African and African Diaspora history," traveling to Africa, the Caribbean, and Latin America (Jackson, 2020). In his interactions with Krug, Scarano said that she never presented herself as Black or Latina. After hearing the news regarding her reverse passing, he was "shocked" by her deception (Jackson, 2020).

Krug's transformation from White to Black likely occurred between graduate school and securing her first academic position at George Washington University. While there, she presented herself as Black. Adding to her performance, she wrote a monograph, *Fugitive Modernities*, which focused on the experiences of people of color. Appropriating an Afro-Latina identity, she won prestigious fellowships targeted for Black and Latinx scholars. Among peers who knew of her deceit, this raised concerns of racial exploitation for profit (Figueroa-Vasquez & Bonilla, 2020).

While masquerading as Black, Krug harassed other individuals of color. Figueroa-Vasquez and Bonilla (2020) reported that Krug "openly bullied, mocked, gaslit and antagonized Black and Latina women she encountered in academic and activist circles as a way to authenticate further and validate her imaginary struggle and holier-than-thou politics." They contended that "[she tore] down those she deemed less 'woke' than herself." The authors suggested that Krug's piece in Medium was a preemptive strike against her unmasking as a fraud.

In Krug's Facebook post, she admits to being a "coward" and a "culture leech" who was "audaciously deceptive" (Krug, 2020). She expressed "remorse" for her dishonesty, insisting that she be "canceled." Once discovered as a fake, Krug apologized. Her duplicity has far-reaching effects, as demonstrated by critical race theory and Afro-pessimism.

The Blackface of White Leadership

Analyzing Dolezal, Cole, and Krug's stories using critical race theory and Afro-pessimism provides several key insights. First, from the perspective of critical race theory, all three demonstrate that race, in this case, racial identity, remains a crucial factor that deserves continued exploration in American society. All three successfully—over differing times—posed as Black individuals by addressing issues pertinent to the Black community and serving in leadership roles in organizations that addressed Black inequality. Furthermore, all three modified their skin tones or hairstyles and "acted" in ways—for example, serving on the NAACP or speaking with exaggerated accents—that led others to believe they were Black.

Through their actions, these individuals demonstrate how race is a constructed category—a central premise of critical race theory. People "read" them as Black because they conveyed markers of Blackness through their attire, physical features, cultural expression, or familial references to Black men. These aspects are culturally defined, and these three people show how race is contextual.

Yet, these cases powerfully illustrate Afro-pessimism. From this perspective, these individuals fetishize and essentialize blackness for their self-interest. They—specifically Dolezal and Krug—express antiblackness, presenting Black womanhood from a caricatured and stereotypical perspective.

In Dolezal's case, blackness is Africanized, kente-cloth wearing, braided hair, Black Latinized vernacular, and an African-inflected name. Dolezal's performance rests on colonialized views of Blacks as "royal" and "pure," seemingly untouched by White civilization. Krug, on the other hand, presents simplistic and racist Latinized Blackness, speaking in exaggerated broken Bronx Spanglish and wearing articles of jewelry supposedly associated with

Afro-Latinas. Krug performs Black Latinidad based on the White racist imagination.

All three cases demonstrated *minstrelsy*, a time during Jim Crow segregation when Whites applied dark makeup to their faces and supposedly acted like Black people. We witness similar parallels with these individuals. Their "blackface" is not as blatant, but they still devalue blackness, presenting it in limiting, exotic, and singular ways.

The motives for passing as Black firmly suggest an antiblackness based on financial and professional gain. All three received material benefits—money, status, honors, or leadership positions—for passing as Black. More insulting, though, these individuals operated under the guise of empowering and helping people of color. Cole received money for their organizations and free press from news outlets. Krug gained a coveted tenure-track position at George Washington University, compensation for speaking engagements, and awards for her research. Finally, Dolezal received a book deal and a Netflix special about her life. These were opportunities not granted to other Black women. Indeed, these White individuals were able to pull off their ploy due to the low status of Black women in the United States—a social dishonor articulated by Afro-pessimism. The racist, one-dimensional, and problematic representations of Black womanhood that these individuals perform are remnants of slavery and Jim Crow.

Conclusion

Based on the actions and public responses to their Black passing, these individuals wanted to make profits from their ruse. They did not want to portray their White identities—although Dolezal contends she is Black—because it would not have placed them in positions to receive compensation or an elevated status.

If they were White individuals on the frontlines of protest movements in Seattle, Ferguson, or Indianapolis, they might not receive the same accolades. Therefore, these individuals presented a distorted type of blackness to gain attention. They were "Black" leaders who profited from Whites' ability to dominate Blacks, a form of White privilege. This is not White allyship. True White allies would listen to marginalized voices and express empathy when needed, not co-opt or appropriate the bodies of Black people for personal gain. That approach continues the domination by Whites against Blacks seen in earlier periods.

References

Beydoun, K., & Wilson, E. (2017). Reverse passing. *UCLA Law Review, 64*(2), 282–354.

Black Indy Live Staff. (2020, September 15). *Shocking details emerge on Indy activist who faked life as a Black woman.* Black Indy Live. https://www.Blackindylive.com/shocking-details-emerge-on-indy-activist-who-faked-life-as-a-Black-woman/

Brubaker, R. (2016). The Dolezal affair: Race, gender, and the micropolitics of identity. *Ethnic and Racial Studies, 39*(3), 414–448. https://doi.org/10.1080/01419870.2015.1084430

Delgado, R., & Stefancic, J. (2001). *Critical race theory: An introduction.* New York University Press.

Dolezal, R., & Reback, S. (2017). *In full color: Finding my place in a Black and White world.* BenBella Books.

Dreisinger, B. (2008). *Near Black: White-to-Black passing in American culture.* University of Massachusetts Press.

Evans, T., & Contreras, N. (2020, September 18). *Satchuel Cole, leader in the fight for racial equality in Indianapolis, lied about her race.* IndyStar. https://www.indystar.com/story/news/investigations/2020/09/18/indianapolis-activist-satchuel-cole-lied-being-black/3486542001/

Figueroa-Vasquez, Y., & Bonilla, Y. (2020, September 9). A White scholar pretends to be Black and Latina for years. This is modern minstrelsy. *The Guardian.* https://www.theguardian.com/commentisfree/2020/sep/09/jessica-krug-white-scholar-Black-latina?CMP=share_btn_tw

Griffin, J. H. (1962). *Black like me.* Signet Book.

Jackson, L. (2020, September 12). The layered deceptions of Jessica Krug, the Black-studies professor who hid that she is White. *The New Yorker.* https://www.newyorker.com/search/q/Jessica%20Krug

Kennedy, R. (2003). *Interracial intimacies: Sex, marriage, identity, and adoption.* Pantheon Books.

Krug, J. (2020, September 3). *The truth, and the anti-Black violence of my lies.* Medium. https://medium.com/@jessakrug/the-truth-and-the-anti-black-violence-of-my-lies9a9621401f85

Larsen, N. (2013). *Passing: A novel.* Oshun Publishing Company.

Lebron, C. (2017). *The making of Black Lives Matter: A history of an era.* Oxford University Press.

Morning, A. (2017). Race and Rachel Dolezal. *Contexts, 16*(2), 8–11.

Oliver, M., & Shapiro, T. (1995). *Black wealth/White wealth: A new perspective on racial inequality.* Routledge.

Ray, V., Randolph, A., Underhill, M., & Luke, D. (2017). Critical race theory, Afro-pessimism, and racial progress narratives. *Sociology of Race and Ethnicity, 3*(2), 147–158. https://doi.org/10.1177/2332649217692557

Summers, J. (2020, September 18). *Here's yet another White activist who lied about their race.* Jezebel. https://jezebel.com/heres-yet-another-white-activist-who-lied-about-their-r-1845110145

Taylor, K-Y. (2016). *From #BlackLivesMatter to Black liberation.* Haymarket Books.

PART IV
ANTIBLACKNESS AND SOCIAL JUSTICE

14

Food Justice

At the Intersection of Policy and Culture

Karen E. Watson

In 2012, I was among the few Black executives at the world's largest market research firm, Nielsen. I was leading a small division that repurposed the company's consumer market research data for insights it could provide to policymakers and nongovernmental organizations. Though best known for its ratings of television shows, Nielsen was founded to collect data about what people purchase in grocery stores. By the time I joined the company, it was collecting data on a much broader range of consumer behavior, including Internet and cell phone usage and video streaming patterns. Nielsen also gathered data on ad placements and analyzed their effectiveness in all mediums, including in stadiums and on billboards.

I had spent 28 years in Washington, DC: first as a journalist, then working in a regulatory agency, and later as a lobbyist on Capitol Hill. It's no secret that regulation can't keep pace with industry in any sector. So when I joined Nielsen in 2006, it soon struck me that policymakers would be much better public servants if they understood and had access to the sophisticated ways in which market researchers study demographic patterns and behaviors.

Most of the data Nielsen collects is licensed by large consumer packaged goods (CPG) companies and is used to advertise highly processed foods in venues where people watch or "consume" entertainment, news, and sports. Increasingly, much of that processed food advertising is targeted very specifically at Black and Brown people living in "food swamps" (Rose et al., 2009), a residential area in which most people live within 5 minutes' walk of four or more fast food restaurants and convenience stores (Hager et al., 2017).

Food swamps are distinct from "food deserts," areas where there are few or no grocery stores or farmers' markets, resulting in a lack of affordable fresh, nutritious food. In fact, living in both types of zones has been linked to obesity (Cooksey-Stowers et al., 2017). However, previous research on the effect

Karen E. Watson, *Food Justice* In: *Antiblackness and the Stories of Authentic Allies.* Edited by: Norman Kim, Carolyn Coker Ross, Mazella Fuller and Charlynn Small, Oxford University Press. © Oxford University Press 2024. DOI: 10.1093/oso/9780197642535.003.0015 of adding grocery stores in residential areas indicated no improvement in diet quality and other health indicators, even though there was increased access to healthy food (Cummins et al., 2014).

Some researchers have argued that it is "the continued accessibility of unhealthy foods" that counters the positive impact of having healthy, less processed foods available (Cooksey-Stowers et al., 2017, § 1.1). Therefore, food swamps may be a more accurate predictor than food deserts of obesity and the chronic diseases that often accompany obesity (Cooksey-Stowers et al., 2017). Research has shown a strong correlation between the concentration of fast food outlets and the concentration of ethnic minorities—generally, Black, Indigenous, and people of color (BIPOC)—regardless of income (Hager et al., 2017; Haynes-Maslow & Leone, 2017; Sanchez-Vaznaugh et al., 2019). Based on this link, Cooksey-Stowers et al. (2017) suggest that "the race and ethnicity of a community shapes the actions of the food industry and community design decision makers, which in turn, influence the food environment" (para. 1.1). In other words, food swamps are actually a deeper problem for BIPOC communities than food deserts are.

When President Obama was re-elected in 2012, I approached Mrs. Obama's chief of staff and inquired about working with the administration to help them understand the importance of the primary research that market research and data analysis could provide to their effort to stem the tide of childhood obesity in America. Understanding the marketplace tools and how they could be used by policymakers for the benefit of the public had become a greater passion after years of witnessing first-hand how low-income BIPOC children, in particular, were targeted through the advertising of highly processed food and sugar-sweetened beverages (SSBs). The childhood obesity epidemic is compounded by the inefficiency of government agencies' efforts to address it and to coordinate on acquiring market research data. Discussions with the White House quickly turned into the Drink Up campaign, which I envisioned, planned, and strategized to employ advanced market research and data to identify the segments of the population that would benefit the most from exchanging their SSBs for water to improve health.

By the time it was published in 2019 in the *Lancet Report*, the findings of the *Lancet* Commission on Obesity were not a surprise to the medical community. The commission's report confirmed what health practitioners and policymakers already knew too well: that obesity is "increasing in nearly every region of the world" (Swinburn et al., 2019, p. 1). Despite the fact that for the past three decades the leading health policymakers who make up the World Health Assembly had endorsed "evidence based policy recommendations to halt and reverse obesity," those recommendations had not been implemented in a way that would result in "meaningful and measurable change" (Swinburn et al., 2019, p. 1).

The commission effectively reframed the global obesity epidemic by linking it to two other inextricably related epidemics: global undernutrition and climate change, renaming this perfect storm the "global syndemic"—a "synergy of epidemics" (Swinburn et al., 2019, p. 1). In its recommendations, the commission called for greater cohesive participation by civil society to combat the forces of commercial interests and put pressure on policymakers to make health a priority.

Then at the end of 2019, the global syndemic came face to face with the global pandemic of COVID-19. Early in the epidemic, medical professionals determined that patients with obesity were second only to patients over 65 in their risk for serious illness or death from COVID-19. The threat of this virus and the 2020 murder of George Floyd by police created global awareness of yet another global risk to public health: racism.

As citizens, leaders, and governments around the world voice a deep and critical need to address entrenched racial hierarchies in our legal, health, housing, and economic systems, few have recognized the transformative potential of tackling nutritional inequality affecting BIPOC communities. Specifically, few are focused on the essential role of advertising and popular culture in influencing our nutrition choices. Nor are they focused on understanding how nutrition norms are modeled by our most admired figures in entertainment media and the ways in which that modeling might be deployed for a greater good, including contributing to creating community agency and well-being. Addressing our popular cultural norms around food is key to unlocking consumer expectation and the support of civil society and policymakers to resist the commercial pressures of the giant multinational corporations that produce highly processed foods that contribute so detrimentally to the undernutrition and obesity epidemics in our communities.

BIPOC Communities in the Eye of the Syndemic

In recent decades, upper-income people (who in the United States are overwhelmingly White, not BIPOC) have become more aware of the damage to their health caused by highly processed foods, much of which has little nutritional value and contains high amounts of added sugars, salt, and fats (Martínez Steele et al., 2016). As a result, CPG companies and fast food chain restaurants have pivoted to targeting their marketing of nutritionally poor products to people with low incomes: in particular, to BIPOC communities. Targeted marketing uses campaigns designed to appeal to a certain group of consumers that a company has identified as particularly lucrative. This "multicultural marketing" is created to be appealing to people of certain racial/ethnic groups (Grier & Kumanyika, 2010). It "uses culturally relevant themes, depicts people of color purchasing and/or consuming advertised products, and/or is placed in media, programming and other venues that are disproportionately frequented by individuals of color" (Rudd Center, 2019, p. 10). Targeted, racialized marketing and the undernutrition that stems from it pose health risks that result in diabetes, heart disease, hypertension, and premature death. New research also suggests that our diets are directly linked to mood, thus affecting mental health as well (Martins et al., 2021).

"Big Food" spends $14 billion a year on advertising, with 80% of that budget promoting fast food, SSBs, candy, and unhealthy snacks. Most of that is spent on TV advertisements for highly processed, nutritionally poor products targeted to Hispanic and Black children and teenagers (Rudd Center, 2019). Black and Hispanic children are a growing segment of the U.S. population and represent an increasing share of the consumer market. Research analyzing Nielsen data on Black and Hispanic consumers concluded that "food-related marketing continues to disproportionately target youth of color with harmful products and contributes to health disparities affecting their communities" (Rudd Center, 2019, 8). Moreover, most food ads seen by Black and Hispanic youngsters were for these unhealthy products. The authors of the *Rudd Report* reiterated what other scientists have found: "Greater exposure to this marketing, both in the media and in their communities, likely contributes to or exacerbates diet-related health disparities affecting communities of color, including obesity, diabetes, and heart disease" (Rudd Center, 2019, p. 10).

The Outsized Role of Advertising in Shaping Popular Culture

The $14 billion mentioned in the *Rudd Report* doesn't include another type of advertising that we as consumers of popular culture absorb every day but in a form we don't recognize as advertising and marketing, because it is hidden within—or even disguised as—entertainment and social media. Since leaving Nielsen, I've come to believe that these covert marketing influences are even stronger than overt advertising. That is, we have little awareness of the role that these food marketers play, as they place advertising in our entertainment and social media.

Advertising is everywhere. Oftentimes, even when we don't know we are watching an ad, we are watching an ad. In the entertainment world, marketing often shows up in the form of product integrations and placements. Product placement is the practice of creative mention, or even incorporation, of a product in narrative storytelling in any entertainment medium under an arrangement with the product's manufacturer. Sometimes this happens without any arrangement, simply because the storyteller/creator thinks the placement is important to the narrative. With each instance, these placements convey to the audience what is acceptable, trendy, important, and cool—or what is verboten, distasteful, and unacceptable.

The inclusion of products in the narrative structure of movies, television shows, sporting events, music videos, and influencers' social media posts is pervasive. But because we don't perceive them as advertisements, we often internalize their messages as socially normative, so their influence is deeper and potentially more harmful than overt advertising and marketing (Shrum, 2012).

Viewers would be wise to pay close attention to the values, norms, and messages that are being communicated in product placements. In most cases, these messages are carefully researched; the impact of the message is not left to chance. They resonate with how we think and feel; they influence our behavior and even what we believe is "normal." Research tells us that the hidden nature of these product integrations means we process them differently than advertising (Shrum, 2012). These placements in narrative format make it harder to realize we are being sold something.

Coca-Cola's manufacturers have been placing that SSB's iconic image into movies almost since the movie industry was created (Coca-Cola Company, n.d.). The company's red-and-white swirl is pervasive in both traditional ads and narrative story structure. Its internal mandate to its employees is to ensure the product is "within an arm's reach of desire" (Business Case Studies, 2020). In other words, the brand's logo and its iconic glass bottle—and their emotive association—are not just a function of our overt and easily recognized advertising environment. We have to recognize that we have been inundated with this brand image, and its carefully crafted association with happiness, since the time we were preverbal.

After the murder of George Floyd, Coke and other corporate brands declared their support of the Black Lives Matter movement. CPG companies decried racism in the United States and around the world. But they continue their targeted marketing of highly processed foods to minority people. If Black and Brown lives matter, do they only matter when it comes to police brutality? Shouldn't they matter even more when it comes to the health effects of these products on BIPOC populations, who suffer disproportionately as a result of these cynical marketing tactics? These companies boast that they spend "generously," supporting Black leadership groups and civil rights organizations, providing scholarships, and so on. That spending, which benefits a very few relative to the enormous harm of consuming their product, has resulted in muting the voices of organizations that represent the civil rights of Black and Brown people.

Some Influencers Push Back

Still, there are hopeful signs that some cultural influencers are conscious of their norm-setting influence on their fans. In 2021, Cristiano Ronaldo, one of the most influential sports figures globally, with half a billion Twitter followers (Sweney, 2021), during a soccer championship press conference very deliberately removed the Coca-Cola bottles from in front of him as he spoke. "'Coca-Cola, ugh,' he said in apparent disgust," and instead, he picked up a bottle of water and showed it to the cameras, saying, "Água!" (water in Portuguese; Lane, 2021, para. 4). Ronaldo thus signaled to all watching that he rejected the sugar-laden beverage and instead embraced water. Coca-Cola shares swiftly dropped $5.1 billion (Gilbert, 2021). While Ronaldo's gesture may not have been the sole cause of this devaluation, it certainly negatively impacted Coca-Cola's image.

Cristiano Ronaldo isn't the only sports celebrity to push back by refusing to allow his influence to be used to promote SSBs or junk food. NBA star Steph Curry played an early part in the Drink Up campaign to promote a healthier choice. During the campaign, Curry declined to sign an endorsement deal with a major SSB manufacturer, signing instead with Brita, the water filter company (Rovell, 2015).

Market Forces

Brand imagery and messaging is the result of careful market research. The brand imagery in front of Cristiano Ronaldo at that press conference was designed to trigger an unconscious, emotional association that Coke has carefully crafted for over 100 years. CPG companies understand that we make most decisions about our health habits unconsciously, almost automatically. It is simply too onerous for us to be self-aware at every moment about our daily choices. Market researchers understand that being healthy is not a motivator for most people. We're more often motivated by the desire to look better, perform better, and feel better, but not necessarily to be "healthy."

Market researchers do not leave to chance whether a message is going to land in the mind and heart where it will make an impact. Using electroencephalogram probes, skin conductance, and eye tracking, they methodically measure and analyze whether––and how effectively—the visuals and narrative of a message work together, triggering the emotion, the memory, the attention, and, critically, the behavioral intention toward a product or a message. Advertisers understand that to be persuaded to change their habits, people need measures that are specific and, more importantly, that they see as achievable. By demonstrating that he rejected an SSB in favor of water, Ronaldo intuitively set an example that an audience could easily internalize and make actionable.

Conversely, another globally popular athlete, Usain Bolt, the 12-gold-medal-winning Olympian, became a spokesperson for Gatorade. Bolt, commonly referred to as the fastest man in the world, signed an endorsement deal with Gatorade, an SSB manufactured by PepsiCo. In 2012, Gatorade released "Bolt!," a video game touted to inspire kids to be their best. According to its creators, the game was a tremendous success, with 4 million online users and 87 million plays by 2013. It even won an industry award for mobile advertising. The object of the game was for Bolt "to run through increasingly difficult levels and grab some Gatorade to keep him fueled while avoiding the dangerous water that might compromise his performance" as a runner (Jones, 2017, para. 2). In other words, the game portrayed water as the enemy of athletic performance.

Advertainment?

Public health practitioners and their allies often focus on the predatory role of advertising to BIPOC communities. But policymakers and public health advocates could increase the effectiveness of their own efforts by paying closer attention to the way advertisers integrate their messages into popular culture. As of mid-2021, 26% of TV viewing was via streaming services (Nielsen, 2021). Streamed content is sometimes free of advertising, but that does not mean it is commercial free. A recent blatant example of product placement in a movie streamed globally on Netflix is a 90-second scene in the film adaptation of August Wilson's *Ma Rainey's Black Bottom*, with Viola Davis, in which Ma Rainey refuses to commence a recording session until the record executives provide her with the Coca-Cola she had stipulated she must have at that time of recording. She demands, "Where is my Coke? I need a Coke!" and sends band members to get her three bottles of the SSB. The film has been seen by millions of viewers—many of them Black—who will be drinking in the influence of the carefully placed product, which in that scene is associated with a Black woman's self-determination and agency.

Product placement built into our cultural narrative has the potential to do great harm. But this practice also presents anyone who cares about creating a culture of health with an opportunity: to begin to understand the power of this practice and how it might be harnessed to set communities on a path to greater vitality and vibrancy.

Creating Demand for Nutritional Equity and Food Justice

The 4-year Drink Up campaign yielded an important understanding of the mechanisms for addressing the most critical question for public health and food justice: *How can we create a climate where citizens value health for themselves and their communities, a climate that gives civil society the opportunity to have public support for policy change?* We need a society that *expects* policymakers to resist commercial interests and prioritize public health.

We are in a time when two major and powerful industries, health care and food, are undergoing a transformation. Consumers are increasingly pressuring the food industry to be more transparent and to provide simpler, unadulterated products, and pressuring the health care industry to address the upstream threat of chronic disease, to improve population health, and to reduce costs. These synergies are especially critical considering that both climate change and COVID-19 disproportionately impact BIPOC communities (Centers for Disease Control and Prevention, 2021; Swinburn et al., 2019).

These transformations are inextricably linked. But the move to greater equality in our food environment, and the wellness in BIPOC communities that would result, cannot accelerate without popular demand for a healthier environment and the reflection of that demand in our popular culture. So the language and images we use to get through to people, and how consistently we infuse them into our cultural milieu, are paramount.

What advertisers and market researchers have perfected, and what health policymakers and doctors should understand, is that it is nearly impossible to move people by appealing to their rational understanding (Kahneman, 2011). Vanity and performance are what drive us to change our behavior: the aspiration of attaining the strength, speed, and magnetism of Ronaldo or the self-assurance and self-determination of Ma Rainey.

Given this, how do we rally support in social justice leadership communities to pay closer attention to the popular cultural and commercial influences that conspire to shape our norms? How do we begin to use these same techniques to infuse *new* images into our culturally influential media in order to create *new* norms around nutrition and create an expectation of health in policymaking? How do we put the *public* back into public health, and the *justice* back into food justice?

The good news is that culture and policy reinforce one another (Daniell, 2014). Armed with data, the latest research, and proven marketing techniques, we can subvert the harmful influences from Big Food and help our BIPOC communities to embrace better nutritional and health habits. As comedian and civil rights activist Dick Gregory said, "Being healthy is a revolutionary act. . . . Changing the world begins with healing your body" (Loggins, 2020, para. 2). Let the revolution begin.

References

Business Case Studies. (2020, February 3). *Within an arm's reach of desire—global marketing.* https://businesscasestudies.co.uk/within-an-arms-reach-of-desire/

Centers for Disease Control and Prevention. (2021, March 22). *Obesity, race/ethnicity, and COVID-19.* https://www.cdc.gov/obesity/data/obesity-and-covid-19.html

Coca-Cola Company. (n.d.). *Coca-Cola red on the silver screen: Exploring the brand's role in movies.* https://www.coca-colacompany.com/news/coca-cola-red-on-the-silver-screen

Cooksey-Stowers, K., Schwartz, M. B., & Brownell, K. D. (2017). Food swamps predict obesity rates better than food deserts in the United States. *International Journal of Environmental Research and Public Health, 14*(11), 1366. https://doi.org/10.3390/ijerph14111366

Cummins, S., Flint, E., & Matthews, S. A. (2014). New neighborhood grocery store increased awareness of food access but did not alter dietary habits or obesity. *Health Affairs (Project Hope)*, *33*(2), 283–291. https://doi.org/10.1377/hlthaff.2013.0512

Daniell, K. (2014). *The role of national culture in shaping public policy: A review of the literature.* HC Coombs Policy Forum, Crawford School of Public Policy, Australian National University. https://coombs-forum.crawford.anu.edu.au/sites/default/files/publication/coombs_forum_crawford_anu_edu_au/2014-08/daniell_2014_the_role_of_national_culture_in_shaping_public_policy_final.pdf

Gilbert, A. C. (2021, June 16). Coca-Cola shares drop $5 billion after Cristiano Ronaldo's gesture to drink water. *USA Today.* https://www.usatoday.com/story/money/2021/06/16/coca-cola-shares-dropper-after-christiano-ronaldo-moves-coke-bottles/5293590001/

Grier, S., & Kumanyika, S. (2010). Targeted marketing and public health. *Annual Review of Public Health*, *31*(1), 349–369. https://doi.org/10.1146/annurev.publhealth.012809.103607

Hager, E. R., Cockerham, A., O'Reilly, N., Harrington, D., Harding, J., Hurley, K. M., & Black, M. M. (2017). Food swamps and food deserts in Baltimore City, MD, USA: Associations with dietary behaviours among urban adolescent girls. *Public Health Nutrition*, *20*(14), 2598–2607. https://doi.org/10.1017/S1368980016002123

Haynes-Maslow, L., & Leone, L. A. (2017). Examining the relationship between the food environment and adult diabetes prevalence by county economic and racial composition: An ecological study. *BMC Public Health*, *17*(1), 648. https://doi.org/10.1186/s12889-017-4658-0

Jones, R. (2017, September 22). *Gatorade to pay $300,000 for using Usain Bolt game to teach kids not to drink water.* Gizmodo. https://gizmodo.com/gatorade-to-pay-300-000-for-using-usain-bolt-game-to-t-1818656349

Kahneman, D. (2011). *Thinking, fast and slow.* Farrar, Straus and Giroux.

Lane, B. (2021, June 15). *Cristiano Ronaldo got rid of 2 bottles of Coca-Cola and replaced them with water at a Euro 2020 press conference.* Insider. https://www.insider.com/cristiano-ronaldo-replaces-coca-cola-bottles-with-water-press-conference-2021-6

Loggins, J. (2020, June 16). *Dick Gregory: Health is a revolutionary act.* https://daretodetoxify.com/dick-gregory/

Martínez Steele, E., Baraldi, L. G., Louzada. M. C., Moubarac, J.-C., Mozaffarian, D., & Monteiro, C. A. (2016). Ultra-processed foods and added sugars in the US diet: Evidence from a nationally representative cross-sectional study. *BMJ Open, 6*, e009892. https://doi.org/10.1136/bmjopen-2015-009892

Martins, L. B., Braga Tibães, J. R., Sanches, M., Jacka, F., Berk, M., & Teixeira, A. L. (2021). Nutrition-based interventions for mood disorders. *Expert Review of Neurotherapeutics*, *21*(3), 303–315. https://doi.org.10.1080/14737175.2021.1881482

Nielsen. (2021, June 24). *Big picture: Getting a clearer view of streaming's part of total TV use.* https://www.nielsen.com/us/en/news-center/2021/big-picture-getting-a-clearer-view-of-streamings-part-of-total-tv-use/

Rose, D., Bodor, N., Swalm, C., Rice, J., Farley, T., & Hutchinson, P. (2009). *Deserts in New Orleans? Illustrations of urban food access and implications for policy.* University of Michigan National Poverty Center, USDA Economic Research Service.

Rovell, D. (2015, December 16). *Warriors' Stephen Curry signs endorsement deal with Brita.* ESPN. https://www.espn.com/nba/story/_/id/14382337/stephen-curry-golden-state-warriors-signs-endorsement-deal-brita

Rudd Center. (2019, January). Increasing disparities in unhealthy food advertising targeted to Black and Hispanic Youth. *Rudd Report*. UConn Rudd Center for Food Policy & Obesity. http://uconnruddcenter.org/files/Pdfs/TargetedMarketingReport2019.pdf

Sanchez-Vaznaugh, E. V., Weverka, A., Matsuzaki, M., & Sánchez, B. N. (2019). Changes in fast food outlet availability near schools: Unequal patterns by income, race/ethnicity, and urbanicity. *American Journal of Preventive Medicine, 57*(3), 338–345. https://doi.org/10.1016/j.amepre.2019.04.023

Shrum, L. J. (Ed.). (2012). *The psychology of entertainment media: Blurring the lines between entertainment and persuasion* (2nd ed.). Routledge.

Sweney, M. (2021, June 18). Coca-Cola's Ronaldo fiasco highlights risk to brands in social media age. *The Guardian*. https://www.theguardian.com/media/2021/jun/18/coca-colas-ronaldo-fiasco-highlights-risk-to-brands-in-social-media-age

Swinburn, B. A., Kraak, V. I., Allender, S., Atkins, V. J., Baker, P. I., Bogard, J. R., Brinsden, H., Calvillo, A., De Schutter, O., Devarajan, R., Ezzati, M., Friel, S., Goenka, S., Hammond, R. A., Hastings, G., Hawkes, C., Herrero, M., Hovmand, P. S., Howden, M., . . . Dietz, W. H. (2019). The global syndemic of obesity, undernutrition, and climate change: The Lancet Commission report. *Lancet Commissions, 393*(10173), 791–846. https://doi.org/10.1016/S0140-6736(18)32822-8

15

Antiblackness and the Black Environmentalist's Conundrum

Ecological Safety or Psychological Surcharge

Joyce Woodson

I am a native Washingtonian, born and raised in Southeast Washington, DC, in the 1960s and 1970s. We moved into a multiracial apartment development when I was 6. It was considered a working-class neighborhood but was spitting distance from the public and low-income housing. Over time, it became entirely African American. I had everything I needed and most of what I wanted. I didn't believe we were poor or even low income. I did know that the area in which I lived was different than others—and not always in a good way.

I attended public schools in my predominately Black neighborhood for prekindergarten and kindergarten. When my mother learned of the desegregation plans, she made sure that my brother and I were the first two on the list to go to a school in the predominately White neighborhood in upper Northwest Washington. I often heard her say, "They won't stop teaching theirs so that they don't teach mine."

Our days were very long. We spent 45 minutes to an hour getting to school in the morning and then again in the afternoon to get home. Sometimes the traffic was really bad so we were late arriving. At 6 years old, I *felt* the difference in where I lived and where I went to school. I felt it in the atmosphere from both people and the physical environment. There were trees and lots of shade where I went to school. The air smelled and felt different. The smell of honeysuckle was palpable at school but never at home. At school, in the spring, it didn't seem as hot on the playground, where there was grass. And there my favorite toys—monkey bars and seesaws—were wood and metal. There were fields and birds of all shades and colors. Wildlife was visible along the bus route and on the playground.

Joyce Woodson, *Antiblackness and the Black Environmentalist's Conundrum* In: *Antiblackness and the Stories of Authentic Allies*. Edited by: Norman Kim, Carolyn Coker Ross, Mazella Fuller and Charlynn Small, Oxford University Press.

My mother was a stay-at-home mom, a civil rights activist who marched and fought battles I never knew about until after I became an adult. Some of them I am just beginning to realize. The microaggressions and macroaggressions inside the Black community and society at large were her lived experience.

She was a dark-skinned woman and explained that education and career opportunities in the 1930s and 1940s were determined by the level of melanin in your skin. She told me about the segregation even within the Black community. The paper bag test was a real thing. As a result, she tried to prepare me mentally and emotionally for the same type of disappointments and frustrations she experienced and was sure I would also experience as a little Black girl in America. I would have to work harder, jump higher, and run faster than all others.

One of my mother's dearest friends, Mrs. Howard, was a Native American of the Cherokee Tribe. My mom didn't drive, but these two stay-at-home moms would pile their kids in Mrs. Howard's VW bus and the nine of us would go to parks, monuments, and museums. We were always outdoors, mostly at public spaces and national parks outside of our neighborhood. Many of these places we visited were free to the public. I don't remember being refused entry or being questioned about it. But I was a kid, and I don't think my mother would have allowed me to know or feel it.

Today, I attribute our access to these places to the unspoken privilege that came to Mrs. Howard, the melanin-challenged driver of that VW bus. When Mrs. Howard moved to a better neighborhood across town, we would go visit on occasion. However, my mother continued our excursions on public transportation, which meant we didn't go very far.

My mother constantly sent or took me to places that many of my friends only read about in books. For example, at age 9, I was sent to a Christian camp in Pennsylvania. This is where my love for nature and the environment really blossomed. Teen Haven Camp provided a rural area with horses and other animals that were not in cages, woods for exploring, and creeks and ponds for swimming in the summer and ice skating in the winter. There was hardly *any* concrete or asphalt there. The air was different. The water was different. It was an atmosphere where nature was free to be nature and I was taught a healthy respect for it.

I was also exposed to all types of recreational activities that were foreign to people in my neighborhood. We ate venison and did lots of arts and crafts. I was exposed to the wonders and pleasures of creation and able to just be a kid.

Water Is Life

My parents did not have access to pools or places where they could learn to swim. Black people were not allowed in public pools, and there were only certain beaches that Black people could enjoy during the 1930s and 1940s. It remained that way into the 1950s and even the 1960s. Consequently, neither of my parents learned to swim growing up. Although they were always renters, mom made sure that all apartments we lived in had a community pool.

According to a Centers for Disease Control and Prevention (CDC) report, the highest-disparity ratio of death from drowning continues to be among people of color (POC; Clemens et al., 2021). Some argue that historical trauma underlies the fear of the water and contributes to this statistic. Others say that it is a lack of *access*, pure and simple. I am a member of the second school of thought. Many Black people I know who lived in middle-class neighborhoods with access to pools as children had the same summer experience I had. We went to the pool when it opened at noon and left when it closed at 5 or 6 p.m. Most of us didn't get formal swim lessons, but because we had access, we were able to learn to swim and have a healthy respect for the water.

It is because of this access that my child and most of my siblings' children are swimmers, employed as lifeguards or in aquatics at some point in their life. In fact, my daughter has made a life for herself in the aquatics field. She is a swim teacher/coach, passionate about teaching Black and Brown kids how to swim, hoping to do her part to chop away at that statistic. She is also a certified pool operator, and when preparing for licensing, she was astonished by how many germs live and thrive in water. She reminds me again and again that our relationship with water is critical to survival, and swimming is a life skill: Water is life. Clean water is life.

The public places where Black people were allowed to visit accumulated stark differences in maintenance and upkeep. This situation continues today in some parts of the state where I currently live. Unfortunately, economic status, racial status, or a combination of the two often stands in the way of many POC when it comes to swimming. This is also true for experiencing and understanding many aspects of the natural world.

Nature Is Healing

Just as swimming is a life skill that often escapes some Black communities, the healing properties of nature are also unrealized or underutilized. While we know that nature is required to survive physically, some don't really understand the crucial role of nature for healing and enabling us to survive and thrive mentally and spiritually. And I can say without fear of contradiction or opposition that most African Americans agree—being Black in America is a traumatic experience.

Research is now revealing what I have known to be true for most of my life: Experiencing nature and the outdoors is healing. It reduces symptoms of trauma, and outdoor activities are beginning to be used as part of many successful treatment plans for posttraumatic stress disorder and anxiety disorders (Anderson et al., 2018). Nature provides the raw materials for our holistic medicines and is beginning to be prescribed by physicians as well as mental health professionals (Elassar, 2022).

There is an immediate and significant disadvantage when people are refused access to its powerful properties for a sound mind, peace, and healing; its stress-relieving properties; recreation; and just plain fun. Today my favorite places are where there is high land and moving water. When I am challenged or having internal struggles, I can give my husband and daughters a look and they will ask, "Time to go to the water? Or is it the mountains this time? All right, when do we leave?!" It's like when you see someone bleeding you ask, "Do you need to go to the hospital? All right, let's go."

Nature is my mental and spiritual hospital. Periodic trips to sit in the presence of Love is a requirement for my peaceful existence on this planet. When in need of guidance, I go sit in Love's presence somewhere in an area where Love's gift—nature—is able to exist free of man's interruption and interpretation. Things become clearer. Love is able to lead me. I find peace from the external and internal struggles I encounter daily. Peace is the offspring birthed from my affair with nature. I recover, reconnect, and recreate using its powers.

The Link Between Ecology and Economy

Contrary to what was once believed and in some places is currently popular belief, Black, Indigenous, and people of color (BIPOC) have great concern for the planet and all that live thereon. I have always been concerned about the air, land, and water that people need for survival.

My love for nature and its bountiful blessings began as a child, but my interest in conservation and the environmental movement was sparked in an environmental economics class required for my undergraduate degree. It was there that the link between what we do as human beings and the impacts on the environment was academically identified and socially reinforced. We are all connected. Due to life circumstances, it took years before I moved fully into a life where I am engaged in my passion. While on my journey, I learned some very unpalatable truths about environmental racism and society's human value gap. As fate would have it, again due to happenstance or grace, a job at a "Big Green" fell into my lap.

Academia opened the door, but my job in conservation is where I really learned of the unfortunate and often combative relationship between economy and ecology. My new employer changed my perspective and shifted my focus. I learned of the segregation in the environmental movement and the environmental inequities and impacts on Black communities.

Discrimination in the environment and access to public resources has been the lived experience of BIPOC communities in North America for centuries. It certainly was a part of my lived experience. For most of my life I have lived in or very close to a fence-line or frontline community. While they are defined differently, they both are disproportionately impacted by pollution—by actual pollution or the outcomes of pollution.

In my early adulthood, my daughter and I lived in a fence-line community that was less than a mile from a water treatment plant. I moved to this area because it was familiar and conducive to my current financial position at the time. (It also had a community swimming pool.) Every Sunday morning, there was an incredible and inescapable stench in my neighborhood. The windows would be closed, but the smell still seeped through as I dressed for church. I often wondered if the smell was on me once I got there.

The water from the faucet didn't always smell great or taste great. I didn't have the resources to purchase bottled water. Assured that it was safe by the landlord, we drank it or, more accurately, we boiled it and made tea. I hate to admit it, but we seldom drank plain water. When my economic situation changed, we moved—still near a superfund site, but to a less polluted area.

The negative impacts of antiblackness and White privilege, while subtle in some areas, are undisputable when it comes to the environment. When people think of or attempt to discuss antiblackness and environmental racism or its more palatable label—*environmental justice*—real estate redlining and unequal housing opportunities are as far as some can go.

Whether in real estate redlining or regentrification, access to national parks or public lands, or water and national resources, antiblackness, discrimination, and White privilege in the environmental sector are issues in America and often cited globally as a major concern. Study after study and report piled upon report go on and on about both the mental and physical health challenges that come from elevated levels of lead and other heavy metals in the bloodstream.

Flint, Michigan, for example, raised awareness of the disparities in access to clean drinking water. While Flint gained national and, I venture to say, even worldwide attention, there are many other areas both urban and rural that are even today experiencing similar conditions. While vacationing in Sedona, Arizona, I learned that the Indigenous Peoples' homes that we could see from the road were without running water or electricity, even though the powerlines were clearly steps away from them. They experienced all the burdens but none of the benefits of the powerlines, with no choice or voice. There are many other cases in which the government has known about hazards but the communities are not told of their risk and consequential impacts until decades later.

A Public Health Concern

Many Black and Brown folks are unhealthy not because of what they have done, but because what has been done and is being done in the environment where they live, learn, work, and worship.

The year 2020 and the worldwide COVID-19 pandemic featured an explosion of these attitudes and outcomes of racism in all its forms. In April 2021, the CDC finally identified racism as a serious public health threat (CDC, 2021). Rochelle P. Walensky, director of the CDC, stated:

> Racism is not just the discrimination against one group based on the color of their skin or their race or ethnicity, but the structural barriers that impact racial and ethnic groups differently to influence where a person lives, where they work, where their children play, and where they gather in community. (CDC, 2021 p. 1, paragraph 4)

This statement in a nutshell identifies environmental racism as a public health threat and acknowledges the health, economic, and environmental disparities caused by racism. There are many who have no choice in where they live and the environment surrounding their homes. Race and/or economic status put them at risk.

Often people limit the racism impact identified in the CDC statement to physical health. However, the mental and spiritual health of human beings are the two other legs of the three-legged health stool upon which all humans sit. Antiblackness in the environment impacts human beings' entire health, relentlessly attacking all sides of the triangle. People in communities targeted by polluters are exposed to toxins from multiple sources: pollution from factories, questionable safety conditions in the plants where they work, broken and/or outdated waste and sewage infrastructure, new waste sites, and more.

The cumulative impacts are passed down from generation to generation. The (polluted) air a mother breathes, the (toxic) water she drinks, and the vegetables she might be planting (in the toxic soil) to supplement the food that she purchases determine not only her health but also the health of her unborn child. The playground is built on land that is toxic, and kids are kicking up toxic particulate matter. As a result, people in vulnerable communities are at a deficit before they are even born. They start the race three paces behind the starting block.

These Black and Brown communities often have more hardscape and less landscape. Fewer trees and foliage create poorer air quality and higher temperatures. Areas in these zip codes are often labeled "heat islands." As a result, there is a disproportionate energy burden for the community. Utility bills are higher, as are irritability, anxiety, and aggression. So the lack of trees has a negative economical, ecological, physiological, *and* psychological impact.

Contamination Without Representation

Discrimination in the environment and access to public resources has been the lived experience of BIPOC communities in North America. But until data was collected, these realities were frequently disputed.

One of the first studies to offer data to support the stories of our lived experiences was published in 1987 and called "Toxic Waste and Race." It revealed that two-thirds of the largest commercial hazardous waste landfills in the United States were located in predominantly Black or Hispanic communities (Commission for Racial Justice, United Church of Christ, 1987, p. xiv). A follow-on study 20 years later found the situation to be graver than earlier reported. With more modern technology and research methods, this study reported that the neighborhoods that host commercial hazardous waste facilities that are clustered close together are 69% POC (Bullard et al., 2008).

These studies have spawned similar studies performed by grassroots environmental justice organizations and educational institutions. A longitudinal study by the University of Michigan in 2016 settled the chicken or the egg dispute that went on for years with regard to demographic communities and waste site decisions.

> The researchers found "a consistent pattern over a 30-year period of placing hazardous waste facilities in neighborhoods where poor people and people of color live." Racial discrimination in zoning and the housing market, along with siting decisions based on following the path of least resistance, may best explain present-day inequities, they concluded.
>
> Minorities and low-income communities are seen as the path of least resistance because they have fewer resources and political clout to oppose the siting of unwanted facilities. (Michigan News, , University of Michigan, 2016, p. 1, Paragraph 9)

This is not just the case for historically low-income communities. These conditions spill into attractive new developments and subdivisions as well, which appear to be areas of promise for more affluent POC. They purchase property in a developed area not fully understanding what was on that land before. They don't check the health of the ground in their front and back yards. They buy a home expecting to pass on wealth to their families, not realizing they are actually passing on contamination.

The negative generational and cumulative impacts are acute and constant. The air may be infected with toxins because of the toxins in the ground where their kids play. The home water supply may be questionable. Yet, government agencies provide permits to developers, who know the condition of the land.

What is the recourse when the homeowners find out their home is on a sinkhole or their water supply is polluted? Charges of violations to Title VI of the Civil Rights Act of 1964 can be filed against the government jurisdiction and/or developers. After years of litigation, orders of restitution and cleanup may result but seldom do.

Homeownership Conundrum

While both my parents were DC government employees, they were renters for all of their lives. As citizens of the District of Columbia, they have been subject to taxation without representation. As members of the African American communities in certain areas of the city, their position and status as renters put them in a state of contamination without representation as well. Property owners had rights; renters were subject to the decisions of the property owners.

My parents did not share their financial status with us, so I often wondered why they chose to continue to rent and not purchase a home. Now I know that there are reasons other than opportunity and financial ability that influence the decision of where to live. For instance, psychological considerations like comfort and community come into play, as does acceptance or avoidance of the constant emotional battle and continued disappointment that come from exclusion, rejection, and deliberate denial of service due to anti-Black attitudes and practices. There is a psychological tax to pay when living in predominately White neighborhoods. But socioeconomic status does not automatically produce privilege or environmental safety.

I always had a desire to live in a more culturally diverse neighborhood, one with more quality amenities and access to nature. My husband was not enthused by this prospect. In fact, he passively fought it. I married a man from the rural South. It only occurred to me recently that he spent all day at work dealing with the impacts of racist systems and attitudes. He didn't want to come home and have to deal with it there as well.

Home is where you go to feel safe. It is not supposed to be a place where you are in a constant state of feeling under impending attack and there is no psychological safety to be found. I am knowledgeable about the environmental hazards that await us in many Black communities and in a financial position that enables us to live in a wide range of neighborhoods in this country that would avoid these hazards.

When the time came to make a decision about the American dream—homeownership—our collective experience as a Black couple with teenage daughters presented us with a conundrum. Do we choose to live where the air and water are cleaner and there are healthy food choices, convenient access to green spaces, options for different types of recreational activities, products and services that are of higher quality, and land that is probably not toxic? Do we choose to avoid the emotional and psychological downside of being away from people who look like us and the culture and community we are familiar with?

If we choose a diverse neighborhood with the convenience of recreation and amenities near where we live, we are also choosing to be ready to defend our right to be in our own yard doing what people do for entertainment and relaxation. We could end up in a place where events and attitudes make it clear that we are not expected or even wanted there.

In my neighborhood, I can sit outside under a tree with my dog, scroll through social media, or read a book without question or raised eyebrows. In non-Black neighborhoods I run the risk of being reported to the police for loitering. In a Black neighborhood, my identity and right to be there are not scrutinized. In a White neighborhood, I risk being denied access to the community pool or other amenities paid for by my fully up-to-date HOA fees. And this is as a Black woman; the risks for Black men grow exponentially. Can our brothers and nephews visit us without concern for their safety?

Studies have shown that making this choice—to risk being constantly in defense mode—presents one with a psychological tax that has biological consequences (Merritt et al., 2006). Our mental health and consequently our physical health inevitably are the price we pay for convenience. We can always get in our cars, like my family did when I was little, and go where these things are available.

So the question is not whether to pay antiblackness taxes. The question is *how many and which ones*. The Black environmentalist's conundrum becomes how to balance their psychological budget.

References

Anderson, C. L., Monroy, M., & Keltner, D. (2018). Awe in nature heals: Evidence from military veterans, at-risk youth, and college students. *Emotion, 18*(8), 1195–1202.

Bullard, R. D., Mohai, P., Saha, R., & Wright, B. (2008). Toxic wastes and race at twenty: Why race still matters after all of these years. *Environmental Law, 38*(2), 371–411. http://www.jstor.org/stable/43267204

Centers for Disease Control and Prevention. (2021, April 8). *Media statement from CDC Director Rochelle P. Walensky, MD, MPH, on racism and health* [Press release]. https://www.cdc.gov/media/releases/2021/s0408-racism-health.html

Clemens, T., Moreland, B., & Lee, R. (2021). Persistent racial/ethnic disparities in fatal un-
intentional drowning rates among persons aged ≤29 years—United States, 1999–2019.
Center of Disease Control and Prevention, Morbidity and Mortality Weekly Report.
June 18. Weekly 70(24), 869–874.

Commission for Racial Justice, United Church of Christ. (1987). *Toxic wastes and race in
the United States*. Public Data Access.

Elassar, A. (2022). *Canadian doctors are prescribing free passes to national parks to treat
patients*. https://www.cnn.com/2022/04/30/health/canada-doctors-prescribe-nature-
wellness/index.html

Merritt, M. M., Bennett, G. G., Jr., Williams, R. B., Edwards, C. L., & Sollers, J. J., III. (2006).
Perceived racism and cardiovascular reactivity and recovery to personally relevant
stress. *Health Psychology*, 25(3), 364–369. https://doi.org/10.1037/0278-6133.25.3.364

Michigan News, University of Michigan. (2016). *Targeting minority, low-income
neighborhoods for hazardous waste sites*. https://news.umich.edu/targeting-minority-
low-come-neighborhoods-for-hazardous-waste-sites/

PART V
ANTIBLACKNESS AND ACADEMIA

16

Fighting for Our Place

Antiblackness in Academia

Chateé Omísadé Richardson

To provide an accurate picture of the way antiblackness manifests and replicates within academia, it is important to trace it back to its origin. Black people have been fighting for their place, for their space, for their sanity, and for the acknowledgment of their humanity in the United States since their ancestors were kidnapped and brought to these shores over 400 years ago. Their very presence gave rise to the idea of whiteness or Eurocentrism in order to keep them subjugated and in check, and antiblackness developed in direct reflection. According to the *Encyclopedia of Diversity and Social Justice* (Thompson, 2015), the creation of Eurocentrism in America simultaneously corresponds with three congruent processes:

> the legitimation of particular peoples and knowledge and the simultaneous illegitimation of other peoples and knowledge, the establishment of the global control of labor via colonization and imperialism, and the social construction of race. (p. 323)

Through a critical race lens, the idea of racism thus is foundational to America, came to saturate all levels of the society as it was being built, and was infused into the laws of the land to reinforce the structure so it continues to replicate itself. Antiblackness in this context, then, is also fundamental to American society. Antiblackness is any behavior or practice that serves to dehumanize Black people or uphold the ideals of whiteness, deeming White as the center of importance and rightness and anything else as deficient. Dr. kihana ross (2020) further identifies it as "the disdain, disregard, and disgust for black existence."

For Black people, the constant fight to simply exist and to create a space of equal footing within this society has been exhausting, has created cultural

Chateé Omísadé Richardson, *Fighting for Our Place* In: *Antiblackness and the Stories of Authentic Allies*. Edited by: Norman Kim, Carolyn Coker Ross, Mazella Fuller and Charlynn Small, Oxford University Press. © Oxford University Press 2024. DOI: 10.1093/oso/9780197642535.003.0017 fissures separating an entire group of people from their ancestral origins, and has caused a deep well of historical trauma that the community has been struggling to swim its way through in myriad contexts and arenas, most notably psychological, social, emotional, physical, and educational. In terms of education, the original American school system solidified in the late 18th century was solely created for the development of White children to legitimate their background and cultural knowledge (Richardson, 2021). Over a century later, the 1954 *Brown v. the Board of Education of Topeka, Kansas* decision integrated classrooms, but it did not integrate the teaching force (which remains 80% White women to this day), nor the curriculum (U.S. Department of Education, 2016).

This is one of the reasons Gloria Ladson-Billings and William Tate (1995) discussed the civil rights movement within the context of a failed project. It asked permission for Black people to participate in structures that were not created with their best interests in mind. It placed Black children in the predicament where what they would learn would be in the hands of others and saturated in an alien ideology. As a result of the decision, people of color were allowed in the classroom; however, space was never actually carved out for them to occupy any sense of importance within it. They were not considered in the educational conversations; they were merely added to what was already there, which served to suffuse the ideas of whiteness and a sense of antiblackness in all participants of the system, including those who are Black, creating oppositional identity.

This trend shows up in all levels of education, all the way up to graduate study and academia, which is the focus of study here. Currently, only about 2% of the total U.S. population has earned a doctorate degree. Only about 6.5% of that small number are Black or Latinx academics. Black, Latinx, and female professors are overwhelmingly underrepresented in U.S. colleges and universities, and the academic job market is very challenging for members of these demographics (Li & Koedel, 2017). The reason for the disproportionate representation of Black and Latinx scholars in academia can be easily and fluently articulated through the lens of critical race theory (CRT).

CRT is a radical departure from typical work on racism and inequity. Normative race work acknowledges the existence of racism but not necessarily at the deep level where it cannot be extracted. The application of CRT seeks out solutions or some type of optimism in one day overcoming this obstacle. Ladson-Billings (2013) explains the anatomy of CRT, which culminated from the extensive study of race literature and legal studies regarding race-based discrimination cases and foundational legal decisions.

From this extensive and intensive deep dive, it was understood that the inequities were not a result of disparate anomalous situations but of systemic, "intractable," and enduring structures that are the very fabric of this country and the laws that form the support beams upholding its foundation (Ballard, 2010; Gildersleeve et al., 2011; Ladson-Billings, 2013).

At the deepest level of definition, CRT acknowledges that racism is the normal mode of functioning in America, it is a common daily occurrence, and it is permanent and endemic in American education at all levels. The ills playing out in society exist within education to an intense degree, because this is where it is taught and perpetuated, and then graduates are sent out into the world to operate as they have been molded, thus continuing the cycle. As such, education is saturated with bias, racist cultural constructs, and inequities (Gildersleeve et al., 2011; Richardson, 2021). There is disproportionate representation because Black people are not truly welcome in this space that is counter to their cultural existence.

Ladson-Billings (2013) further asserts that those who situate their scholarship within the frame of CRT ascribe to five underlying principles related to the endemic nature of racism:

1. the belief that racism is not an aberration
2. interest convergence or material determinism
3. race as a social construction
4. intersectionality and antiessentialism
5. voice or counternarrative

These tenets are interwoven through the ivy halls of academia. The first principle is self-explanatory, as the connection has already been made to education in general. Racism is exacerbated in academia as it is simultaneously the bedrock and pinnacle of American education. Even though hundreds of studies have dissected and reported on the racist underpinnings of the system, people become hostile in response to a critical race analysis of the phenomenon. Part of the reason there is such a strong negative response to CRT is because people, particularly those in power, do not want to acknowledge it, but also because it connects directly to the second tenet, the idea of interest convergence.

On one hand, the thought that racism is an endemic issue brings a sense of frustration and hopelessness to White scholars who come to equate it with the feelings of guilt they experience when confronted with the history of White people and the myriad ways they have oppressed people of color. They do not want this guilt transferred to their children. It may also be that they do not want to acknowledge the truth, because then it would have to be changed.

On the other hand, and in direct connection to this point, interest convergence connotes that White people will seek racial justice only to the extent that they will benefit from enacting the change. The current system, whether or not it is acknowledged, serves to teach and reinforce their perspective, holding up the base and very existence of power and privilege. Changing the system would shake that foundation and dismantle their way of life. Even with this admission, if CRT is engaged correctly, it is not about making White children or parents feel guilty, nor is to make them dislike themselves. The focus is on acknowledging the existence of racism and the impact that it has on all aspects of society to make conditions better for people of color.

It is important to heed Ladson-Billings (2013), who cautions anyone engaging in dialogue connected to CRT to ensure that race is indeed of primary concern to the subject of the conversation. Scholars must truly understand what it is and must be willing to, and even further able to, acknowledge what CRT *is not*. They must be honest when there is another explanation for the phenomenon in question or the outcome.

In other words, one cannot show up in a mediocre capacity and blame their lack of success on racist people or structures. Engaged correctly, CRT ensures that the race card cannot be pulled when race is a nonfactor. It is not an easy out or failsafe. It is not another form of affirmative action that perceptibly gives credit or opportunity when it is not earned or deserved. The work of a critical race theorist must be beyond rigorous. Stellar scholarship is a part of guarding the integrity of this work. There must not be an opportunity to question the work, as the focus should be on authentically bringing attention to endemic racism—which in academia shows up as antiblackness.

Antiblackness manifests directly in academia in several ways, including elitism, socialization, racial aggressions (micro and macro), liberal White supremacy, discrimination in the research process, discrimination in the promotion and tenure process, and the salary gap (Gildersleeve et al., 2011). Elitism is at the base of academia, and it directly connects back to both Eurocentrism and a perceived "disdain, disregard, and disgust" for Black graduate students and faculty (ross, 2020). Unfortunately, the higher one climbs up the educational ladder, the closer they get to the pinnacle of Western thought, and the more saturated they become in the foundational ideas of Eurocentrism, the essence of whiteness. It is in this space where the core of elitism exists.

This is where people become the representation of intellectualism, where they begin to separate themselves and others belonging to the exclusive 2% of people in America who have earned doctorate degrees from the folks who have not accomplished this monumental feat. The separation becomes us versus them, a privileged space of judgment.

Then even inside of this exclusive space there is another division where the presence of melanin denotes intellectual inferiority. The more the melanin, the greater the inferiority is, as people of color with lighter complexions are sometimes more accepted. A person's proximity to whiteness, both externally and internally, determines their intellectual ability, their level of professionalism, and their degree of belonging. This is also part of the third tenet, the social construction of race in the creation of whiteness, Eurocentrism, and othering categories of existence that (as explained through the fourth tenet of CRT) come to overlap with the understanding that any part of our identities could be the focus of negative conceptualization and reaction (Ladson-Billings, 2013; Thompson, 2015).

This "disdain, disregard, and disgust" does not come solely from White scholars (ross, 2020). It also comes from people of color who, over time and through depth of connection, internalize this ideology and come to buy into the idea that melanin somehow makes you less able, less capable, or less intelligent. The higher one climbs up that ladder, the more they risk losing pieces of themselves and disconnecting from the community. This is also directly connected to how graduate students are socialized in doctoral programs toward those foundational ideas of whiteness, and how they are alienated and isolated through the racial aggressions they must silently endure, because once they acknowledge them or complain, they become the problem.

Racial aggressions (both micro and macro) can be defined as common racial indignities experienced by both Black graduate students and faculty (Gildersleeve et al., 2011). These seem to be small annoyances but build up over time and cause exhaustion as a normative response to racial trauma. At times Black students may be called on to represent their race in course conversations. It is understood that White students have singular identities because they are fully human, but students of other racial backgrounds are sometimes perceived to share a hivemind with other members of their race, as their humanity is never fully actualized in society as a result of Eurocentrism and reflective antiblackness.

An example of a microaggressive rebuff for a Black faculty member might be the refusal to use their title (i.e., addressing them by their first name yet referring to White academics as Dr. so-and-so). This denial of their earned identity shows a direct level of disdain and underestimation. Similarly, both student and faculty might be called articulate, which is an off-handed microaggressive compliment connecting back to them being considered elite members of the culture who can form a coherent thought. This articulation ability is seen as anomalous.

In many instances, these aforementioned rebuffs are not perpetrated by overt racists but by well-meaning White scholars who honestly believe themselves to be liberal, progressive, and promoters of inclusivity. They do not see how supremacist ideology both lives within them and alters their view of students of color. They may believe that they are authentic allies to the Black community with an understanding of and appreciation for the Black experience. White scholars get racism in its overt manifestation. They do not, however, realize that they actually create silencing environments that are hostile to Black students. These students find themselves in a situation where they are damned if they speak out and damned if they do not, so many mute themselves and continue to endure or suffer in silence so as not to be further targeted and, once again, not to become problematized (Bell et al., 2020; Gildersleeve et al., 2011).

These progressive faculty also may not realize that they are discriminating against their students in their quest to uphold academic rigor, as they may not see the direct correlation that their idea of rigor has to elitism. This connects to the issue of discrimination and antiblackness in the research process (Bell et al., 2020). Now, uplifting the lived experiences and personal (counter) narratives of Black scholars directly connects back to CRT's fifth focus on demystifying dominant ideologies (Gildersleeve et al., 2011).

One Black academic shared her personal story of the overt discrimination she experienced in her doctoral program that was disguised as superior research acumen and the concern for academic rigor by the department but was exposed as discrimination by her brave attempt to open the faculty's eyes to their treatment of students of color. Whenever she wrote research proposals that had a cultural focus, her idea was always shot down and called either too narrow or not rigorous enough in front of her cohort. To expose the underlying racism in their thought processes, she rewrote the proposal and removed the cultural aspect of the study. The professor raved about her proposal after reading it and approved it. When she pointed out to the professor that it was the same exact idea minus culture, the professor became upset and denied that bias played a roll in her decision.

This same professor also later accused this student of plagiarism because her work was so well written. She had to be cheating because this could not be her work. There was no way this was her intellectual property. This assumption was rooted in the professor's internal disdain, disregard, and disgust for Black students, whether the professor knew it was there or not. Her internalized antiblackness caused her to academically harm this student by placing unnecessary obstacles in the student's path and prolonging her program. The department also failed this student because it allowed the harassment to continue. The department required the student to complete another residency study.

Another graduate student spoke of her mentor professor, who was a Black male, hindering her dissertation process and showing no regard for the harm he was causing in the process. He would have her work in his possession for 3 months, then call her the night before her defense and tell her he did not think she was going to pass, then give her copious notes about what was wrong with her work and what he felt needed to be fixed. When she passed anyway, he told her, "Well, I did not think you could do it."

The professor threw hurdles at her during every phase of the process. He told her to change her methodology, then during the defense the methods faculty asked her why she changed it and reprimanded her. The mentor remained silent and cosigned the chastisement knowing full well it was his error, yet he did not take responsibility. This professor is a prime example of one who has internalized anti-Black ideology regarding intellectual ability and, in turn, practiced research discrimination. This student persevered in the face of these faculty-imposed obstacles to become one of the 2%.

A third example was shared by a professor from her days as a graduate student in a counseling psychology doctoral program in the Midwest. She self-identifies as African centered and explained that she did at the time of this incident as well. She got along well with everyone in her program and was widely known to be congenial. One day she was called into her professor's office to discuss an issue that was reported by her doctoral-level counseling supervisor. She was confused because she did not know of any issue or conflict. The doctoral supervisor, a White woman, claimed that the graduate student did not listen to her recommendation, nor apply her expertise with the graduate student's client (as she had been instructed to) because she did not like White people. The student was completely caught off guard. She asked if she had done or said something to make the supervisor feel this way. The supervisor said, "No, but you are African centered, so you do not like White people."

The graduate student was floored. She took a breath, looked at the professor, then looked at the supervisor and explained that her identity did not depend on hating or disliking anyone, saying, "because then, my identity would be about you and not loving myself and my culture. You are not in the equation."

The student then explained that the supervisor made her recommendation after only watching 5 minutes of one recently taped session, but she had been working with this client for months, seeing him twice a week. She had gotten to know him, his specific circumstances, and his needs. She was employing a client-centered approach that was grounded in his best interest, and at no time did the supervisor ask her about her treatment plan choices. The supervisor went directly to the professor to complain that she was not being obeyed.

The accused graduate student had to remain calm and explain herself in the face of a baseless accusation that was grounded in Eurocentrism and antiblackness. The supervisor had not had enough conversations with her or any social encounters to know who or what she liked or disliked. She made an ignorant assumption. And still, the student could not express her frustration because her reaction could be misconstrued and tied back to the original complaint. Thankfully, the professor was satisfied with the student's explanation.

Even once on the other side of graduation, Black students experience difficulty finding academic appointments, specifically in predominantly White institutions (PWIs) that might question their expertise and credentials. When they get past this monumental obstacle and are accepted in tenure-track positions, Black academics face two additionally significant challenges: the racial pay gap and issues in the promotion and tenure process that make it difficult for them to advance to higher positions within academia. This can be its own type of glass ceiling. In terms of salary, Black faculty are paid significantly lower than their White counterparts with equivalent expertise. This gap becomes even wider when controlled for both race and gender (the space of intersectionality and antiessentialism).

In addition, faculty at historically Black institutions receive about $18,000 less annually than those at PWIs (Clery, 2021; Ladson-Billings, 2013; Li & Koedel, 2017). These faculty are not being compensated adequately for their level of expertise, nor their workload. They are also asked to complete free labor at a higher rate than White academics. Several colleagues have mentioned being contacted by White scholars, whom they do not know and have never met, and asked to give them their hard-won research or to teach them some concept with no offer of compensation and the expectation that it would be done. There is a sense of entitlement there, entitlement to their time, energy, and resources with nothing in return.

Issues in the tenure promotion process also connect to elitist ideas of what type of work and publications are acceptable. The work can show up as books versus articles, or articles versus book chapters being considered acceptable (Bell et al., 2021). In terms of publications, some journals will not accept manuscript submissions dealing with culture and racism, which disenfranchises some scholars of color, who have been found to write about their experiences in the system more often than disconnected subjects. There is also an issue with journal editors or publishing bodies discriminating against names that are perceived to be ethnic, creating hurdles in the path to publishing and thus tenure. Black faculty at PWIs are also targeted and specifically preyed on by some White students who purposefully give them negative course evaluations knowing that it presents another obstacle for those scholars (Richardson, 2021).

When thinking of scholarship, Black professors have accomplished a lot and come a long way. On the other hand, it is ludicrous that 422 years after the formation of the education structure in America, there are still many positions and spaces that Black people have never been allowed to occupy. America is still experiencing many "firsts," which would not be the case if racism were not the bedrock of the nation. This will not change until we are openly allowed to engage in critical race–based conversations about the academy that route out and dismantle racist structures and ideologies permeating the profession. Until this is done, antiblackness will persist.

In the meantime, Black scholars can make a concerted effort to engage in critical race scholarship and hold each other accountable to remaining culturally present as they traverse academia. It is important for students to encounter and engage with faculty who look like them and are clear about who they are and what they stand for.

References

Bell, M. P., Berry, D., Leopold, J., & Nkomo, S. (2021). Making Black Lives Matter in academia: A Black feminist call for collective action against anti-blackness in the academy. *Gender Work Organization, 28*(S1), 39–57.

Clery, S. (2021). The calm before COVID: The last look at faculty salaries before the tumultuous Pandemic. *NEA Higher Education Faculty Salary Analysis 2019–2020, 39*(1), 1–36.

Gildersleeve, R. E., Croom, N. N., & Vasquez, P. L. (2011). "Am I going crazy?!": A critical race analysis of doctoral education. *Equity & Excellence in Education, 44*(1), 93–114. https://doi.org/10.1080/10665684.2011.539472

Ladson-Billings, G. (2013). Critical race theory—What it is not! In M. Lynn & A. D. Dixson (Eds.), *Handbook of critical race theory in education* (pp. 34–47). Taylor & Francis Group.

Ladson-Billings, G., & Tate, W. (1995). Toward a critical race theory of education. *Teachers College Record, 97*(1), 47–68.

Li, D., & Koedel, C. (2017). Representation and salary gaps by race-ethnicity and gender at selective public universities. *Educational Researcher, 46*(7), 343–354. https://doi.org/10.3102/0013189X17726535

Richardson, C. O. (2021). *Tomorrow's super teacher: Changing teacher education to nurture culturally sustaining educators.* Rowman & Littlefield.

ross, k. (2020). Call it what it is: Anti-Blackness. *New York Times.* Retrieved from https://www.nytimes.com/2020/06/04/opinion/george-floyd-anti-blackness.html

Thompson, S. (2015). Eurocentrism. In *Encyclopedia of diversity and social justice* (Vol. A–I). Rowman & Littlefield.

U.S. Department of Education. (2016). *The state of racial diversity in the educator workforce.* Office of Planning, Evaluation and Policy Development, Policy and Program Studies Service. https://www2.ed.gov/rschstat/eval/highered/racial-diversity/state-racial-diversity-workforce.pdf

17

The Dearth of Black Male
School Psychologists

Charlynn Small

I am a Black female school psychologist, and I must have sat at the same table more than 100 times, in different K–12 buildings, in different cities, wondering various versions of: *What is wrong with this picture? Where are this child's parents? Why is his grandmother here for the school support team (SST) meeting? How did she get here? Did she drive? Did she walk all that way using her walking stick? How did she manage with that other sweet little baby in tow? Does she understand the purpose of today's meeting? Where is Omar's grandfather? Amid all of this pomp and circumstance and important-looking people crowded around the table, I hope she doesn't think Daunte is in some kind of trouble again.* Always, though, I'd think, *This just isn't fair, having to raise or be responsible for people this young again.*

Of course, there isn't anything new about grandparents raising grandchildren. In fact, their numbers are increasing (U.S. Census Bureau, 2019), so much so that places like Washington, DC, Boston, and the Bronx have created housing developments to aid grandparents in caring for their grandchildren. These projects have been instrumental in keeping families together, by keeping children out of foster care. The reasons grandparents find themselves in these circumstances aren't new either. The long list of usual reasons includes one or both parents abusing substances (including opioids, which is being called an epidemic now, since so many young White women have developed opioid dependency problems, though it has always been in Black communities); abusing their child; being incarcerated; being absent; being too young and immature to be parents; having mental health concerns due to biology, adverse childhood experiences, or other trauma; or having been murdered.

Charlynn Small, *The Dearth of Black Male School Psychologists* In: *Antiblackness and the Stories of Authentic Allies.* Edited by: Norman Kim, Carolyn Coker Ross, Mazella Fuller and Charlynn Small, Oxford University Press. © Oxford University Press 2024. DOI: 10.1093/oso/9780197642535.003.0018

What Is a School Psychologist?

According to the National Association of School Psychologists (NASP, 2021):

> School psychologists are uniquely qualified members of school teams that support students' ability to learn and teachers' ability to teach. They apply expertise in mental health, learning, and behavior, to help children and youth succeed academically, socially, behaviorally, and emotionally. School psychologists partner with families, teachers, school administrators, and other professionals to create safe, healthy, and supportive learning environments that strengthen connections between home, school, and the community. (p. 1, paragraph 1)

School psychologists are often confused with school counselors, who generally serve a broader student population and are less focused on addressing mental health concerns (Saalmuller, 2022). Typically, a student is seen by a school psychologist upon referral by a teacher or other pupil personnel worker to the school's multidisciplinary team. That team will make the determination of whether an evaluation is necessary. The student's legal guardian must consent to services.

School psychology graduate programs offer three levels of study:

1. master's degree: allows for work as an educational diagnostician or psychometrist
2. specialist degree: allows for employment in most states as a practitioner and administrator (may require additional administrative credentials)
3. doctoral degree: allows for practice as a practitioner, administrator, and faculty/researcher (NASP, 2021)

The required school psychology training curriculum established by the NASP includes advanced graduate-level coursework in psychology and education, as well as other applied experiences (i.e., practicum). A 1,200-hour, supervised internship is also required. School psychologists most often are credentialed by the state in which they practice, or they may also apply for nationwide certification endorsed by the National School Psychology Certification Board, established by the NASP.

Competencies and skills used most frequently by school psychologists include data collection and analysis, consultation and collaboration, assessment, special education services, and crisis preparedness, response, and recovery. The NASP (2021) recommends a ratio of 500 students to one school psychologist. This ratio is consistent with research showing that school psychological services decrease as ratios of students to school psychologists increase (Eklund et al., 2017). The national ratio for the 2020–2021 school year was 1,162 students to one school psychologist. The NASP (2021) reports that the majority of school psychologists work in public school settings (85%). They can be found in many other settings, including colleges and universities (8%) and private schools (4%; Goforth et al., 2021). Salary ranges average between $53,760 and $103,240 (NASP, 2021).

Why Do Black Men in School Psychology Matter?

I worked for several years in three different jurisdictions—District of Columbia Public Schools, Prince George's County (MD) Public Schools, and Chesterfield County (VA) Public Schools. One of the things these systems have in common is that they each have populations of urban learners. Even Chesterfield County, though primarily suburban, has some pockets of urban communities. Quite often, students from these urban communities, mostly Black and Brown children, are those who could benefit most from having Black male role models. Yet, I encountered only one Black male school psychologist (BMSP) colleague during the entirety of my service in those three counties.

While Black women's numbers in the discipline are utterly meager, accounting for about 2.3% of all school psychologists, they are still double that of Black men, who make up an abysmal 1% (Zippia, 2022). An increase in the numbers of BMSPs can make important differences in the lives of children—Black children in particular—in so many ways. According to my own survey of four BMSPs, three of whom work in large, urban school districts, children could be positively impacted by an increase of BMSPs in public schools in the following ways:

- Many Black boys don't have a positive male figure in their homes or one in their schoolhouse, and a BMSP could fill that role.
- Black male students stand to benefit most from the guidance and mentorship of a positive, affirming Black male role model.

- Black male students would know that a school psychologist is a job to which they can aspire.
- BMSPs are more likely than non-Black school psychologists to consider cultural concerns when working with Black children (including caution regarding the use of culturally biased assessment procedures) and their families (R. Mitchell, personal communication, October 10, 2022); this approach speaks to the notion of cultural competence.
- BMSPs offer a certain built-in relatability, because someone who looks like the student or is representative of the student's culture is opposite them.
- With the built-in relatability comes a greater ease when addressing behavioral and emotional health concerns.
- BMSPs provide a certain level of comfort for the families of these students as well (R. Mitchell, personal communication, August 8, 2022).

This last point is not anecdotal. Specifically, there appears to be a greater sense of relief for parents and caregivers as they attempt to navigate school support services and interdisciplinary team processes (Goforth et al., 2021) when someone who looks like them is also seated at the decision-making table.

Cultural Competency

Cultural competency isn't just a bullet point—it's a grave matter. As an example, one day during my internship, our school psychology division attended a professional on-site visit at an intensive outpatient treatment facility for teens located in a very wealthy Washington, DC suburb. I asked one of the facilitators about the population of children who were served by the facility. Her curt response was that they served "children." The implication was that all children are the same and should be treated thusly. Because I'm sure she meant well, I didn't tell her how idiotic she sounded, or that she was broadcasting her cultural incompetence and prejudice. And I didn't want to embarrass my supervisors. We were invited guests, after all.

What this person didn't know is that cultural competence has everything to do with acknowledging that people are different; it's *not* about taking a color-blind approach to assessment and interactions when working with people from different populations and cultural backgrounds (Small, 2021).

A color-blind approach merely relieves a therapist of their obligation to address racial difference and difficulties (Williams, 2011).

Because it is critical for any discussion on mental health to be considered in terms of culture and context (Kelly & davis, 2021), a valuable benefit of having BMSPs in school settings is that because of their own lived experiences and training, they can be instrumental in advancing the knowledge of cultural competence of non-Black school psychologists who work with Black children. Nationally certified school psychologist and survey participant Ronald J. Mitchell (personal communication, August 8, 2022) stated that the lived experiences of BMSPs make them uniquely qualified to understand the impact of race-related stress (Kelly and davis, 2021) and systemic racism in the United States on the education of Black students, rendering them well positioned to advocate for and to support Black male students in particular.

Representation matters. And many Black children are starved for attention—the kind that BMSPs can provide. I can recall numerous occasions when I would go to pull a young person out of class to conduct an assessment and several other children would run over to me, hopeful that I was there to pull them out as well. It wasn't important whether I was there to dole out consequences or other discipline for getting into trouble. They just wanted some attention. And of course, it should go without saying, that these same precious children would have been equally as happy to garner attention for positive behavior.

Affinity Groups

In addition to providing individual mental health services, including a variety of support groups (e.g., trauma, grief, attention deficit hyperactivity disorder, interpersonal), for children, BMSPs can be of tremendous value in creating affinity groups for Black boys in particular, where they can speak, be heard, and listen to others like them. In these groups they can discuss issues that pertain to them expressly. BMSPs can be the catalyst for facilitating dialogue on students' thoughts and feelings about tough topics, such as why consequences are more severe for Black boys than for any other demographic of children, like the way they receive two-thirds of all school suspensions nationwide (AP, 2014), or why Black children account for almost 50% of all preschoolers suspended from school-based preschool programs more than once, despite making up only about 18% of preschool children (AP, 2014).

In BMSP-led affinity groups, Black boys can:

- gain knowledge about and discuss how stiffer penalties for people like them factor into the development of the preschool-to-prison pipeline;
- discuss seeing Black men and boys dying senseless, needless, violent deathsin their neighborhoods and across the nation—murders committed following what might've initially appeared to be a routine traffic stop by a few bad apples sworn to protect and serve them, or murders resulting from domestic or other violence;
- learn to regulate their energy and anger and pain about such concerns, especially when they are directly impacted by such;
- learn adaptive strategies and skills for coping with their feelings, enhance their mental health literacy, and reduce the stigma for seeking mental health support;
- have a safe space to discuss healthy and safe sex, COVID-19, LGBTQ+ concerns, and jobs and careers;
- talk about their dreams and be recognized for and celebrate academic achievements and behavioral accomplishments and goals met; and
- create new rituals and rights of passage.

BMSPs can rely on their own community platforms to create additional mentorship and guidance opportunities through their club memberships and fraternal organizations.

Why Are Black Men Missing From the School Psychology Discipline?

A review of the scant literature on the reasons for Black men's absence from the discipline includes Black people's historical mistrust (albeit with good reason) of U.S. health care systems. In a recent interview with National Public Radio (Salhotra, 2022), Celeste Malone, Howard University associate professor of school psychology and NASP president, said she believes that the disproportionate rate at which Black children have been referred for special education services may be a factor in discouraging Black persons from pursuing careers in school psychology. Specifically, Black students with disabilities are more likely to be identified with intellectual disability or emotional disturbance than all students with disabilities and more likely to receive a disciplinary removal than all students with disabilities (Office of Special Education Programs, 2021). As such, the NASP President concluded that "It could be hard to reconcile wanting to be in a profession and wanting to support kids that look like you . . . ," with the role that school psychology ". . . has played in the special education evaluation system."

In addition, there remains some stigma around seeking help for mental health–related concerns, which is another possible reason for the under-representation of Black men in the discipline. Fortunately, though, the stigma seems to be declining (Kelly and davis, 2021) as many Black men appear to be becoming increasingly more concerned about their mental health status amid so many adverse national events that are impacting them directly.

Others assert that the primary reason Black men are missing from school psychology is a lack of timely exposure to it as an area of career interest in the K–12 curriculum. I certainly had never heard of school psychology, nor had others in my circle. It wasn't until a year after graduating with a master's degree in clinical/community psychology and I began considering to which schools I would apply for my doctorate in clinical psychology that a supervisor of mine suggested I look into Howard University's School Psychology program. That was the very first time I had ever heard of this specialty area of psychology. Still, my master's degree was in clinical, so I had no interest in whatever this other miscellaneous branch of psychology was. *Was this school guidance counseling?* I wondered.

Best Practices for Recruiting Black Men Into the School Psychology Discipline

The NASP advocates for the early awareness of the discipline as a recruitment strategy aimed at high school students (NASP, 2016). To increase interest in the discipline, the NASP suggests implementation of some very prudent and specific recommendations such as increasing visibility of school psychologists and their roles in school settings, incorporating school psychology material into high school advanced placement (AP) courses, creating scholarship incentives (I was the first student to receive a paid internship in the Howard University–Prince Georges County Public Schools School Psychology Collaborative), and encouraging high school affiliate membership in school psychology professional organizations.

Still, despite the NASP's clarion call, they may be missing their recruitment mark in two ways. First, the applicability of their recommendations to the entire population of students (*as they should be*) does not address the problem of the underrepresentation of BMSPs. Kelly and Davis (2021) argue that the recommendations put forth must be contextualized based on the circumstances of Black male students. They note as an example, and it should come as no surprise, that these students have typically been underrepresented in AP psychology courses (Whiting & Ford, 2009), among others, and that as such, our governing organizations should take some action to assist Black students in gaining greater access to these courses. Given that our governing organizations have acknowledged the dearth of Black men in the discipline, and having made substantive and apropos recommendations (i.e., incorporating school psychology material into AP courses) for recruitment of high school students and college undergraduates in general—which includes Black males—I believe it is incumbent upon us to bear some of the responsibility of helping to increase AP course access for these students.

The second way the NASP may be missing the recruitment mark is that high school may be too late to begin their campaign. By high school, many students have already embarked upon a career interest or path (Kelly and Davis, 2021). Students are increasingly more often selecting a high school based on their chosen career aspirations (Kelly and Davis, 2021; Pottiger, 2022), which may have begun in middle school. For example, in middle school, my son, Chuck, was a member of the Technology Students Association's VEX IQ Robotics team. During that time, his sixth grade team was 11th in the World Championship—Middle School Division, and he participated on two national championship teams. In eighth grade, Chuck took the next logical step in his career path, which was to apply to our county's High School Engineering Specialty Center, where, like the NASP recommends for high school students interested in school psychology, Chuck took AP courses in his specialized areas of interest and applied for student memberships in professional organizations. Subsequently, Chuck continued to nurture his interests in the STEM fields. He's currently a college sophomore and is a recently licensed private airplane pilot minoring in astronomy. While Chuck's success in his area of interest demonstrates that the NASP's recruitment formula is a good one, I think it also clearly shows that it's one that should begin before high school.

In addition to Black students' relatively limited exposure to and awareness of school psychology as a discipline, a lack of cultural competence and neglect by persons in the position to do the recruitment and hiring may be a barrier to Black men entering the field. For instance, my Black colleagues and I had been lobbying for Black school psychologists or residents to join our team of predominantly White school psychologists. When none were forthcoming, we inquired about the status of the search. Our supervisor told us with great pride—secure in the knowledge that they had truly put forth a great effort—that they had attempted recruitment from many schools, including, most notably, the University of Nebraska. At that time, that school had a very strong School Psychology program. The problem was that that program didn't have a history of training very many Black people. Meanwhile, nearby Howard University with its program specializing in Urban School Psychology had not been a consideration. Later, two other women residents from Howard did join our team.

Another suggestion for recruiting Black students into the field includes career mentoring, either in person or virtually. Ideally this would be provided by Black men in the discipline because they would be able to provide a more authentic perspective (Kelly and davis, 2021).

Finally, in a study on the experiences of BMSPs, survey respondents indicated that the desires of Black students in school psychology programs "trended heavily toward wanting to make a difference for Black students in particular" (Cooper, 2021). Unfortunately, few historically Black colleges and universities offer degrees or training in school psychology despite having education and psychology programs.

Urban Learners, the Pandemic, and BMSPs

Staggering numbers of children in grades K–12 are experiencing significant increases in stress, anxiety, depression, suicide ideation and gestures, self-harm, eating disorders, and other mental health issues since the pandemic began (Murthy, 2021; U.S. Department of Education, 2021). Less than favorable preexisting circumstances (e.g., racism, poverty, violence, homelessness, abandonment) have compounded the impact for many Black children.

Yet, in many school systems, testing and assessment continue and will likely continue to be a primary function of some school psychologists. However, because school psychologists are well prepared to help enhance student skills development in many ways, BMSPs are best situated to work with these children to address traumas resulting from isolation and devastation following the pandemic. A temporary shift from assessment to counseling and consultation will allow for greater opportunities for positive interactions between Black students and BMSPs, particularly for those children who have not had the benefit of positive male role models.

As one member of a school's multidisciplinary team, my primary responsibilities as the school psychologist did indeed consist of conducting psychological testing and assessments, the purpose of which was usually to determine whether a student was eligible for special education services. Unfortunately, though, the list of students referred for assessment was always staggeringly high. What this typically meant was that the equally staggering number of children who could have benefited from emotional mental health care—who, by the way, were often the same children referred for educational testing—didn't get it.

In the wake of the pandemic, children from some of the often disenfranchised communities would benefit from counseling to an even greater degree. The virus has disproportionately affected low-income Black communities in so many ways. We died at rates much greater than other groups for numerous and varied reasons. In addition to less access to health care, preexisting immunocompromised conditions, and fewer financial resources, many persons in these communities lived in homes with several generations of their families represented and thus weren't always able to quarantine sufficiently. Black women, many of whom are single mothers, made up many of the low-wage, frontline workers (e.g., hospital or health care aids, housekeeping staff), which further increased the risks of transmitting the virus to their families. During this time, many children's parents lost employment, and an estimated 200,000 children lost a parent or caregiver due to COVID (Chuck et al., 2022). Not surprisingly, trepidation about the future yielded more acute stress, anxiety, and depression. These concerns may exceed or at least rival the demand for academic assessment.

If school systems aren't able to shift the focus of services from testing to counseling or consultation entirely, perhaps the percentage of time allocated to various duties could shift. If students had greater access to help for emotional concerns, their academic performance would improve, decreasing the need for so many initial special education referrals. Gassman-Pines et al. (2020) suggested that students would best be served if school administrators made provisions for counselors to maintain a focus on emotional and mental health care for the foreseeable future as students continue to return to school following the period of virtual learning.

Given what we know about the impact of trauma and individual responses made to trauma, it is not a stretch to assume that children will continue to behave in myriad ways during this period. We should be less reactive and not automatically conclude that they should be evaluated for a disability (Arundel, 2021). Because the pandemic-related misidentification of numerous students with disabilities can yield programming, staffing, and financial difficulties, careful consideration should be given to special education referrals and identifications made during catastrophic moments in time (Arundel, 2021).

Conclusion

One day my professor assigned me to ask White school psychologists of goodwill what they needed to know to provide competent, effective care to Black children. As luck would have it, my clinical supervisor where I was working at the time was a White male school psychologist. He told me it was important to know where their families lived, where they worked, what kind of parties they attended, what they ate, what kind of music they listened to, and what they did for fun. Specifically, he said that White school psychologists needed to learn everything they could about the Black families they served.

After that time, I began driving newly graduated White school psychologists who joined our team around the communities where some of the children we served lived, and we dialogued about some of those children's experiences. My aim was to facilitate the advancement of social justice by demonstrating the importance of cultural context whenever engaging with Black children and when interpreting their test responses (Small, 2021).

It is my hope that in helping to promote cultural competence I succeeded in some small measure in bridging the culture gap so that we as school psychologists can best meet our students' needs with compassion, integrity, reliability, and understanding. I also remain hopeful that continued support of initiatives such as the NASP's Exposure Project yields more BMSPs in school settings. In the meantime, I call for all school psychologists to do what they can to meet their students where they're at.

References

AP. (2014, March 21). *Black students more likely to be suspended—even in preschool.* CBS News. https://www.cbsnews.com/news/education-department-black-preschoolers-more-likely-to-be-suspended/

Arundel, K. (2021). *Why having too many or too few special education students matters.* K-12 Deep Dive. https://www.k12dive.com/news/why-having-too-many-or-too-few-special-education-students-matters/600659/

Chuck, E., Breslauer, B., & McFadden, C. (2022, March 7). *More than 200,000 kids have lost a parent or caregiver to Covid.* NBC News. https://www.nbcnews.com/news/us-news/200000-us-children-lost-parent-caregiver-covid-efforts-help-haphazard-rcna16140

Cooper, J. (2021). *The experiences of Black school psychologist* [Thesis proposal, University of Dayton].

Eklund, L., Meyer, L., Way, S., & McLean, D. (2017). School psychologists as mental health providers: The impact of staffing ratios and Medicaid on service provisions. *Psychology in the Schools, 54*(3), 279–293. 0https://doi.org/10.1002/pits.21996

Gassman-Pines, A., Ananat, E. O., & Fitz-Henley, J. (2020). COVID-19 and parent-child psychological well-being. *Pediatrics, 146*(4). https://doi.org/10.1542/peds.2020-007294

Goforth, A. N., Farmer, R. L., Kim, S. Y., Naser, S. C., , psychology in 2021: Part 1, demographics of the NASP membership survey. *NASP Research Reports, 5*(2), 1–17.

Kelly, K., & Davis, J. (2021). Increasing representation of Black men in school psychology through early exposure. *Penn GSE Perspectives on Urban Education, 19*(1).

Murthy, V. H. (2021). *Protecting youth mental health: The U.S. surgeon general's advisory.* https://www.hhs.gov/sites/default/files/surgeon-general-youth-mental-health-advisory.pdf

National Association of School Psychologists (NASP). (2016). *Addressing shortages in school psychology: Resource guide.*

National Association of School Psychologists (NASP). (2021). Who are school psychologists? https://www.nasponline.org/about-school-psychology/who-are-school-psychologists

Office of Special Education Programs. (2021, August 9). *Fast facts: Race and ethnicity of children with disabilities served under IDEA Part B.* https://sites.ed.gov/idea/osep-fast-facts-race-and-ethnicity-of-children-with-disabilities-served-under-idea-part-b/

Pottiger, M. (2022). *#WordinBlack: Black men are missing from school psychology—that matters.* AFRO News. https://afro.com/wordinblack-black-men-are-missing-from-school-psychology-that-matters/

Saalmuller, L. (2022). *School psychology vs. school counselling: What's the difference?* Northeastern University Graduate Programs.

Salhotra, P. (2022, July 29). *There's a nationwide shortage of Black male school psychologists.* National Public Radio. https://wusfnews.wusf.usf.edu/2022-08-14/theres-a-nationwide-shortage-of-black-male-school-psychologists

Small, C. (2021). Eating because we're hungry, or because something's eating us? In C. Small & M. Fuller (Eds.), *Treating Black women with eating disorders: A clinician's guide* (pp. 13–32). Routledge.

U.S. Census Bureau. (2019). *American Community Survey 2019.*

U.S. Department of Education. (2021). *Supporting child and student social, emotional, behavioral, and mental health needs.* https://www2.ed.gov/documents/students/supporting-child-student-social-emotional-behavioral-mental-health.pdf

Whiting, G. W., & Ford, D. Y. (2009). Multicultural issues: Black students and advanced placement classes: Summary, concerns, and recommendations. *Gifted Child Today*, *32*(1), 23–26. https://doi.org/10.4219/gct-2009-840

Williams, M. (2011). Colorblind ideology is a form of racism. *Psychology Today*. https://www.psychologytoday.com/us/blog/culturally-speaking/201112/colorblind-ideology-is-form

Zippia. (2022). *School psychologist demographics and statistics in the US*. https://www.zippia.com/school-psychologist-jobs/demographics/

18

Systems Failure

Black Children Left Behind

Randy B. Nelson, Kideste Yusef, and Felecia Dix-Richardson

Anti-Black Racism

This analysis moves beyond discrimination, the unjust treatment of an individual or group based on prejudice or bias, within educational and justice systems and instead focuses on the impact of anti-Black racism on the creation and continuation of the school-to-prison pipeline. Racism is best understood as the progenitor of every other system of oppression, including sexism, classism, homophobia, and Islamophobia (Omi & Winant, 2014). Critical race theory (CRT) and its derivative, intersectionality, is utilized in this work to examine how race, class, and gender contribute to the disproportionate push of Black children out of schools and into the juvenile and criminal justice systems.

Prefaced by the realization that the gains of the civil rights movement have stalled, CRT offers a set of antiracist tenets that target the subtle and systemic ways racism and White supremacy operate outside of overt racist expressions. Although the current discourse around CRT is highly charged and hyperpartisan, it is the most appropriate lens through which to analyze and address the disproportionality in academic achievement and system involvement among Black youth. The failure to seriously acknowledge the influence of race on education and justice system outcomes will prevent the implementation of effective and sustainable strategies. Hence, CRT offers the most suitable framework by which to achieve this end.

The subsequent sections will examine the role of race in educational performance, followed by analyses of school discipline and juvenile justice system involvement. Given that Florida is the third largest state in the nation and a recognized leader in data collection in the areas of education and juvenile justice, the authors center the discussion on Florida.

Randy B. Nelson, Kideste Yusef, and Felecia Dix-Richardson, *Systems Failure* In: *Antiblackness and the Stories of Authentic Allies*. Edited by: Norman Kim, Carolyn Coker Ross, Mazella Fuller and Charlynn Small, Oxford University Press. © Oxford University Press 2024. DOI: 10.1093/oso/9780197642535.003.0019

Race and School Performance

By most educational achievement measures, Black youth in general and Black males in particular perform at a level lower than their White counterparts and other racial/ethnic groups (National Assessment of Educational Progress [NAEP], 2021). It is well documented that one's educational level directly impacts their income level. The NAEP was analyzed to assess fourth- and eighth-grade reading and math proficiency; results for 2019 are presented in Charts 18.1 and 18.2. Regardless of the grade level analyzed, Black children did not perform as well as their peers (NAEP, 2021).

Similar to national data, Florida educational data also reveal racial disparities. Unlike NAEP data, the Florida Standard Assessment (FSA) begins

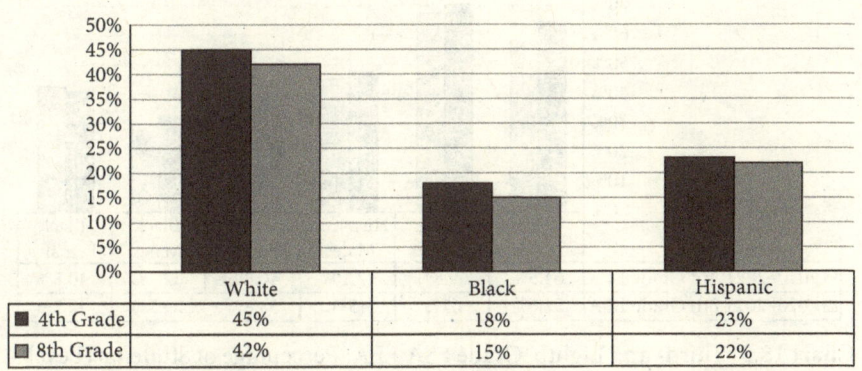

	White	Black	Hispanic
■ 4th Grade	45%	18%	23%
▨ 8th Grade	42%	15%	22%

Chart 18.1 NAEP Reading: Percentage of Students at or Above Proficiency

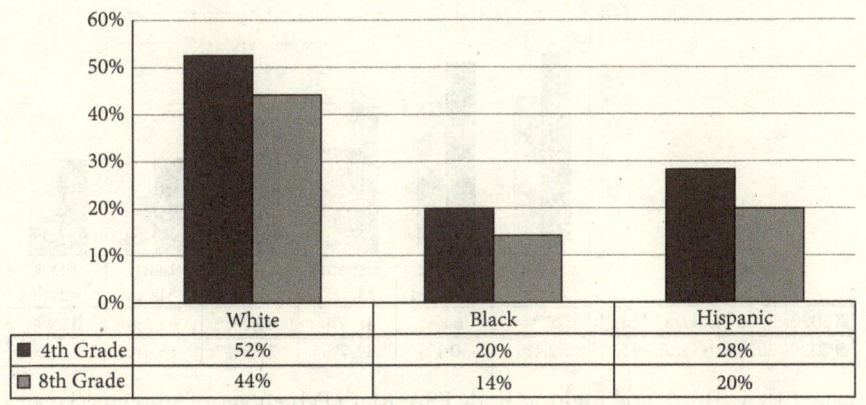

	White	Black	Hispanic
■ 4th Grade	52%	20%	28%
▨ 8th Grade	44%	14%	20%

Chart 18.2 NAEP Math: Percentage of Students at or Above Proficiency

at third grade. Data from the Florida Department of Education over the past academic years have consistently indicated disturbingly low performance rates among Black students on the FSA English language arts (ELA) and math assessments. To address this pattern of performance, third- and eighth-grade-level proficiency in FSA ELA and math results were analyzed and are presented in Charts 18.3 and 18.4. As indicated in these charts, the ranking of Florida's Black children mirrored national reading and math proficiency rates.

Research has consistently concluded that there is a correlation between poor school performance, school disciplinary sanctions, and delinquency (Blomberg & Pesta, 2017). When racial/ethnic groups disproportionately fail to meet proficiency in the fundamental areas of reading and math at critical

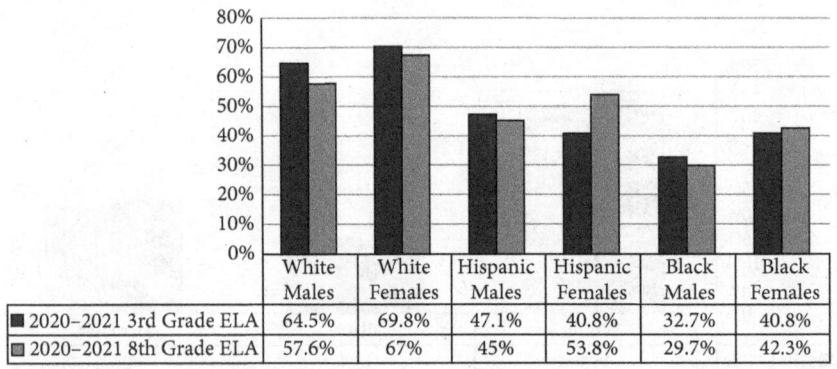

	White Males	White Females	Hispanic Males	Hispanic Females	Black Males	Black Females
2020–2021 3rd Grade ELA	64.5%	69.8%	47.1%	40.8%	32.7%	40.8%
2020–2021 8th Grade ELA	57.6%	67%	45%	53.8%	29.7%	42.3%

Chart 18.3 Third- and Eighth-Grade FSA ELA: Percentage of Students (Level 3 and Above)

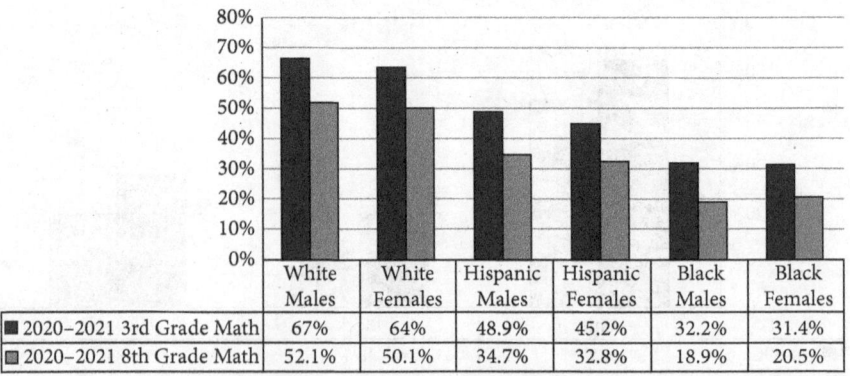

	White Males	White Females	Hispanic Males	Hispanic Females	Black Males	Black Females
2020–2021 3rd Grade Math	67%	64%	48.9%	45.2%	32.2%	31.4%
2020–2021 8th Grade Math	52.1%	50.1%	34.7%	32.8%	18.9%	20.5%

Chart 18.4 Third- and Eighth-Grade FSA: Math Percentage of Students (Level 3 and Above)

grade levels, they are more likely to be overrepresented in negative outcomes such as school disciplinary sanctions and delinquency.

Black males in Florida have historically performed lower on most primary and secondary school standardized educational achievement tests (Florida Department of Education, 2021). More than 90% of the public primary and secondary schools identified by the Florida Department of Education as low-performing schools are located in or serve minority communities (Florida Department of Education, 2021). School performance and school-related arrests are factors that are often researched as catalysts to the school-to-prison pipeline. For many children who struggle academically, successfully completing high school becomes a challenge and involvement within the juvenile justice system becomes a reality. Since academic proficiency in reading and math sets the trajectory for academic success or failure, national and Florida data will be presented to reveal racial/ethnic and gender differences across these measures.

Antiblackness: Perception Fuels Reality

As a primer to our analysis of disciplinary practices in schools, it's important to recognize America's inseparable association of blackness, White hysteria, and fear. This nexus is illuminated by the barrage of news stories detailing the latest shootings of unarmed or nonaggressive Black men and boys, and to a lesser degree Black women and girls, who are killed at the hands of police or White citizens. Since its 19th-century inception, the Black-crime myth has functioned to project a universal culpability onto Black people while withholding empathy of victimization. The extrajudicial tradition of policing blackness binds Blacks of all ages to a perpetual suspect status, often resulting in guilty treatment in the absence of a violation or crime.

A 2016 Yale University Child Study of educator implicit bias revealed that as early as preschool, Black children are singled out by educators and expelled at disproportionately high rates. This study assessed the gaze of preschool teachers when instructed to look for challenging behaviors among children aged 3 to 5 on video. Although recordings did not actually include any challenging behaviors, teachers gazed longer at Black children, especially Black boys. Nationally, Black children make up about 19% of preschool enrollment but represent 47% of preschool suspensions. In addition, "Black preschoolers are 3.6 times as likely to receive one or more suspensions relative to White preschoolers" (Gilliam et al., 2016, p. 2).

Another study found that participants exhibited implicit racial bias with Black male faces as young as 5 years old (Todd et al., 2016). The association of blackness, gender, and crime was consistent for adults and children. Black male children lead the country in suspensions, expulsions, and arrests, with suspension rates three times that of White youth. Possible explanations for this pattern include implicit bias among teachers and inadequate training to identify and address biases. Other likely factors are discriminatory discipline practices and school racial climate (Gilliam et al., 2016).

Studies also highlight how race coupled with adultification bias, the false evaluation of Black and female children as older than their biological age, contributes to beliefs of increased culpability of Black children, positioning them as a threat to the safety of *other* children (Okonofua & Eberhardt, 2015). Consequently, Black children are viewed by teachers and administrators as more deserving of severe punishments including suspension and expulsion.

Kimberle Crenshaw's (1989) seminal work on intersectionality explains how race, gender, social class, and other characteristics function collaboratively to create varied modes of discrimination and privilege. Historically, Black women and girls have been subjected to a host of pejorative stereotypes that link sexism, racism, and poverty to produce caricatures of immortality, promiscuity, and aggressive behavior. Black girls are particularly vulnerable to these stereotypes within academic settings. According to a *New York Times* analysis of Department of Education data, "Black girls are over five times more likely than White girls to be suspended at least once, and seven times more likely to receive multiple suspensions than White girls and three times more likely to receive referrals to law enforcement" (Green et al., 2020, para. 10).

Just as racism and bias play a direct role in the criminalization of Black girls, adultification bias leads to less empathy, presumed early maturity, and harsher surveillance and treatment including dress code enforcement (Epstein et al., 2017). The removal of young Black girls from Florida's elementary schools is not uncommon. For example, 5-year-old Ja'eisha Scott was handcuffed and taken into custody by St. Petersburg police. She remained in custody in the back of the police cruiser while the police tried to get the state attorney to approve her arrest on charges of assault and battery of a school official, disruption of school function, and resisting a law enforcement officer ("Arresting Development," 2006).

Race and School-Related Arrests

As part of the broader "get tough on crime" movement, zero-tolerance policies exacerbated educational inequities and increased strict

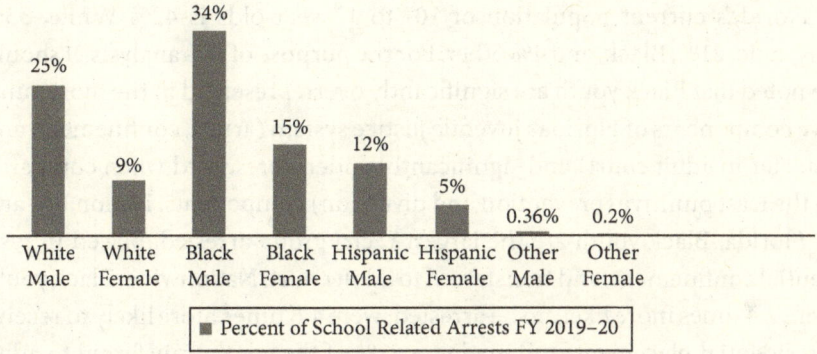

Chart 18.5 Percentage of School-Related Arrests, FY 2019–2020

disciplinary practices within schools. Simultaneously, media-driven hysteria in the 1980s regarding youth crime, including Hilary Clinton and others' promotion of the "super predator" hypothesis, coupled with the popularity of Wilson and Kelling's broken windows theory, fueled zero-tolerance policies in schools. This required administrators to aggressively enforce minor school infractions without consideration of individual factors, guided by the belief that high-level enforcement would prevent major offenses. Under zero tolerance, the role of law enforcement in schools expanded, resulting in higher rates of school suspensions, expulsions, and school-based arrests.

Based on data obtained from the Florida Department of Juvenile Justice, there were over 1.5 million 10- to 17-year-old children enrolled in Florida schools during 2019–2020 (July 1, 2019–June 30, 2020). Slightly more than 5,200 of these students were arrested at school. There was clear evidence of racial disparity in the Florida school arrest data. Black males exceeded the arrest rate of all other groups, followed by White males and Black females. When isolated by gender, Black females made up 52% of all female arrests (Florida Department of Juvenile Justice, 2021a; see Chart 18.5).

Race and Justice System Involvement

Since the creation of the Florida Department of Juvenile Justice in 1992, racial disparities among youth arrested, confined, and transferred to adult court have existed. The failure of the educational system may contribute to the school-to-prison pipeline. Some contend that if Black youth are less likely to matriculate through the educational system, their disproportionate representation and involvement in the juvenile justice system is expected.

Florida's current population of 10- to 17-year-olds is 42% White, 33% Hispanic, 21%, Black, and 4% other. For the purpose of this analysis, it should be noted that Black youth are significantly overrepresented in the most punitive components of Florida's juvenile justice system (arrest, confinement, and transfer to adult court) and significantly underrepresented when compared to the least punitive (prevention and diversion) components. Nationally, and in Florida, Black youth are the largest racial group arrested, placed in residential confinement, and transferred to adult court. Nationwide, Black youth were 2.4 times more likely to be arrested, were 4.6 times more likely to receive a residential placement, and made up 52% of the youth transferred to adult court (Azalia et al., 2021).

According to data obtained from the Florida Department of Juvenile Justice, statewide racial disparities exist across its entire continuum of care. When youth become involved within the juvenile justice system, the likelihood for them to become involved within the criminal justice system increases. For minority youth in particular and for Black males specifically, this path often becomes difficult to avoid. The overrepresentation of Black youth is evident in every stage of Florida's juvenile justice continuum (see Chart 18.6). Black male representation exceeded all other racial/gender groups at every stage. After diversion, as Black males move further into the other more serious continuums, their representation and rate of disparity increased significantly. Although Black males make up the largest group of those diverted, they are more than twice as likely to be transferred to adult court (Florida Department of Juvenile Justice, 2021b).

Conversely, patterns of racial disparity for Black girls cannot be ignored. Black girls in Florida experience disparate outcomes with respect to justice

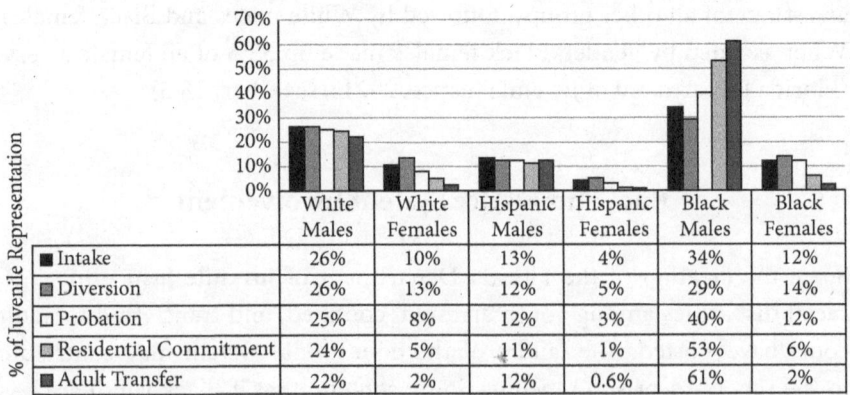

	White Males	White Females	Hispanic Males	Hispanic Females	Black Males	Black Females
■ Intake	26%	10%	13%	4%	34%	12%
▨ Diversion	26%	13%	12%	5%	29%	14%
☐ Probation	25%	8%	12%	3%	40%	12%
▨ Residential Commitment	24%	5%	11%	1%	53%	6%
■ Adult Transfer	22%	2%	12%	0.6%	61%	2%

Chart 18.6 Juvenile Justice Outcomes, FY 2019–2020

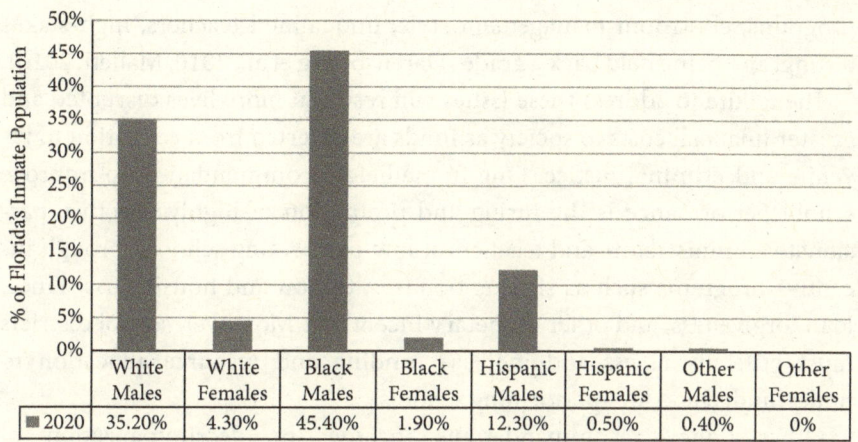

	White Males	White Females	Black Males	Black Females	Hispanic Males	Hispanic Females	Other Males	Other Females
■ 2020	35.20%	4.30%	45.40%	1.90%	12.30%	0.50%	0.40%	0%

Chart 18.7 Florida Inmate Population, FY 2020

system involvement. Black females were overrepresented in every category; however, the disparity rate between Black females and White females was not as glaring as the disparity rate between Black males and White males (Florida Department of Juvenile Justice, 2021b).

Youth who underperform academically, experience severe school discipline, and are involved in the juvenile justice system are more likely to enter the adult correctional system. To illustrate, the imprisonment rate for Black adults was five times that of White adults and almost twice the rate of Hispanics (Carson, 2020). When age is taken into consideration, "Black males ages 18 to 19 were 12 times as likely to be imprisoned as white males of the same ages, the highest black-to-white racial disparity of any age group in 2019" (Carson, 2020, p. 16). At this age, this group should be graduating from high school and entering the workforce or college.

The data presented in Chart 18.7 reflect the 2020 Florida Department of Corrections prison population (Florida Department of Corrections, 2020). Black males represent the largest group of the incarcerated population in the United States and Florida.

Where Do We Go From Here?

Researchers have sought plausible explanations to better understand the school-to-prison nexus. Some of the causes presented in the literature include failing public schools, zero-tolerance policies, increased out-of-school suspensions and expulsions, placement in restrictive special education programs, classroom management style, unqualified teachers, high-stakes testing, and being held back a grade (Darensbourg et al., 2010; Mallett, 2016).

The failure to address these issues will result in more lives disrupted and greater financial costs to society as funds are diverted from education to juvenile and criminal justice. One immediate recommendation to improve school performance is the hiring and promotion of highly effective, passionate administrators and teachers at low-performing schools through incentive programs such as signing bonuses, tuition and housing assistance, loan forgiveness, and other monetary incentives. Moreover, school districts must critically assess and increase funding and resource allocation to underfunded and low-performing schools.

Other policy recommendations include the decriminalization of minor infractions, enforcement of age limits on school arrests for non-violent offenses, and critical examination of disciplinary referrals, expulsions, suspensions, and school arrests for potential bias. Additional recommendations within academic settings include expanding alternatives to zero-tolerance policies such as positive discipline approaches including those centered in restorative justice, early intervention, increased use of community referrals and resources, gendered mentoring teams, reduced overreliance on school resource officers (SROs), and de-escalation, cultural bias, and adultification training for SROs, teachers, and administrators.

Nationally, juvenile justice leaders must seek innovative best practices to address the disproportionate representation of minority youth in general and Black youth in particular within the juvenile justice system. Some of these may include expanding the use of diversion programs, identifying overt and covert discriminatory practices, and ensuring the use of culturally validated risk and protective factor assessment instruments.

One innovative program that was implemented in Florida is the High-Risk Delinquency and Dependency Educational Research Project, funded by the Florida legislature, in 2017. This project utilized the situational environmental circumstances (SEC) mentoring model as a core component. The SEC mentoring model involved the delivery of targeted mentoring services to Black elementary-age males by Black male college students attending one of Florida's four historically Black colleges and universities and select predominantly White higher learning public institutions. Many of the mentors had experienced attending low-performing schools, residing in disadvantaged communities, living in single-family households, and having family members with justice system involvement. Among project sites that implemented the SEC mentoring component with fidelity, the mentees showed an improvement in school grades, behavior, and/or attendance.

Closing Thoughts

There are distinct differences in the opportunities, resources, and privileges afforded to Americans based on their racial and ethnic identity. The nation's rapidly changing racial and ethnic demographics will require meaningful conversations and sustainable strategies to ensure equity and inclusion sooner rather than later. The recent global movement for racial and social justice has been met with opposition, primarily fueled by White anxiety and a desire for self-preservation.

Recently released 2020 census data reveal two significant facts relative to the country's changing demographics. The primary finding revealed a decade-long loss in the number of White Americans for the first time in history. In fact, all the nation's growth over the past decade is attributable to people of color. In 1980, Whites made up almost 80% of the nation's population; today, that figure is 58%. The second significant finding involved the growth in the non-White youth population. People of color now make up more than half of the total youth population under age 18. This finding further supports the need for sustainable strategies to ensure equity, diversity, and inclusion across every facet of American life.

As a nation, we are as deeply divided along racial and cultural lines now as any time before or since the civil rights movement in the 1960s. If some elements of the White community continue to promote an agenda that suppresses the minority vote or bans the teaching of America's true history and its treatment of people of color for the purpose of retaining political power in the short term, then their fears of receiving the same treatment as a numerical minority may be justified. To this end, the authors put forth an antiracism approach that is grounded in the fundamental principles of equity, diversity, and inclusion.

This chapter focused on the operation and practice of the educational and juvenile justice systems, but the authors fully recognize that the historical and lingering effects of racism, discrimination, and institutional racism permeate every institution and facet of American life. For this reason, we must ensure that Blacks and other racial/ethnic groups have unfettered opportunities and the necessary resources to live, grow, prosper, and raise their families free from the barriers of what some consider America's original sin—racism. If Whites wait until they are the numerical minority population to promote equity, diversity, and inclusion as the standard for America, it will likely ring hollow.

References

Arresting development: Addressing the school discipline crisis in Florida. (2006). Florida State Conference NAACP, Advancement Project, NAACP Legal Defense and Educational Fund.

Azalia, L., Campbell, S., Dawson, B., Davis, M., Gardner, E., Hatch, T., King, K., Mehrabi, E., Olender, S., Martin, B., Sowa, A., Sprow, S., & Tilly, Z. (2021). *The state of America's children*. Children's Defense Fund. http://www.childrensdefensefund.org

Blomberg, T. G., & Pesta, G. B. (2017). Education and delinquency. In C. J. Schreck, M. J. Leiber, H. V. Miller, & K. Welch (Eds.), *The encyclopedia of juvenile delinquency and justice* (pp. 1–5). Wiley. https://doi.org/10.1002/9781118524275.ejdj0044

Carson, E. (2020, October). *Prisoners in 2019* (NCJ 255115). U.S. Department of Justice, Office of Justice Program, Bureau of Justice Statistics. https://bjs.ojp.gov/content/pub/pdf/p19.pdf

Crenshaw, K. (1989). Demarginalizing the intersection of race and sex: A Black Feminist critique of antidiscrimination doctrine, feminist theory, and antiracist politics. *University of Chicago Legal Forum, 140*, 139–167.

Darensbourg, A., Perez, E., & Blake, J. (2010). Overrepresentation of African American males in exclusionary discipline: The role of school-based mental health professionals in dismantling the school to prison pipeline. *Journal of African America Males in Education, 1*(3), 196–211.

Epstein, R., Blake, J., & Gonzalez, T. (2017). *Girlhood interrupted: The erasure of Black girls' childhood*. Georgetown Law Center on Poverty and Inequality.

Florida Department of Corrections. (2020). Institutions/inmate populations. In *Strategic plan & annual report* (p. 47). http://www.dc.state.fl.us/pub/annual/1819/2020-2021-Strategic-Plan.pdf

Florida Department of Education. (2021). *K-12 assessments. Florida Standards Assessments (FSA) results. Interactive reporting.* https://www.fldoe.org/accountability/accountability-reporting/interactive-reporting

Florida Department of Juvenile Justice. (2021a). *Delinquency in Florida's schools dashboard*. https://www.djj.state.fl.us/research/reports-and-data/interactive-data-reports/delinquency- in-schools

Florida Department of Juvenile Justice. (2021b). *Florida Department of Juvenile justice delinquency profile*. https://www.djj.state.fl.us/research/reports-and- data/interactive-data-reports/delinquency-profile

Gilliam, W. S., Maupin, A. N., Reyes, C. R., Accavitti, M., & Shic, F. (2016). *Do early educators' implicit biases regarding sex and race relate to behavior expectations and recommendations of preschool expulsions and suspensions?* Yale Child Study Center.

Green, E. L., Walker, M., & Shapiro, E. (2020, October 1). A battle for the souls of Black girls. *New York Times.* https://www.nytimes.com/2020/10/01/us/politics/black-girls-school-discipline.html

Mallet, C. (2016). The school-to-prison pipeline: A critical review of the punitive paradigm shift. *Child and Adolescent Social Work Journal, 33*(1), 15–24. https://doi10.1007/s10560-015- 0397-1

National Assessment of Educational Progress (NAEP). National Center for Education Statistics, National Assessment of Educational Progress. 2019/2021 Reading and Math Assessment. U.S. Department of Education. Institute of Education Sciences. https://nces.ed.gov/nationsreportcard/data/

Okonofua, J. A., & Eberhardt, J. L. (2015). Two strikes: Race and the disciplining of young students. *Psychological Science, 26*(5), 617–624. https://doi.org/10.1177/0956797615570365

Omi, M., & Winant, H. (2014). *Racial formation in the United States.* Taylor & Francis.

Todd, A. R., Thiem, K. C., & Neel, R. (2016). Does seeing faces of young black boys facilitate the identification of threatening stimuli? *Psychological Science, 27*(3), 384–393. https://doi:10.1177/0956797615624492

PART VI

ANTIBLACKNESS AND HEALTH CARE

19

The Impact of Systemic Racism on Mental Health Care

Delbert R. Wigfall

Much has been written on the issue of the impact of systemic racism on disparities in health care, and the recent COVID pandemic only underscored the appreciation of this reality. While the contributing issues have been acknowledged and reviewed, little has been done to constructively effect change. Adequate health care, especially in provision of mental health services, is dependent on having well trained compassionate providers, along with inclusion of providers who share commonality in culture and community.

"Poverty, housing discrimination, mental health disparities, community violence, low levels of educational attainment, and anti-immigrant sentiment are some ways that racism continues to impact communities of color today" (Santiago-Rivera et al., 2016, p. 229) and contributes to the persistent disparities of care. For clarity, let's consider the conditions that impact occurrence and care and those that create a paucity of providers.

Systemic Conditions That Impact Mental Health Care

A History of Mistreatment

Persons of color have been the targets of health and social inequities since their arrival to the United States. Authors have well documented the manipulation and experimentation with Black lives in the history of medicine. For one example, James Sims, credited as the "father of modern gynecology," used enslaved women to perfect his operative techniques related to women's reproductive health. He performed his procedures initially on Black women without the benefit of anesthesia, often lasting hours. As a founding father

Delbert R. Wigfall, *The Impact of Systemic Racism on Mental Health Care* In: *Antiblackness and the Stories of Authentic Allies*. Edited by: Norman Kim, Carolyn Coker Ross, Mazella Fuller and Charlynn Small, Oxford University Press.
© Oxford University Press 2024. DOI: 10.1093/oso/9780197642535.003.0020

of the American Gynecological Society, he has been lauded for his procedural acumen, though he caused untold suffering and death to hundreds of enslaved women.

According to Brynn Holland (2017), "Sims's decision to not use (anesthesia)—or any other numbing technique—was based on his misguided belief that Black people didn't experience pain like white people did" (p. 1). In addition, Holland reported that Sims had warped ideas about developmental differences between African Americans and White people, namely, that African American "skulls grew too quickly around their brain," making them less intelligent (Holland, 2017, p. 1).

Such beliefs contributed to continued experimentation with Black lives after the legal end of slavery. But because Sims's research was conducted on enslaved Black women without anesthesia, medical ethicists, historians, and others say his use of enslaved Black bodies as medical test subjects falls into a long, ethically bereft history that includes the Tuskegee syphilis experiment and Henrietta Lacks. Critics say Sims cared more about the experiments than providing therapeutic treatment (Holland, 2017).

The misinformation about Black lives and Black health has continued into the 20th century. In 2016, Hoffman et al. revealed "that a substantial number of white laypeople and medical students and residents hold false beliefs about biological differences between blacks and whites and [this] demonstrates that these beliefs predict racial bias in pain perception and treatment recommendation accuracy" (p. 4296). In her words:

It also provides the first evidence that racial bias in pain perception is associated with racial bias in pain treatment recommendations. Taken together, this work provides evidence that false beliefs about biological differences between blacks and whites continue to shape the way we perceive and treat black people—they are associated with racial disparities in pain assessment and treatment recommendations. (Hoffman et al., 2016, p. 4296).

Mistrust

It is not surprising that this history of abuse and scientific misinformation and misperception would contribute to mistrust and, as such, prevent ill persons from seeking the care they need. Thus, the very individuals we wish to treat may not seek help yet be more severely affected because of the enduring systemic racism that might give rise to their disorder.

Cultural Incompetence

With regard to depression, major depressive disorder (MDD) is among the most prevalent disorders in the United States that often goes underdiagnosed and untreated. The burden of disability among those untreated is heaviest among untreated minority populations. Among African Americans, those with socioeconomic stress are less likely to report psychological symptoms or remain compliant with initiated treatment. While overall population studies suggest major depression is slightly less common in Black persons, persons who are of African-American ancestry tend to have depressive episodes that are more disabling, more persistent, and more resistant to treatment relative to their white counterparts (Hankerson et al., 2015). Part of the problem of underdiagnoses lies with the provider. Many providers today are unable to notice subtleties in presentation or recognize uncommon presentations of disease (Bailey et al., 2019).

Bias

Studies have demonstrated that black Americans are diagnosed with higher rates of schizophrenia than white Americans. Researchers found that black people are 2.4 times more likely to be diagnosed with schizophrenia than their white counterparts, and that pattern has been consistent for the past three decades. Other studies put that rate at three to four times more likely (Cohen & Marino, 2013; Olbert et al., 2018; Rutgers University, 2019; Schwartz & Blankenship, 2014).

Stigma

There is a strong stigma attached to mental disorders that prevents those affected from getting psychological help. The consequences of stigma are worse for racial and/or ethnic minorities compared to racial and/or ethnic majorities since the former often experience other social adversities such as poverty and discrimination within policies and institutions (Eylem et al., 2020).

Insurance

Equally problematic in the effective diagnosis and treatment of mental health disease is access to care because of insurance coverage and provider availability. Lee et al. looked qualitatively at the convergence of racial and income disparities in insurance coverage in the United States.

> Results of the study showed that while income was a significant predictor of health insurance coverage, race/ethnicity was independently associated with lack of insurance. At the same income level, minorities were significantly more likely to be uninsured than white persons. Moreover, minorities were more likely to be insured for part of the year than white persons. The combined effect of income and race on insurance coverage was devastating as low-income minorities with bad health had 68% less odds of being insured than high-income white people with good health. It is also noteworthy that minorities were disproportionately over-represented in the low-income or bad health groups so that any adverse association between income, bad health, and insurance status would more adversely affect minorities than white people. (Lee et al., 2021, p. 96)

Systemic Conditions That Impact Mental Health Occurrence

Sociocultural and Economic Factors

"Research suggests that African American and Latino adults may develop disease and posttraumatic stress disorder (PTSD) at higher rates than White adults and that the clinical course of PTSD in these minority groups is poor. One factor that may contribute to higher prevalence and poorer outcomes in these groups are sociocultural factors and racial stressors, such as experiences with discrimination" (Sibrava et al., 2019, p. 101).

The U.S. Office of Health and Human Services Office of Minority Health reports that in 2019, suicide was the second leading cause of death for blacks or African Americans, ages 15 to 24. The death rate from suicide for black or African American men was four times greater than for African American women, in 2018. Black females, grades 9–12, were 60 percent more likely to attempt suicide in 2019, as compared to non-Hispanic white females of the same age. Black or African Americans living below the poverty level, as compared to those over twice the poverty level, are twice as likely to report serious psychological distress. (U.S. Surgeon General, 2001)

The Substance Abuse and Mental Health Services Administration published a comparison of use of mental health services by race and/or ethnicity. In each age group, White adults were more likely than their Black, Asian, and Hispanic counterparts to use any mental health service. When ethnic minorities were compared, estimates of mental health service utilization were similar among ethnic minorities at a rate half that of Whites (6% vs. 16%; Substance Abuse and Mental Health Services Administration, 2015).

Police Violence

While the United States grapples with the effects of persistent systemic societal racism, it is also important to note that there is a disproportionate impact of police violence in Black communities. Law enforcement's function as a stopgap for mental health care access has deadly consequences: Approximately 25% of fatal police shootings involve people exhibiting signs of mental illness. Furthermore, according to the Federal Bureau of Investigation's National Use of Force Data Collection, in 2019, 54% of people who died as a result of harm from police and whose race was identified were people of color—including Asian, Black, Hispanic, Native American, and Pacific Islander individuals (Agbafe et al., 2020).

Racism

Although discrimination is the most studied aspect of racism, racism can also affect mental health through structural/institutional mechanisms and racism that is deeply embedded in the larger culture (Williams, 2018). While the genetic origin of mental health conditions remains a focus of medical research, the environment has catastrophic effects on the expression and outcome of mental health disease. Years of systemic racism have amplified the expression of disease and prevented access to care for a population at increased risk.

Therefore, what results is a complex interplay of racism, violence, and stigmatization of mental health precluding effective access and treatment of these health concerns. Effective treatment of mental health diseases is dependent on recognition and acceptance of disease and a willingness to seek help.

Systemic Conditions That Create Disparities Among Mental Health Providers

Paucity of Providers

There is a well-documented shortage of providers, as noted recently by the American Association of Medical Colleges (AAMC). According to new data published by the AAMC, the United States could see an estimated shortage of between 37,800 and 124,000 physicians by 2034, including shortfalls in both primary and specialty care (IHS Markit, 2021). At present, there is a limited pool of individuals motivated to pursue health careers.

Lack of Diversity

While the United States is already home to tremendous racial and ethnic diversity, projections suggest that our nation is on track to become even more diversified. By 2040, non-Hispanic Whites will be the minority race in this country, and by 2060, about one in five Americans is anticipated to be foreign born. The U.S. health care system will need to cultivate a more diverse physician workforce to address these changing demographics. This need is even greater in psychiatry, where culture disproportionately impacts key aspects of care including symptom expression and attribution, care-seeking behaviors, stigma, and access to mental health services (Lokko et al., 2016).

The American Psychiatric Association reports that while African Americans make up 13% of the U.S. population, only 2% of the 41,000 psychiatrists in the country are Black ("Demographic Characteristics"). Racial concordance has been shown to improve perceived care, and recently

Takeshita et al. (2020) demonstrated this finding using Pres Ganey survey scores, finding that higher scores and associated patient satisfaction were "associated with racial/ethnic concordance between patients and their physicians" (Takeshita et al., 2020, p. 1001).

Morris et al. (2021) examined the diversity of medical school applicants and enrollees over the past four decades, hoping to demonstrate progress. This group examined the number of matriculates in medical school between 1978 and 2019. During this period, it was noted that the number of women increased markedly, and now women represent over half of students in medical school. "This upturn has been attributed largely to an increase by a factor of 12 in the enrollment of Asian women" (Morris et al., 2021, p. 1661). They also noted a "decrease in the percentage of male enrollees, most notably White men, but this was offset by an increase by a factor of approximately five in the enrollment of Asian men. The percentages of enrollees from Black, Hispanic, and other racial and ethnic groups that are underrepresented in medicine remain well below the percentages of these groups in the national Census" (Morris et al., 2021, p. 1661).

Given the realization that culturally concordant care helps to improve health outcomes, there is a natural extension of thought that to properly address the mental health needs of the Black community, it is imperative that a significantly more diverse pool of trainees be brought into health careers. Beyond these benefits for direct patient care, increased workplace diversity exerts positive effects on group performance, education, and clinical care (Lokko et al., 2016).

Academic Barriers

For Black individuals, there is limited academic mentoring and preparation; what does exist is ameliorated by the creation of educational pipeline programs. These programs are designed to assist underrepresented minorities (URMs) in becoming a part of the needed diversity efforts. The programs target underrepresented racial/ethnic minorities from low socioeconomic backgrounds to address health disparities in the United States, and through these efforts we might reduce health care inequality (Boekeloo et al., 2015; Smith et al., 2009a).

To that end, members of the Joint Working Group on Improving Underrepresented Minorities (URMs) Persistence in Science, Technology,

Engineering, and Mathematics (STEM) were charged with the creation of specific pathway programs. The National Institute of General Medical Sciences and the Howard Hughes Medical Institute convened the group, which noted that "self-determination theory suggests that it is the intrinsic characteristics of careers which are most likely to sustain pursuit of a health science-related career and lead to job satisfaction" (Estrada et al., 2016, p. 7).

This group suggests expanding to include a stronger focus on the institutional barriers that need to be removed and the types of interventions that "lift" students' interests, commitment, and ability to persist in STEM fields. Using Kurt Lewin's planned approach to change, the committee describes five recommendations to increase URM persistence in STEM at the undergraduate level (Smith et al., 2009b). These recommendations include increased institutional accountability with regard to interests, matriculation, and average graduation rates. Equally important in this effort is identifying other factors that might influence acceptance and matriculation, including gender, socioeconomic status, and first-generation status.

It is important to create partnerships and programs that promote interest and acumen. The curriculum may need to be expanded to encourage appropriate skill acquisition and address student disparities in resources and preparation. Finally, the programs need to inspire, encourage, and sustain interest (Smith et al., 2009b).

Barriers in Medical School and Training

There is an ever-increasing appreciation of a disproportionate decline in the number of Black men in medicine (Laurencin & Murray, 2017). Laurencin and Murray (2017) noted:

> Research data continues to reveal continuing trends in the areas of discrimination, incarceration, health disparities and mortality with respect to Black males. The lack of increase in Black male medical school applications and matriculation contrasted by the continuing trends mentioned above illustrates that there is in fact an American crisis. (p. 317)

They promoted a need to examine the "medical school data specifically in the areas of: qualification barriers, race/ethnic classification and the impact of diversity on quality of healthcare in the U.S." (Laurencin & Murray, 2017, p. 317).

While recent data from the AAMC has demonstrated a modest increase in the absolute percentage of Black applicants (10% of the total number of applicants) and matriculants (9% of the total number of enrollees; AAMC, 2020), these percentages are unchanged from 1975 (Nivet, 2010). Further, admitting a diverse class is not the sole solution to these inequities. Inequities continue to exist once students have matriculated.

There is a growing body of evidence pointing to the disproportionate prevalence of mistreatment and microaggressions toward racial/ethnic minorities in medical school and clinical training. These covert occurrences serve to deliver condescending messages that negatively affect learning, academic performance, and well-being. As described by Daher et al. (2021), a recent study examining stress coping and resiliency among Black men in medical school reported that perceived academic inequities such as lower academic expectations, less access to academic resources, and social isolation caused tension for Black medical students, creating an environment in which the general stress of medical school was compounded by additional race-related stress.

The endpoint of this mistreatment is disparate rates of graduation of ethnic minorities. In published data from the AAMC, in the years 1987, 1992, and 1995, there were approximately 16,000 medical students. Within this group, the average attrition of White students due to academic reasons was less than 1%, while that of Black students was 7%. Similar rates (3%) were observed across this period in Latino and Native American students ("Medical School Graduation and Attrition Rates," 2007).

URM students suffer in part from performance evaluations. Rojek et al. (2017) found that many words and phrases used in subjective evaluations reflected students' personal attributes rather than competency-related behaviors. They observed a significant difference in narrative evaluations associated with gender and URM status, even among students receiving the same grade. For Rojek et al. (2017), this raised concerns of implicit bias in narrative evaluation, the basis of grading in the clinical year. Even in graduation letters of assessment, "white applicants were more likely to be described using 'standout' or 'ability' keywords (including 'exceptional', 'best', and 'outstanding') while Black applicants were more likely to be described as 'competent'" (Ross et al., 2017, p. 1371).

The training of providers specifically in psychiatry is especially fraught with difficulty. First, there are barriers to becoming a successful candidate for residency training. Second, there are the aforementioned concerns of evaluation and summative comments in letters of support. Third, there is the need to perform well on a standardized test, the U.S. Medical Licensing Examination (USMLE).

These test scores had been postulated to be an indication of whether a student had highly educated parents, attended well-resourced schools, had exposure to years of test preparation and summer science programs, and had access to professionals who served as role models and mentors. Standardized exams can be the great equalizers they are purported to be only if everyone has access to the resources required to excel on them. Otherwise, they remain markers of generations of unequal opportunities for underrepresented students (Youmans et al., 2020).

One portion of that examination is going to be reported as pass/fail going forward, but subsequent segments are numerically scored. Although the original intent of these exams was licensure alone, they have become a mode of discerning the credibility of students for residency training. Since these examinations are fraught with experiential bias, they may prove to be a stumbling block to entry into training, preserving the inadequacy in the mental health providers in our communities.

One would hope that successful entry into residency training might signal an end to barriers of success. Yet, a review of data from the Accreditation Council for Graduate Medical Education in 2015–2016 revealed that there were 27,495 medical school graduates nationally, of whom 47.3% were White and 5% were Black, a proportion that had remained unchanged for 20 to 30 years. Of the 1,375 Black students who entered training, 7% withdrew or were terminated, compared to 2.4% of White students.

Specifically, in psychiatry, there was a 4.2-fold higher percentage of Black residents who were dismissed or withdrawn compared to White residents ("Databook," 2019). The American Board of Psychiatry report a first-time failure rate for accreditation in this same time of 12%. Bishop et al. (2016) noted a 10% decline in the number of practicing psychiatrists per 100,000 residents in hospital referral regions in the preceding decade (2003–2013). The result of all of these academic impediments is that currently, "within psychiatry, historically underrepresented minorities in medicine (URMs) had less representation as residents (16.2%), faculty (8.7%), and practicing physicians (10.4%) compared with the US population (32.6%), Ps < 0.0001" (Bishop et al., 2016, p. 4).

Even given the difficulties students face, there is still a need for the U.S. mental health care system to increase the training and retention of racial/ethnic minorities. This is particularly true in order to improve mental health care. As noted by Lokko et al. (2017), patients often prefer and report greater satisfaction with racially matched providers, particularly in the field of mental health.

Legal Barriers

We are now seeing a resurgence of state-supported voter suppression legislation and have had ongoing cases of anti–affirmative action litigation that has reached the Supreme Court. Anti–affirmative action legislation and state-sponsored anti–affirmative action voter initiatives have the potential to limit the number of underrepresented minorities in the health professions and create even greater opportunity gaps and educational disparities. As a society, we need to foster collaborative communication that reframes the dialogue involving affirmative action and move to intentionally addressing historical and contemporary health disparities (National Academies of Sciences, Engineering, and Medicine, 2018).

Addressing Systemic Racism Is Key

Systemic racism is a provocative agent in the disproportionately higher occurrence of mental health disease among the Black population. And that disease is inadequately addressed in part due to cultural stigma, as well as a distrust of the medical profession that is centuries old. At the same time, socioeconomic barriers, including lack of insurance coverage and access to care, are manifestations of the social isolation that racial discord brings.

There is perpetuation of racism in more subtle forms that limits the education, preparation, and mentorship of underrepresented youth. Successful entry into medical school does not guarantee success in attaining the desired or needed training due to long-lasting stereotypes that impair professional assessment and development. Even the desire that medical graduates have for training may be limited by poor progression, higher rates of dismissal, and limitations imposed by accreditation board examinations.

Black physicians also professionally face inequities in advancement, high levels of burnout, reduced career duration, and elevated risk for mental health problems (including suicide). These adverse factors only further undermine the medical profession (Silver et al., 2019). Therefore, the root cause of mental health disparities in provider availability, diagnosis, and therapy lies in systemic racism, which will need to be addressed more fully by all segments of society in order to ameliorate this problem.

References

Agbafe, V., Boles, W. R., & Gee, R. E. (2020, November 20). *Bridging the Black mental health access gap*. Health Affairs. https://www.healthaffairs.org; 10.1377/hblog20201113.817116

American Association of Medical Colleges. (2020). *2020 facts: Applicant and matriculants data* (Tables A8–A14).

Association of American Medical Colleges. Medical school graduation and attrition rates. (2007). *Analysis in Brief, 7*(2).

Bailey, R. K., Mokonogho, J., & Kumar, A. (2019). Racial and ethnic differences in depression: Current perspectives. *Neuropsychiatric Disease and Treatment, 15*, 603–609. https://doi.org/10.2147/NDT.S128584

Bishop, T. F., Seirup, J. K., Pincus, H. A., & Ross, J. S. (2016). Population of US practicing psychiatrists declined, 2003–13, which may help explain poor access to mental health care. *Health Affairs, 35*(7), 1271. https://doi.org/10.1377/hlthaff.2015.1643.

Boekeloo, B. O., Jones, C., Bhagat, K., Siddiqui, J., & Wang, M. Q. (2015). The role of intrinsic motivation in the pursuit of health science-related careers among youth from underrepresented low socioeconomic populations. *Journal of Urban Health, 92*(5), 980–994. https://doi.org/10.1007/s11524-015-9987-7

Cohen, C., & Marino, L. (2013). Racial and ethnic differences in the prevalence of psychotic symptoms in the general population. *Psychiatric Services, 64*, 1103–1109. https://ps.psychiatryonline.org/doi/pdf/10.1176/appi.ps.201200348

Daher, Y., Austin, E. T., Munter, B. T., Murphy, L., & Gray, K. (2021). The history of medical education: A commentary on race. *Journal of Osteopathic Medicine, 121*(2), 163–170. https://doi.org/10.1515/jom-2020-0212

Databook of the Accreditation Council for Graduate Medical Education. (2019). ISSN 2473-8670.

APA Member Profiles. (2018). *Demographic characteristics of APA members by membership characteristics.* https://www.apa.org/workforce/publications/17-member-profiles/table-1.pdf

Estrada, M., Burnett, M., Campbell, A. G., Campbell, P. B., Denetclaw, W. F., Gutiérrez, C. G., Hurtado, S., John, G. H., Matsui, J., McGee, R., Okpodu, C. M., Robinson, T. J., Summers, M. F., Werner-Washburne, M., & Zavala, M. (2016). Improving underrepresented minority student persistence in STEM. *CBE Life Sciences Education, 15*(3), es5. https://doi.org/10.1187/cbe.16-01-0038

Eylem, O., de Wit, L., van Straten, A., Steubl, L., Melissourgaki, Z., Danışman, G. T., de Vries, R., Kerkhof, A. J. F. M., Bhui, K., & Cuijpers, P. (2020). Stigma for common mental disorders in racial minorities and majorities a systematic review and meta-analysis. *BMC Public Health*, *20*, 879. https://doi.org/10.1186/s12889-020-08964-3

Hankerson, S. H., Suite, D., & Bailey, R. K. (2015). Treatment disparities among African American men with depression: Implications for clinical practice. *Journal of Health Care for the Poor and Underserved*, *26*(1), 21–34. https://doi.org/10.1353/hpu.2015.0012

Hoffman, K. M., Trawalter, S., Axt, J. R., & Oliver, M. N. (2016). Racial bias in pain assessment and treatment recommendations, and false beliefs about biological differences between blacks and whites. *Proceedings of the National Academy of Sciences*, *113*(16), 4296–4301. https://doi.org/10.1073/pnas.1516047113

Holland, B. (2017, August 29). The 'Father of Modern Gynecology' performed shocking experiments on enslaved. https://www.history.com/news/the-father-of-modern-gynecology-performed-shocking-experiments-on-slaves

IHS Markit. (2021). *The complexities of physician supply and demand: Projections from 2019 to 2034*. AAMC.

Laurencin, C. T., & Murray, M. (2017). An American crisis: The lack of black men in medicine. *Journal of Racial and Ethnic Health Disparities*, *4*(3), 317–321. https://doi.org/10.1007/s40615-017-0380-y

Lee, D. C., Liang, H., & Shi, L. (2021). The convergence of racial and income disparities in health insurance coverage in the United States. *International Journal for Equity in Health*, *20*, 96. https://doi.org/10.1186/s12939-021-01436-z

Lokko, H. N., Chen, J. A., Parekh, R. I., & Stern, T. A. (2016). Racial and ethnic diversity in the US psychiatric workforce: A perspective and recommendations. *Academic Psychiatry*, *40*, 898–904.

Morris, D. B., Gruppuso, P. A., McGee, H. A., Murillo, A. L., Grover, A., & Adashi, E. Y. (2021). Diversity of the national medical student body—Four decades of inequities. *New England Journal of Medicine*, *384*, 1661–1668. https://doi.org/10.1056/NEJMsr2028487

National Academies of Sciences, Engineering, and Medicine. (2018). *An American crisis: The growing absence of Black men in medicine and science: Proceedings of a joint workshop*. National Academies Press. https://doi.org/10.17226/25130

Nivet, M. A. (2010). Minorities in academic medicine: Review of the literature. *Journal of Vascular Surgery*, *51*(4 Suppl), S53–S58. https://doi.org/10.1016/j.jvs.2009.09.064

Olbert, C. M., Nagendra, A., & Buck, B. (2018). Meta-analysis of Black vs. White racial disparity in schizophrenia diagnosis in the United States: Do structured assessments attenuate racial disparities? *Journal of Abnormal Psychology*, *127*(1), 104–115. https://doi.org/10.1037/abn0000309

Rojek, A. E., Khanna, R., Yim, J. W. L., Gardner, R., Lisker, S., Hauer, K. E., Lucey, C., & Sarkar, U. (2017). Differences in narrative language in evaluations of medical students by gender and under-represented minority status. *Journal of General Internal Medicine*, *34*(5), 684–691. https://doi.org/10.1007/s11606-019-04889-9

Ross, D. A., Boatright, D., Nunez-Smith, M., Jordan, A., Chekroud, A., & Moore, E. Z (2017). Differences in words used to describe racial and gender groups in medical student performance evaluations. *PLoS ONE*, *12*(8), e0181659. https://doi.org/10.1371/journal.pone.0181659

Rutgers University. (2019, March 21). African-Americans more likely to be misdiagnosed with schizophrenia, study finds: The study suggests a bias in misdiagnosing blacks with major depression and schizophrenia. *Science Daily*. www.sciencedaily.com/releases/2019/03/190321130300.htm

Santiago-Rivera, A. L., Adames, H. Y., Chavez-Dueñas, N. Y., & Benson-Flórez, G. (2016). The impact of racism on communities of color: Historical contexts and contemporary issues. In A. N. Alvarez, C. T. H. Liang, & H. A. Neville (Eds.), *The cost of racism for people of color: Contextualizing experiences of discrimination* (pp. 229–245). American Psychological Association. https://doi.org/10.1037/14852-011

Schwartz, R. C., & Blankenship, D. M. (2014). Racial disparities in psychotic disorder diagnosis: A review of empirical literature. *World Journal of Psychiatry*, 4(4), 133–140. https://doi.org/10.5498/wjp.v4.i4.133

Sibrava, N. J., Bjornsson, A. S., Pérez Benítez, A. C. I., Moitra, E., Weisberg, R. B., & Keller, M. B. (2019). Posttraumatic stress disorder in African American and Latino adults: Clinical course and the role of racial and ethnic discrimination. *American Psychologist*, 74(1), 101–116. https://doi.org/10.1037/amp0000339

Silver, J. K., Bean, A. C., Slocum, C., Poorman, J. A., Tenforde, A., Blauwet, C. A., Kirch, R. A., Parekh, R., Amonoo, H. L., Zafonte, R., & Osterbur, D. (2019). Physician workforce disparities and patient care: A narrative review. *Health Equity*, 3(1), 360–377. http://doi.org/10.1089/heq.2019.0040

Smith, S. G., Nsiah-Kumi, P. A., Jones, P. R., & Pamies, R. J. (2009a). Pipeline programs in the health professions, part 1: Preserving diversity and reducing health disparities. *Journal of the National Medical Association*, 101, 836–840.

Smith, S. G., Nsiah-Kumi, P. A., Jones, P. R., & Pamies, R. J. (2009b). Pipeline programs in the health professions, part 2: The impact of recent legal challenges to affirmative action. *Journal of the National Medical Association*, 101, 852–863.

Substance Abuse and Mental Health Services Administration. (2015). *Racial/ethnic differences in mental health service use among adults*. HHS Publication No. SMA-15-4906. Substance Abuse and Mental Health Services Administration.

Takeshita, J., Wang, S., Loren, A. W., et al. (2020). Association of racial/ethnic and gender concordance between patients and physicians with patient experience ratings. *JAMA Network Open*, 3(11), e2024583. https://doi.org/10.1001/jamanetworkopen.2020.24583

U.S. Surgeon General. (2001). Mental health: Culture, race, and ethnicity: A supplement to mental health: A report of the surgeon general. http://www.ncbi.nlm.nih.gov/books/NBK44251

Williams, D. R. (2018). Stress and the mental health of populations of color: Advancing our understanding of race-related stressors. *Journal of Health and Social Behavior*, 59(4), 466–485. https://doi.org/10.1177/0022146518814251

Youmans, Q. R., Essien, U. R., & Capers, Q., IV. (2020). A test of diversity—What USMLE pass/fail scoring means for medicine. *New England Journal of Medicine*, 382(25), 2393–2395. https://doi.org/10.1056/NEJMp2004356

20

The Fight for Civil Rights and
Its Connection to Mental Health
in Black Communities

Ceewin N. Louder, Alexis R. Franklin, Marisol L. Meyer,
Gabrielle M. del Rey, Melissa A. Gutierrez, Joelle Dorsett,
Brandon Wise Masters, and Guerda Nicolas

Protests are not senseless. They are an oft-neglected cry of pain and anger that has troubled the United States. That pain has several causes, including biased policing; discriminatory effects of segregation affecting education, job opportunities, and health; unequal opportunities to build wealth; an unequal criminal justice system; and unjust voting laws. Many of the inequities Black communities in the United States experience are a byproduct of a long history of discriminatory laws dating back to African enslavement that has fueled inequalities in every structure of society. Our society's core structures—labor, housing, education, voting, health care, and justice—are all formed around these laws and policies.

The civil rights movement is a centuries-long effort of Black Americans to resist racial oppression and to advance their civil rights in the United States. Nat Turner's slave rebellion. The Montgomery bus boycott. The March on Washington for Jobs and Freedom. The Stonewall riots. Black Lives Matter. The protests and the organizations behind them garnered media attention and national sympathy to shift the political, social, and cultural fabric of America.

While these movements have inched the United States closer to living up to its purported principles of liberty and equality, the toll on the individuals participating in such protests is less understood. With the threat of violence, imprisonment, or even death, Black Americans continue to organize, protest, and demonstrate. While protests can change society, much remains to

Ceewin N. Louder, Alexis R. Franklin, Marisol L. Meyer, Gabrielle M. del Rey, Melissa A. Gutierrez, Joelle Dorsett, Brandon Wise Masters, and Guerda Nicolas, *The Fight for Civil Rights and Its Connection to Mental Health in Black Communities* In: *Antiblackness and the Stories of Authentic Allies*. Edited by: Norman Kim, Carolyn Coker Ross, Mazella Fuller and Charlynn Small, Oxford University Press. © Oxford University Press 2024. DOI: 10.1093/oso/9780197642535.003.0021 be understood regarding the individual benefits of participating in protests, specifically as it pertains to mental health and well-being. While cultural change can be the long-term goal, short-term benefits can result from engaging in these movements as well.

Defining Protests

Imagine a protest. You may see large-scale rallies, indignant protesters, and hand-painted signs. These images are only one expression of protest. Merriam-Webster (2023) defines protest as "a solemn declaration of opinion and usually of dissent," "the act of objecting or a gesture of disapproval," and "a complaint, objection, or display of unwillingness usually to an idea or a course of action." While the literal definition of protest centers on the idea of objection and dissent, the notion of protest has a rich and complex history in the United States.

The spirit of *protest* is innate to America, a country founded through rebellion. Yet the spirit of protest is only celebrated and protected when the vessel that carries it speaks and looks a certain (i.e., White) way. Inherent in the idea of protest is some minority dissenting against an upheld status quo. In a country built on White supremacy, Black folks and historically marginalized groups have been protesting since America's conception. Living in a country designed to exploit you, not support you, is to live a life of protest.

Protests take on many shapes. There are large-scale social movements that define the cultural zeitgeist, like the civil rights and Black Lives Matter movements. Protests can include nonviolent resistance, peaceful acts, symbols such as graffiti and flag burning, or physical acts such as rioting, "looting," hunger strikes, and imposing physical barriers. Protests can include one person or millions. History illustrates different forms of protest and expands our understanding of protest. In this exploration, we ask that you both uphold and suspend your automatic thoughts on what it means to protest.

Nonviolent Resistance

Nonviolent resistance or civil disobedience is a common form of protest, characterized by a commitment to utilizing creative nonviolent means to resist violent forces and influencing and encouraging social change. Typically, nonviolent protests are symbolic acts of peaceful opposition or attempted persuasion to demonstrate that the protestors are against something. A prolific example is people peacefully refusing to cooperate; however, there are several other types of nonviolent protests. In *The Politics of Nonviolent Action* (1973), Gene Sharp lists various methods of nonviolent actions ranging from formal statements to symbolic public acts to public assembly, and we have highlighted a few below to expand your understanding of protests.

Formal Statements

Formal statements are a verbal expression of opinion, dissent, or intention that may be for or against some issue, regime, system, policy, or condition (Sharp, 1973). They take various forms such as public speeches, letters of opposition, public statements, and petitions. Formal statements are primarily used to address the body that is being supported or opposed but in turn may have effects on the larger society (Sharp, 1973). Dr. Reverend Martin Luther King Jr. inspired, and continues to inspire, people with the power of his speech and letters. More specifically, his "I Have a Dream Speech" was critical for the civil rights movement and was effective in persuading Congress to pass the Civil Rights Act of 1964.

Communications With a Wider Audience

The protests that fall within this classification are used primarily to communicate ideas or viewpoints to a larger audience (Sharp, 1973). The most common forms of visual and oral statements are slogans, symbols, and caricatures. They may be written on social media, painted on a wall, or spoken at a protest to influence the opposing body or gain support for the cause. While visual and oral statements are commonly part of marches and larger group protests, they can stand alone as a form of protest. A family might place a "Black Lives Matter" poster in their yard, or a racial equity organization may hand out pamphlets highlighting the injustices happening in the community.

Symbolic Public Acts

Many viewpoints and stances are expressed in symbolic behavior. The National Association for the Advancement of Colored People (NAACP) created a flag as a way to protest against the lynching of Black people in the United States. The flag read, "A MAN WAS LYNCHED YESTERDAY" and was flown from the NAACP building the day after the news of a lynching reached them. Die-ins are another form of a symbolic public act, defined as participants lying motionless on the ground in a public space to represent physical reminders of the lives taken. After the killings of Michael Brown and Eric Garner by White police officers, students and other organizers staged die-ins to call attention to police brutality.

Withdrawal and Reunification
Withdrawal and reunification protests are defined as forms in which people withdraw from usual behavior or renounce an honor they hold (Sharp, 1973). Walkouts, in which a group or an individual can express a stance by walking out of a conference, a meeting, a class, or an assembly before it has been officially adjourned, are common protests. Similarly, a group or an individual can choose to withdraw from certain practices, such as kneeling during the National Anthem, as spurred by Colin Kaepernick.

Noncooperation
Noncooperation is a type of protest in which the organizer intentionally withdraws from their usual form of cooperation with a person, institution, or organization with which they do not agree (Sharpe, 1973). Individuals can refuse to buy certain products, shop at certain stores, or go to work or school. The organizer performs their protest by ceasing their normal cooperation or by withholding new forms of assistance, which results in the slowing down of normal operations (Sharp, 1973). In sum, noncooperation includes the resistance to existing social, economic, or political relationships (Sharp, 1973).

Violent or Destructive Protests

While some say violence has no place in the fight for racial equity, the United States was founded on violence. Between the genocide of Native Americans and the enslavement of Africans, author Casey Gerald put it best: "Violence is really the only language that America understands" (Wiley & Proehl, 2020, para. 15). The entire civil rights movement began in response to violence against Black individuals, and this violence has been used to draw attention to the plight of Black folks in America and demand change. While most protests remain nonviolent, there have been violent incidents. Violent or destructive protests tend to occur after several nonviolent acts of protests have gone unheard. Riots, looting, and vandalism can lead to more attention and potentially bring about change. As Dr. King said in 1966, "A riot is the language of the unheard" (CBS News, 2013, para. 8).

Mental Health and Protesting

While protesting is valuable in and of itself, protesting may, directly and indirectly, have positive implications for mental health. We posit that protesting may (a) create or increase one's sense of belonging, (b) contribute to one's development of a stable and clear self-concept, (c) enhance one's sense of autonomy, (d) create opportunities for catharsis, and (e) promote feelings of hope.

Belonging

The psychological need to belong is remarkably powerful (Fiske, 2000). Belonging allows an individual to address both the psychological and physical need for safety and security (Brewer, 2007). When humans feel as though they belong, they can nurture trustful, cooperative relationships without expending psychological resources worrying about the possibility of being exploited (Kramer & Goldman, 1995; Turner et al., 1987). Alternatively, when humans feel as though they do not belong, they may experience "othering," or intentional exclusion from a group and its resources (Brewer, 2007). Myriad research has demonstrated that belonging or being othered has a variety of implications for mental health, including experiences with depression, anxiety, self-esteem, physical well-being, and identity development (e.g., Begen & Turner-Cobb, 2015; Cook et al., 2012; Hawkley & Cacioppo, 2010; Steger & Kashdan, 2009).

One of many ways racism causes significant harm is by inciting and perpetuating the systematic exclusion (or othering) of Black individuals from access to resources and protections offered to White Americans. While engaging in protest might not immediately correct the injustice of being excluded or othered, it is likely that it sustains a sense of belonging within the community one is advocating for (May, 2011).

Theoretical work by May (2011) posits that this process is iterative: Engaging in advocacy and liberatory action for one's community strengthens one's sense of belonging to that community, and a powerful sense of belonging increases one's inclination to advocate for their community. Belonging to a democratic community that co-constructs transformational change necessitates the recognition that those in the community "experience a linked fate" (Powell & Toppin, 2021, p. 55; Dawson, 1994). It is this linked fate and the protests Black individuals engage in to decide this fate that create the psychologically protective experience of belonging (Dawson, 1994).

Self-Concept Development

Self-concept is how an individual understands themself and the extent to which that understanding is consistent and clear (Campbell et al., 1996). A stable and coherent self-concept can significantly contribute to both mental and physical health, whereas a muddled or turbulent self-concept is associated with a variety of negative outcomes (Richman et al., 2016).

A dimension of self-concept is one's understanding of their heritage (i.e., "inherited traditions, monuments, objects, and culture" as well as "contemporary activities, meanings, and behaviors"; UMass Amherst Center for Heritage and Society, n.d., para 1). Leaders in the fight for Black liberation have cited the identification and celebration of Black heritage as foundational to the flourishing of the Black community.

As expressed by Malcolm X to the Organization of Afro-American Unity in 1964, "We must recapture our heritage and our identity if we are ever to liberate ourselves from the bonds of White supremacy" (Blackpast, 2007, section 5, para 24). Heritage, self-expression, and connection to the Black community are all elements of self-concept that are intertwined with protesting.

For example, soul music is a form of artistic expression created by the Black community to celebrate Blackness, communicate the various injustices Black people experience, and provide messages of hope (Maultsby, 1983). Creators and consumers of this form of protest are provided with the opportunity to reflect on and connect to both the Black community and their personal Black identity (Adelakun, 2019).

Further, engaging in protest, regardless of the form of protest, may be considered informative for one's self-concept development. El-Khoury (2012) theorizes that in the United States, the Black experience is in part defined by resistance. Resistance to the multiple systems of oppression that Black individuals face daily may contribute to the development of a sociopolitical identity that unites individuals to engage in collective action (Pender et al., 2019).

Relatedly, various movements for Black liberation across time have differed in their approach to protest, but many have centered on the cruciality of developing Black identity and feeling prideful of that dimension of one's self-concept (Zangrando & Zangrando, 1970). Connecting to one's Black identity and to others who are prideful of their blackness and advocate for Black liberation may have a substantial positive impact on one's self-concept.

Autonomy

Resistance, in seeking the power to decide and act independently, involves a struggle for autonomy (Williams, 2008). Williams (2008) states that "the prerequisite of resistance is a certain autonomy, that of the social movement itself and that of individual activists" (p. 67). Autonomy is said to be one of the variables that are expected to have direct effects on an individual's health; higher levels of autonomy are associated with psychological well-being (Keyes, 2009; Reis et al., 2000).

However, autonomy is highly suppressed by discrimination (Keyes, 2009), which is often experienced by the Black community. Williams (2008) shares that a person may experience a form of autonomy that initiates in the mind as one receives an increased awareness of injustice. Thereafter, they can function as advocates for their well-being and freedom through a variety of autonomy-promoting actions. Social movements involve a fight for justice and the promotion of equality. Protests allow individuals to collectively enhance their autonomy as they experience racial socialization that promotes self-development (Keyes, 2009). Protests can be one of those actions as it creates spaces that facilitate autonomy development and self-advocacy for Black individuals (Reis et al., 2000), which can contribute to better mental health in the Black community.

Catharsis

Collective actions may serve as a cathartic experience when a group of people express similar grievances (Ni, 2020). Catharsis can be defined as a process that provides relief from restrained emotions or an attempt to resolve pain from an experience (Kettles, 1995). Catharsis may happen spontaneously, such as bursting into tears, or it can be a cognitive release when an individual realizes that an event is affecting the way they feel (Kellermann, 1984).

The inability to release emotion is said to be a feature of "early socialization processes and a product of cultural oppression, including institutionalization" (Kettles, 1995, p. 76). Expression of emotions in a sincere form has been found to reduce feelings of anger and aggressive behavior (Doob & Wood, 1972). Catharsis has been considered valuable in the treatment of severe mental diagnoses, such as posttraumatic stress disorder, personality disorders, and somatoform disorders (Kellerman, 1984). It has also been considered a curative factor in group therapy processes when combined with other techniques (Yalom, 1975).

Emotions participate in every stage of protests and social movements (Jasper, 1998). According to Jasper (1998), social movements create a space for negative emotions to be allowed and are even useful to promote change, as these are opportunities to consider negative emotions as rational. Catharsis not only allows for healing and growth to occur (Kettles, 1995) but also creates a space where negative feelings can produce a positive outcome. Jasper (1998) states that "passion for justice is fueled by anger over existing injustice" (p. 414), which supports the claim that catharsis can lead to more than improved mental health for individuals.

Protests may be one of the few spaces where the Black community can release emotions in force since systems have not allowed it otherwise. Symbolic public acts and nonviolence resistance allow for individuals to express their opinions and release restrained emotions in a way that promotes positive change. These social movements are creating opportunities for healing amid oppression.

Hope

Hope is an enigmatic concept in psychology research, as it has traits of both an emotional and a cognitive framework. Hope, the emotion, is described as a desire and optimism for a different situation in the future. Hope, the cognitive framework, however, speaks more to an active component, as one's actions, individually or collectively, can achieve the desired situation. Wlodarczyk and colleagues (2017) describe hope as "a bridge between collective action frames and actual action" (p. 201). Succinctly, hope the emotion gives us a "why," and hope the cognitive framework helps us figure out our "how."

As it relates to mental health, a large body of research demonstrates a positive relationship between hope and various aspects of positive mental health, and a negative relationship between hope and various aspects of negative mental health. Increased hope is associated with increased self-efficacy, positive experiences, optimism, eudaimonia, and improved well-being (Gallagher et al., 2020; Griggs, 2017). Further, hope has a positive association with self-worth and satisfaction in adolescents and children and has been shown to predict posttraumatic growth (Griggs, 2017). Academically, hope is positively related to higher grades, resiliency, thriving, and adaptive coping (Griggs, 2017). Those with increased hope demonstrate decreased suicidal ideation and risk (Griggs, 2017).

As hope relates to the fight for civil rights and protesting, the relationship may be bidirectional. For some, hope can be a precursor to engaging in acts of protest and resistance. Individuals with higher levels of hope believe there is a better future that is attainable through their actions. Hope is what shifts anger about social injustices into collective action to foster the change that should and will be (Wlodarczyk et al., 2017). In coping with the pain, burden, and thwarted belongingness imposed by racism, increased hope allows one to adaptively cope with these feelings and maintain flexibility toward achieving civil rights goals (Gallagher et al., 2020; Griggs, 2017).

The emotion of hope allows one to tap into cognitive resources that are initiative-taking in seeking and bringing about change. Hope allows one to connect one's efforts to their successes, which is motivating to continue working for social change. Additionally, hope can also be contagious; when participating in collective forms of protests, feelings of affiliation, belongingness, hope, and social support can spread from the group to the individual, increasing the hope of the individual (Wlodarczyk et al., 2017).

In the ongoing fight for civil rights, participating in protests and acts of resistance is necessary for fostering, sustaining, and maintaining hope: hope for a desired better future, and hope that one's actions, collectively and individually, can bring about that desired change.

Conclusion

The fight for civil rights is a long and arduous one, making the protection of mental health an important goal for Black individuals and communities.

Fortunately, protests remain a key method of supporting mental health through advocacy, self-transformation, and inspiration.

Healing work is often thought of as an individual process, but the systemic nature of many issues faced by Black communities warrants simultaneous community work. Action moves us from the individual to the collective, which can provide support for individuals as they wrestle with feelings of helplessness in the face of racism. Thus, mental health professionals should consider how protesting, in its many forms, can serve as a unique community-centered coping resource for clients.

Similarly, educators should consider the immense potential for learning inherent in protesting. Protests, as the language of the unheard, can illuminate the voices, stories, and perspectives of Black communities that have been marginalized for centuries. For many, protests are a form of meaningful alternative education, providing knowledge about the self and the history of one's people. There is power in people and power in knowledge, and protests provide a distinctive way to use these powers for the betterment of Black individuals, communities, and futures.

References

Adelakun, A. A. (2019). Black Lives Matter! Nigerian Lives Matter!: Language and why Black performance matters. *Genealogy, 3*(2), 19.

Begen, F. M., & Turner-Cobb, J. M. (2015). Benefits of belonging: Experimental manipulation of social inclusion to enhance psychological and physiological health parameters. *Psychology & Health, 30*(5), 568–582. https://doi.org/10.1080/08870446.2014.991734

BlackPast, B. (2007, October 15). *(1964) Malcolm X's Speech at the Founding Rally of the Organization of Afro-American Unity.* BlackPast.org. https://www.blackpast.org/african-american-history/speeches-african-american-history/1964-malcolm-x-s-speech-founding-rally-organization-afro-american-unity/

Brewer, M. B. (2007). The importance of being we: Human nature and intergroup relations. *American Psychologist, 62*(8), 72.

Campbell, J. D., Trapnell, P. D., Heine, S. J., Katz, I. M., Lavallee, L. F., & Lehmann, D. R. (1996). Self-concept clarity: Measurement, personality correlates, and cultural boundaries. *Journal of Personality and Social Psychology, 70*, 141–156.

CBS News. (2013, August 25). *MLK: A riot is the language of the unheard.* 60 Minutes Overtime, CBS Interactive Inc. https://www.cbsnews.com/news/mlk-a-riot-is-the-language-of-the-unheard/

Cook, J. E., Purdie-Vaughns, V., Garcia, J., & Cohen, G. L. (2012). Chronic threat and contingent belonging: Protective benefits of values affirmation on identity development. *Journal of Personality and Social Psychology, 102*(3), 479.

Dawson, M. C. (1995). *Behind the mule: Race and class in African-American politics.* Princeton University Press.

Doob, A. N., & Wood, L. E. (1972). Catharsis and aggression: Effects of annoyance and retaliation on aggressive behavior. *Journal of Personality and Social Psychology, 22*(2), 156–162. https://doi.org/10.1037/h0032598

El-Khoury, L. J. (2012). "Being while Black": Resistance and the management of the self. *Social Identities, 8*(1), 85–100.

Fiske, S. T. (2000). Stereotyping, prejudice, and discrimination at the seam between the centuries: Evolution, culture, mind, and brain. *European Journal of Social Psychology, 30*(3), 299–322.

Gallagher, M. W., D'Souza, J. M., & Richardson, A. L. (2020). Hope in contemporary psychology. In C. Blöser & T. Stahl (Eds.), *The moral psychology of hope* (pp. 189–207). Rowman & Littlefield International.

Griggs, S. (2017). Hope and mental health in young adult college students: An integrative review. *Journal of Psychosocial Nursing and Mental Health Services, 55*(2), 28–35. https://doi-org.access.library.miami.edu/10.3928/02793695-20170210-04

Hawkley, L. C., & Cacioppo, J. T. (2010). Loneliness matters: A theoretical and empirical review of consequences and mechanisms. *Annals of Behavioral Medicine, 40*(2), 218–227.

Jasper, J. (1998). The emotions of protest: Affective and reactive emotions in and around social movements. *Sociological Forum, 13*(3), 397–424. http://www.jstor.org/stable/684696

Kramer, R. M., & Goldman, L. (1995). Helping the group or helping yourself? Social motives and group identity in resource dilemmas. In D. A. Schroeder (Ed.), *Social dilemmas: Perspectives on individuals and groups* (pp. 49–67). Praeger.

Kellermann, P. F. (1984). The place of catharsis in psychodrama. *Journal of Group Psychotherapy, Psychodrama & Sociometry, 37*(1), 1–13.

Kettles, A. (1995). Catharsis: A literature review. *Journal of Psychiatric and Mental Health Nursing, 2*, 73–81. https://doi.org/10.1111/j.1365-2850.1995.tb00146.x

Keyes, C. L. (2009). The Black-White paradox in health: Flourishing in the face of social inequality and discrimination. *Journal of Personality, 77*(6), 1677–1706. https://doi.org/10.1111/j.1467-6494.2009.00597.x

Maultsby, P. K. (1983). Soul music: Its sociological and political significance in American popular culture. *Journal of Popular Culture, 17*(2), 51.

May, V. (2011). Self, belonging, and social change. *Sociology, 45*(3), 363–378.

Merriam-Webster. (2023). Protest. In Merriam-Webster.com dictionary. Retrieved February 25, 2023. https://www.merriam-webster.com/dictionary/protest

Ni, M. Y., Kim, Y., McDowell, I., Wong, S., Qiu, H., Wong, I. O., Galea, S., & Leung, G. M. (2020). Mental health during and after protests, riots, and revolutions: A systematic review. *Australian & New Zealand Journal of Psychiatry, 54*(3), 232–243.

Pender, K. N., Hope, E. C., & Riddick, K. N. (2019). Queering Black activism: Exploring the relationship between racial identity and Black activist orientation among Black LGBTQ youth. *Journal of Community Psychology, 47*(3), 529–543.

Powell, J. A., & Toppin, E., Jr. (2021). Uprooting authoritarianism: Deconstructing the stories behind narrow identities and building a society of belonging. *Columbia Journal of Race and Law, 11*(1), 1–82. https://doi.org/10.7916/cjrl.v11i1.8019

Reis, H. T., Sheldon, K. M., Gable, S. L., Roscoe, J., & Ryan, R. M. (2000). Daily well-being: The role of autonomy, competence, and relatedness. *Personality and Social Psychology Bulletin, 26*(4), 419–435. https://doi.org/10.1177/0146167200266002

Richman, S. B., Pond, R. S., Jr., Dewall, C. N., Kumashiro, M., Slotter, E. B., & Luchies, L. B. (2016). An unclear self leads to poor mental health: Self-concept confusion mediates the association of loneliness with depression. *Journal of Social and Clinical Psychology*, *35*(7), 525–550.

Sharp, G. (1973). *The politics of nonviolent action* (3 vols.). Porter Sargent.

Steger, M. F., & Kashdan, T. B. (2009). Depression and everyday social activity, belonging, and well-being. *Journal of Counseling Psychology*, *56*(2), 289.

Turner, J. C., Hogg, M. A., Oakes, P. J., Reicher, S. D., & Wetherell, M. S. (1987). *Rediscovering the social group: A self-categorization theory*. Basil Blackwell.

UMass Amherst Center for Heritage and Society. (n.d.). *What is heritage?* University of Massachusetts Amherst. https://websites.umass.edu/infochs/about/what-is-heritage/

Wiley, M., & Proehl, A. (2020, July 4). *"Violence is really the only language that America understands": Author Casey Gerald on Frederick Douglass and the Fourth of July*. KQED. https://www.kqed.org/news/11827442/violence-is-really-the-only-language-that-america-understands-author-casey-gerald-on-frederick-douglass-and-the-fourth-of-july

Williams, G. (2008). Cultivating autonomy: Power, resistance, and the French alterglobalization movement. *Critique of Anthropology*, *28*(1), 63–86. https://doi.org/10.1177/0308275X07086558

Wlodarczyk, A., Basabe, N., Páez, D., & Zumeta, L. (2017). Hope and anger as mediators between collective action frames and participation in collective mobilization: The case of 15-M. *Journal of Social and Political Psychology*, *5*(1), 200–223. https://doi-org.access.library.miami.edu/10.5964/jspp.v5i1.471

Yalom, I. D. (1975). *The theory and practice of group psychotherapy* (2nd ed.). Basic Books.

Zangrando, J. S., & Zangrando, R. L. (1970). Black protest: A rejection of the American dream. *Journal of Black Studies*, *1*(2), 141–159.

21

Mental Health Industry Challenges and the Need for Black Psychological Allyship

Alonzo C. DeCarlo

Black Psychological Allyship Defined

Black psychological allyship (BPA) is a person, group, or institution engaged in activity explicitly designed to eliminate disparities in mental health assessment, diagnosis, and treatment and to promote mental health well-being among Black Americans. On the other hand, *antiblackness* is actions undertaken to obstruct or regress Black people's development or culture. Few phrases are as unpalatable to mainstream America as "antiblackness." It is an expression that many White Americans find discombobulating and that others meet with disbelief. Nevertheless, the phenomenon is as organic as the Black Lives Matter protests that sprouted uvp across the country, seemingly daily, in 2020.

The historicity to which Black American life has been psychologically and physically subjugated is circuitously chronicled in nearly every discipline in the academic enterprise and beyond. Equal treatment in mental health services for Black Americans has been impeded by a paucity of institutional BPA. Black American livelihood in the United States continues to be vulnerable to premature demise due to structural and institutional indifference, a sizable intractable strain on American ideals.

Hence, the psychology of thriving for Black Americans is fraught with mental impositions. Indeed, at the intersection of race and *mental health*—defined as a state of emotional well-being in which persons can function comfortably within their society and in which their achievement and characteristics are satisfactory to them (Sadock et al., 2017)—Black Americans find uncertainty, unease, and unfairness.

Like Black American boys in the juvenile court system, Black Americans in general suffer extreme bias at every level of the mental health system, from

Alonzo C. DeCarlo, *Mental Health Industry Challenges and the Need for Black Psychological Allyship* In: *Antiblackness and the Stories of Authentic Allies*. Edited by: Norman Kim, Carolyn Coker Ross, Mazella Fuller and Charlynn Small, Oxford University Press. © Oxford University Press 2024. DOI: 10.1093/oso/9780197642535.003.0022 assessment to intervention. Black Americans are about half as likely to obtain mental health care as their White counterparts, despite having equal or more significant mental health needs (Marrast et al., 2016). When Black Americans do seek and receive services, the outcome is often inadequate (Leslie et al., 2003; Merikangas & Burstein, 2011; Rue & Xie, 2009).

The empirical literature cites several explanations for Black Americans' timid approach to and outcome of mental health interventions. One of many contributing factors is the problem of uninsured and underinsured status. Still, even after controlling for this, Black Americans are more likely to be referred to public rather than private treatment facilities, suggesting racial bias in assessment and treatment recommendations (Sadock & Ruiz, 2017). Thus, it is reasonable to assert that ethnopsychopharmacological factors may account for a small amount of the variance in differential response disparities to mental health medication and treatment across racial groups that disfavor Black Americans.

Similarly, clinician cultural incompetence—and perhaps more powerful factors at work—also plays a prominent role in Black Americans' poor mental health outcomes in diagnosis and treatment.

Mental Health Equity

As it relates to Black Americans, mental health equity remains one of the most challenging issues facing licensed mental health practitioners (LMHPs). According to the U.S. Department of Health and Human Services Office of Minority Mental Health (2017) , Black Americans are 10% more likely to report severe psychological distress than White Americans. However, a recent study showed that only 25% of Black Americans seek mental health services, compared to 40% of non-Hispanic Whites (Marx, 2019). According to the Substance Abuse and Mental Health Services Administration (SAMHSA, 2020) mental health equity is the right of all populations to access quality mental health care regardless of race, ethnicity, gender, socioeconomic status, geographical location, or social conditions.

The American Psychiatric Association (APA) is the largest psychiatric organization internationally, and its influence on mental health equity is one of the most prominent in the United States. To a large extent, all mental health–providing disciplines—including counseling, social work, psychology, and psychiatry—are affected by major APA mental health policy and practice changes that play a definitive role in shaping approaches to diagnosis and treatment.

The APA has a clear definition of *mental disorders* but not *mental health*. The APA is responsible for publishing the *Diagnostic and Statistical Manual of Mental Health Disorders*, fifth edition (DSM-V), the go-to manual for the codification of mental health disorders. In this manual, you can locate nearly 300 mental illnesses. However, you will not find data on how these mental disorders are discernibly juxtaposed to mental health. The principal objective of the DSM-V is to empower clinicians to reliably diagnose patients who may struggle with what appears to be mental disorder symptomology.

The consistency with which clinicians diagnose patients may have a slight variance, which is understandable, but the substantial differential in the rate of misdiagnosis for Black Americans is unacceptable. Black Americans experiencing significant mental health disparities is no longer surprising, but the milquetoast explanations offered in the empirical literature are puzzling. Indeed, the notion that the mental health industry may be viewed as a guiding light in their psychological well-being is viewed with cynicism by Black Americans.

Mental Health Disparities

In this chapter, mental health disparities are considered within the classification of the Institute of Medicine's (IOM's) notion of disparities in health care that are "racial or ethnic differences in the quality of health care that are not due to access-related factors or clinical needs, preferences, appropriateness of interventions" (Stith & Nelson, 2002, p. 666). These disparities also contribute to other inequalities associated with the psychological well-being of Black Americans. The concern is considerably more pronounced than an inability to navigate the cultural distance between clinicians and patients effectively.

Part of the mistrust of seeking psychological or psychiatric services is based on the inclination of clinicians to pathologize behavior resulting from economic struggles, racism, and discrimination in the schools, workplaces, and communities of Black Americans. The issue is not that Black Americans are iaotrophobic; rather, they have legitimate iatrogenic concerns. Black Americans will continue to be essentially a psychological enigma to clinicians so long as they are concerned that their mental health status will worsen after an office visit to a professionally licensed behavioral clinician.

Empirical studies consistently reveal that the disparities in diagnosing serious mental disorders for Black Americans have been problematic for several decades. In a review of research on race and diagnosis of psychotic disorders spanning 24 years, Schwartz and Blankenship (2014) found a clear and pervasive pattern wherein Black Americans are diagnosed with psychotic disorders at a rate of three to four times higher than White Americans. A robust meta-analysis confirms that Black American adult clients are 2.4 times more likely to be diagnosed with schizophrenia than White American individuals and indicates that more meticulous diagnostic procedures are unsuccessful in eradicating this racial inequality (Villatoro et al., 2018).

Moreover, Black Americans are significantly more likely to be prescribed higher dosages of antipsychotics and are less likely to receive second-generation antipsychotics than White Americans (Kreyenbuhl et al., 2003; Kuno & Rothbard, 2002). Second-generation drugs are critical to the treatment regimen as they are linked with less severe side effects.

These biases extend to Black American children as well. For example, Black American children are two and a half times more likely to receive a diagnosis of conduct disorder (CD) than attention deficit hyperactivity disorder (ADHD). Black American children who are disproportionately and often inaccurately diagnosed with CD will not receive the educational accommodation, pharmacotherapy, and behavioral treatment intervention commonly prescribed for ADHD. Studies have shown that physicians who have diagnosed Black American children with CD rather than ADHD are significantly more likely to ascribe to pessimistic forecasts for their future concerning criminality (Mizock & Harkins, 2011; Rockett et al., 2007).

Mental Health Professionals, Pedagogy, and Credentialing

The training grounds of counselors, social workers, psychologists, and psychiatrists include multicultural-related pedagogy, which is now largely subsumed by the phrase *diversity, equity, and inclusion* (DEI). The cultural zeitgeist in American institutions, especially in the academic enterprise, is the promotion of DEI. The rationale is that teaching the individual to understand elements of DEI as a critical factor in their interface with consumers would mitigate against unfair treatment of Black Americans and other marginalized groups. The DEI initiatives were supposed to be to discrimination and disparities what penicillin is to infections. A prudent question would be, why is it necessary to inject and enforce DEI as a function of effective institutional engagement with Black Americans?

It is expected that mental health professionals are well acquainted with the variety of ways people from different cultures report ailments, behavioral responses to livelihood threats, and other idioms of distress. The pedagogical prowess of cultural causal attributions related to perceived pathology is readily available in the training of mental health professionals in graduate programs across the country. Yet, it is clear that the appropriate use of this cross-cultural training is not effectively evoked in an orthogonal context with Black Americans in mental health settings.

For more than 50 years, prospective Black American patients have continued to complain that there are not enough Black American mental health professionals, with a particular emphasis on the lack of Black American male behavioral clinicians. This complaint stems from feelings that many non-Black American clinicians generally do not have an understanding of their culture or the institutional bigotry contribution to their conditions and that therefore it is simply not worth talking to them. The unspoken insight for Black Americans is often that White American clinicians are a part of the system that has contributed to the psychological problem they are trying to overcome and that their implicit bias is problematic.

Naturally, the concern regarding the litany of long-term misdiagnoses and treatment disparities in mental health for Black Americans beckons the question: What are the sustaining mechanisms of this misdiagnosis and mistreatment? The culprit ranges from institutional biases to institutional bigotry and more. Moreover, what would an individual or institution have to gain by engaging in such unjust tactics?

Wittingly or unwittingly, the mentality of many licensed mental health practitioners, who are predominantly White American, is a microcosm of the wider American society, which is replete with racism, discrimination, prejudice, and stereotypical thinking and behavior. White Americans seem to be obsessed with holding on to their dominance through status, wealth, and power. Others, including "want-to-be Americans," are fixated on removing this power structure or preoccupied with access to it.

Thus, one hypothesis to the question mentioned earlier is that there exists an inverse relationship between the socioeconomic success of Black Americans and other people of color and the identity achievement of White

Americans. For example, as Black Americans substantially increase their social–economic standing, White Americans begin to question their place and roles in society at the micro, meso, and macro levels. This stage of self-definition, in which the stability and well-being of White American selves are predicated on the ebb and flow of that of people of color, is called *White identity fragility*. In other words, the clarity with which White Americans navigate their political and socioeconomic world becomes cloudier as Black Americans' socioeconomic standing becomes noticeably elevated.

To prevent this opaqueness from threatening the dominance of ideological and interpersonal mainstays of White identity, institutional bigotry is engaged throughout American institutions, including the mental health industry. This is one tactic employed to mitigate against the existential angst of White identity fragility. The second method involves a newly named concept for an old phenomenon: *opprejudice*, which is when members of the dominant group support human subjugation through actions and attitudes in a manner thought to be so subtle, ambiguous, or complex that the victim is unaware of it (DeCarlo, 2021).

The protection mechanisms are so subtle and deeply embedded in the White American consciousness and fabric of our institutions that White Americans may not be aware that they are using this implicit psychological defense against White identity fragility. The application of opprejudice (DeCarlo, 2021) as a mechanism against White identity fragility can be seen in nearly every facet of American life and is particularly damaging in the mental health industry.

One of the most sensible places to begin addressing this problem is on the training grounds of mental health professionals. Graduate programs across the country have made many efforts to tackle the shortcomings in the mental health professions. However, we face multiple challenges when addressing this problem through our academic enterprise:

1. Teaching students about this issue has little impact on their professional or personal opprejudice bandwidth, so they simply do what is necessary to pass the coursework to obtain their advanced graduate degree.
2. Academic institutions providing the training only support invoking the tenants of what is minimally necessary to accommodate the idea that they are genuinely interested in DEI in support of Black Americans.

3. Professors are simply uninformed as to how to best convey the material on the subject of DEI in behavioral mental health settings.
4. Accrediting bodies for the mental health professions in academe do not mandate enough rigorous curriculum coursework requirements, hands-on mentorship, and intrapersonal assessments to counter institutional bigotry and opprejudice as a function of training graduate programs.

Indubitably, the cross-cultural mental health guidance and mentorship offered to graduate students has been a step in the right direction to improve the psychological well-being of Black Americans. Many faculty members, university staff, and partnering agencies and organizations have continued to be commendably dedicated to this cause. The good work performed in the past cannot be ignored due to the present struggles in mental health. Further addressing the aforementioned challenges will require a targeted approach aimed unambiguously at the mental health needs of Black Americans. In countering antiblackness in the mental health industry, actions such as those promoted in BPA can effect the change needed to support Black American mental health well-being.

The Role of Black Psychological Allyship

Consider BPA a function of protecting and benefiting the public by setting standards of qualification, education, training, and experience as a function of professional mental health practice in individual, family, and group settings. Mental health policies at the state and federal levels have the power to reshape the narrative of mental health service delivery outcomes for Black Americans. The oversight level in Table 21.1 suggests macrolevel adjustment to open new possibilities to fill in gaps of mental health service shortcomings for Black Americans. The underrepresentation of Black Americans in mental health clinical trials also adds to the difficulty of providing adequate services. Substantial increases in support for Black scholars, researchers, and practitioners could significantly improve Black Americans' participation in the research necessary to improve practice standards.

There are many ways to address the mental health concerns of Black Americans at the state level. Presently, in a largely capitated mental health care system, Black Americans are disadvantaged considering their mental

Table 21.1 Black Psychological Allyship and Mental Health Services Retooling Plan.

O V E R S I G H T	Level 1 Federal	1. Federal regulatory agencies should provide the necessary resources for clinical social service, mental health organizations, and other community stakeholders to support Black Americans with serious and persistent mental illness to be treated by Black clinicians. 2. Incentivize clinical and psychosocial research for Black American scholar-practitioners to engage in clinical services (individual-level) research and service structures (systems-level) research to accelerate the translation of empirical findings to practice in mental health services for Black Americans. 3. Include within the strategic plan of the National Institute of Mental Health goals to support BPA fiscally and technically as a function of translational research and services and interventional research.
	Level 2 State	1. Establish a BPA monitoring mechanism for mental health services for Black Americans to evaluate aggregate data in an iterative and collaborative fashion with all stakeholders. 2. Include a definition of BPA within the statutes, public acts, and/or legislative glossary at the state level for all LMHPs. 3. Create and sustain funding for comprehensive mental health services for Black Americans for qualified service providers.
I N T E G R A T I O N	Level 3 Licensure	1. Clinicians who are mandated to maintain certification and licensure at the state level should be required to attend training programs regarding Black psychological well-being annually as part of their continuing professional education credit. 2. State-required licensing platforms for practicing clinicians should include a testing section to ascertain the examinee's knowledge and skill-based tenets necessary to effectively address Black American psychological well-being in individual, family, and group settings. 3. Licensing bodies at the state level should provide credentialing indicating that the mental health practitioner has obtained certification with specialized training to provide services to Black patients.
	Level 4 Accreditation	1. University-specialized accrediting bodies for licensed practitioners in counseling, social work, psychology, and psychiatry (i.e., Counseling for Accreditation of Counseling and Related Educational Programs, Council for Social Work Education, American Psychological Association, and American Board of Psychiatry and Neurology) should include a content section with specific accrediting criteria associated with BPA. Failure to comply at the program level should result in a temporary suspension of program accreditation. 2. University-specialized accrediting bodies for mental health licensed practitioners should require that a number of professors commensurate to a graduate program's size are identified as experts in the subject matter related to BPA to provide pedagogical guidance to candidates as a requirement for graduation. Failure to do so should result in a temporary suspension of program accreditation. 3. Institutional accrediting bodies should temporarily suspend university accreditation status when the institution fails to maintain Black staff and faculty proportional to societal representation.

health needs may be more culturally nuanced, which may cause LMHPs to shy away from providing services and Black Americans to be reticent about utilizing mental services. Part of these service inadequacies may be related to LMHPs rarely receiving training specifically relevant to Black Americans' emotional and mental well-being.

Academic, accreditation, and licensing institutions must make a substantial, measurable investment in BPA if we are to move beyond surface need recognitions to counter the anti-Black sentiment and subcompetency ratings of LMHPs. In addition, we need to move from an informal unsystematized teaching platform around the issues of BPA to a highly regulated didactic model of training to push the disparities needle in the mental health sector for Black Americans. Presently, no established standards within the mental health industry or academic education assert actionable steps to counter the shortcomings of assessments and treatment for Black Americans. However, the interface of accreditation inclusions and licensing accommodations for BPA can significantly boost the service competency for Black Americans' mental health status.

These industry changes will be significantly less effective if they take place in isolation. Collective work, an attitude of responsibility, and behavioral responses from all parties involved are needed, including the Black American public as responsible change agents in concert with the BPA movement.

Conclusion

Unfortunately, the clinical principles of training have a propensity to lag the needs of Black patients in the mental health industry. Still, it would be intellectually irresponsible to attribute all of the mental health industry's shortcomings in assessing, diagnosing, and treating Black Americans to antiblackness sentiments. On the other hand, it would be dangerous to pretend that a profoundly impactful amount of the variance in assessment, diagnoses, and treatment is not born out of antiblackness sensibilities. Indeed, the mental health industry's in/outpatient practice habits have become ingrained in its service institutions, especially where Black patients are concerned. Like structural racism, the politics of change in mental health professional training is resistant.

Moreover, the habitual comfort and reliability routine of LMHPs in the mental health industry will remain immutable without meaningful incentives or disincentives. A substantive retooling of part of the LMHP labor force training is not easy, but it is necessary. This is particularly challenging because social work, psychology, psychiatry, and counseling mental health professionals have a self-concept of being separate and unequal, yet they all converge on the notion of healing.

Even if we invoke the tenants of equipotential of each of the disciplines mentioned above to adequately serve Black Americans, reimagining this process will be necessary. BPA is merely the first step of several to move this transformational needle. The Inline figure Black Psychological Allyship and Mental Health Services Retooling Plan provides a top-down approach to remedying the evolution of antiblackness in the mental health industry. The bottom-up portion is for readers and contributors to the field like you to support the BPA plan.

References

DeCarlo, A. C. (2021). *The culture of education and experiential polemics.* AuthorHouse.

Kreyenbuhl, J., Zito, J. M., Buchanan, R. W., Soeken, K. L., & Lehman, A. F. (2003). Racial disparity in the pharmacological management of schizophrenia. *Schizophrenia Bulletin, 29*, 183–194.

Kuno, E., & Rothbard, A. B. (2002). Racial disparities in antipsychotic prescription patterns for patients with schizophrenia. *American Journal of Psychiatry, 159*, 567–572.

Leslie, L. K., Weckerly, J., Landsverk, J., Hough, R. L., Hurlburt, M. S., & Wood, P. A. (2003). Racial/ethnic differences in the use of psychotropic medication in high-risk children and adolescents. *Journal of the American Academy of Child & Adolescent Psychiatry, 42*(12), 1433–1442.

Marrast, L., Himmelstein, D. U., & Woolhandler, S. (2016). Racial and ethnic disparities in mental health care for children and young adults: A national study. *International Journal of Health Services, 46*(4), 810–824.

Marx, A. (2019). *Barriers faced by Black Americans in receiving mental health care.* Families USA. https://familiesusa.org/resources/barriers-faced-by-african-americ ans-in-receiving-mental-health-care/

Merikangas, K. R., He, J. P., Burstein, M., Swendsen, J., Avenevoli, S., Case, B., Georgiades, K., Heaton, L., Swanson, S., & Olfson, M. (2011). Service utilization for lifetime mental disorders in US adolescents: Results of the National Comorbidity Survey–Adolescent Supplement (NCS-A). *Journal of the American Academy of Child & Adolescent Psychiatry, 50*(1), 32–45.

Mizock, L., & Harkins, D. (2011). Diagnostic bias and conduct disorder: Improving culturally sensitive diagnosis. *Child and Youth Services, 32*, 243–253.

Rockett, J. L., Murrie, D. C., & Boccaccini, M. T. (2007). Diagnostic labeling in juvenile justice settings: Do psychopathy and conduct disorder findings influence clinicians? *Psychological Services, 4*(2), 107–122.

Rue, D. S., & Xie, Y. (2009). Disparities in treating culturally diverse children and adolescents. *Psychiatric Clinics of North America, 32*(1), 153–163.

Sadock, B. J., Sadock, V. A., & Ruiz, P. (2017). *Kaplan & Sadock's comprehensive textbook of psychiatry* (2 vols., 10th ed.). Wolters Kluwer Health.

Schwartz, R. C., & Blankenship, D. M. (2014). Racial disparities in psychotic disorder diagnosis: A review of the empirical literature. *World Journal of Psychiatry, 4*(4), 133.

Stith, A. Y., & Nelson, A. R. (2002). *Unequal treatment: Confronting racial and ethnic disparities in health care*. Institute of Medicine.

Substance Abuse and Mental Health Services Administration. (2020). *Behavior health equity*. https://www.samhsa.gov/behavioral-health-equity

U.S. Department of Health and Human Services Office of Minority Mental Health. (2017, September). *Mental health and Black Americans*.

Villatoro, A. P., Mays, V. M., Ponce, N. A., & Aneshensel, C. S. (2018). Perceived need for mental health care: The intersection of race, ethnicity, gender, and socioeconomic status. *Society and Mental Health, 8*(1), 1–24.

22

Environmental Racism in Rural America

Shannon Z. Jones

"America is segregated, and so is pollution," said famed sociologist and environmental activist Dr. Robert Bullard at a historically Black college and university (HBCU) climate change conference. During this session, he reflected on his life's work of highlighting and uncovering systemic oppression in the form of environmental racism. For the last several years, I too have focused my research and teaching on the investigation of environmental injustice across America.

Having access to the natural resources that are necessary to sustain health and livelihood is an essential and basic human right. Yet, certain populations have not been afforded this right for a variety of reasons. Several studies have demonstrated that communities of color and those from lower socioeconomic backgrounds are disproportionately impacted by air and water pollution. A recent study demonstrated that poor people and minoritized people of color are much more likely to live near polluting industries and therefore breathe in more polluted air (Tessum & Marshall, 2021). The study also shows that people in poverty are exposed to more fine particulate matter ($PM_{2.5}$) than people living above poverty. This holds true at the county, state, and national levels. An earlier study from 2016 (Bravo & Miranda, 2016) reported that long-term exposure to particulate matter is associated with racial segregation, with more highly segregated areas suffering higher levels of exposure. All across the country, impoverished communities and communities of color face higher risks for exposure to both air and water pollution. Furthermore, marginalized communities are often excluded from environmental policy decision-making. Since the civil rights movement of the 1960s, the environmental justice movement has been gaining momentum in order to shed light on the environmental inequities faced by communities of color.

I recently developed an interdisciplinary science course at the University of Richmond that provides a safe space for young learners to interrogate and investigate issues relating to environmental justice. In this course, students

Shannon Z. Jones, *Environmental Racism in Rural America* In: *Antiblackness and the Stories of Authentic Allies.*
Edited by: Norman Kim, Carolyn Coker Ross, Mazella Fuller and Charlynn Small, Oxford University Press.
© Oxford University Press 2024. DOI: 10.1093/oso/9780197642535.003.0023

examine the social, political, and economic factors that contribute to this disparity. In addition, we also discuss the biological impact that pollution has on the health of exposed populations. Our essential question is this: How is it that certain groups of people do not have access to basic natural resources or are systematically burdened with pollution or environmental hazards to a greater extent than other groups? To say that this teaching experience has been transformative and enlightening is an understatement. Not only have I benefited from my students' perspectives, but also teaching this course has provided me with ample opportunities to reflect on my own personal investment in the topic of environmental racism.

Superfund Sites Near Marginalized Communities

Since the 1980s, the Environmental Protection Agency (EPA) has been tasked with protecting human health and the health of the environment by organizing and managing the cleanup of our country's most hazardous waste sites. In the late 1970s, the health impacts of toxic waste sites were gaining national attention. In response, Congress established the Comprehensive Environmental Response, Compensation, and Liability Act (CERCLA). CERCLA is informally known as the Superfund taskforce and was created for the purpose of cleaning up contaminated sites across the United States. This legislation holds the responsible parties accountable by forcing them to either perform the cleanup themselves or reimburse the EPA for the costs of cleanup. CERCLA has also provided temporary emergency federal funding for toxic waste cleanup if responsible parties can't be found or are unable to cover the costs.

Since the formation of the Superfund, hundreds of toxic waste sites have been identified all across the country, and a significant amount of these sites have been successfully remediated. As of 2022, there were 1,329 Superfund sites on the National Priorities List (NPL) in the United States. Approximately 452 of these sites have been remediated, or cleaned up and removed from the list. Unfortunately, African Americans are more likely to live in or near a Superfund site. Black Americans are 75% more likely to live near waste-producing facilities, or within fence-line communities, when compared to the average American (Bullard, 1994). Furthermore, 70% of the Superfund sites in the United States that are listed on the NPL are located within a mile of government-assisted housing (Shriver Center on Poverty Law, 2020). In each of my undergraduate toxicology courses, I ask my students to investigate whether their hometown is located near or on a Superfund site. They are often surprised to learn about the close proximity of these sites. I experienced a similar feeling years ago, when I learned that I grew up near a Superfund site.

Humble Beginnings and Early Pursuits of Knowledge

People often ask me why/how I became involved in the field of toxicology and environmental justice, and I often reply that it's because of my lived experience. I grew up in Roper, North Carolina, a small, rural, and predominantly African American community in the most northeastern corner of the state. Roper is located in Washington County, North Carolina, where almost 48% of the population is African American and 25% of the residents live below poverty level (based on the most recent census data). I have the most vivid, wonderful memories of growing up in those quiet woods. I was raised in a very close-knit family and in a household full of love. It never occurred to me that my family or any of the surrounding families were lacking financial resources and also facing systemic oppression. It always seemed that we had what we needed. After all, I hail from a family of proud and independent Black women who provided for their families without complaint.

It wasn't until I left home for college, and especially while in graduate school, that I realized the great divide between the haves and the have-nots. While I was coming of age and while my education and knowledge of the world were expanding, I became acutely aware of the gross inequities that are faced by African Americans in the rural South. One of the most important motivating factors in my decision to study toxicology in graduate school was my interest in understanding how exposure to toxic chemicals can ultimately impact one's health. My family has been riddled with chronic health issues for as long as I can remember, and I've always been curious as to whether this was due to exposure to some unknown toxicant.

After I gained expertise in toxicology, it became especially clear that there are significant disparities related to pollution exposure in poor and/or Black and Brown communities. These knowledge gains continue to fuel my passion for spreading awareness about issues of environmental racism and injustice.

My Family's Experience With Environmental Justice

I grew up as part of a very large extended family. My fondest memories include sitting around the dinner table at my grandmother's house with my brother and my mom, her eight siblings, and a host of cousins. I listened eagerly as my mom and her siblings discussed what it was like for them to grow up in Roper. My grandfather raised chickens and had a small garden. This was the primary source of food for the family. With nine children in rural North Carolina, financial resources were scarce. So, my mom's family truly lived off of the land. Because they were located in such a remote part of the county, my family did not have access to treated water. Instead, they relied on groundwater from a well. This well water was used not only for bathing but also for cooking, cleaning, and watering the garden.

During my graduate studies, I learned that groundwater from a well is often contaminated with many toxicants that can impact human health. With no means to test for toxic contaminants, my family, as well as other families nearby, was especially at risk for exposure to many water pollutants including heavy metals, infectious microorganisms, nitrates, fluoride, and other organic waste material. Today, my mom and her siblings all suffer from chronic health conditions. My mom has chronic joint pain, and her siblings suffer from metabolic disorders, autoimmune diseases, and even cancer. Some of these conditions may be related to other lifestyle factors, but I can't help but wonder how much of their health issues stem from repeated exposure to chemicals contaminating the groundwater. I can see that suffering from chronic physical illnesses for an extended length of time has also taken its toll on the mental health of my family members.

Although the water was never formally tested by the county, we eventually purchased an in-home extensive water testing kit. Results from this Tap Score™ analysis revealed excessive levels of lead, aluminum, and other heavy metals. Today, my family only uses the tap water for bathing.

In addition to potential chemical exposures at home, many of my family members were also at risk for occupational exposure to hazardous chemicals. Whereas my mom and her sisters continued their education after high school thanks to a nearby HBCU (Elizabeth City State University), my uncles decided to enter the workforce immediately after high school. Four of my five uncles began working at the local paper mill and manufacturing facility. At the time, this was considered a great achievement that would lead to great financial gains. Working at the paper mill turned out to be one of the most lucrative jobs in Washington county. Although none of my uncles were able to receive a college education, they were able to earn a higher than average salary to support their own families until retirement. Most would say that my uncles were lucky to achieve such financial success. But no one ever really considered the ultimate cost: years of chronic exposure to hazardous chemicals and its toll on human health (both physical and mental).

The Kieckhefer-Eddy Company began operating this paper mill and a paper products manufacturing facility in Washington County in 1937. The Weyerhaeuser Company would later manage the mill from 1957 to 2007. Currently, Domtar Corporation owns and operates the facility. For as long as I can remember, the operation of the mill has been associated with an awful stench that permeates throughout the county. When traveling back home to visit family, I could always tell when I was nearing my hometown, based on the distinct odor that I could smell when crossing over the county line. When others (usually those from out of town) would comment on the awful stench, people that worked at the mill (including my uncles) would often reply, "Oh, that's the smell of money." At the time, I never considered the significance of this odor and the potential chemical hazards posed by the operation of the paper mill.

Occupational health and safety has always been a central part of the environmental justice movement. In fact, the earliest public protests for environmental justice in the United States were on behalf of Black sanitation workers in Memphis, Tennessee, who were facing deplorable work conditions with very little pay. The death of two of the workers (African American men) prompted peaceful protests led by Reverend Dr. Martin Luther King Jr. The toxic properties and health effects of many environmental pollutants were originally identified in workplace settings, where workers were repeatedly exposed to high doses of such contaminants. One of the most famous and devastating examples of this is illustrated by the high incidence of oral cancers in the "radium girls," the women who worked with radium-containing paint at Timex watch factories in the 1920s.

Superfund Site in Washington County, North Carolina

Unbeknownst to local community members, waste from the paper mill in Washington County had been discharging into the nearby Roanoke River since 1937. Residents of Washington County were promised jobs and prosperity with the opening of the paper mill. They were never informed of the hazards that would be associated with its operation. Investigations by the EPA in the 1990s found that the paper mill's waste disposal practices had contaminated groundwater, sediment, soil, surface water, and fish in the Roanoke River. The river had been polluted with wastes from the site that contained toxicants such as dioxins, organic solvents, and the heavy metal mercury (EPA, n.d.). Many of these chemicals are known carcinogens. There is no safe level of exposure to dioxin or heavy metals. In 1990, the state imposed a fish advisory for fish consumption because of the dangers of dioxin and mercury, which both tend to bioaccumulate in water-dwelling organisms. In other words, high levels of both dioxin and mercury can accumulate in the tissue of living organisms, especially fish. Consuming fish from these waters would expose residents to very high levels of this dangerous poison. This fish consumption advisory would later be extended to include the Albemarle Sound in 1990. My family's home is located no farther than five miles from the sound. For reasons that weren't explicitly stated, the EPA did not list the site on the NPL but considers it an NPL-caliber site.

Although the paper mill was identified as a Superfund-level site over 30 years ago, my family and other residents had never been informed of the high levels of pollution. I was quite shocked to learn about the Superfund site during my studies in graduate school in 2016, approximately 20 years after the contamination was uncovered. I would never have guessed that there would be a Superfund site in my own backyard. After sharing this information with my mother and the rest of my family, I received mostly looks of shock and disbelief. It was clear that they felt betrayed by the town's governance as well as the operators of the paper mill. My uncles had a much more conflicted response. They had worked at the mill an average of 45 years. They'd spent more than half of their lifetime in paper and pulp mills. Upon retiring, they were enjoying a comfortable retirement thanks to the paper mill. Although they are grateful for the financial stability provided to them by their jobs, they were also quite troubled to learn about the environmental damage and pollution caused by the operation of the facility. They also began to consider what other harm may have been inflicted by working at the mill for 45 years.

Several men who worked at the paper mill received compensation from the Weyerhaeuser company for asbestos exposure and increased risks for mesothelioma. My grandmother's neighbor of many years died of mesothelioma. He worked at the paper mill for most of his life. When my uncles first began working at the mill, ear protection was not provided as part of their personal protective equipment. According to my uncles, many of the men working at the mill were operating loud, heavy machinery (like jackhammers) with only paper towels to stuff into their ears. Many of my uncles now suffer from significant hearing loss due to the operation of the loud machinery during paper manufacturing. The paper mill has since agreed to a financial settlement for this as well.

I also learned from my uncles that many of the men who worked at the mill could barely read or write. Therefore, it is unlikely that they truly understood the safety risks they faced while working at the mill. The psychological toll of this experience is incalculable. There is now a great sense of mistrust of the town governance by many members of the community. There is also a great sense of betrayal, hopelessness, and abandonment. In addition to increased risk for disease, many of the employees of the paper mill also missed out on time with their loved ones due to the inflexible, 12-hour work shifts to which they were subjected. My uncles also share that they regret missing so many memorable moments with their families because of their work schedules. To this day, they often comment on the tremendous amount of loss they feel. As they continue to age, their concerns about their health and the health of their families continue to grow. In addition to their own health issues, their spouses also suffer from significant chronic health issues as well. The story of pollution in Washington County is, unfortunately, not unique. The feelings of my family greatly mirror the emotions felt by members of fence-line communities all over the nation.

The Dangers of Dioxin

Dioxin is the most common contaminant found in the Roanoke River and in the Albemarle Sound of Washington County. Dioxin belongs to a category of toxicants referred to as persistent organic pollutants or "forever chemicals." It is formed as an unintentional byproduct of many industrial processes such as waste incineration, chemical and pesticide manufacturing, and pulp and paper bleaching (Kurwadkar et al., 2020). Dioxin was a toxic component of Agent Orange, and it was also found at the Love Canal Superfund site in Niagara Falls, New York. Severe dioxin pollution was also responsible for mandatory evacuations in Times Beach, Missouri (Little, 2022), as well as Seveso, Italy (Eskenazi et al., 2018).

Because it is a "forever chemical," dioxin does not break down easily in the environment. Instead, it bioaccumulates. Over time, continual low-level exposures will "build up" until subtle adverse health effects start to occur. Dioxin is highly lipophilic (or fat-loving) and accumulates in the fatty tissues of the human body. Therefore, once a person has been exposed, dioxin can persist in the body for a very long time.

Because it is a common byproduct of manufacturing, dioxin can easily contaminate our water supply. Humans usually come into contact with dioxin through direction ingestion. Over 90% of human exposure to dioxin occurs through food products, primarily meat and dairy products, fish, and shellfish. For this reason, dioxin exposure in the general population is practically inevitable.

Dioxin is a known human carcinogen and can also have other devastating effects on human health. In addition to causing cancer, exposure to dioxin can lead to severe reproductive and developmental abnormalities (at levels 100 times lower than those that are associated with its cancer-causing effects). It is also well known for its ability to damage the immune and endocrine systems. Dioxin exposure has been linked to a variety of pathologies including birth defects, spontaneous abortion (miscarriage), decreased fertility in men and women, endometriosis, diabetes, learning disabilities, immune system suppression, lung and skin disorders, and lowered testosterone levels (Kurwadkar et al., 2020).

After learning so much about dioxin in my graduate studies, and to later learn that my family and other members of my community were unknowingly exposed to this dangerous chemical, I was overwhelmed and saddened to say the least. I'm sure these feelings are similar to those experienced by marginalized communities all across the United States living in or near Superfund sites. The psychological toll of those living in or near Superfund sites must be considered.

The Long Road to Justice

The environmental justice movement grew out of the fight for civil rights in the 1960s. Led almost exclusively by African Americans, Latinx individuals, Native Americans, and Asians and Pacific Islanders, this movement continues to address the disturbing fact that the people who live, work, and play in America's most polluted environments are likely to be poor people of color.

Reverend Benjamin Chavis coined the term "environmental racism" in 1982 in response to the poly-chlorintated biphenyl (PCB) landfill siting in Warren County, North Carolina. PCBs are another of example of extremely toxic forever chemicals. Chavis referred to environmental racism as discrimination in environmental policymaking. Since then, the environmental justice movement has gained significant momentum. Today activists across the county (and the world) continue to spread awareness of environmental justice and advocate for changes in environmental policies that would lead to a more just society.

I am incredibly inspired by the activists who have devoted their life and livelihood to the pursuit of a more just society with regard to environmental pollution. Initially, it seemed as if the voices of those impacted by environmental justice were unheard. Protest after protest was often followed by inaction at the local, state, and federal levels. After watching several documentaries about environmental justice, it's easy to see the despair and hopelessness felt by marginalized communities. But recent national events inspire hope that the tide is turning.

For the first time in U.S. history, the federal government, led by the Biden administration, has set a goal that 40% of the overall benefits of some federal investments be received by communities that are underserved and overburdened by pollution. Some examples of these investments include climate change, clean energy and energy efficiency, clean transit, affordable housing, workforce development, and the development of clean water and wastewater infrastructure.

This historic piece of legislation, known as the Justice40 initiative, was put into action when President Biden signed Executive Order 14008 within just days of taking office (White House, 2022). It remains to be seen whether this legislation will provide the impacted communities with the support they so desperately need. But for now, the future looks brighter.

References

Bravo, M., Anthopolos, R., Bell, M., & Miranda, M. (2016). Racial isolation and exposure to airborne particulate matter and ozone in understudied US populations: Environmental justice applications of downscaled numerical model output. *Environment International*, *92–93*, 247–255. https://doi.org/10.1016/j.envint.2016.04.008

Bullard, R. D. (1994). *Dumping in Dixie: Race, class, and environmental quality.* Westview Press

Environmental Protection Agency (EPA). (n.d.). *Superfund site: WEYERHAEUSER CO PLYMOUTH WOOD TRTNG PT PLYMOUTH, NC.* https://cumulis.epa.gov/superc pad/SiteProfiles/index.cfm?fuseaction=second.contams&id=0403156

Eskenazi, B., Warner, M., Brambilla, P., Signorini, S. Ames, J., & Mocarelli, P. (2018). The Seveso accident: A look at 40 years of health research and beyond. *Environment International, 121*(Pt 1), 71–84. https://doi.org/10.1016/j.envint.2018.08.051

Kurwadkar, S., Mandal, P., & Soni, S. (2020). *Dioxin: Environmental fate and health/ecological consequences.* CRC Press.

Little, J. (2022). *A town, a flood, and Superfund: Looking back at the Times Beach disaster nearly 40 years later.* U.S. Environmental Protection Agency. https://www.epa.gov/mo/ town-flood-and-superfund-looking-back-times-beach-disaster-nearly-40-years-later

Shriver Center on Poverty Law. (2020). *Poisonous homes: The fight for environmental justice in federally assisted housing.* https://www.povertylaw.org/wp-content/uploads/ 2020/06/environmental_justice_report_final-rev2.pdf

Tessum, C., Paolella, D., Chambliss, S., Apte, J., Hill, J., & Marshall. J. PM$_{2.5}$ polluters disproportionately and systemically affect people of color in the United States. *Science Advances, 7*(18). eabf4491 (2021) https://doi.org/10.1126/sciadv.abf4491

White House. (n.d.). *Justice40: A whole-of-government initiative.* https://www.whiteho use.gov/environmentaljustice/justice40/

U.S. Census Bureau. (n.d.). *QuickFacts: Washington County, North Carolina.* https://www. census.gov/quickfacts/fact/table/washingtoncountynorthcarolina/PST045221

23

Making Space When Black Voices Speak Their Truth

Camilla W. Nonterah

Black voices have been fighting to be heard for centuries. America's history is saturated with examples of people of African descent fighting for equal rights to extinguish the identity of second- or third-class citizenship.

The racial pandemic in America was at center stage during the death of George Floyd at the hands of Derek Chauvin. The video footage and pictures of this incident gave credence to Black voices who have been emphasizing the unfair treatment of people who identify as Black or African American (B/AA),[1] especially at the hands of the police, for numerous years.

The COVID-19 pandemic allowed for a pause, which resulted in White America having to face the reality of racism via police brutality, as it was documented on the news and numerous media outlets. This resulted in demonstrations all over the United States as well as internationally. Black Lives Matter (BLM) signs and posters were everywhere, with companies and organizations making statements to demonstrate their support.

Some of these acts seemed genuine, whereas others appeared to be perfunctory, seemingly a product of virtue signaling. For example, many tech companies who wrote pledges associated with BLM had 20% fewer employees who identified as B/AA relative to those who did not (Heut & Toulon, 2021).

A renewed dedication to fighting against racial injustice was evidenced by the increase in education on White privilege, institutionalized and structural racism, and microaggressions, among others. Conversations about racial injustice were being held at the individual level, on the campuses of different

---

[1] In this chapter, I use the term "Black/African American (B/AA)" to account for people of African descent from different parts of the diaspora such as Continental Africa, Northern America, South America, and the Caribbean, given the similarities of their social identity, regardless of their ethnic background or country of origin.

Camilla W. Nonterah, *Making Space When Black Voices Speak Their Truth* In: *Antiblackness and the Stories of Authentic Allies*. Edited by: Norman Kim, Carolyn Coker Ross, Mazella Fuller and Charlynn Small, Oxford University Press.
© Oxford University Press 2024. DOI: 10.1093/oso/9780197642535.003.0024

organizations, with discussions about what it means to be an ally or accomplice and how to be antiracist.

A Forbes article reported a 2,000% growth in the sales of antiracism books after the BLM protests, with critics expressing skepticism given that these acts do not necessarily translate into actual systemic change (McEvoy, 2020). From a health perspective, organizations such as the American Public Health Association (APHA) and the American Psychological Association (APA) released statements about the impact of racism on mental and physiological health outcomes (APA, 2020; APHA, 2020).

Visions of hordes of people from numerous racial and ethnic backgrounds fighting for Black lives during the protests and the increase in dedication to anti-Black racism may have evoked emotions of hope and solidarity for many people. Nevertheless, B/AAs, other people of color (POC), and White accomplices with a thorough understanding of the different forms of racism—from apparent or deemed unacceptable, such as the murder of B/AAs by White nationalists, to systemic, such as redlining and mass incarceration—acknowledge the depth of the work that remains to be completed to achieve true equality for Black lives.

The insidious systemic forms of racism contribute significantly to the mental and physical health disparities between B/AAs and White individuals (C. P. Jones, 2000; NeMoyer et al., 2019). As a counseling psychologist whose research and pedagogy focus on behavioral medicine and understanding the effects of social determinants of health (e.g., the ways in which factors such as a person's social and occupational environments, region of birth, and income influence their health), I have a heightened level of awareness of how different forms of racism impact the health outcomes of B/AAs as well as people from other minoritized racial groups.

Moreover, intersections of other forms of minoritized statuses—such as one's gender identity, sexuality, and disability status—as a result of sexism, homophobia, and ableism may magnify or produce a novel experience, which could result in additional inequities.

Racism's Effect on Black Lives

Historical hurts have contributed to and continue to generate many of the health inequities that are apparent today. Health disparities between people of African descent and their European counterparts have been documented for centuries in the areas of maternal health and chronic conditions such as diabetes, hypertension, and kidney disease (Braverman et al., 2011). Many of these disparities were previously attributed to racial differences, without accounting for the effects of different forms of racism, such as *personally mediated* racism (e.g., discrimination and microaggressions) and *institutionalized racism* (e.g., practices and regulations that produce unequal access to opportunities based on one's phenotype), that produce race-related stress (C. P. Jones, 2000). *The Bell Curve*, published almost three decades ago, claimed B/AAs were of genetically lower intelligence, indicating any interventional work to improve outcomes for B/AAs would be futile (DeFreitas, 2020).

Certain pioneers in the field of psychology perpetuated the ideology of phenotypical racial differences, with former president of the APA, Henry Garett, reporting support for racial segregation based on the belief in the diminished complexity and size of a Black man's brain (Guthrie, 1998). In fact, in October 2021, the APA issued an apology for the organization's role in contributing to racial inequities. These are just a few of numerous cases of how perceived inherent racial differences have been used to justify differential treatment of B/AAs and other POC from Whites, resulting in severe health repercussions.

Social determinants of health have only gained recognition over the last few decades, causing scientists to engage in critical assessments of the ways neighborhood conditions, education, income, and residential segregation systematically disenfranchise Black lives in the United States. Despite being armed with this knowledge, many psychologists and scientists in the field of medicine and public health continue to operate and conduct research using European samples as the "standard," with viewpoints that are heavily skewed toward Eurocentric values and epistemologies, while the values of POC are relegated to a diversity and inclusion category.

Much of the psychological literature and theories established over multiple decades are saturated with Western, educated, industrialized, rich, democratic (WEIRD) samples that center individualism (DeFreitas, 2020), even though POC make up the global majority. Our current practice of science is analogous to cooking, in which one prepares the main meal (everything Eurocentric) and then adds spices (the experiences of POC) for additional flavor. It is unsurprising that many POC and especially B/AAs are on the receiving end of significant disenfranchisements, given that their experiences and cultural practices (e.g., collectivism) are not studied from a vantage point.

Researchers have established connections between racism experienced from one's social environment and physiological changes, such as the activation of the amygdala and increases in the stress hormone cortisol, resulting in poor physical and psychological health (S. C. T. Jones & Neblett, 2019; Raque et al., 2021). Countless implications of racism on Black lives and their well-being underscore the significance of people of African descent being able to use their voices, especially when they are in predominately White settings, where their experiences are rarely viewed as valid or central. This is magnified by the fact that many B/AAs must undergo a lot of thought processes and personal dialogues about whether and when to use their Black voice.

The Complexity of Using Your Black Voice

Given the history of the United States, B/AAs have learned that using their voices comes with a range of responses. Even the successful demonstrate that using one's minoritized voice has consequences. Although Martin Luther King Jr. has been heralded in mainstream media as being the prime illustration of a template for fighting for civil rights, many people fail to acknowledge that despite his use of peaceful protests and other strategies, he was assassinated. Moreover, he was perceived as radical by many during his time.

There are numerous examples of other Black leaders, such as Ella Baker, John Lewis, and Rosa Parks, who were "punished" in some form (e.g., experienced psychological distress, life endangerment, were imprisoned) for being on the right side of history. With these famous examples in mind, we are left to imagine the magnitude of B/AAs who tried to use their voices for change without the same level of authority, power, and/or status.

B/AAs who navigate predominately White spaces (PWSs) have a keen understanding of the advantages and disadvantages of using their voice. A shared awareness exists among many B/AAs that one must be cognizant of the tone of their voice and demeaner. A simple display of one's passion may be perceived as "threatening" and "aggressive," although anger, particularly about injustice, is well justified. Black women, having to manage the intersections of racism and sexism, are especially cognizant that being labeled "an angry Black woman" is somewhat of a death sentence, especially when that anger results in a White woman crying.

We have all been primed and programmed to care for White women and their discomfort via *cultural racism*, a term used by James Jones in 1997 to explain the manner in which Eurocentric values and viewpoints are viewed as superior to other ethnic values, such as Afrocentrism, Asian, or Indigenous American culture. Cultural racism is represented in media and imagery that sustains stereotypes (S. C. T. Jones & Neblett, 2019).

When most of us think of an angel or princess, we are more likely to think of White women because we have been primed to do so, in part because most of us grew up watching Disney princesses with long blond hair and pale skin. It is no wonder that even POC are prone to subconsciously protect a White woman over her Black counterpart. When I reflect on some of my personal experiences, I recognize moments in which I was susceptible to this myself, even though I am a Black woman.

One depiction of the centering of whiteness in popular media was an encounter between Sheryl Underwood and Sharon Osbourne on the television show *The Talk* in March 2021. Osbourne became defensive as she challenged the notion that her friend, Piers Morgan, was racist based on his comments about Megan Markle. Osbourne reprimanded Underwood, telling her not to cry because she (Osbourne) should be crying and demanded that Underwood educate her about racism. Throughout the entire encounter, Underwood and Welteroth, both Black women on the show, remained calm although they were talked over and undermined. These women's cognizance of perpetuating the stereotype of an "angry Black women" resulted in the use of vital emotion regulation strategies in that moment. Osbourne, a woman of significant socioeconomic status and White privilege, was completely unaware of the depths of her problematic behavior, partly because she is used to being centered in most of her social experiences. This example illustrates a common experience among B/AAs who exist in PWSs.

Recognizing potential ramifications of standing up to injustice, B/AAs consistently engage in personal negotiations about which battles to fight when they experience an injustice or witness inequitable practices. Some become comfortable with being labeled the "troublemaker" and as a result may be shunned by their peers and colleagues, including other POC. The "diplomats" learn the politics of the organization and may use strategic approaches to delicately address the issues they face, accepting that they may have turned a blind eye to one issue to preserve their energy for another issue of greater importance. The "fatalists" become numb to injustices because they have been silenced in their past; they avoid using their voices because they do not believe it will make a difference. Notably, there is a category of B/AAs I refer to as "yielders," who ascribe to antiblackness and seek to maintain the status quo.

In listing these different protypes, I seek to draw attention to the multifaceted ways in which B/AAs make negotiations about when and whether to use their voice while acknowledging that there are pros and cons to each prototype. These consequences range from disruptions to one's mental and physical health as well as occupational status. B/AAs with *internalized racism*, a form of racism that causes a Black person to devalue their blackness and internalize stereotypes and negative messages about their abilities and others who look like them (C. P. Jones, 2000), have been reported to experience more psychological symptoms and depleted levels of self-esteem (Belgrave & Allison, 2019).

In contrast, Black people who are comfortable with their racial/ethnic identity are more likely to experience positive mental health outcomes (Belgrave & Allison, 2019). Yet, a person with a positive view of their Black identity could be susceptible to negative occupational consequences (e.g., reduced compensation and promotion) in their efforts to speak against the status quo in PWSs, despite civil right protections.

The Weaponization of Black Courage

Fear of retaliation often comes with challenging any status quo. This retaliation could range from fear of being ostracized to losing a relationship and/or the stability of one's employment. A prime example is the case of Nikole Hannah-Jones, decorated journalist, Pulitzer Prize winner, and creator of the 1619 Project. Hannah-Jones was appointed as a Knight Chair in Race and Investigative Journalism and was supposed to join the University of North Carolina (UNC) as a tenured professor in fall 2021. Instead, she was offered a 5-year teaching contract by the board of trustees. This teaching contract came with the option for future review of her tenure case, in spite of unanimous recommendations for tenure from her department and the university tenure committee.

Pressure from conservative groups expressing concerns about the nature of her work, namely, her work on the 1619 Project, highlighting how slavery was used to fund the American Revolution, was allegedly the catalyst for Hannah-Jones's tenure denial, although the UNC board of trustees originally attributed their denial to her being a professional rather than a career professor. This made Hannah-Jones the first person in the position of the Knight Chair to not be offered tenure, although other predecessors with professional journalism backgrounds were offered tenure.

Ultimately, UNC reversed its decision after pushback from the UNC faculty, staff, and students and prominent critics, protests, and lawsuits (Folkenflik, 2021). Her case is indicative of how Black courage can be weaponized. All over the United States, race scholars and those whose research focuses on centering the experiences of POC, thereby challenging the status quo, are faced with minor to significant complexities, including criticisms about researching topics that emphasize the study of "self," teaching evaluations that state that the professor "talks too much about race," reviewers criticizing a researcher of color's work because it deviates from the "norm," and cyber harassment.

Black courage can also be weaponized in interpersonal relationships, in seemingly innocuous ways. Most of us seek to protect our interpersonal relationships. In doing so, we may avoid conflicts or ignore and/or provide explanations for a friend's behavior to maintain the harmony of that relationship. In an interracial friendship dynamic, particularly between a B/AA individual and their White counterpoint, observations of antiblackness or racism can be particularly difficult to navigate, especially when revealed after a deeper bond has been established.

B/AAs with a thorough understanding of racism recognize that racism can present in myriad forms. For the most part, POC do not inherently expect perfection but rather dedication to antiracism, especially when confronted about one's unconscious behaviors that perpetuate racism. A personal experience is when I observed a range of behaviors from a friend with whom I had established a strong bond. I viewed this friend and her partner as my family due to years of support and dedication to our friendship. This friend expanded my knowledge of certain issues pertaining to the LGBTQ+ community and women.

Yet, I had observed incidents that made me question the depth of her understanding of what it meant to be antiracist. I did not always have the terminology to describe or process incidents that stirred up some discomfort within me. I finally addressed my concerns with her because I perceived our friendship as having built enough security to withstand honest, authentic, and vulnerable conversations. Unfortunately, this resulted in a domino effect in which my Black courage became the catalyst for the demise of our friendship because she concluded that I perceived her and her partner as "racists." Hence, there was nothing she could do about that.

I came to realize that, like many White people, her fear of being perceived as "racist" was far worse than challenging any internalized racism she may possess. All I wanted was for her to confront the imbedded racist ideologies within her so that I could continue to feel safe and secure within our friendship. Motivated by the 2020 BLM protests, I wrote a letter, entitled "A Love Letter to My White Friend," which I shared with her and others. Here are some excerpts from the letter:

> I never expected you to be perfect. After all, we are all a part of this messed up system that is inherently racist. I do have to share some of my most vulnerable thoughts and feelings.
>
> I do know that I need a type of radical love from you. . .
>
> I need you to love me enough to hear me and engage with me when I talk about racism.
>
> I need you to love me enough not to be complacent about racism even if it is deep within you.
>
> I need you to love me enough to be uncomfortable because you understand that my humanity is more important than your discomfort.
>
> I need you to love me enough to do your antiracist work so that I can feel safe in your presence because I do not feel safe in the world most of the time.
>
> I need you to love me enough to fight for racial justice with the same passion as you fight for LGBTQ+ and women's rights.
>
> I need you to love me enough to disrupt the status quo at your job because you value my humanity.
>
> I need you to love me enough to stand against the racism you see in your family and friends.
>
> I need you to love me enough to weather my anger about the racial injustice I experience because you will never understand what it is like to be me.
>
> I need you to love me enough to see that underneath that anger lies deep hurt and pain so I need the type of love from a friend who will protect my Black body.
>
> Know that I love you enough to forgive you when you get it wrong because I see you working hard to get it right. However, I cannot exist in a space that invalidates my Blackness because that is my gift of radical love that I need to give myself.

How to Truly Create a Space for Black Voices

Without recognizing this, White people who perceive themselves to be allies or accomplices in the fight against antiblackness can engage in problematic behaviors that reinforce them being the focal point. This was evident in the BLM protests in which some self-proclaimed allies became the faces of the movement or the loudest voices, instead of centering the needs of Black protestors. Other examples include "White allies" who have not yet developed a thorough understanding of the numerous ways in which antiblackness is apparent in areas such as their rhetoric, policies they support, their history of interpersonal relationships, and behaviors in the workplace yet make declarations about their commitment to anti-Black racism and proceed to take the "proverbial mic" away from Black voices.

To become a true ally or accomplice, one must first recognize that they cannot achieve this goal by taking up space. *Authentic allyship* includes leading with a significant amount of humility, and always being open to constructive criticism and feedback, while acknowledging one's privilege and power. It is important to emphasize that Black people and other POC are the ones who get to determine whether someone is truly an ally. A White ally can only be authentic when they are driven by a deep desire for a just world and radical love for humanity rather than seeking approval from others.

Much of our global history is Eurocentric, such as the perceived superiority of the English language and the prioritization of White Anglo-Saxon Protestant values in the United States. White accomplices who are used to being at the forefront of everything may take away from the same voices they seek to elevate without realizing it. White guilt about racism, for instance, shifts the focus away from Black voices.

As a psychologist, I recognize that feelings of guilt and sadness are a normal part of the human experience. Nonetheless, it is imperative that a White ally engages in important emotion regulation skills to avoid taking away space from a Black voice. Examples include crying about a racist event or act, especially to the point where the Black person sharing their experience stops talking because you are inconsolable, or relating a Black person's experience of antiblackness to a personal experience that is incomparable.

Being antiracist is not simply about being a good person—good people can engage in behaviors that promote antiblackness. To be an authentic accomplice, an individual must be prepared to do the work and recognize that this work would likely occur over the course of a lifetime. To make space for Black voices, one must "walk before you run," spend more time listening and learning and less time talking, and avoid the complex of being a "White savior."

Black people are the experts of their experience and have been navigating antiblackness and racism for centuries. Thus, they should be heard when they use their voices. Many Black authors have expended time, knowledge, and emotional labor to provide pedagogy on anti-Black racism as well as provide solutions. In making space for Black voices, prioritization of the scholarly work of Black authors is key because of their scholastic abilities and personal expertise. Antiracism training developed by Black experts, and those developed by White accomplices vetted by Black antiracist experts, facilitate the elevation of Black voices.

In positions of power, a White accomplice can create spaces for Black voices by using their voices to advocate. Bell and colleagues (2021) provide a list of examples within academia, such as advocating for appropriate compensation, mentorship, and protecting Black faculty from engaging in excessive service because they are the only POC in a specific department.

Advocating for the well-being of Black students includes creating safe spaces for expressing their opinions without repercussions, including physical spaces representative of their culture and the achievements of people who look like them. Of note, Black people in PWSs are burdened with the task of having to "speak for all Black people." This is taxing and perpetuates the notion that Black people are monolithic. Thus, an authentic ally should not wait for the only Black person to bring up an issue related to diversity.

Creating a space for Black voices also entails rest and self-care. Navigating race-related stress is exhausting. B/AAs cannot continue to use their voices when they are burned out. Allies can support Black voices by enabling environments that offer periods of recuperation. This could include ethnically affirming therapeutic services and time off from engaging in antiracist or diversity initiatives.

References

American Psychological Association (APA). (2020, May 29). *We are living in a racism pandemic, says APA president.* https://www.apa.org/news/press/releases/2020/05/racism-pandemic

American Public Health Association (APHA). (2020, October 24). *Structural racism is a public health crisis: Impact on the Black community.* https://www.apha.org/policies-and-advocacy/public-health-policy-statements/policy-database/2021/01/13/structural-racism-is-a-public-health-crisis

Belgrave, F. Z., & Allison, K. W. (2019). *African American psychology from Africa to America* (4th ed.). Sage Publications.

Bell, M. P., Berry, D., Leopold, J., & Nkomo, S. (2021). Making Black Lives Matter in academia: A Black feminist call for collective action against anti-blackness in the academy. *Gender Work Organ, 28*(S1), 39–57. https://doi.org//10.1111/gwao.12555

Braverman, P., Egerter, S., & Williams, D. R. (2011). The social determinants of health: Coming of age. *Annual Review of Public Health, 32,* 381–398.

DeFreitas, S. C. (2020). *African American Psychology: A positive psychology perspective.* Springer Publication Company.

Folkenflik, D. (2021, June 30). *After contentious debate, UNC grants tenure to Nikole Hannah-Jones.* NPR. https://www.npr.org/2021/06/30/1011880598/after-contentious-debate-unc-grants-tenure-to-nikole-hannah-jones

Guthrie, R. V. (1998). *Even the rat was white: A historical view of psychology* (2nd ed.). Allyn & Bacon.

Heut, E., & Toulon, K. (2021, May 17). *Tech companies that made #BlackLivesMatter pledges have fewer Black employees.* Blomberg News. https://www.bloomberg.com/news/articles/2021-05-17/blm-pledges-came-from-companies-with-fewer-black-employees

Jones, C. P. (2000). Levels of racism: A theoretic framework and a gardener's tale. *American Journal of Public Health, 90*(8), 1212–1215.

Jones, S. C. T., & Neblett, E. W., Jr. (2019). The impact of racism on the mental health of people of color. In M. T. Williams, D. C. Rosen, & J. W. Kanter (Eds.), *Eliminating race-based mental health disparities: Promoting equity and culturally responsive care across settings* (pp. 76–98). Context Press.

McEvoy, J. (2020, July 22). *Sales of "White Fragility"—and other anti-racism books—jumped over 2000% after protests began.* Forbes. https://www.forbes.com/sites/jemimamcevoy/2020/07/22/sales-of-white-fragility-and-other-anti-racism-books-jumped-over-2000-after-protests-began/?sh=4afc6c9f303d

NeMoyer, A., Alavarez, K., & Alegría, M. (2019). Understanding mental health disparities. In M. T. Williams, D. C. Rosen, & J. W. Kanter (Eds.), *Eliminating race-based mental health disparities* (pp. 9–26). Context Press.

Raque, T. L., Mitchell, A. M., Coleman, M. N., Coleman, J. J., & Owen, J. (2021). Addressing racial equity in health psychology research: An application of the Multicultural Orientation Framework. *American Psychologist, 76*(8), 1266–1279. https://doi.org/10.1037/amp0000888

24

Racial Disparities Within Black Maternal Health

Ashanda Saint Jean

Racial disparities in health care delivery have affected both a patient's experience and outcome. In maternal health, racial disparities tell a tale of health inequity and systemic racism for Black birthing people.

The Institute of Medicine defines disparities as racial or ethnic differences in the quality of health care that are not due to access-related factors or clinical needs, preferences, and appropriateness of intervention (American College of Physicians, 2010). The staggering statistics of racial disparities during the birthing experience for Black people have come to the forefront and been labeled a public health priority. The American Public Health Association has diagnosed this a public health crisis, and the Centers for Disease Control and Prevention (CDC) has acknowledged racism to be a "fundamental driver of health disparities."

Black birthing people are three to four times more likely to die in childbirth than their White counterparts in the United States. In New York state, the pregnancy mortality rate for Black birthing people is five to six times higher, and in New York City 9.4 times higher, than the national average—despite Black births representing only 15% of total births.

This is the present landscape in the United States for Black birthing people as they embark on their pregnancy journey—one that should be filled with joy and expectation but is often terrifying and permeated with fear and anxiety, which stains the maternal experience and can affect the overall maternal mental state.

A History of Black Maternal Health

Understanding the role history has played in overall Black health helps to explain the current state of emergency for Black maternal health. The history

Ashanda Saint Jean, *Racial Disparities Within Black Maternal Health* In: *Antiblackness and the Stories of Authentic Allies*. Edited by: Norman Kim, Carolyn Coker Ross, Mazella Fuller and Charlynn Small, Oxford University Press.

of social, birth, and reproductive injustice for Black people dates to the trans-Atlantic slave trade in the United States and provides roots for present-day medical distrust.

In the 1800s, Dr. J. Marion Sims, the "father of modern gynecology," developed surgical techniques in gynecology, specifically in vaginal repairs after childbirth and bladder/rectal reconstruction. Dr. Sims used slave women to trial and perfect his techniques and often did not provide anesthesia during the surgical procedures. Three slave women—Betsy, Anarcha, and Lucy—were often the subjects of his medical research; they endured repeated surgeries and unimaginable pain while Dr. Sims performed surgical experimentation and fed his desire to perfect his surgical skills. He performed 30 surgeries on Anarcha alone, the most of any enslaved woman, all without anesthesia (Zhang, 2018).

In the South during the 1950s, Henrietta Lacks, a Black woman, was diagnosed with cervical cancer after having persistent vaginal bleeding. She entrusted her care to medical professionals to treat and diagnose her illness; however, her cancer cells—named HeLa cells—were taken and used without her consent for medical research. Today, 60 years later, HeLa cells are continuously used worldwide to study various diseases and medical conditions, for cancer research, and to create vaccinations. Sadly, Lacks died at the age of 31 years old, never knowing her immortal contribution to medicine for generations to come nor ever receiving any financial compensation for her cells, which changed the blueprint for biomedical research, disease pathophysiology, and pharmacology.

At the heart of this travesty, Lacks was never afforded the opportunity to give informed consent. This failure, while permitted by the ethical norms of the time, has affected the Lacks family in profound ways, including limiting the comfort, pride, and satisfaction that come with knowing a deceased loved one made an important contribution to science (Wolinetz & Collins, 2020).

Informed consent is a principal pillar of medical ethics and respectful care. This premise is grounded in one receiving sufficient medical information regarding their medical condition from their health care professional. This medical information should include the risks, benefits, and alternatives of any proposed medical procedure and/or medical intervention. This enables a patient to arrive at a balanced decision regarding their medical care. Informed consent should occur at every juncture in one's medical journey, especially when a medical decision must be made, thus allowing transparency and reinforcing the trusted relationship between provider and patient.

From the 1920s to 1980s, a "Mississippi appendectomy" was a surgical procedure performed on women of color in the South. In fact, it was not an appendectomy—the removal of the appendix—at all; it was a hysterectomy, the removal of the uterus that results in permanent sterilization and cessation of menses. Informed consent was not obtained for these procedures, and again, women of color were used for medical experimentation.

Mississippi appendectomies were performed by doctors in training—interns, residents, and medical students—affording them the opportunity to practice and fine-tune their surgical skills. It also allowed population control and impeded the growth of communities of color. This unwanted surgical castration performed without informed consent, or any consent at all, forced sterilization on women of color, who were unable to ever bear children again. These shameful, federally funded sterilization programs took place in 32 states throughout the 20th century (Wolinetz & Collins, 2020).

One of the noted Mississippi civil rights activists from the 1960s, Fannie Lou Hamer, was also a victim of surgical sterilization without consent. She underwent a minor surgical procedure to remove a benign fibroid tumor but was later discharged from the hospital unable to ever conceive again. A hysterectomy was performed without her knowledge or consent; she discovered her uterus was absent during an infertility evaluation shortly after marrying her husband. They wanted to conceive and strongly desired children. This experience ignited her activism in both civil and women's rights in the South. They later adopted two children.

The relationship of Black people and medicine continued its fractured path with the Tuskegee experiment, in which the U.S. Public Health Service and the CDC conducted a study of untreated syphilis on approximately 400 Black men from 1932 to 1972 in Tuskegee, Alabama. Black men, their families, and their offspring suffered the debilitating effects of primary, secondary, and tertiary syphilis, unknowingly. Fifteen years into the study the antibiotic penicillin became the recommended treatment. However, researchers convinced physicians to not treat the participants in order to track the disease's full progression. No effective care was provided as the men went blind or insane, experienced other severe health problems, or even died due to untreated syphilis (Nix, 2020).

Medical research and human experimentation in this study allowed the inhumane treatment of Black men and their families to occur for decades. This study violated several medical ethics and principles, including the right of informed consent; violated the Hippocratic Oath taken by medical doctors to "first do no harm"; and, lastly, only included a cohort of Black men, targeting this specific race to be used as human subjects for medical research that resulted in a multitude of harmful irreversible effects.

Factors in Maternal Health Inequity

While reviewing the historical events that have contributed to medical mistrust allows us to fully explore the present-day health care crisis of racial disparities in maternal health in the United States, it is pivotal to acknowledge other factors that contribute to this health care crisis. Studies have shown that income, financial wealth, education, private insurance, and social status contribute to Black birthing people having a much higher pregnancy mortality ratio than their White counterparts (Howell, 2018).

Systemic and structural racism are both major contributors to racial disparities in maternal health. The effects of institutional racism—racism that began with the enslavement of Black people—were embedded in our earliest institutions and have continued to influence policies and practices ever since (National Institute for Children's Health Quality, 2022).

Racism impacts the birthing journey and is a significant barrier to equitable health care, quality of health care, and overall health care access. Black birthing people have experienced interactions with medical professionals that are racially biased and have changed the trajectory of their birthing experience. These negative birthing encounters have led to toxic medical experiences and birthing trauma. It is those experiences that contribute to poor outcomes and leave a lasting stain on what should be the best day of a patient's life—bringing a life into the world.

Implicit bias and discrimination have played major roles in poor outcomes leading to severe maternal morbidity and mortality. These invisible but mentally and physically palpable behaviors can instantly change the course of one's health care experience. Black birthing people confront these behaviors in health care spaces even though they should be nurturing, supportive, and encouraging environments.

These interactions are major contributors to reluctance and fear of medical systems and the desire to have a doula present at delivery, for that extra layer of support. A doula is a trained labor support professional who provides continuous physical, emotional, and informational support to a mother before, during, and shortly after childbirth to help achieve the healthiest, most satisfying experience possible (DONA International, 2022). Evidence shows that the addition of doulas to obstetric health care teams can improve both maternal and infant outcomes. They contribute to "shorter labor time, earlier initiation of breastfeeding and longer duration of breastfeeding, enhanced mother-baby bonding, and overall positive feeling about their birth experience" (City of New York, Department of Health, 2022).

The intersection of social status and health care plays a significant role in racial disparities in maternal health. There lie the barriers to health care access and equity. Those barriers are recognized as social determinants of health, which, when identified and addressed, can truly balance the scale for underserved and marginalized communities. Social determinants of health include health care access, health care literacy, unstable housing, education, income, food insecurity, transportation deficits, immigration status, and environmental conditions. When social determinants are corrected, it can change the course of health care outcomes, specifically reducing pregnancy-related mortality and morbidity.

Medical deserts exist because there are regions where medical health care services are unavailable. This can pertain to overall medical care or certain types of medical disciplines or subspecialties. For example, many hospitals in rural settings do not have maternity health services or a maternal birthing facility. This presents a major barrier for maternal care in these communities and limits health care access. Patients in these regions must commute to neighboring towns, counties, or even states to receive maternal health care.

Health care access can also be impacted by a lack of health insurance or the type of health insurance plan. Often, private sector health care providers don't accept health care plans associated with Medicaid, a U.S. federal and state program that helps with health care costs for lower-socioeconomic individuals. Thus, the social determinant of health corresponding to income can impact one's health care access.

Community health workers have been key to facilitating health care services and coordination of care for low-income individuals and Medicaid recipients. A community health worker is a frontline public health worker who serves as a bridge between their community, the government, the health care industry, and social service systems by using outreach, community education, counseling, and social advocacy to increase public health knowledge in underprivileged and marginalized communities where people lack access to affordable and quality health care (Indeed, n.d.).

Poor environmental conditions and lower socioeconomic status are both social determinants that contribute to racial disparities, not only in maternal health but also in all facets of health care.

Redlining is an environmental discriminatory practice that puts services (financial and otherwise) out of reach for residents of certain areas based on race or ethnicity; the policy of redlining is felt most by residents of minority neighborhoods (Hayes, 2021). Redlining further ostracizes underserved communities' resources for healthy living, for example, by not providing public parks and other community spaces.

In addition, these communities have fewer nutritious food-purchasing options. Known as food deserts, these geographic areas lack convenient options for affordable and healthy foods—especially fresh fruits and vegetables. Food deserts are disproportionately found in high-poverty areas and create extra everyday hurdles that can make it harder for kids, families, and communities to grow healthy and strong (Annie E. Casey Foundation, 2021). The opportunity to make healthy eating choices, which should be easy, is often impeded by the lack of grocery and farmers markets, hindering the ability to purchase fresh produce including fruits, vegetables, meats, poultry, and seafood in these communities.

A Call to Action

So how do we strive for change? How do we course correct or alter the path? How can we improve maternal outcomes for Black birthing people? There are several proposed ideas to combat this public health crisis, but how do we thread equity and social justice into those concerted responses and revolutionary efforts?

Our call to action must combine a unity of purpose, community, social justice, and health collaborative partnerships. Together, we can impact change and alter the course for Black birthing people. There must be a present-day application of birth justice that combines holistic approaches to maternity care with both culturally matched and competent care. Only through truly understanding Black birthing people, their past traumas, intergenerational stress, environmental stressors, and their resilience will the medical community make strides in providing medically just care, free of racism and discrimination.

A patient should have agency and opportunities for informed, respectful care via judgment-free communication with their health care provider during their birthing journey. The patient should participate in shared decision-making with their provider, in which the patient and clinician work together to make optimal health care decisions that align with what matters most to the patient (Massachusetts General Hospital Health Decision Sciences Center, 2022).

The addition of midwifery services to obstetric health care teams can also benefit Black birthing patients. Midwifery-led care has proven results and positive outcomes for both birthing people and newborns. For instance, midwifery-led care is associated with an increase in vaginal births, higher breastfeeding rates, reduction in use of epidural anesthesia, fewer episiotomies and instrumental births, and a lower likelihood of preterm birth or losing a baby before 24 weeks' gestation (Van Meerdervoort 2022).

Shared best practices from the midwifery community applied to populations at risk can bring about substantial positive change in improved birth outcomes, especially for Black birthing people. The inclusion of doulas on obstetric care teams provides an extra layer of support to all birthing people, but especially Black birthing people. Enhancing doula access across the entire birthing journey—prenatal, antepartum, and postpartum—is another modality that can alter the course of Black maternal health. In New York City, several efforts have been made for insurance plans to cover the cost of doulas, thus providing universal access to all birthing people. This citywide doula initiative also includes increasing access through offering no-cost doula care, Medicaid-covered doula care, and birthing facility–covered doula care.

Health care is a human right, one that needs community and intentional efforts to ensure healthy outcomes and positive birth experiences. A first step toward addressing social determinants of health in any community is learning about the lived experience of residents. Care providers need to understand the social factors that impact their patients, and universal screening for social determinants of health can help programs determine the best strategies for addressing them (Rural Health Information Hub, 2017). With community outreach resources and referrals for all patients, we can uplift marginalized communities, including Black birthing people.

Pregnancy-related mortality is defined as "the death of a woman while pregnant or within 1 year of the end of pregnancy from any cause related to or aggravated by the pregnancy" (CDC, 2022). Given this, many efforts have been made to ensure birthing people have health care coverage that extends to 1 year postpartum, instead of lasting only through the 6-week postpartum course. Sadly, many pregnancy-related deaths occur after the 6-week postpartum period, when Medicaid coverage is no longer effective. In 2022, New York state extended Medicaid coverage for new mothers from 60 days to a year postdelivery for all birthing people (Burnett, 2022).

Cardiovascular disease and mental health conditions are the top two causes of pregnancy-related mortality in the United States. Both conditions require close medical attention and follow-up care, especially during the postpartum period. Nearly all deaths that happen after the 6- to 12-week mark after birth are from cardiovascular disease (Burnett, 2022).

Legislation that extends Medicaid health insurance until 1 year postpartum would be a lifesaver for many birthing people and enable access to health care and treatment. This mandate is needed nationwide, and we will continue to strive for federal legislation like the Black Maternal Health Momnibus Act of 2021, a bill that utilizes multiple agencies to improve maternal health, especially among racial and ethnic minority groups, to change this maternal health crisis.

A maternal death cause analysis provides an opportunity of transparency of why the maternal death occurred, an understanding of why and charters a path toward corrective actions and accountability. The CDC developed maternal mortality and morbidity review boards to examine maternal deaths in 31 states and jurisdictions. Most review boards include clinicians, community members, doulas, midwives, and community health workers. They are tasked with dissecting each maternal death and determining contributing factors, preventability, and whether racism or discrimination played a role in the patient's death. These review boards provide clarity for all aspects of a sentinel event, evaluate any errors made, and identify areas of improvement at the patient, provider, and facility levels. They also offer solutions for future prevention and improvement on a systems level. With increased attention to maternal mortality rates and disparate rates of death by race, many states have renewed or strengthened their review of pregnancy-related deaths (Burnett, 2022).

Partnerships, community collaborations, and structural change are needed to effectively change the state of Black maternal outcomes in the United States. It must be a public health priority to arrive at racially balanced outcomes and save the lives of Black birthing people. There are several strategic approaches that amplify agency, community, cultural sensitivity, and cultural competence and embrace holistic care models with midwifery and doula care. We must continue these multilayered approaches to address the thoughts, concerns, and fears Black birthing patients have throughout their birthing journey.

References

American College of Physicians. (2010). *Racial and ethnic disparities in health care, updated 2010.*

Annie E. Casey Foundation. (2021, February 13). *Food deserts in the United States.* https://www.aecf.org/blog/exploring-americas-food-deserts

Burnett, K. (2022, May 10). *Medicaid postpartum care for new moms extended to 1 year from 60 days.* Spectrum News 1. https://spectrumlocalnews.com/nys/central-ny/news/2022/05/10/medicaid-postpartum-care-for-new-moms-extended-to-1-year-

Centers for Disease Control and Prevention (CDC). (2022, June 22). *Pregnancy mortality surveillance system.* Division of Reproductive Health, National Center for Chronic Disease Prevention and Health Promotion. https://www.cdc.gov/reproductivehealth/maternal-mortality/pregnancy-mortality-surveillance-system.htm

City of New York, Department of Health. (2022). *Doula care.* https://www1.nyc.gov/site/doh/health/health-topics/doula-care.page

DONA International. (2022). *What is a doula?* https://www.dona.org/what-is-a-doula/

Guttmacher Institute. (2022, July 1). *Maternal mortality review committees.* https://www.guttmacher.org/state-policy/explore/maternal-mortality-review-committees

Hayes, A. (2021, October 21). *Redlining.* Investopedia. https://www.investopedia.com/terms/r/redlining.asp

Howell, E. (2018, June). Reducing disparities in severe maternal morbidity and mortality. *Clinical Obstetrics and Gynecology, 61*(2), 387–399.

Indeed. (n.d.). *What does a community health worker do?* https://www.indeed.com/career/community-health-worker?

Massachusetts General Hospital Health Decision Sciences Center. (2022). *What is shared decision making?* https://mghdecisionsciences.org/about-us-home/shared-decision-making/

National Institute for Children's Health Quality. (2022). *The impact of institutional racism on maternal and child health.* https://www.nichq.org/insight/impact-institutional-racism-maternal-and-child-health

Nix, E. (2023, December 15). *Tuskegee experiment: The infamous syphilis study.* History. https://www.history.com/news/the-infamous-40-year-tuskegee-study

Rural Health Information Hub. (2017). *Tools to assess and measure social determinants of health.* Center for Health Care Strategies. https://www.ruralhealthinfo.org/toolkits/sdoh/4/assessment-tools

Van Meerdervoort, L. (2022). *Definition of the midwife.* International Confederation of Midwives. https://www.internationalmidwives.org

Wolinetz, C. D., & Collins, F. S. (2020). Recognition of research participants' need for autonomy: Remembering the legacy of Henrietta Lacks. *JAMA, 324*(11), 1027–1028.

Zhang, S. (2018, April 18). The surgeon who experimented on slaves. *The Atlantic.*

PART VII
AUTHENTIC ALLYSHIP

25

Authentic Allyship

A Call to Action

Mazella Fuller

The support I received during my formative years appropriately sums up my perception of *authentic allyship*, a genuine effort by a person or persons who exert privilege to achieve justice for Black, Indigenous, and people of color (BIPOC) who are marginalized in the workplace and in the wider society. I am a baby boomer who was born into a nurturing family in a coastal plain region of eastern North Carolina. In that predominantly Black community where Black people were bound together by intimate social, cultural, economic, and political ties, I was prepared for the racist, sexist, and oppressive society in which I lived.

My strongest institutional weapon of survival was my family. My family bore the responsibility of helping me maintain kinship ties, embrace formal and informal cultural practices, and thrive in my community. My family helped me form three pillars that embody my personal core: confidence, competence, and integrity. Equally important, from my family I acquired a hunger for justice.

My maternal great-grandfather and maternal grandmother intensified my hunger for justice when they deeply immersed me in Black history. They taught me that my enslaved ancestors shaped my family's dogged determination to thrive in a society that perpetuates racial, class, and gender oppression. From my ancestors, I acquired the capacity to perceive Black women's dual vulnerability as I learned about the assaults on the Black female body. Historically, the Black female body has been subjected to rape, experimentation, and murder—violence that has continued throughout the 21st century.

Listening to my grandparents' stories of courage ignited my inner activist. Subsequently, following Dr. Martin Luther King Jr.'s assassination, I, a 9½-year-old child, participated in protests in my hometown. The police rewarded my efforts with a free bus ride to jail. Yes, when I was 9 years

Mazella Fuller, *Authentic Allyship* In: *Antiblackness and the Stories of Authentic Allies*. Edited by: Norman Kim, Carolyn Coker Ross, Mazella Fuller and Charlynn Small, Oxford University Press. © Oxford University Press 2024. DOI: 10.1093/oso/9780197642535.003.0026 old, I was arrested for expressing my human right to a life free of racism, sexism, and oppression. Can you imagine your 9-year-old child living in a hostile society that provokes her to protest and that then thrusts her into the criminal justice system after she peacefully advocates for her human rights?

Furthermore, my nuclear family was not the only Black social institution that supported me in my struggles to realize equality in an unjust world. My extended family of loyal teachers, principals, neighbors, and church members created spaces for me to develop academically, professionally, and spiritually. After all, those loyal Black leaders and I lived in the same community: They understood my culture because it was their culture.

Aware of my needs, my teachers invested in my success by delivering a high-quality education to me, building my self-confidence, and developing my professional skills. In a similar vein, leaders in my Black church nurtured my professional skills when they appointed me to leadership positions in the youth choir, on the usher board, and in the young adult missionary society. At the age of 15, I represented youths at an all-Black conference in Hempstead, New York.

In essence, my initial authentic allies were Black people who gifted me the tools I needed to diversify and enrich the dominant culture outside the safety of my familial environment. One primary reason the Black community fights for justice is for their entry into the dominant culture, particularly the professions.

The Professions: Authentic White Allyship, Diversity, Equality, Equity, and Inclusion

As BIPOC transition into the professions, more White people must help them smoothly navigate spaces that historically have rejected them. In other words, the time has come for more White people to admit that racism is a White problem and that another kind of allyship is needed to combat systemic racism.

Within the helping professions of psychology, mental health counseling, nursing, and social work is a commitment to a culturally competent practice that demands diverse thoughts and environments. As practitioners, we take pride in our professional skills and in the service we deliver to our diverse clients. To deliver competent care to clients, authentic allyship is important for the professional development of specialists from disenfranchised communities.

However, many of these professionals face multiple challenges and structural barriers that result in missed opportunities for mentorship, sponsorship, and advancement. Authentic allyship can eliminate these barriers and challenges.

Authentic White allies shift the current paradigm from segregation and aggression to integration, inclusion, equality, and equity. Authentic allies call out racism. They eschew the ideology that Black progress thwarts White progress: Authentic allies recognize that their non-White colleagues add value to organizations. Additionally, authentic allies recognize that the institution of slavery and structural racism have pushed their non-White colleagues to the periphery of society. Finally, authentic White allies acknowledge their non-White colleagues' trauma and acknowledge how being disenfranchised and a person of color manifest as a double-edged sword in a racist society. When authentic White allies eliminate racism and other structural barriers, they cultivate a positive, healthy work culture.

One persistent structural barrier that impedes a positive work environment is communication. When Black people express their discriminatory treatment to their White coworkers, many of their White coworkers label them as complainers (Rasinski & Czopp, 2010). Rasinski and Czopp explored how race and stereotypes affect responses to interpersonal confrontations of bias. They found that "because targets who speak out are perceived as complainers, their confrontations may be less effective than those made by nontargets" (Rasinski & Czopp, 2010, p. 10). Rasinski and Czopp (2010) define "targets" as Black people and "nontargets" as White people (p. 10).

Many White people harbor unconscious stereotypes; thus, they often struggle to self-regulate, particularly when Black people express egalitarian norms (Rasinski & Czopp, 2010, p. 9). Raninski and Czopp's findings demonstrate that BIPOC still need authentic White allies to support them in their enduring fight for equality, equity, and inclusion.

Authentic Allyship Versus Performative Allyship

Though we have made some progress, for the most part, we are fighting an uphill battle because too many White people who verbally identify as allies expect BIPOC to fight the battle alone. For this reason, those White people are not authentic allies; instead, they are *performative allies*. Performative allyship is drastically different from authentic allyship. Performative allyship shows up as mere words without action, and performative allies avoid discomfort and engagement. History informs that some White people with good intentions experience guilt and defensiveness that feed disengagement. When White people abstain from evoking their own power to eradicate racism, their disengagement fuels White privilege.

Rothenberg (2012) maintains that "White privilege is the other side of racism" and that White people must "welcome a degree of discomfort in [their] lives and feel short-changed if it is not present" (p. 1). Rothenberg (2012) insists that White privilege must be dismantled on personal and institutional levels as White privilege perpetuates "unearned advantages" and inequalities (p. 1). To dismantle White privilege, White people must use a critical lens to identify their blatant and implicit biases and accept differences between and among other human beings. White people who deeply engage these practices do a better job of initiating the transformative process of creating sustainable change in the workplace and in the wider society where everyone progresses.

A Call to Action From Authentic White Allies: Becky Thompson and Joshua Miller

Since entering the profession, I have experienced the sting of racial discrimination and microaggressions. Experiencing the loneliness of being the only Black woman in predominantly White spaces and navigating the intersectionality of gender, race, and class became the norm for me. Anyone familiar with these situations will agree that authentic White allies can help their colleagues of color not only survive but also thrive in predominantly White professional spaces.

More than 25 years ago, Becky Thompson and Joshua Miller influenced my decision to dismantle inequities in my profession. Thompson is a sociology professor at Simmons University in Massachusetts. In her classrooms and scholarship, she addresses Black women's trauma and the harsh realities of systemic racism. Similarly, Miller is a professor of social work at Smith College in Massachusetts. In his graduate courses and in his scholarship, Miller discusses the deviating impact of racism on Black people and teaches White people how to become authentic allies.

Both Thompson and Miller make their privilege visible and speak back to their legacy of intergenerational silence. They know that racism is a White problem and foster identities as authentic allies. If you are struggling to situate yourself as an ally, pay close attention to Thompson's and Miller's calls to action.

Thompson: Kiss Whiteness Goodbye

What White allies have taught me over the years is to unpack my own biases and to ask a lot of questions. They have taught me to consider where I worship, shop, vacation, live, send my children to school, and eat. Seeking integrated spaces and shifting to avoid White-dominated spaces except to conduct antiracist business have been a part of my learning process. My learning process necessitates inquiry. Thus, I ask myself the following questions: How do I hold my body with White coworkers and with Latina coworkers? What might that reveal? Whose books do I review, promotions do I support, committees do I serve on? When do I act as if there are only so many seats at the antiracist table? How can I elongate the table and cultivate White rebellion?

I refuse to write anonymous evaluations. White people have said and written all kinds of things without being held accountable.

I keep learning: listening to Black women's anger. Their anger comes from centuries of harm. If Black women are willing to share their experiences in my presence, I am doing something right. I don't take their experiences personally. Instead, I take ownership of what's mine but don't center myself in their stories. White people aren't the center. We were just taught that we are the center.

Authentic White allies must keep seeking out the history of slavery and settler colonialism in our family histories. I search for my mother's rebellious gardens. We must learn the distinct history of Black women globally: Haiti was the first country in the Western Hemisphere to abolish slavery; Ethiopia is a country in Africa that was never colonized; and Black lesbians are at the forefront of liberation struggles across the globe.

I speak up because it is the right thing to do even when there are no Indigenous people there to validate me. Guilt is a waystation with no train leading in or out. Cultural humility includes getting it wrong, making amends, and committing to learning more. We must show up at demonstrations and watch consciousness expand. People are not inferior. Oppression breeds resistance. When a few doors close, the whole world opens up.

Turn the world map upside down, the global south at the top, the global north at the bottom. All of us White people must accept that White people are one-eighth of the world population—the minority. Kiss whiteness goodbye!

Miller: Being an Authentic White Ally Against White Supremacy and Antiblackness

Every day, I think about being a White ally for BIPOC. Because I am White and more specifically a White male, I always benefit from White supremacy in so many aspects of my life even though I did not choose or wish for this. I say this because White supremacy and antiblackness are baked into every institution and policy in the United States.

White supremacy shapes our communities, organizations, discourses, and epistemologies, and it colonizes our minds through our educational processes, the media, and our practices. Although this might sound like a strong statement to some, I am, if anything, understating the extent that the United States is saturated with White supremacy. It is part of our nation's history from the very beginning to the present, and it structures today's society.

The web of institutional racism (see Garran et al., 2002) affects Black people's lives, while White people pass through this web often without noticing its impact on Black people. This web affects all aspects of our lives. This web of institutional racism influences where people live, where they go to school, and where they go to work. This web affects people's relationships with the police and the criminal justice system, their quality of health care, their exposure to toxic environments, their life expectancy, and their ability to accrue assets. Finally, this web determines who gets paid more or less for the same job, who experiences upward mobility, and who exercises their right to vote and much, much more.

Given this context, I would like to suggest eight aspects of being an authentic White ally:

- *The work is never finished: I have been an antiracism activist all my adult life and teach and write about it. My work is ongoing, and I believe that this is true for all White authentic allies. We never finally "get it" because we have internalized White supremacy from birth and experience it in the way society is structured. White supremacy is the default. Anytime we are not paying attention or actively working against White supremacy, it seeps back into our lives. Thus, unlearning racism is an ongoing process with no endpoint as long as racism persists. White allies will make mistakes and hopefully will reflect on and learn from them; this is part of the process.*

- *Although White supremacy is structural, being an ally involves inner work: As one of my White students once said, racist stereotypes, which are the internalization of structural White supremacy, bubble up into White people's consciousness like pop-up screens on a computer and our first impulse is to click the "x" and shut them down. But it is important to leave them up on our screen of consciousness to know that they are still there, interrogate where they come from, and work to substitute our values and all of the evidence that contradicts the stereotype to nullify their impact. If this is not done, then well-meaning White people will enact microaggressions and aversive and implicit racism.*

- *Accept feedback from other people without defensiveness: There is often a sense of shame when White people are confronted about racist behaviors, ideas, or interactions. Sometimes White people challenge the veracity of Black people's experience: justifying, explaining, minimizing, and reframing that experience. This not only invalidates Black people's experience in the world but also gets in the way of authentically reflecting on how White supremacy has been internalized. It is better to be grateful for feedback and to thoughtfully and nondefensively consider it.*

- *Accept personal and collective accountability: Authentic White allies need to hold ourselves accountable, without beating ourselves up but also without letting up. Accountability is often more effective when it is held collectively, such as in a White affinity group exploring internalized White supremacy. It is important to not burden Black people with having to witness this or to expect them to teach White people about our racism.*

- *Do your own work and do not attack other White people: I have often seen "woke White students" aggressively attacking other White students whom they perceive as being less enlightened. This not only shuts down another White person but also deflects the aggressor from continuing to do their own work.*

- *Guard against recreating White supremacy in multiracial coalitions: Multiracial coalitions are important vehicles for racial justice and social change. Since White people are used to seeing themselves in leadership positions, it is important to be mindful of this and to follow the lead of BIPOC in multiracial coalitions.*

- *Radical work necessitates radical self-care: Antiracism work takes physical, emotional, and social energy. White allies need to be in it for the long haul, and the journey necessitates self-care. Self-care includes compassionate accountability—holding yourself accountable without being punitive to yourself.*
- *Do it for your liberation: While I engage in antiracism work for all my BIPOC friends, colleagues, and students, I also do it for my own liberation and for that of my family and friends. White supremacy wounds everyone in some way. If we want to live a life that expresses our values and ideals and our commitment to equality, justice, and equity, then we must liberate ourselves and engage in antiracism work on behalf of others.*

Conclusion

As Thompson insists in her call, authentic White allies open the door for BIPOC and invite them to have both a seat and a voice at the table. BIPOC do not expect unearned privileges. However, they expect fair treatment and equal opportunities as Miller points out in his call. The measures that Thompson and Miller outline above are imperative to BIPOC's well-being because positive human interactions have positive physical and mental health benefits.

Historically, too few White people have acknowledged that White privilege and racism are a White problem that makes Black people sick. Accordingly, out of Black enslaved women's determination to survive in the midst of adversity, they birthed the strong Black woman syndrome (SBWS), and the signs and symptoms manifest themselves in Black women today. Many researchers and health professionals link superwoman syndrome to success rather than to survival.

Yet, several Black women clinicians (Conley, 2021; Mann, 2021; McMillian, 2021; Ross, 2021; Watson, 2021) examine how SBWS operates as a survival mechanism that has detrimental health outcomes for Black women. These clinicians examined links among racism, sexism, and mental health. They concluded that Black women experienced conditions such as hypertension, depression, eating disorders, and stress that are triggered by racial discrimination.

"Similarly, Allen et al. (2020) examined the connection among SBWS, racial discrimination, and allostatic load," which is the way that stress negatively affects the body (pp. 104–105). They found that "racial discrimination becomes biologically embedded" in Black women's bodies (p. 117), thus making them sick. The physical and psychological effects of racism on Black bodies is deafening. So is White people's silence!

Though we have made progress toward creating humane work environments for BIPOC, my White allies and I call for more aggressive actions in the workplace.

The time is right for authentic allies to not only restructure workplaces but also promote social action within, across, and beyond workplace boundaries. I trust that my allies and I have inspired you to act by centering non-White voices and bodies in predominately White spaces.

References

Allen, A. M., Wang, Y., Chae, D. H., Price, M. M., Powell, W., Steed, T. C., Black, A. R., Dhabhar, F. S., Marquez-Magaña, L., & Woods-Giscombe, C. L. (2020). Racial discrimination, the superwoman schema, and allostatic load: Exploring an integrative stress-coping model among African American women. *Annuals of the New York Academy of Sciences, 1457*(1), 104–127. https://doi.org/10.1111/nyas.14188

Conley, J. (2021). Creative training approaches for clinicians-in-training working with African American women with eating disorders. In C. Small & M. Fuller (Eds.), *Treating Black women with eating disorders: A clinician's guide* (pp. 165–173). Routledge.

Garran, A. M., Werkmister-Rozas, L., Kang, H. K., & Miller, J. (2002). *Racism in the United States: Implications for the helping professions* (3rd ed.). Springer Publishing.

Mann, W. C. (2021). The skin I'm in: Stereotypes and body image development in women of color. In C. Small & M. Fuller (Eds.), *Treating Black women with eating disorders: A clinician's guide* (pp. 67–74). Routledge.

McMillian, D. (2021). Only a dog wants a bone! The other end of the eating spectrum: Overweight and obesity. In C. Small & M. Fuller (Eds.), *Treating Black women with eating disorders: A clinician's guide* (pp. 133–139). Routledge.

Rasinski, H. M., & Czopp, A. M. (2010). The effect of target status on witnesses' reactions to confrontations of bias. *Basic and Applied Social Psychology, 32*(1), 8–16. https://doi.org/10.1080/01973530903539754

Ross, C. C. (2021). An integrative approach to understanding and treating disordered eating in African American women. In C. Small & M. Fuller (Eds.), *Treating Black women with eating disorders: A clinician's guide* (pp. 88–102). Routledge.

Rothenberg, P. S. (2012). *White privilege: Essential readings on the other side of racism.* Worth Publishers.

Watson, K. (2021). Black women's presence in eating disorder treatment facilities. In C. Small & M. Fuller (Eds.), *Treating Black women with eating disorders: A clinician's guide* (pp. 143–149). Routledge.

26

Owning Our Unconscious on a Path of Antiracism Work

One White Woman's Travelogue

Mardy S. Ireland

"No matter where you go, there you are" is a salient phrase for racism, allyship, and antiracism, all because of what goes into the words "there you are."

This is a personal narrative concerning my journey with what these words mean about race, as well as what it means that "words matter" in their power to transform human experience—for better or worse! For example, "otherness" is a relative and complicated term, and the what, who, and where this "other" is located, along with how people deal (or don't deal) with "otherness," are central to how each person's lived experience of being human is perceived and felt. It is a central element, therefore, in "there you are."

Let me begin with a story that takes place in the South. A small girl—8 or younger—is walking downtown with her dad when she sees two water fountains. One fountain reads "WHITES," and the other reads "COLOREDS." Though thirsty, she becomes confused. She knows she is White, but she wonders, *Isn't White a color too*?

"What's the difference?" she asks her dad.

"There is no difference," he sighs as he turns to look around the street to see both Whites and some Blacks nearby.

"Why are there two?"

"Some people have problems with skin color and think people should stay separated by color. They also think that if you are not White, you are not as good as them."

Ah, this explains the mystery as to why there are two different ladies rooms in buildings too.

The father, with greater intensity, says, "*That* is *not* how our family sees things—people are people, period."

Mardy S. Ireland, *Owning Our Unconscious on a Path of Antiracism Work* In: *Antiblackness and the Stories of Authentic Allies*. Edited by: Norman Kim, Carolyn Coker Ross, Mazella Fuller and Charlynn Small, Oxford University Press.

"It doesn't matter then if I drink from the colored one?"

The father sighs again. "No, but since you are White and some White people set these things up this way, it may feel to a colored person who sees you do that that you are showing disrespect because you can drink wherever you want and they cannot without risk and danger. AND, that same kind of White person may also feel you are humiliating yourself—and THEM somehow—by simply drinking from the colored fountain."

The little girl only understands some of this, but she certainly understands that she does not like the feelings of it—*at all*! So, to rid herself of confusion, she takes a drink of water from each fountain. They walk away with the father's hand on the girl's head, the father just shaking his own head.

Only later in adulthood does the little girl understand her father's fierce intensity and her own strivings to make something understood in a feeling sense.

That little girl was me.

The 1950s Southern Context

In the segregated days of the 1950s, such a father would be described benignly using the word "unprejudiced" or malignantly using words we were not allowed to say in our family then or now. Yet, throughout my southern childhood and adolescence I often heard these ugly words from children and adults directed at my family. In 21st-century language my father would likely be called an antiracist in his active fight against the prevailing interdiction of "don't cross the color line," that is, by being the first to hire Black lab technicians in his medical center research lab and then having to fight again to get his techs equal pay to White lab technicians.

There are many such stories from my upbringing that would illustrate the conscious—and at times not well-thought-through—efforts my parents made to raise "unprejudiced" children when it came to race and class. And yet, because the conscious mind of intentions is only one part of the human equation of what goes into the "there" of "there you are," another part always includes what appears to be "not there." So, another story is needed.

I was raised in a White community in what was designated an "other" family due to having nonsouthern parents, and upon leaving the South after college I thought it would be for the rest of my life. After all, the South was "not me." To say I felt both insecure and self-righteous in my differences would be apt.

My summer job was lifeguarding, but I also served as a swim instructor for the primarily Black community of Anacostia, Washington, DC. I remained the only White person on staff that entire summer. My conscious attitude was "no problem." My conscious sense of myself as nonracist was soon to be decentered by the unconscious entitlement I carried concerning both my personal safety and the respect I expected to automatically receive as a staff member entering the scene—in a word, I was delusional! It was shocking the many ways the naivete and arrogance of my assumptions and presumptions were challenged—and the resultant anxiety and shame I experienced as my emotional understanding and thinking deepened and broadened concerning what constituted racism.

I taught lessons to children of different ages several mornings a week. My favorite class was a group of 8- to 10-year-old boys. They listened attentively, tried hard, and joined in with gusto when at the end of the lesson I would jump into the pool and engage in a "them against me" 5-minute splashing fight. It seemed liked they always won! For weeks I called them "my boys," until one day my pool manager and assistant manager called me into their office. After that conversation I never again called them "my boys"—but they were still my favorites. There were other consciousness-raising stories from this summer at the pool, but this one was particularly potent because it underscored the tremendous power of language to destroy as much as it can create, gather, and lift up humanity. On my path to becoming a clinician, language would become a primary medium of change.

No Matter Where You Are—There You Are!

Really, there was no such thing as fleeing the South as "not me"—because no one can truly leave behind what has been unconsciously internalized from the environment into which one is thrust at birth and lives through in childhood (and beyond). Even if you have a family who strives to consciously raise you as a nonracist, the culture in which they themselves grew up and lived within is not organized as such. Therefore, my parents unconsciously communicated—in their silences, unpacked ideas or actions, assumptions of place, etc.—all the White privilege presumptions I took to the all-Black community pool.

These lessons I learned from the swimming pool when I was 22 years old were just the beginning of a lifetime of lessons to be learned when you realize you have to consider elements of the unconscious in yourself—even when it seems as if nothing is there. In other words, "No matter where you go, there you are" by definition includes the structural reality that the unconscious lives in "there" in every person. And unconscious group identifications (e.g., being White or Black, poor or rich) that each person carries within are a part of what is "there."

Often unconscious things within us push to become known and connected to our conscious selves; the "there" in "No matter where you are, there you are" includes both negative and positive things you may wish to deny or defend against owning. One way of warding off these things is through *projection onto other people*—but there are other ways to defend against knowing one's unconscious self. (Racism, sexism, and classism lie at one end of a pole, while idealizing and aggrandizing others—i.e., movie/Internet stars, political leaders—lie at the opposite end.)

There really are no purely altruistic conscious motives. My father came from a poor family with an alcoholic, abusive, philandering father and a loving but aggrieved, passive mother. He was taunted by peers, pitied or scorned by adults, and left feeling helpless, causing his psyche to become organized around values of fairness, truth, dignity, and care for those who had less—but he carried an unquenchable rage that meant unconsciously he was always in search of an enemy to marshal his resources to fight against. He tried to shield (not always successfully) his family from this deeper anger and the fierce intensity I felt at the water fountains. Only as an adult did I see this, but I felt it all in my childhood emotions and confusion. My confusion surrounding the water fountains when I was 8 years old perhaps makes evident how it was no accident that I consciously pursued psychology, but perhaps it more unconsciously determined my becoming a psychoanalyst.

Passage From the Mainland to the Islands

Despite these powerful lessons learned at the pool, a remnant of fantasized escape from both gender and racial conflicts persisted. Fortunately, this escape did not last long because challenges arose again in Hawaii, where several years of graduate school awaited. In Hawaii only about 25% of the population is what we would call White. Those anticipated several years turned into a decade, however, and in that time I learned much about living within a racially diverse and racially stratified society.

For the first time I could not be invisible in a crowd—I could not blend in as a blond-haired, blue-eyed woman there. In addition, I did not seem to talk right or occupy personal space or move among others quite right. I felt awkward in so many ways. In essence, I suddenly became an outsider—so "other"—in the very place that was supposed to become my home for years! I was a person regarded with suspicion, even hostility at times, no matter how I presented myself. The overall effect was that I felt "less than" others as well as "unseen."

The periodic open hostility in Hawaii for Whites was understandable. The smallest racial group had somehow pushed the Indigenous people to one small island of Niihau to call their own. The White men of the U.S. government had simply ignored international and U.S. law and annexed a free republic of Hawaii as a U.S. territory in the years after the Spanish-American War. During World War II, an internment camp was established in Hawaii for prisoners of war. In contrast to the mainland, where all Japanese Americans were interned, only those citizens perceived as "disloyal" were interned in Hawaii—most likely because there were simply too many of them to put them all in one camp! Thus, even underneath my surface experience of "otherness" there, I still carried a deeper White privileged status.

What unconscious pressure must White people carry within us that this bullying pattern repeats itself? Below the skin level all human beings, unlike any other species, have a profound infantile dependence requiring years of devoted care to keep us alive and nurture our growth or we simply don't survive and continue. But no one really wants to own the scaredy-cat baby inside, so projection remains ongoing on many levels, in many places, toward many people, as in that all-American unconscious racial contract tilted in favor of whiteness.

The longer I lived in Hawaii, the more I came to believe that every White American would benefit by living on the island for a year or more to viscerally *grok* (a term coined by Robert Heinlein in 1961 meaning to understand profoundly and intuitively) something about being "otherized" and its pernicious effects on all humanity. Was it by chance, conscious intention, or unconscious currents that I ended up in psychology training there and stayed 10 years to learn such lessons?

Do the best you can until you know better. . . . Then when you know better, do better.

—Maya Angelou

The Link Between the Individual and Their Group

There are psychic nodules knotting together an individual's unconscious mind and the collective/societal unconscious mind. The terms "White fragility," put forward in recent years, and "microaggression," described in 1970 but more popularly cited now, make up one such prominent nodule. When a White person responds defensively because they feel embarrassed, exposed, and perhaps even shamed by a comment they have made "without thinking," we see "White fragility" in action. In the momentary pulse of this person's unconscious "microaggressive" statement, they are speaking for their group from the internalized racism of the privileged group of whiteness. Such an interaction is often noted as a "calling out" of the White person. In this interpersonal moment there is an unconscious repetition of American society's preferred unconscious "racial contract" that has endured across generations and simply made itself visible to both people in that encounter—the unconscious microaggression of the white person—followed by a "calling out" response by the Black person.

Thinking the trauma of being "called out" mirrors centuries of Black trauma at the hands of Whites, however, has the effect of emotionally freezing both people within their traumatic state of mind and body. What is needed more by all of us is to be able to move in such moments from a feeling of trauma to experiencing emotional empathy and mourning for the pain and loss experienced throughout our history, which could lead us toward a substantive group reparative process. What also lives in these moments of "calling out" is the opportunity to be "called in." In such encounters a Black person is also saying unconsciously, if not consciously, "Come into my experience." Many times I have that feeling of embarrassment, shame, and being less than—not only for myself but also for the generations behind me who were violated far worse.

In such moments there is a call for White accountability, yes—but also *collaboration* at both the conscious and unconscious levels for an American history denied or minimized. It can be a present and direct call for human reconnection, the start of the emotional work of mournful recognition and repair. White and Black mourning is necessary before any meaningful group reparation can begin.

Our work is to move toward feelings of shame, anxiety, confusion, and guilt for the hurt caused and to bear it—and then to give, as well as ask for, more words to flesh out the experience. Such work moves us toward establishing "a third place" beyond the outer binary of Black and White racism toward the "awaiting humanness" inside the skins of both people.

And yet this is not so easy to do. Why is it so hard?

As a country we overprivilege the conscious mind of the individual as part and parcel of our national insistence on "rugged individualist freedom." It is as if that freedom somehow also means that you can and should know all of your own mind. In other words, culturally we act as if there is no such thing as an unconscious layer of mind—or if acknowledged, as in "Freudian slips," it certainly is not of real consequence. As a result, we often act as if we do not need to be fully accountable for unconscious expressions or actions—after all, consciously those "microaggressions" were not our intent! In my mind, the biggest fuel sustaining systemic racism (as well as sexism and all "isms") is our individual and societal systemic resistance to and projection and denial of all our own "unconscious stuff," so to speak.

Thus, in my pool story, I did not intend to be racist or aggressive in calling my students "my boys," and yet I basically was by using a word that is saturated in violence and humiliation for Black men, but so easy for me to say. I wish I had been more attuned and thoughtful to turn inward and more able to link my conscious intention with my own unconsciously identified stance of White superiority transmitted across America's centuries of Black enslavement, exploitation, and violent humiliation by deed and word. If that had been possible, I could have made a small effort to "own" the violence of the past by not continuing it. But I did not have such a presence of mind at that time in my life.

It was not only the children who heard me say "my boys"—other adults were around and it landed on them too! The pool manager and his assistant manager together spoke to me directly in emotionally laden language about why I should not and could not ever talk like that again. I listened and I learned how much words matter, mark bodies, shape minds, and set the terms by which a society exists—now and in the future.

It is a difficult *truth* that all of us live within the space between two minds: the unconscious and the conscious. The unconscious is a layer of the human mind that is not stationary—it pulses at times. Such pulses let us know that what is out of our conscious mind may need tending. For example, you forget where your keys are; once, twice, three times in a week you forget the milk your partner asked for; or you make a "microaggression" against a colleague, and not for the first time. Depending on how serious the issue, the frequency of pulses may increase or the pulses may become bigger ruptures into our conscious minds. Importantly, this is true not just for individuals but for groups/societies as well!

My sense is that America entered an intense period of inflection in 2020 and into 2021 regarding systemic racism and classism. Addiction to prescription medications across classes, increasing mass shootings (school shootings began in the 1990s), burgeoning incarceration rates, ongoing police shootings of Black men, and more polarization of political parties all appear to me as pulses of our social unconscious calling attention to what is ailing us as a country and needs tending.

The 2020 election was a test, and then a sign, to White citizens that our country can move toward addressing the darkest aspects of America's unconscious racist history—and its conscious but often minimized racist present. Surely we must transition from *the surface* of skin color or of protruding (or not) exterior body parts, in the case of gender, to *the interior* workings of what makes us most human in our shared and fragile humanity.

Home Is Where "There You Are" Really Lives

Thomas Wolfe said you can't go home again, but if that place never felt like home, when you do return, can you make it a home? If you have fled a place and labeled it as "not me" only to find out in many respects "it is you," is reconciliation ever possible? Over 40 years later I began to answer that question.

I was sitting at the Raleigh-Durham International Airport. Airports are special transitional spaces within which we travelers hover in what is, has been, and could be. Eating breakfast alone, I was feeling a tug of depression and was glad for the silence. I did not notice a group of women seated elsewhere until I heard their excited joy-filled voices. I hunkered down to armor myself. Were they really talking loudly or was it my brittle state of mind? Ah, these were friends anticipating a girls' weekend away—no partners or children to attend to, just freedom to do whatever.

The ocean and beach were calling them together somewhere beyond driving distance. I felt a little bit of sunshine inside and then their easy laughter and teasing brought a little more lightness. The undertow of emotional darkness began to recede. Gate time was approaching, yet I simply could not leave without telling them how they had "shifted my day" to finding a better emotional footing.

I walked to them and said, "Excuse me, ladies."

An array of looks came my way, from *Uh oh, is criticism coming?* and *Don't even think about giving us attitude!* to a shielded blankness and a cautious smile.

I explained that their joy had lifted me from the pull of depression so I simply needed to thank them. The initial mixed emotional tenor shifted toward engagement and we exchanged where we were going and why. Then I stepped back to leave. One woman jumped up and said, "Oh, let's take a picture for the beginning of our trip."

I offered to take one, but no, they wanted me in it too. Surprised, I stepped forward again and the waitperson became photographer.

This is a more complicated story than it might be simply because these women were Black and I am White. It really could not yet be a simple snapshot of an early 21st-century airport scene of women. When I heard their louder voices, I also heard the racist inner voices of my past saying how Black people can just talk too loudly, just take up too much social room, and another voice in me saying, *No, it's a sign of life force speaking. I am still here after 400 years of aggression and I will not be annihilated.*

If I were a Black person, would I have even felt okay approaching a group of White women? Was I just one more White person "expecting" Black women to take care of me or entertain me out of my funk? Was the group photo a moment of true humanity shared or a record taken of my being a token White person actually being human and connected? Though we lived in our area of racial diversity, we were traveling to locations of our separate racial tribes, so to speak: Jamaica, an originating place of enslavement, and northern Michigan, a chosen place of Scandinavian immigration.

In Closing: A Process

There will be a day when that airport story will not need unpacking. It will just be a memory of a palette of feelings that were experienced by us all, where in the span of 20 minutes, we went from a segregated twosome to become one group of vacationing women. For now, though, "no matter where you go, there you are" requires more wondering and thinking on "what about race?"

In matters of race, I have come to believe that being a good "working collaborator" is actually more to the point than being a "good ally," because in allyship there is a sense that one can reach a static state of arrival—"Okay, now I am here: a good ally." *Ally* also evokes a quality that you are outside the problem of racism, whereas in *collaboration*—even when it only resides in one's intrapersonal work of airport thinking versus behavioral interpersonal action—you know there will always be another experience with more to work with and through.

As I have learned in becoming and working as a psychoanalyst, in large measure to take on that identification means you have consciously put yourself on a lifetime path of being humbled through learning from your own and others' unconscious material. It seems a similar journey to becoming and working as a collaborator in antiracism—it is a never-ending process of learning and working to do better by leaning into owning and making conscious America's unconscious racial contract, of which we White people are each a part. This does not always feel good or even satisfying.

We need to be willing, however, to step onto a path of knowing that even your best antiracist intentions will be interrupted by unconscious pulses at times to let you know "what else" you need to take into account, acknowledge, grieve the loss of, and perhaps make reparation for to move toward reweaving a viable social web that holds all and has structures that are more equitable and just. In the final analysis, we must not avoid or disavow that "no matter where you go, there you are" by leaving out the unconscious mind. We must accept all of it—the good, the creative, the bad, the beautiful, and the racist ugly—from both regions of our minds and do better.

References

Crenshaw, K. (1989). Demarginalizing the intersection of race and sex: A Black feminist critique of antidiscrimination It wadoctrine, feminist theory and antiracist politics. *University of Chicago Legal Forum, 1989*(1), Article 8.

DiAngelo, R. (2018). *White fragility*. Beacon Press.

Layton, L. (2019). Transgenerational hauntings: Toward a social psychoanalysis and an ethic of dis-illusionment. *Psychoanalytic Dialogues, 29*, 05–121.

Menakem, R. (2021). *My grandmother's hands*. Penguin.

Oluo, I. (2018). *So you want to talk about race*. Seal Press.

Pierce, C. (1970). Offensive mechanisms. In F. Barbour (Ed.), *The black seventies* (pp. 265–282). P. Sargent.

Van der Kolk, B. (2015). *The body keeps score*. Penguin.

Wilkerson, I. (2020). *Caste*. Penguin.

27

Authentic Allyship Through Cross-Cultural Mentoring

A Personal Journey

Betty Neal Crutcher

Mentorship can prepare us to be strong allies; cross-cultural mentoring can give us both the skills and ideals to create the beloved community throughout our ever-expanding world.

An examination of the roots of "mentor" and "ally" tells us that mentorship precedes allyship. "Mentor" comes from ancient Greek. We first encounter the term in Homer's *Odyssey,* when Odysseus leaves his only son under the guidance and care of one he trusts named Mentor. My own introduction to mentoring came first-hand from another Homer—my father. What the classical literature wrote about, my father actually put into practice. Proud of his work as an electrician trained and employed by Tuskegee Institute, Mr. Homer L. Neal Sr. mentored students and even brought them home for lunch.

My father also showed me how to transform a stranger into an ally. "Ally" derives from the Latin word *alligare*, meaning to bind, to protect each other, and to act together. This is related to the Old French word for "alliance," which some centuries ago was used to describe marriage. Often those who become allies begin with little in common. This was the experience for both my father and me.

Growing up in a predominately Black community, I watched my father find an ally in Mr. P., a white electrician. Together they worked on projects, taking turns guiding, supporting, caring for, and learning to trust each other. As allies in their work who became friends in the process, they would become a model for me in the development of my passion for mentoring and cross-cultural mentoring (Crutcher, 2014). Bridges could indeed be crossed and we could all begin to move forward together.

Betty Neal Crutcher, *Authentic Allyship Through Cross-Cultural Mentoring* In: *Antiblackness and the Stories of Authentic Allies.* Edited by: Norman Kim, Carolyn Coker Ross, Mazella Fuller and Charlynn Small, Oxford University Press.
© Oxford University Press 2024. DOI: 10.1093/oso/9780197642535.003.0028

Rich Roots in Tuskegee

In the best of circumstances, we begin by being mentored by our family members and community leaders as the values and virtues that sustain us are passed from one generation to the next.

I was born on a college campus at the John A. Andrew Hospital on the grounds of Tuskegee Institute, now Tuskegee University, a place where my parents, Homer L. Neal Sr. and Rosea Carpenter Neal, both studied and worked—my father as an electrician and refrigeration specialist and my mother in elementary education. My place in the family was the oldest of four children, followed by Peggy Ann, Jacqueline Denise, and Homer Lewis Jr., now known as "Omar," who remains in Tuskegee and is a former mayor.

My mother grew up in Eutaw, Alabama, in a large family of eight living siblings. Her family owned many acres of wooded land that included timber. Enthusiastic as they were entrepreneurial, the family businesses included farming, chopping and marketing lumber, trimming and styling hair, selling Blair products, and doing whatever they could to take care of their family.

My father, one of 11 children, was proud of his service during World War II as a cook for the Navy in Cuba; he sent back money for his mother to buy property. We grew up on what we called "Neal-Tyson Hill," surrounded by the love and support of relatives and my father's mother, Maggie Gunn Neal, widowed at an early age when my father was 9 years old. She grew and sold vegetables and was also a midwife.

On Sunday afternoon, after church, the grandchildren would gather for a presentation to our elders. We would sing songs and recite poetry we learned in school or church. Then we would rush down the hill to our Aunt Ella and Uncle Frank's house for coconut and chocolate cake. We were a close-knit family who shared attention and appreciation while looking out for each other. This gave me a deep sense of belonging and willingness, even eagerness, to share with everyone in a spirit of trust.

From my childhood through most of my undergraduate years, the segregated town of Tuskegee, Alabama, was a tightly connected community that represented the pride of the swift-growing South. We took pride in remembering the Tuskegee Airmen who trained around our town to fight in World War II, and in how Eleanor Roosevelt, the wife of Franklin Roosevelt, the 36th president of the United States, had flown in the sky with one of the Tuskegee Airman, C. Alfred "Chief" Anderson, who carried our hopes and dreams for a better day. Tuskegee Institute was central to our lives, in many ways woven into our very being. The great spirit of founder and former slave Booker T. Washington, with his emphasis on education and industry and giving back, infused the campus: "Nothing ever comes to one, that is worth having, except as a result of hard work." "We all should rise above the clouds of ignorance, narrowness, and selfishness." "If you want to lift yourself up, lift up someone else." For most of my time in Tuskegee, Luther H. Foster was the president of Tuskegee Institute (1953–1981). He had earned an MBA and had a quiet kind of confidence. He was also an eloquent speaker, sharing wisdom and inspiration, such as "The successes of Tuskegee, often under trying circumstances, are rooted in the Institute's commitment to human dignity. Our operational style seeks to elicit from others high expectations and committed service for the common good" (Tuskegee University Presidents, 2002, paragraph 4).

In my all-Black high school I won a contest for "Miss Personality"—the prize included an afternoon visit at the Tuskegee Institute President's Residence, with President Foster and his wife, first lady Vera Foster. Mrs. Foster and my mother knew each other, admired each other, and had a friendship. Mrs. Foster, I would later learn, was a Phi Beta Kappa of Fisk University with a master's degree in sociology from the University of Nebraska. She served as a social worker for the Veterans Administration and would sit on the national boards of the YWCA, Common Cause, and Planned Parenthood. She was a founder of the Alabama chapter of the American Association of University Women. Details from that visit over 50 years ago are hazy now. I'm sure my mother dressed me in my Sunday best. Feeling a bit nervous, however, I was welcomed into the president's home and shown a special kind of hospitality that made me feel comfortable and gave me a sense of belonging. Words such as "allyship" and "mentoring" were not part of the vocabulary. The Tuskegee campus community promoted its values of service to each other and the outside world.

Looking back on that date, it was as if this was an audition for a higher purpose, for a later role for me to play, as presidential spouse for 10 years at Wheaton College in Norton, Massachusetts, and for 6 years at the University of Richmond in Richmond, Virginia. The Fosters gave me a model of a presidential couple that had strengthened town and gown relationships. When the opportunity presented itself almost four decades later, I could walk with a certain measure of confidence in the role of presidential spouse with my husband, Ronald A. Crutcher, serving as the first Black president for both these institutions.

Recently I was honored and humbled to receive a special acknowledgment from a White university department chair, who wrote, "Dr. Betty Neal Crutcher is always ready to step in and step up to foster growth and connections and positivity across so many different levels, including same-aged peers and colleagues, new mentees and educators, especially in the African American/Black community. She is a champion of women in academia." My intent to embody the Tuskegee ideal of service to others now embraced the new words of allyship and mentoring in my desire to help create a better world.

From the Warmth of the South to the Cold of the Midwest

Because of an administrative error in the Tuskegee registrar's office, my early graduation was delayed and my advisor offered me a place in an exchange program between Tuskegee Institute and the predominantly White University of Michigan. When the flight landed at the Detroit Metro Airport, there outside the window was the shock of my young life—a foot of snow! As a young Black woman from the South, my mind and body were actually traumatized with fear. Would I lose my footing and fall into a deep valley?

Gratitude fills my heart for the then-new community of students, staff, and professors of different ethnic backgrounds who, by listening, caring, supporting, building trust, and offering wise counsel, became for me the bridge to a world unknown.

Navigating new experiences in the Midwest, I felt as if I were on another planet. People didn't speak like me, they didn't dress like me, and in many ways, our thoughts and our values appeared to be so different. How could anyone get to know, trust, and understand people who didn't serve grits and bacon at breakfast and collard greens and cornbread at dinner?

I was still lost in that snow—yet people continued to be bridges and help shake the snow from my clothes, hold me steady, and give me new hope and assurance to stand on my own. They became mentors to me; their wisdom and guidance found a home in my head and in my heart. Here was also a new experience: My new mentors who helped me understand this strange new world were not always of the same race, gender, or religion. Differences that had been perceived as barriers became a foundation of strength. I no longer felt disoriented or isolated; a new sense of belonging was given to me by people from different backgrounds and races. My new White mentors helped

me understand the majority viewpoint and grow personally and professionally, and my Black mentors stretched me to reach new heights.

Henry "Hank" T. Johnson, who was a Morehouse College graduate and
vice president for student services at the University of Michigan, welcomed
me to his staff and helped to give me a sense of belonging in a predominately
White institution. The university would later describe him as having a

> unique management style, characterized by an unusual compassion and
> understanding for the students who were the primary beneficiaries of his
> services.... Henry T. Johnson has demonstrated an enthusiasm, a gracious-
> ness, and an energy that have enabled those associated with him to aspire
> and to achieve high levels of accomplishments. (University of Michigan
> Regents Proceedings, 1991, paragraphs 2 and 4)

Another early bridge builder was Clyde Briggs, a Black educator who
encouraged me to pursue a graduate degree in the School of Public Health.
He said to me, "I see more in you than you see in yourself." My mentor's
ability to perceive a vision of my future and to believe in the possibility of its
being realized would become part of my own mentoring toolbox.

**My encounters with Vice President "Hank" Johnson and counselor Clyde
Briggs helped to build my self-worth. I would need every ounce of the confidence they and others had given me to overcome the next roadblock.**

A Time Without Allies

Not every experience at the University of Michigan included people who were
recognized as allies and mentors. Encouraged to apply to the master's program at the School of Public Health, I was told that this professional domain
could use "more of my tribe." My studies included biostatistics and hospital
administration. While my grades were better than passing, some in the school
accused me of studying too much. A group of White male professors asked
to meet with me and put me in the middle of their circle. Coming from the
segregated South, this was a frightening experience. They told me that my time
would not include a role in their department at the School of Public Health.
The White professors agreed that if another program in the School of Public
Health would accept me, then I could stay at the school. Knock on doors, they
told me, with a laugh, and see if anyone else might have a place for me.

What the professors did not know was something deeper inside me. My mother and grandmother had knocked on doors, selling Avon and Blair products. Knocking on doors was a pleasure and part of the entrepreneurial success of my family. It was a best practice. There was no fear, and rejection was part of the process. I knocked on many doors, and I heard only nos. No other options presented themselves—except to keep knocking. Who could return to a hometown such as mine having failed at the University of Michigan School of Public Health? Not I.

Finally, behind the last door was another White professor, Dr. Michael Decker. He was a very tall man and his stature and expression were intimidating, but he welcomed me with a gentle voice, and he listened. He apologized for his colleagues, and he invited me to study public health administration under his leadership, indicating that if my grades could equal my previous work, he would accept me into his program.

My gratitude to Dr. Michael Decker for giving me a special chance to prove myself is beyond my capacity to express. Professor Decker would be remembered as a kind and gracious ally. He later had a long career at the University of Texas School of Public Health in Houston. For his *Houston Chronicle* obituary in 2010, a student wrote, "He was the quintessential scholar, educator, mentor and was my friend" (Houston Chronicle, 2010, Paragraph 4).

Invisible Mentoring by Cabinet Member Patricia Roberts Harris

A few years after receiving my master's in public health from the University of Michigan and serving in the Michigan State Department of Public Health, I met my husband, Ronald A. Crutcher, a classical cellist who had begun his work as a professor of music. My aspirations were made clear: to receive a doctorate and to become secretary of health and human services, like Secretary Patricia Roberts Harris, a lawyer, educator, and the first Black woman to serve in the U.S. Cabinet. In 1977, Harris was first appointed as secretary of housing and urban development. At her confirmation hearing, she was queried as to her ability to represent the interests of the poor. Her response was:

I am one of them. You do not seem to understand who I am. I am a Black woman, daughter of a dining-car worker. I am a Black woman who even eight years ago could not buy a house in some parts of the District of Columbia. . . . I started, Senator, not as a lawyer at a prestigious law firm, but as a woman who needed a scholarship to go to college. If you think that I have forgotten that, you are wrong. (GW Today, 2017, Paragraph 6)

I was so impressed with Secretary Harris, who was raised by a single mother. My father had left to migrate for a better opportunity during my early high school years, so Secretary Harris shared with me a special bond.

My recollection is that my meeting with Secretary Harris in Washington, DC happened during a tour with staff from the state of Michigan. I was impressed with everything about her—her clothes, her voice, her sense of command, even how she walked. Just thinking about Secretary Harris gave me courage in my professional life. If she could become secretary of health and human services, then maybe someday so could I.

The accomplishments of others have given me and continue to give me strength. They carry me on their shoulders as I carry others, and together, we can reach new heights.

A New Best Practice

After our marriage, my husband took a job as a music professor at the University of North Carolina (UNC) at Greensboro. I left my profession in public health and was recruited to be assistant to the UNC chancellor. This was followed by my serving as assistant to the president at Guilford College, also in Greensboro, and then as director of community relations at the Cleveland Clinic in Cleveland, Ohio, where my time was also spent mentoring medical students, interns, doctors, and community members and setting up the first exchange program between the Cleveland Clinic and the Morehouse School of Medicine. My next academic appointment was the University of Texas–Austin, serving as an assistant to the President and community relations specialist. This was followed by 5 years at Miami University in Oxford, Ohio, where my husband served as provost. As community outreach coordinator, my specialty became the mentoring of students at risk, working in recruitment and retention of local students of color. My unspoken work as an ally and mentor was based on what I learned at Tuskegee and someday to be called "church" ground rules: the best practices of welcoming, listening, showing kindness, giving respect, building bridges, and building community.

With our daughter Sara off to college, my activities at Miami included a women of color luncheon to highlight successful stories of women of color on campus. With the success of that and other similar events, I began to feel the tug toward a long-ago aspiration: to receive a doctorate. After spending almost 20 years in higher education and community relations, mentoring and being mentored with my husband at every campus institution where we served, now at age 50, a new path was opening.

A PhD in education administration seemed appropriate, and it would be about mentoring. The process for me to apply for consideration for a PhD at the Miami School of Education seemed unusual; I was given a blue book and told to sit at a desk in an otherwise empty room without a purse or any other papers. The purpose was to write in that blue book my reasons for wanting a doctorate and what my line of research would add to the already expansive literature on mentoring. My decision on my area of study was clear: the attributes that made mentors and mentoring successful.

Sitting alone in this room, I began to think about all the people who had tapped me on the shoulder and helped to move me forward. *How did that happen? What were the ingredients for mentoring success?* I'd been educated in and out of the classroom. People of both the same and different ethnic backgrounds had helped me learn, grow, and become more of myself. *What were the qualities and actions that others had shown me to propel me toward success?*

In this bare and empty room with not so much as a curtain at the window, my mind could not have been more full. Flooded with a rush of realization of all that had propelled me forward, my soul brought forth a type of vision, an understanding of the heart of successful mentoring. I instinctively called it "the three Vs"—the *values* mentors had shared with me that showed our commonalities, the *virtues* that give us the ability to navigate new terrain and overcome barriers, and the holding of the *vision* "I see more in you than you see in yourself."

After receiving my doctorate on "Cross-Cultural Mentoring: An Examination of the Mentors" (Crutcher, 2006), my mentoring work would be defined by these new best practices—"the three Vs" of values, virtues, and vision. This could also be a pathway for building allies, a way to move the heart to soften the head for greater understanding and acceptance.

Mentoring faculty, staff, students, community members, and even trustees as a presidential spouse would be my major role for 10 years at Wheaton College in Norton, Massachusetts, and for 6 years at the University of

Richmond in Richmond, Virginia. Now my toolbox was fuller and included listening with the three Vs and expanding the circle of belonging to help create inclusive excellence for all.

Building Allies to Transform a 40-Year Tragedy

Moving toward inclusive excellence can be stunted by the past. Growing up in Tuskegee, I had no idea that my relatives were involved in a 40-year tragedy—four decades without allies—as mistreated participants of the U.S. Public Health Service Syphilis Study at Tuskegee (Centers for Disease Control and Prevention, 2022) and Macon County. The infamous government study took place from 1932 through 1972 at the John A. Andrew Hospital in Tuskegee, the very hospital of my birth, where more than 600 Black men were told, perhaps some on the very morning of my birth, that they were being treated for "bad blood." My own relatives—including Rufus Neal, Rueben Neal, and Uncle Freddie Lee Tyson—took part in this study under false pretenses, deceived by their own government.

Even a public apology from William J. Clinton, the 42nd president of the United States, in 1997 could not undo this damage that bred widespread mistrust (Newsome, 2021), evidenced most recently by the reluctance and refusal of many in Black communities across the country to seek the COVID-19 vaccine, thus adding to the health disparities we already face.

The coming of COVID-19 would make the finding of new allies and the need for mentoring people of color as medical students, doctors, nurses, and other health care professionals a paramount concern. My time spent as board member of the Voices for Our Fathers Legacy Foundation and cochair and chair of the Scholarship Committee included our goal of lifting up 623 new Black voices in health care. My work also included serving on the board of the Cobb Institute/National Medical Association, as cochair of the Cobb Pipeline/Pathways Committee, and as a member of the Cobb Scholars Advisory Committee.

As co-founder and board member of the Seeds of Hope Mentoring Program in Boston, I serve with allies that include both Harvard medical school students and faculty to encourage underrepresented minority students of all ethnicities to consider careers in the health care field. As a cross-cultural mentor at Seeds of Hope, I mentor Latinx and other students of color with the goal that together we can help to eliminate health care disparities that harm minority communities.

Cross-Cultural Mentoring Today

One of my University of Richmond mentees, Dr. Leslie Mark, recently wrote an article called "The Power of a Mentor" for the *University of Richmond Magazine* and wrote about her experiences in cross-cultural mentoring.

As a Black woman interested in pursuing surgery, I knew I could not assume that I would find only mentors who looked like me. . . . I also did not want only mentors who looked like me because I would be treating a diverse population of people. It became important for me to find mentors from as many backgrounds as possible. (Mark, 2021, Paragraph 12)

Dr. Mark (2021) also said, "On the pathway to my M.D., my family, Dr. Crutcher, and other mentors reminded me of my potential, and their support inspired me to never give up." (Paragraph 14)

The Tuskegee emphasis on service and the church-based ground rules of welcoming, listening, showing kindness, giving respect, building bridges, and building community continue to guide my work. As an ally and mentor, these best practices for me now include the three Vs: values, virtues, and vision. My aim is to continue to be one of the bridges of hope and healing with allies and mentors in unity with one another and for the betterment of our global community.

References

Centers for Disease Control and Prevention. (2022). Tuskegee Study and Health Benefit Program. http://www.cdc.gov/tuskegee/index.html

Crutcher, B. N. (2006). *Cross-cultural mentoring: An examination of the perspective of mentors.* http://rave.ohiolink.edu/etdc/view?acc_num=miami1151683574

Crutcher, B. N. (2014). Cross-cultural mentoring: A pathway to making excellence inclusive. *Liberal Education, 100*(2) , 26–31. dgmg81phhvh63.cloudfront.net

GW Today. (2017, March 29). *In her own words: The First African-American woman to become a cabinet secretary.* https://gwtoday.gwu.edu/her-own-words-first-african-american-woman-become-cabinet-secretary

Houston Chronicle. (2010, November 24). *Dr. Michael Decker.* https://www.legacy.com/us/obituaries/houstonchronicle/name/michael-decker-obituary?id=22852244

Mark, L. (2021, February 4). The power of a mentor. *University of Richmond Magazine.* https://urnow.richmond.edu/magazine/article/-/19494/the-power-of-a-mentor.html

Newsome, M. (2021, March 3). We learned the wrong lessons from the Tuskegee "experiment." *Scientific American.*

Tuskegee University Presidents. (2002). *Dr. Luther Hilton Foster, Jr., Fourth president of Tuskegee Institute.* https://www.tuskegee.edu/discover-tu/tu-presidents/luther-h-foster

University of Michigan Regents Proceedings. (1991, December). https://apps.lib.umich.edu/staff-memoir/apps.lib.umich.edu/staff-memoir/faculty/henry-t-johnson.html

28

Intersections

A Cross-Cultural Conversation

Keith W. McIntosh

Conversations about race happened often in my household growing up. For me, having a father in the military meant we lived in different countries and various parts of the United States. I attended multiple grade schools, middle schools, and high schools. Looking back, I can see how diverse and rich my childhood was and how it shaped my adult life. My parents instilled in my sisters and me a deep care and respect for others, a strong work ethic, and the value of education.

They also gave us **THE TALK**—the talk many if not all Black kids receive from their parents, the same talk I gave my son and daughter. They made sure we understood the challenges and dangers of racism, prejudice, and hatred based on the color of our skin. More importantly, they discussed our role and responsibility as Black kids in all situations with all people, especially those in authority or leadership positions, before, during, and after a situation or incident. There was a strong emphasis on how we spoke, how we carried ourselves, and how to handle specific situations to ensure our safety and to prevent escalation. Years later, I would learn that some people can go their entire lives without ever really having to think about race—let alone have conversations about the topic.

Although I was shy and an introvert growing up, as a child, and especially as a teen, I was mindful of those who were excluded, those who needed support or an ally. It pained me to see the marginalization of others. My empathy and love of people, coupled with a curiosity about other cultures, led to a focus on diversity, equity, and inclusion in my adult life, particularly in the practice of inclusive leadership. It also led me on a journey to bring people together to learn and share in uncomfortable conversations about race and other aspects of a person's identity and abilities.

Keith W. McIntosh, *Intersections* In: *Antiblackness and the Stories of Authentic Allies.* Edited by: Norman Kim, Carolyn Coker Ross, Mazella Fuller and Charlynn Small, Oxford University Press. © Oxford University Press 2024. DOI: 10.1093/oso/9780197642535.003.0029

I also believe racial equity is achievable. In 2017, I initiated a cultural conversation at the University of Richmond that came to be called *Intersections*. Intersections is a weekly, cross-cultural conversation open to all staff, faculty, and students. Our attendance ranges from 15 to 20 people each week. It increases to over 200 people for hot topics such as the deaths of George Floyd, Breonna Taylor, and Ahmaud Arbery or the 2022 shootings in Buffalo, New York, and Uvalde, Texas. I share my experiences on this journey with the hope that it will inspire others to start up similar conversations in their institutions, organizations, families, or communities.

The Genesis and Origins of Intersections

Our cultural conversation group was formed after the tragic events of the Unite the Right rally in August 2017. This White supremacist rally was held in Charlottesville, Virginia, about 65 miles west of the University of Richmond—about an hour's drive away. The world witnessed the acts of hatred and violence that occurred, including the death of Heather Heyer, who was killed by a motorist who drove his car into the crowd of counter-protestors. My wife, Penny, and I had visited Charlottesville for the first time just a few weeks prior and had walked those same streets.

When my staff, a team of 70-plus information technology professionals, came to work on Monday, August 14, 2017, it was all anyone could talk about, but they didn't really know how or what they wanted to share. My assistant, Melody Wilson, brought this to my attention. It was then that I decided to host a meeting for members of our division to discuss what happened. My intention was to create an opportunity for the team to share their thoughts, reactions, and feelings about what they had witnessed.

I got the idea of hosting a discussion from Gerald Hector, executive vice president and chief business officer at the University of Central Florida. I worked for Hector from 2014 to 2016 when we served at Ithaca College. While at Ithaca College, he initiated diversity and inclusion discussion circles in response to student criticism that diversity and inclusion were not prioritized at the college. He started these conversations on campus during lunch to provide a space where many faculty and staff could come to learn more about what they did not know with regard to race and racism. I also participated in these conversations.

During our first discussion meeting at the University of Richmond, those in attendance decided as a group to limit attendance to our division: Information Services. We did this for three reasons: to ensure privacy, to establish trust, and to build on our familiarity with each other. We felt that the subject matter would be sensitive and uncomfortable. It was and still is!! We focused the first half-hour of our first meeting on discussing why we were meeting, establishing some rules of engagement, and answering two questions: *What are your highest hopes for the outcome of these conversations?* and *What are your most realistic expectations?* Then we moved to sharing our thoughts and feelings about what we witnessed in Charlottesville.

We purposely focused our initial conversations about race, as the Unite the Right rally was a White supremacist rally. Our first meeting was awkward and uncomfortable. So were our second, third, and fourth meetings. Our first few months in the fall of 2017 were challenging primarily because people were not comfortable sharing or using their voice to discuss race. Many people had never had open or serious conversations about race. They were showing up, which was great, but they were reluctant and hesitant to speak. I did most of the talking. I realized that for the discussions to be productive and beneficial, it would be important for participants to actually participate. But how?

Once we selected a book to read and discuss, the conversation really started to flow, and that's when I knew we had something special. Our first book was *Overcoming Bias: Building Authentic Relationships Across Differences*, by Dr. Tiffany Jana and Matthew Freeman (2016). Their book uses vivid stories and fun (yes, fun!) exercises and activities throughout the seven chapters and a little over 100 pages to help us reflect on our personal experiences so we could uncover how our hidden biases are formed.

The authors tell us that we are all biased and it is "our human tendency to prefer some things and people more than others" (Jana & Freeman, 2016, p. ix) We also decided that someone other than me would guide each chapter discussion. We were fortunate, since the authors reside in Richmond, to have one of them, Dr. Jana, visit and speak with us at the conclusion of reading and discussing the book. We also were fortunate to have our university president, Dr. Ronald A. Crutcher, and presidential spouse, Dr. Betty Neal Crutcher, in attendance for this discussion.

Word was getting out about our conversations within our division, and folks began to inquire if they could join us. We posed this question to the team about 6 months into our journey. However, the team was not ready to open it up at that time. But after about a year into our journey, the team was ready to invite staff from other divisions.

As a group we chose the name *Intersections* because it accurately represented who we are and what we desired to be. The name derives from the concept of intersectionality originated in 1989 by civil rights activist and legal scholar Kimberlé Crenshaw. Intersectionality refers to the combination of certain aspects of who you are (your identities) and how your identities impact you. It is not just the identities but also the intersection of identities that provide an advantage or disadvantage to someone. We wanted to explore the myriad dimensions of identity to include gender, sex, race, class, sexuality, religion, disability, physical appearance, and beyond. We also wanted to be a place and a space where all were welcome.

A key aspect of our efforts and success has been using the entire community to curate the topics, to build a topic schedule, and having members facilitate discussions. During our first full year in 2018, we were discussing a different topic each week. We were rapidly moving through topics, but at a very high level. Although we met from noon to 1 p.m., we would often continue the conversation to 1:30 or 1:45 p.m. because we needed to go deeper. We also used the last few weeks of the year and beginning of the next year to identify our topics and build a schedule. In 2019 we decided to create monthly themes so we could dive deeper into topics. Typically the first week would be a primer to build a foundation, and then we would progress through the month, where the fourth week was a focus on actions we could take individually.

I received several inquiries to facilitate conversations and lead another group discussion on a different day, time, and location on campus because they were interested but couldn't attend on Wednesdays at noon. I realized I could not, but I thought it would be better if we shared what we were doing in the hope to inspire others to do the same. We decided to host a panel for the campus instead.

We hosted a lunch and learn session, "Talking About Race," in our Heilman Dining Center on February 14, 2019. The event was sponsored by the President's Advisory Committee for Making Excellence Inclusive and Information Services. We were pleased to have approximately 40 to 50 faculty and staff in attendance who were interested in learning how to start a cross-cultural intergroup dialogue in their own office or department. I think it helped that we also provided lunch!

During this lunch and learn we convened a panel that included Information Services division staff and new members from outside our division. We (Information Services) shared that we had been hosting weekly lunchtime dialogues on race and racism for over a year and it had garnered interest and attention from faculty and staff around campus. Our Intersections panel discussed the formation of the group, the challenges we faced, and the lessons we learned individually and collectively.

Our panelists shared thoughts about how these conversations affected them, preconceived notions they may have had prior to attending, what they had learned, why they kept attending, and what had been most challenging for them. We concluded with fielding audience questions following the panel discussion. It was important for us to show others how we did it so they could do it too. Basically, we were teaching others how to fish, so to speak.

This was also the moment when faculty in attendance asked if they could participate in our discussions, to which we agreed. Additionally, Blake Stack, assistant director, student engagement and operations, asked if we could include students in our discussion. He led the meeting where students were first included, on July 17, 2019, and on July 31, 2019, we began advertising weekly meetings in SpiderBytes, our daily university e-mail digest.

"Social Change Requires Social Exchange"

Dr. Robert Livingston, a social psychologist and diversity consultant who is a leading expert on the science of bias and racism, released a wonderful book in early 2021 called *The Conversation*. I highly encourage you to get it, read it, and read it again. Dr. Livingston (2021) states, "Social Change requires Social Exchange" (p. 20). I couldn't agree more. I believe conversations, purposeful and intentional, provide each of us the ability to learn so much about others as well as ourselves. It is through these conversations that we can build awareness and understanding, which in turn can lead to action and change. Change cannot occur without awareness and understanding.

Not only are conversations a key component of strong and healthy relationships, but also they are at the core of our ability to develop our cross-cultural intelligence and cross-cultural communication skills. Now I am not talking about casual conversations. Do not get me wrong— casual conversations serve a purpose. But we need to have direct, open, candid, informed, and truthful conversations that make us uncomfortable.

These conversations include discussions on racism, sexism, homophobia, Islamophobia, anti-Semitism, and ageism, just to name a few.

The Center for Creative Leadership (2022)—a top-ranked global provider of leadership development headquartered in Greensboro, North Carolina—says that our "inability to have meaningful conversations contributes significantly to the unproductive relationships that can sometimes develop across diversity divides." We need to be comfortable, confident, and capable of having meaningful conversations with folks from vastly different backgrounds, perspectives, or lived experiences.

We endeavor to have these types of conversations in Intersections. Our conversations have not always been easy or comfortable. For example, most of us avoid the topic of racism throughout our lives. Racism exists and it impacts us all—some much more than others. Our ability or inability to have a conversation about race, racism (individual and structural or systemic), White privilege, whiteness, prejudice, stereotypes, and biases enhances or deters our effectiveness in working with others. These are all topics we tend to avoid.

Attendance has always been and always will be voluntary. We have had people come once and not come back. We have had people come regularly until we discuss a topic that was too much for them at that moment and they did not return. We have had people leave and come back. We also continue to have new people join us. The key is persistence. We need to persist through our discomfort so we can learn and grow.

Intersections has helped each of us grow and develop. First and foremost, we have learned more about ourselves. We have learned about our own biases, prejudices, and stereotypes. We identify and determine where they come from as well as how they have impacted and are impacting our thoughts, words, and actions. We have also learned more about others, especially those who are different from us.

We have exposed histories that we did not know existed and how they have shaped and continue to shape the country and communities we live in today. We have learned about policies, processes, and structures that negatively impact some while positively impacting others. We have learned how to look at the person in the mirror so we can address our discomfort with topics and issues while building our ability to persist despite how they make us feel. We also have grown in our ability to handle difficult conversations and situations. While our focus has been and continues to be education, awareness, and understanding, many Intersections participants have been moved to action in their personal lives, in their families, and in their communities.

People participate in Intersections for a variety of reasons. Some attend for the education they receive about other cultures, orientations, and ideologies. Some remark how Intersections challenges, expands, and develops their understanding of their own beliefs and thinking while appreciating the diversity of viewpoints. One participant, Austin Jones (Pseudonym)shared that "It is an opportunity to learn; garner the perspective of others; be an inspiration as well as be inspired; to seek and contribute in a manner that is constructive, meaningful, and for the betterment of all who engage" (A. Jones, personal communication, July 2, 2020).

I Am Confident You Can Start Your Own Discussion

I often hear people say they would like to create something like Intersections but they do not know how or they do not possess a position or title to be able to do so. People also say, "Well, I am not a person of color" or "I am not from an underrepresented group." Several will tell me that they are not this or they are not that, so they are not sure if they can or should lead such an effort. They also say they do not have any experience with these issues, nor do they have any formal education on these topics. I respect and understand these statements and concerns, but I also challenge folks to not let any of those statements or any other excuses hold them back from pursuing this if they are called or feel called to do so. Perhaps you may be wondering if you can start something like this at your campus, and the short answer is yes, you can.

Remember our first panel discussion? One of the attendees was Hilary Brown Appleton, assistant director, donor relations, who works in our Advancement division. Hilary was inspired to start a group in her division after attending our panel discussion. In her words, "I left that panel discussion fired up!" (H. Appleton, personal communications, July 2, 2020).

She and I met the following week and I shared our meeting structure, topic history, recommended reading, and rules of engagement; answered her questions; and provided advice. I advised her to get approval from her leadership and to find someone who can partner with her. She spoke with her vice president and asked for her support, which she gave enthusiastically. Then she identified a cofacilitator, Emily Saunders, assistant director, Student & Young Graduate Program, Office of Alumni Relations. The two of them completed 3 days of facilitator training with a local organization in Richmond.

Before launching their discussions, they did a lot of planning. Hilary stated:

> We knew we had to make our conversations relevant to our division's business purpose—engaging alumni and donors to raise money and advance the University's strategic plan. We wrote a mission statement, goals, and guiding principles, and we also adopted the rules of engagement you graciously shared. (H. Appleton, personal communications, July 2, 2020)

They thought carefully about the people in their division and what would make them want to attend. They officially launched their meetings in December 2019 and have been meeting every other week since then. I am super proud of these two because although they did not have any experience leading these types of discussions, they had an abundance of courage, commitment, curiosity, and compassion.

Hilary, along with her longtime friend in Richmond, Virginia, Christine Wu, recently launched a podcast called "I Might Be Biased," which grapples with identity, bias, and the way we view others. I was honored when they asked me to be their first guest. What we have done at the University of Richmond can be done anywhere.

Learning as You Listen

The events of 2020, in particular the tragic deaths of Ahmaud Arbery, Breonna Taylor, and George Floyd, sparked a social justice movement. Many in the Black community have long been aware of such attacks on our brothers and sisters. Now the world became aware as a young man was violently chased and gunned down while jogging in his neighborhood. A young woman lost her life while asleep in her home. A man lost his life after someone knelt on him for 8 minutes and 46 seconds, which was caught on video.

The world witnessed the rioting and violent attack on the U.S. Capitol on January 6, 2021. They watched again the senseless and violent attacks on our brothers and sisters in the Asian American and Pacific Islander (AAPI) community that occurred without retribution across the United States. We still see continued hatred and violence directed at the Jewish and Muslim community.

All of these examples serve as a reminder of the need for dialogue to lead to action to stamp out hate and build bridges within and among communities. Although I have not been a victim of such physical and violent attacks, I have experienced profiling; been pulled over and detained for no reason, including once with my wife in the car; and received verbal insults and racial slurs. These incidents have occurred and continue to occur in our communities. Intersections has been there for participants to learn and understand more about such events.

Each of us learns or gleans information during these conversations. Not only do we learn about others, but also we learn more about ourselves. Intersections is seen as a brave and sometimes therapeutic space for attendees to be with others who are open to learning how to understand and address biased behavior. It is also a space where folks have identified and interrogated their biases, stereotypes, and prejudices. Additionally, participants have been inspired to do more in their personal lives, within their families, or even in their communities with respect to developing their cross-cultural awareness.

I received an e-mail from someone who had been attending Intersections for a few months and has yet to speak in any conversation, which is perfectly okay. They wrote:

> I would like to say the work that you're doing through "Intersections" is amazing. I feel like I've learned so many different perspectives of how others feel and how they have been treated. I apologize for not speaking much in these conversations. I have never had to deal with racism before because I grew up in Rural Pennsylvania. We were a small community made up of Polish and Italian ethnicities. Anyway, my point is I am learning as I listen to everyone's stories and just can't fathom how people can be so cruel and inhumane to one another. I am honestly at a loss of words most times. Also, you all speak more eloquently than I ever could. Again, thank you for having the courage to stand up for people who just do not have the words to speak (Anonymous or Emery Smith (pseudonym), personal communications, March 24, 2021).

Intersections is successful in large part due to those who attend. Attendees contribute and receive valuable information during our weekly exchanges. These conversations are not always easy or comfortable, but I learned a phrase from a former colleague, Dr. Belisa Gonzales: "We must get comfortable with being uncomfortable." It is through the discomfort that awareness, understanding, and growth happen.

Keith Webb, associate director/career advisor in Career Services, captured the spirit of Intersections when he stated:

> I appreciate the efforts by you and your team to create a space for dialogue. It has the community talking and we need that! People do not know what they do not know, and Intersections has given folks from a variety of backgrounds, beliefs, upbringings, etc., to join the Intersections community once a week and take a deep dive into a subject, with the intent of each participant leaving with at least one thing they were unaware of prior to the meeting.(K. Webb, personal communications, February 14, 2021)

Perhaps you are reading this and thinking, "Hey, I am a good person. I am open minded. I treat people fairly. I am not a racist." Ibram X. Kendi (2019), author of *How to Be an Antiracist*, defines a racist as "one who is supporting a racist policy through their actions or inaction or expressing a racist idea" (p. 13) and an antiracist as "one who is supporting the antiracist policy through their actions or expressing an antiracist idea" (p. 13).

The key outcome of these cross-cultural conversations is enabling participants to move from being nonracist to antiracist (antisexist, antiageist, etc.). Several Intersections members have remarked how they are more knowledgeable, confident, and prepared to take antiracist actions. For some it was having conversations with their family or friends for the first time around uncomfortable topics. For others it was writing letters to elected officials about policies. For still others it was seeking to proactively support traditional marginalized groups with their time, talent, or treasure.

The most precious resource we have is each other. We do what we do for and with people, whether they are family, friends, coworkers, community members, or even strangers. I encourage you to step out of your comfort zone, develop your own cultural intelligence, and start having honest, real conversations about racism and all forms of marginalization. I hope you will take the necessary steps to educate yourself about the lived experiences of others so you can build an awareness and understanding of different backgrounds, and most importantly so you will take appropriate and necessary actions to build an equitable and inclusive community.

References

Center for Creative Leadership (CCL). (2021, June 2). *5 powerful ways to take REAL action on DEI (diversity, equity & inclusion).* https://www.ccl.org/articles/leading-effectiv ely-articles/5-powerful-ways-to-take-real-action-on-dei-diversity-equity-inclusion/

Jana, T., & Freeman, M. (2016). *Overcoming bias: Building authentic relationships across differences.* Berrett-Koehler Publishers.

Kendi, I. X. (2019). *How to be an antiracist.* Penguin Random House.

Livingston, R. (2021). *The conversation: How seeking and speaking the truth about racism can radically transform individuals and organizations.* Penguin Random House.

29

Liberatory Training and Authentic Allyship

Clinical Supervision of Mental Health Interns

Rebecca Hurst

A Call for Liberatory Training

In concert with liberation movements in psychotherapy, liberatory training environments are fundamental to advancing the field of mental health practice. Training experiences that promote antiracism and embrace liberation are paramount to affirmative and growth-enhancing experiences for clients and clinicians of color and serve to humanize a field that purports to center diversity and humanity while struggling to do so in action.

Although there have been efforts to increase the diversity of graduate training programs, the racial/ethnic identities of mental health providers and trainees do not mirror the population they serve. In a survey of health service psychology doctoral programs in 2015, 64.5% of students were White, while 11.9% were Hispanic/Latinx, 7.6% Asian, and 7.0% Black, with even smaller numbers of Alaska Native or American Indian, Pacific Islander, and multiracial students (Page et al., 2017). In the same study, nearly 73% of doctoral program faculty were White, which is significant given the influential role that faculty play in the teaching, advising, and mentoring of graduate students.

There have been some recent gains in diversifying graduate mental health training programs. In the wake of intentional recruitment efforts, the percentage of psychology graduate students who identify as racial/ethnic minorities has increased from 27% in the 2006–2007 academic year to 35% in 2016–2017 (Bailey, 2020). Moreover, the fields of social work and mental health counseling demonstrate greater diversity in their student populations. In 2019, 50.2% of master's of social work students were White, while 20.1%

Rebecca Hurst, *Liberatory Training and Authentic Allyship* In: *Antiblackness and the Stories of Authentic Allies*.
Edited by: Norman Kim, Carolyn Coker Ross, Mazella Fuller and Charlynn Small, Oxford University Press.
© Oxford University Press 2024. DOI: 10.1093/oso/9780197642535.003.0030

were Black, 16.3% were Hispanic/Latinx, and 3.5% were Asian, while in practice-oriented doctoral programs in social work, 36% of students were White, 35.8% were Black, 10.5% were Hispanic/Latinx, and 3.3% were Asian (Council on Social Work Education, 2020). Similarly, in a 2017 survey, 59.8% of Council for Accreditation of Counseling and Related Educational Programs–accredited master's students were White, 18.4% were Black, 7.9% were Hispanic/Latinx, and 2.1% were Asian. In CACREP doctoral programs, 55.3% were White, 25.1% were Black, 5.7% were Hispanic/Latinx, and 3% were Asian (Council for Accreditation of Counseling and Related Educational Programs, 2018).

Experiences of Trainees of Color

While these gains in diversifying mental health training provide hope, graduate programs, which have been developed, structured, and implemented within ethnocentric, Western European philosophies and values and predominantly staffed by White faculty and clinicians, continue to struggle with providing affirming and multiculturally informed training experiences for students. Moreover, mental health internships are embedded within larger systems (e.g., colleges and universities, health care systems, military settings) that uphold and engage in White supremacist processes as the status quo way of doing business.

Graduate students of color commonly describe experiences of racial microaggressions, including oversensitivity to White student denial of racism, questioning of credibility, ascription of intelligence (assigning intelligence based on race and gender), and assumptions of criminality, isolation, marginalization, and tokenization (Linder et al., 2015). Psychology interns have framed their experiences during internship training utilizing Smith's (2004) framework of racial battle fatigue (RBF), which describes the social–psychological stress responses associated with being a person of color and the target of systemic racial oppression (Wang et al., 2020). These stress responses may include frustration, anger, exhaustion, physical avoidance, emotional withdrawal, escapism, and acceptance of racist attributions.

Likewise, interns of color report a number of problematic experiences in clinical supervision spaces that are not dissimilar to experiences described by clients of color in mental health treatment. For example, Constantine and Sue (2007) identified themes of microaggressions experienced by Black supervisees from White clinical supervisors in the fields of clinical and counseling psychology. These themes included invalidation from the supervisor when discussing racial issues, supervisor reluctance to provide feedback due to their own fears of being viewed as racist, intrapsychic blame toward clients of color rather than recognizing systemic factors, experiencing stereotypical assumptions about Black supervisees and clients, and receiving culturally insensitive treatment recommendations. Additionally, power dynamics inherent in supervisory relationships can complicate an already tenuous positionality for trainees of color. This results in increased emotional and intellectual labor due to real concerns of being misunderstood at one end of the continuum and being discriminated against on the other.

Trainees benefit from liberatory training environments that offer divergent ways of thinking and experiences with colleagues and supervisors with diverse racial identities. However, cross-racial engagement of antiracism and White supremacy within systems, while necessary, often presents challenges, and the bulk of negative impact is experienced by trainees of color. This is consistent with research showing that graduate-level psychology diversity courses disproportionately benefit White students when compared to students of color and that the experiences of students of color are often disregarded in these courses (Curtis-Boles & Bourg, 2010). Moreover, Black graduate students in predominantly White clinical and counseling programs report experiencing RBF across graduate student roles (i.e., as students in classrooms, as advisees, and as supervisees; Ragland Woods et al., 2021).

Recommendations to Support Liberatory Training

How can mental health training programs offer a more liberatory training experience for trainees? How can White staff serve as authentic allies in this process? These are essential questions we should be asking ourselves—and continuing to ask as we learn and revise processes. In this chapter, I offer some recommendations that are informed by both the literature and my experience as a clinical supervisor and member of training committees in university counseling center settings over the past decade. I address both systemic/structural considerations and ways that White clinicians can serve as authentic allies to trainees of color.

I am a White cisgender queer woman and counseling psychologist who has had the privilege of working with a diverse, knowledgeable, and engaged group of psychology, counseling, and social work interns over the years. I have also been fortunate to have worked with training directors and colleagues who are committed to training environments that promote the growth and development of trainees with a range of identities and lived experiences. This work has been imperfect, and there have been many challenges and missteps along the way. However, I can honestly say that the commitment to antiracist, liberatory training has been consistent.

Liberatory Training Must Be Held Collectively

This brings me to the most important component of a liberatory training program: It must be held and nurtured collectively. This means that the agency, including leadership, clinical, and nonclinical staff, needs to have the support, skills, and motivation to engage in creating an antiracist environment. This also means that upper-level administration must commit to funding and creating professional time and space for ongoing antiracism work. Without the financial, educational, and temporal resources, the work of antiracism is too easily subsumed by the ever-present currents of the status quo.

In mental health settings, emotional (Dishop et al., 2019) and service (Center for Collegiate Mental Health, 2017) demands can be quite high. In the context of increased demand, systems respond by uplifting values of productivity motivated by narratives of scarcity and self-sacrifice. In such work cultures, everyone is vulnerable to reverting to the ways of White supremacy as a means of survival. A critical, antiracist, liberation lens must be employed to challenge and interrupt these implicit and explicit values. Agencies that do not engage in the consistent work of challenging industrial, White supremacist norms will be vulnerable to inflicting harm on trainees whose positionality typically places them with less power in hierarchical systems. Staff and trainees of color are disproportionately burdened in these systems, often resulting in great harm.

Representation Is Necessary but Not Sufficient

Liberatory training programs also require representation of people of color in varying positions on the staff. Increased representation of staff of color can infuse the agency with diverse perspectives and increase the complexity and nuance with which we, for example, talk about clinical work or hiring processes. It invites challenges to predominantly White, patriarchal, and White supremacist ways of thinking and practicing. It also gives trainees the opportunity to interact with and learn from mentors and supervisors who share diverse identities and lived experiences. It creates the possibility for support and community with experiences and perspectives that may have formerly been kept in isolation without the possibility of witnessing, validation, and collective problem solving.

While representation is a prerequisite, it is not sufficient in and of itself. A major challenge for training programs is whether the agency has the leadership, systemic support, and skill to adjust values and processes to support and affirm a more diverse staff. Without these important shifts, staff and trainees of color are continually subjected to inequities within the system, while White staff are vulnerable to defensiveness, denial, and reversion to the status quo.

Having a Seat at the Table

Creating a culture of antiracism within an organization requires leadership who not only are willing but also have the skills and resources to support the collective work. For training programs, this means that training leadership (e.g., coordinators and directors of training) must have a real seat at the table and be meaningfully engaged in the overall leadership of the agency, including organizational antiracism work. Too often, training is relegated to a lower tier within the organizational hierarchy, which limits the potential for trainees to experience genuine systemic support and to express their own agency within the organization, and for the organization and trainees to grow from their mutual engagement.

Agency leaders should be involved in training and consultation to grow their skills and to continually clarify and refine their commitment to antiracism. Training directors have the unique opportunity to infuse diversity, equity, and antiracism throughout the training program. For example, seminar series and all-staff continuing education provide a platform for thoughtful selections that uplift antiracist practice across domains and populations while also attending to the developmental needs of both trainees and the agency. Additionally, consultative spaces for clinical supervisors offer the potential for rich dialogue and consistent collective support in honoring the identities and lived experiences of trainees in clinical supervision and in their interactions within the system. Didactic training and intentional consultative spaces help provide a scaffolding of knowledge and experience that allows staff and trainees to respond more constructively to racism when it occurs.

Without the awareness and skill development that comes from both education and experience engaging one another around issues of race and racism, there is no foundation to support the often difficult and potentially harmful responses (or lack or responses) to racism within an agency. The secondary trauma that can come from inappropriate and inadequate responses is yet another potentially harmful consequence of racism.

Evaluation Within the Training Program

The evaluation process is another salient area to consider within the training program. Trainees often talk about being in a "fishbowl," which is a reference to the intense scrutiny they experience throughout their graduate training programs through continuous evaluation and feedback. I have worked with several trainees who have experienced significant harm from feedback received from supervisors and professors. While any form of critical feedback can be challenging, it is important to acknowledge the deep limits to the content and process of evaluation within the field of mental health.

For example, content domains often reflect theoretical preferences of the particular training program, interpersonal behaviors deemed most appropriate within these types of therapeutic encounters, and/or developmental considerations from traditional models of clinical supervision. One challenge with this is that the vast majority of the theory and research supporting these clinical skills is developed through a Western European value system using research with predominantly White clinicians and clients (Henrich et al., 2010). Add to this the reality that trainees of color are often receiving feedback from supervisors who do not share similar lived experiences and may also be functioning from a limited understanding of their own racialized biases, and you can see the tenuous position in which trainees find themselves.

Let this sink in. Trainees of color are repeatedly met with evaluation that is set up to miss who they are in the encounter. This is a dehumanizing experience in a field that relies on the mental health clinician developing an understanding of themselves within the therapeutic space and being able to bring who they are into encounters with clients who also present with a range of lived identities and experiences. From a pedagogical perspective, we are doing a disservice to trainees when we do not create the opportunity for them to be accurately seen and supported through the evaluation process.

Evaluation in a liberatory training environment presents the opportunity to engage trainees in a clear, collaborative, and mutual process that honors their ways of being and gives them a voice in the process. It involves trainee-led goal development that invites self-evaluation from the outset. It requires that clinical supervisors engage in continuous self-examination and consultation about their reactions to supervisees. It is predicated on the development of a collaborative and trusting supervisory relationship that invites supervisees to openly share their experiences and to provide honest feedback to the supervisor, training program, and agency.

Finally, it requires intentional refining of the content of the evaluation that honors divergent ways of being and is anchored in behavioral observations rather than conjectures or interpretations of behavior. Ideally, the training program will seek feedback from trainees about the content and process of evaluation to more fully inform the refinement of the evaluation process.

What Is Authentic Allyship in Clinical Supervision?

Embedded within mental health care systems and training programs are the clinical supervisors who are directly responsible for supporting trainees of color in the development of their clinical skills and professional identities. This uniquely positions supervisors to engage in authentic allyship with trainees of color. White supervisors are tasked with the important work of self-exploration, curiosity, and informed action as they work to develop collaborative supervisory relationships with interns. They are presented with the opportunity to challenge their own biases and develop and practice skills in antiracism that may feel contradictory to their own training and cultural norms.

Recommendations for Engaging in Authentic Allyship With Mental Health Interns

While we can all agree that there is no "right way" to develop a strong supervisory relationship, here are some recommendations to consider:

Talk About Race and Other Salient Identities

It is important to engage this dialogue with openness and explicit permission for the supervisee to have agency in what they choose to share with you. The power dynamics at play within the supervisory relationship and with respect to racial (and other) salient identities must be honored. Often, an organic situation will invite dialogue about racial identities. For example, I worked with a supervisee who had been assigned to supervision with me and then assigned to cofacilitate a group with me as well. There were several clinicians of color on staff, and I was curious about her reaction to not getting to work with them in these contexts. So I asked her how she was feeling about it with explicit curiosity about her identity as a Black woman, my identity as a White woman, and her training goals. She was able to name her disappointment, and I was able to validate this and explicitly invite her emotions and needs into our relationship.

It was important for me to explicitly communicate openness, curiosity, and nondefensiveness. This opened us to important ongoing dialogue about ways that we each show up in the space together as group cofacilitators and within the supervisory relationship. This conversation was the first of many we had about her needs as a trainee and the ways that I could best support her development as an emerging psychologist in all of her identities.

Encourage Support Seeking and Mentorship

Explicitly encourage supervisees to connect with, consult, and seek mentorship from staff with whom they can be honest and from whom they have the potential to experience understanding. This may come from participating in a cultural affinity group of other staff members who share identities or from specific mentorship from colleagues of color. This sends an important message that it is healthy to seek out perspectives and support from those the trainee feels may best understand their experience. It demonstrates the values of humility and collaboration while also supporting the collective spirit of the training environment.

There have been multiple occasions in which the mentorship a trainee of color received from another staff member significantly deepened their understanding of an experience and helped them clarify options to most authentically express agency moving forward. An important secondary benefit to this is that I have been able to grow and expand my awareness as well, which has a direct positive impact on my work with colleagues, trainees, and clients.

One caution I will offer in this area is to not unintentionally place more burden on colleagues of color to do your job as clinical supervisor or to take on more than they are already holding. It is common for clinicians of color to experience differential burden within systems related to caring for clients and trainees of color.

Honor Emotional Expression—and Lack Thereof

When interns experience conflict, microaggressions, negative systemic impact, and/or even abusive behavior within the system, it is imperative to make explicit space for their emotion. However, it is equally imperative not to demand or expect that they emotionally share with you. Based on histories, identities, and lived experiences, trainees may experience varying degrees of safety with sharing vulnerability with a White supervisor. Inviting them to share and then honoring where the trainee is without pathologizing based on their expressed emotions—or lack thereof—is a respectful and ethical relational stance.

Provide Active and Attuned Support

Beyond holding space for their emotional experience, it is important to actively support the trainee in processing and responding to any negative experiences in the agency. This is an area where consultation with colleagues is very helpful—for both the trainee and the supervisor. However, it is important to obtain consent from the trainee for you to more directly address these concerns on their behalf. It can easily be disempowering for a White supervisor to take over this process—even when it comes from a sincere want to support and protect. We can be vulnerable to assuming the role of the "White savior," which implicitly centers our own needs and identities rather than authentically working to support the agency of the person of color.

Recognize Nuances of Power Dynamics

Name and attend to the dynamics of power within the supervisory relationship and the larger system. Power is an inherent factor in all organizational settings and professional relationships. Invite it into the dialogue so that you and the supervisee can engage in mutual curiosity about its influence on experiences within the training environment and in interactions with clients, colleagues, and other stakeholders.

One of the challenges to interrogating power is that we can sometimes fall into a dichotomous way of thinking (e.g., "This person has more positional power, which means that the other person is disempowered"). This really misses the intersectionality and nuances of power and its impact on the humanity present in the interaction and within the system. I have been consistently in awe of the capacity for trainees to empower themselves within the system to speak out and engage the training program through their own grounding in their identities and unique positionality as temporary employees. Some of the most fruitful organizational growth I have witnessed has come through the voices and actions of trainees.

Uplift Strengths

Get to know the trainee as a whole person and actively uplift and celebrate their strengths. There is not a single trainee that I have worked with who has not had unique gifts to offer the field of mental health. Unfortunately, clinical training and supervision can be largely oriented toward identifying and shoring up areas of deficiency—or as we like to call them in the counseling center world, "growth edges." As supervisors, particularly when working with a trainee who is experiencing some challenges, we can get overly fused with our role as gatekeeper.

Clearly, we want to do everything we can to ensure that clients and students are not harmed by their encounters with mental health professionals. However, losing sight of a trainee's strengths is problematic in at least two ways:

1. As referenced earlier, the goalposts of counselor development are limited in their own right due to their predominantly Western European foundation. An uncritical focus on this without interrogating the assumptions of these theories and the lived identities of the supervisee and client is educationally unsound and dangerous.
2. My experience has been that inviting and celebrating areas of strength give trainees the opportunity to inhabit these parts of themselves and from this place be more open to curiosity about areas that may need more attention and growth. It is through embracing one another's gifts that we are able to meet one another in struggle.

Do Not Avoid Constructive Feedback

While uplifting strengths and caring for the supervisee as a whole person, it is important not to shy away from providing constructive feedback. I was once challenged by a trusted colleague to consider the impact of not providing this feedback. In my role as clinical supervisor, I struggle with the weight of piling more stress onto a supervisee who is already navigating current and historical racialized stressors. However, when I am honest with myself in these moments, my avoidance of potentially difficult feedback is more motivated by my desire to protect my (perceived) role as a "safe" White person for the trainee.

In reality, my fear of engaging authentically with the trainee centers my own anxieties and my own fantasies of my role (i.e., "White savior"), which makes me decidedly less safe for the trainee. Clear constructive feedback in the context of a caring supervisory relationship demonstrates my commitment to the trainee and their professional development.

Show Up Professionally

Explicitly name and challenge norms of White supremacy and advocate for antiracism in the agency. Antiracism cannot be contained to our interactions with trainees and within the training program. Walking the walk in dynamic organizational spaces where we often experience more personal vulnerability can be challenging. Lack of positional power, role demands, lived identities, relational histories, and financial concerns can all contribute to an increased sense of risk and leave us susceptible to silence and collusion with White supremacy.

Because White supervisors are steeped within a culture of White supremacy, we are forever vulnerable to reverting to White supremacist behaviors and beliefs, particularly during times of stress and when our personal motivations are at the forefront. White supremacy can be intoxicating when it promises us personal safety, comfort, or advancement. We must persist in returning to our values of antiracism and taking accountability when we fall into the trance of White supremacy. This means taking risks, speaking up, holding space, and being uncomfortable.

Practice Self-Development, Consultation, and Accountability

It is our responsibility to continue to develop ourselves as culturally informed, aware, and adaptive professionals. Our professional roles demand that we engage in our own individual work to increase our understanding of ourselves and others culturally. We should utilize affinity spaces, like White accountability groups, to engage in authentic dialogue about our experiences, vulnerabilities, and behaviors as White professionals (and humans) and develop trusting relationships with colleagues who are our accountability partners in this ongoing work. We must invest in our own humanity through our antiracism work.

A Call for Action

As we take important steps to diversify the field of mental health, we must challenge ourselves to both reflect inward and actively disrupt the White supremacy that pervades our educational theories, practices, and spaces. Authentic allyship as a clinical supervisor is defined by systems- and relationally oriented work to create liberatory training environments that uplift and celebrate the voices and lived experiences of racially minoritized trainees.

References

Bailey, D. (2020, January). Enticing new faces to the field. *Monitor on Psychology*. https://www.apa.org/monitor/2020/01/cover-trends-new-faces.html

Center for Collegiate Mental Health. (2017, January). *2016 annual report* (Publication No. STA 17–74). https://sites.psu.edu/ccmh/files/2017/01/2016-Annual-Report-FINAL_2016_01_09-1gc2hj6.pdf

Constantine, M. G., & Sue, D. W. (2007). Perceptions of racial microaggressions among black supervisees in cross-racial dyads. *Journal of Counseling Psychology*, 54, 142–153.

Council for Accreditation of Counseling and Related Educational Programs. (2018). *CACREP vital statistics 2017: Results from a national survey of accredited programs.* http://www.cacrep.org/wp-content/uploads/2019/05/2017-CACREP-Vital-Statistics-Report.pdf

Council on Social Work Education. (2020). *2019 statistics on social work education in the United States.* https://cswe.org/getattachment/Research-Statistics/2019-Annual-Statistics-on-Social-Work-Education-in-the-United-States-Final-(1).pdf.aspx#:~:text=There%20were%20more%20than%205%2C600,6.8%25%20were%20Hispanic%2FLatinx

Curtis-Boles, H., & Bourg, E. (2010). Experiences of students of color in a graduate level diversity course. *Training and Education in Professional Psychology*, 4(3), 204–212.

Dishop, C. R., Green, A. E., Torres, E., & Aarons, G. A. (2019). Predicting turnover: The moderating effect of functional climates on emotional exhaustion and work attitudes. *Community Mental Health Journal*, 55, 733–741.

Henrich, J., Heine, S. J., & Norenzayan, A. (2010). The weirdest people in the world? *Behavioral and Brain Sciences*, 33(2–3), 61–83.

Linder, C., Harris, J. C., Allen, E. L., & Hubain, B. (2015). Building inclusive pedagogy: Recommendations from a national study of students of color in higher education and student affairs graduate programs. *Equity & Excellence in Education*, 48(2), 178–194.

Page, C., Buche, J., Beck, A. J., Stamm, K., Lin, L., & Christidis, P. (2017). *Understanding the diversity of students and faculty in health service psychology doctoral programs.* Behavioral Health Workforce Research Center. https://www.behavioralhealthworkfo rce.org/wp-content/uploads/2018/02/BHWRC-Supplemental-APA-Diversity-Hea lth-Service-Psychology-Programs-Full-Report.pdf

Ragland Woods, C. C., Chronister, K. M., Perez Grabow, A., Woods, W. E., & Woodlee, K. (2021). Racial battle fatigue: The experience of Black/African American, Biracial Blacks, and Multiracial Black identified graduate students. *Journal of Black Psychology, 47*(4–5), 219–243.

Smith, W. A. (2004). Black faculty coping with racial battle fatigue: The campus racial climate in a post-civil rights era. In D. Cleveland (Ed.), *A long way to go: Conversations about race by African American faculty and graduate students at predominately White institutions* (pp. 171–190). Peter Lang Publishers.

Wang, S. C., Hubbard, R. R., & Dorazio, C. (2020). Overcoming racial battle fatigue through dialogue: Voices of three counseling psychologist trainees. *Training and Education in Professional Psychology, 14*(4), 285–292.

30

Rx Racial Healing Through Authentic Narratives

A Tool for Allyship and Collective Healing

Gail C. Christopher

Since the 2020 police killing of George Floyd in Minneapolis, segments of the American population have demanded a reckoning on race in the United States. There have been marches and protests, corporate- and philanthropic-driven solutions, and other earnest efforts to grow racial equity and justice. I fear, however, that an important ingredient is missing, or at least is not prominent enough to fuel the real change needed.

President Abraham Lincoln understood the importance of public sentiment to American democracy when he debated his opponent, Stephen Douglas, back in 1858. "In this and like communities, public sentiment is everything," Lincoln noted. "With public sentiment, nothing can fail. Without it, nothing can succeed" (Davis & Wilson, 2008, p.1).

More than a century later, the Kerner Commission investigated the racism and violence erupting throughout the country and reached a similar opinion as President Lincoln. In its 1968 final report, the commission stated:

> The need is not so much for the government to design new programs as it is for the nation to generate new will. Private enterprise, labor unions, churches, foundations, universities, and all our urban institutions must deepen their involvement in the life of the city and their commitment to its renewal and welfare. (Report of the National Advisory Commission on Civil Disorders, 1968, p. 230)

Today, the more things have changed, the more the underlying factors have remained constant. The Kerner Commission cited institutional racism, police brutality, and lack of employment opportunities as the root causes of

Gail C. Christopher, *Rx Racial Healing Through Authentic Narratives* In: *Antiblackness and the Stories of Authentic Allies.*
Edited by: Norman Kim, Carolyn Coker Ross, Mazella Fuller and Charlynn Small, Oxford University Press.
© Oxford University Press 2024. DOI: 10.1093/oso/9780197642535.003.0031

the 1967 uprisings. Since then, there have been monumental judicial and legislative civil rights victories, but communities of color continue to face barriers from systemic and structural racism that perpetuate police killings and myriad inequities in health care, housing, education, transportation, and most of the social determinants of well-being.

In our country and throughout the world, racism, extreme nationalism, anti-Semitism, and other forms of ethnic and religious bias are often sustained by an antiquated notion that the human family can be divided and ranked based on physical characteristics and ascribed traits—an ill-conceived belief in a hierarchy of human value. This belief is alive today, as is the racism it has perpetuated and ingrained in communities from coast to coast.

Our nation must have a strategy for uniting a multiracial, critical mass of people who stand in solidarity to eradicate the false ideology of a hierarchy of human value and its harmful consequences. Our society must shift away from permitted hatred, indifference, and lovelessness toward unity and systemic human compassion for all.

What I call "Rx Racial Healing" can enable people to conceptualize and experience a new model for relating to each other as an extended human family, one that is capable of perspective taking and seeing ourselves in the face of the perceived "other," feeling empathy, and demonstrating compassion with one another. We get there by encouraging the sharing of authentic narratives. In our homes, with neighbors, with colleagues, in communities, and in organizations, this is how trust is built, and that trust, in turn, spurs the transformation our nation needs.

Narratives have always helped to shape human societies, ranging from creation and ancestral mythologies of Indigenous cultures to religious and scriptural allegories to world-changing novels and great epic tales. To minimize the power of story is to have a major blind spot for what drives real social change. Most successful political candidates begin to convey their personal and life story as an important onramp for their campaigns. The book market is flooded with authentically penned and ghostwritten autobiographies during the years that lead up to presidential elections. The entertainment industry, in its myriad forms, was built on the power of story to engage and indeed to compel viewers and listeners.

With narratives as its base, Rx Racial Healing is a conceptual framework for action. It includes a circle methodology, which guides people from diverse backgrounds and perspectives through a story-telling process that leads them to recognize and embrace each other's humanity.

The Rx Racial Healing Circle experience involves up to 26 participants per circle and is facilitated by two trained individuals, usually of different identities (gender, race, ethnicity, etc.), so that they model the desired state of connecting across differences. Each circle experience lasts for no less than 2 hours and includes breaking into dyads to invite more intimate sharing of authentic narratives; everyone responds to the same prompt.

For example, participants might share a story about an important time in their lives when they needed to be seen or heard and that need was met. They might share how the experience made them feel and what impact it had on their lives.

Then the dyads return to the full circle and share their stories within the broader group. They benefit from a specifically designed feedback process that helps to optimize their sense of belonging and resonance with one another. Thus, the healing circle focuses on our collective humanity and lifts up the qualities that unite us rather than divide us. It is a compassionate space that engages participants in discovering, respecting, and honoring the unique experiences of each person. It's a unique opportunity for diverse people to heal together.

In one Rx Racial Healing Circle, a renowned Black economist tearfully shared that his choice of career was driven by witnessing the premature, violent deaths of many of his friends on the streets of his neighborhood as a teenager. Economic and employment racial inequities are a hallmark of America. This researcher's work took on new and lasting meaning as a result of the personal narrative he shared.

This healing work does not replace advocacy for systemic or structural change—quite the contrary. Both are needed to eliminate racism, but social justice will not happen without healing, and healing cannot happen without social justice. This is the cycle of transformation that the 21st century demands.

When we take a helicopter view of the landscape for social change, we have to recognize that as change agents and advocates, we are swimming against a powerful tide of dominant narratives about the issues, as well as groups of people. Only through a process like healing circles, or other environments where we can openly reveal to others the authentic narratives that have shaped us, can we collectively heal our wounds and progress together. These compassionate spaces encourage authentic sharing and deep listening to individual stories of life experiences that reflect personal agency in the face of challenge. Here are my stories.

The Harm Racism Generates

When I was 15, I journeyed from an African American community in Cleveland, Ohio, to a White enclave—a summer arts encampment in Chautauqua, New York, where I was the second person of color in the town. My roommate was White, and I recall feeling a deep sense of separation and alienation.

I woke up early every morning and walked, alone, to the wooded area in this quaint western region of New York. I discovered a love of nature and learned to appreciate the simple beauty of trees. I sat on a picnic table for what seemed like hours listening to the sound of water flowing in a nearby brook and staring at the pale sky sneaking through the treetops.

Over time, I learned about the healing effects of nature and how forested areas can actually help the body reduce levels of the stress hormone cortisol. Later, I became a champion for the global movement to engage children with nature and opened the Ntianu Center for Healing and Nature in a three-acre forested location fed by an artesian spring. That summer, however, I only knew that my early morning hours with the trees and the brook eased my tension, helping me through my days in Chautauqua.

My White roommate and I became friends. We came from completely different worlds in a racially divided Cleveland, but we built a strong connection, sharing meals and attending classes together. At night, we told stories about our families. My father was a truck driver, hers a police officer; she was an only child, while I had an older brother and younger sister. She lived in the working-class, predominantly White West Side of Cleveland, while I lived in the poorer, mostly Black East Side. Our paths would have never crossed back home, but here we bonded, just two teenagers learning new things, having fun, and sharing a space uninterrupted by the outside world.

Heavily scheduled days and evenings filled with concerts and shows made the weeks pass quickly. Soon the once-in-a-lifetime summer arts experience drew to its end. On one of the camp's last days, as I walked past all the charming Victorian houses on our little street, an ambulance appeared in front of our yellow house. Hurrying to see what was going on, I reached the front stairs in time to see my roommate being carried out on a stretcher. She was unconscious.

I asked our house parents what had happened, and they said she had taken pills in an attempted suicide. I ran up to our room, which suddenly seemed unbearably small. There I found a note she had written: "I don't want to go home. My father has taught me to hate black people. I now know that is a lie. I don't want to live like that anymore."

Deeply conflicted by the hatred she was taught and the happiness she experienced with a Black person, she tried to take her own life.

I assumed they saved her life that day, but we both returned to our segregated existences, so I never learned her fate. But I never forgot how it felt to have lived a brief moment within an innocent and authentic friendship that, unbeknownst to me, had pierced the veneer of racial hatred. I came face to face with my roommate's deep pain, the child within me wanting to know why people believed in, taught, and acted upon racial hate. The adult and eventually the healer in me learned the answer to that question.

Our inability as individuals and as a society to value all human beings equally, or as Albert Einstein once said, to "see ourselves in the face of the other" (Jerome & Taylor, 2005, p. 33), is causing deep harm to individuals and to societies as a whole. The harmful results are disproportionately experienced by communities of color that also face limited opportunities. Even more important, this incapacity keeps us from experiencing optimal well-being and happiness.

As mammals, we evolved from and for connection to one another. Our hearts and brains are designed to resonate within harmonious relationships. The opposite—fear and anxiety, separation, alienation, and hate—induces stress and distress. Distress causes a cascade of illness-related changes within our very cells in our physical bodies and within our body politic. This inability is not unlike the design flaw in the Boeing 737 Max Jet airliner that contributed to the 2018 and 2019 plane crashes that caused the needless tragic deaths of hundreds of passengers. Researchers estimate that 265 people die every day from racial health disparities in the United States (Williams, 2016). This is the equivalent of a 737 jet crashing on a daily basis.

Trauma Created by Racial Disparities in Medical Treatments

In 1972, we lost our baby girl, Ntianu, 6 weeks after she was born. On reflection, I now realize there was a clear inconsistency between the words of the doctors and the weight of their facial expressions. But their words had offered hope. What new parents wouldn't cling to hope? The doctors' words were: "When she is older, we will perform open heart surgery to correct the defect."

She died of tetralogy of Fallot, which is better known as "blue baby syndrome."

Decades later I learned the story of Vivien Thomas, who created the complex surgical procedure that could have saved her life. As a lab assistant in partnership with Dr. Alfred Blalock, Thomas was the first person to figure out how to divide the subclavian artery and sew it into the pulmonary artery that supplies blood to the lungs (Thomas, 1998).

The arteries of infants are tiny compared to those of the animals in the laboratory on which Thomas had perfected the procedure, so he had to design special needles that could make sutures small enough to heal properly and ensure that the lungs would become reoxygenated—turning blue babies healthy again and able to live long and normal lives.

In fact, in 1950, the year I was born, Blalock and Thomas operated on their 1,000th blue baby. In subsequent years hundreds of thousands of other infants were saved by their procedure. So how was it that 22 years later in 1972, my African American blue baby was denied this life-saving operation, which had, ironically, been created by an African American genius?

One can only speculate about why the doctors in a small hospital on the East Side of Cleveland, Ohio, did not use it: Our daughter was African American. We lived in a racially segregated neighborhood where the hospital was located. The physicians were White. It was not a large teaching hospital. The list could go on.

However, my loss pales in comparison to the immeasurable human potential that goes unrealized every day because of our failure to remove the scourge of racism, and the denial of the humanity of anyone perceived as the other. Its shadow looms large today in racial and ethnic violence, as well as in those institutional and structural forms of racism and exclusion that I may have been dealing with in that inner-city hospital.

Vivien Thomas managed to do the impossible for a Black man of his era, though it was the pragmatic kindness of a White man, Alfred Blalock, that made possible their shared success. When the rules and norms of the time said no to Thomas having a meaningful place in the laboratory, Blalock recognized his talent and fought to keep him at his side, and to get him paid more than the janitor's salary that was allowed by university policies.

The surgical procedure that Thomas perfected and that Blalock performed successfully ushered in the entire field of cardiac surgery in the United States. Thomas went on to train a generation of African American cardiac surgeons and was eventually awarded an honorary doctorate from Johns Hopkins

University. Thomas's life story is a penetratingly sharp illustration of the costs that racism imposes on individuals and societies. How many other geniuses of color have been marginalized, forgotten, or never realized?

Changing Minds Can Help Change Behavior

The fundamental premise of Rx Racial Healing is that we must replace the antiquated belief in human value hierarchy with a heartfelt appreciation for our interconnected and equal humanity. This requires a seismic shift in our collective ethos, changing hearts and minds. How can we change, eliminate, and replace a deeply held cultural belief and norm in individuals and in society?

Renowned Harvard psychologist Howard Gardner (2006) has identified seven key factors in his book, *Changing Minds: The Art and Science of Changing Our Own and Other People's Minds*. I applied his factors in the design of a multi-million-dollar multiyear investment strategy of the W. K. Kellogg Foundation beginning in 2007, America Healing. This was an ambitious initiative for helping people through organizations and communities across the United States begin to face and eliminate racism and its harmful consequences.

Gardener's key factors that can be leveraged for changing our own and others' minds are:

- reason
- research
- resonance
- redescription
- resources and rewards
- real-world events
- resistance

In large measure, these are cognitive factors and influence thinking or thought patterns. However, Gardner does emphasize that the purpose of changing people's minds is to change behaviors. The seven factors listed above are applied to stimulate change at varying levels in society. These include individuals; organizations; communities; identity groups such as racial, religious, ethnic, or gender; and within corporations or society as a whole. The goal is to stimulate action and bring about needed behavioral change.

The ABCs of racial healing—appreciation, belongingness, and consciousness change—are concepts that become real through experiences, through doing. They are also fundamental human motivational and psychological needs. But they can only be actualized through interaction with others.

The healing takes place through the experience of being appreciated and affirmed, of feeling a sense of belongingness, and of experiencing a consciousness change or level of personal growth that deepens our sense of connection and relatedness as a human family. In this regard, the Rx Racial Healing Circle models and embodies a desired state of human interaction in which we are respectful and kind to one another, can listen deeply, and can affirm and appreciate our diverse experiences while finding commonality and valued human connections.

The etymology of the word "heal" is "to make whole." Albert Einstein's quote reminds us that wholeness is a fundamental concept for humanity: "A human being is a part of a whole ... [but] he experiences himself, his thoughts and feelings as something separated from the rest" (Einstein, 1950, p. 1). This delusion is a kind of prison for us, restricting us to our personal desires and to affection for a few persons nearest to us.

Our task must be to free ourselves from this prison by widening our circle of compassion to embrace all living creatures and the whole of nature in its beauty. Nobody is able to achieve this completely, but striving for such achievement is, in itself, a part of the liberation and a foundation for inner security (Einstein, 1950, p. 1).

Ironically, despite Einstein's iconic status as a genius, humanitarian, and fighter for social justice, recent publication of his 1920s travel diaries in 2018 reveal clearly xenophobic, racist, and what can be interpreted as misogynistic comments about perceived others (Rosenkranz, 2018). These travel diaries were written between 1922 and 1923, reflecting on a trip he and his wife took to Asia. This surprising revelation of racist reflections in his early years contrasts with his antiracist actions decades later, after he immigrated to America and became a U.S. citizen.

In 1946, Einstein accepted an invitation from singer and activist Paul Robeson to cochair the American Crusade to End Lynching. The Federal Bureau of Investigation considered this group a subversive organization because its members included radicals trying to pressure President Harry Truman to support a federal law against lynching.

How do we acquire, or reconnect with, what I believe is an innate urge or need to see ourselves in the face of the other? Like any other skill or capacity, it is acquired through practice. The Rx Racial Healing Circle experience is designed to provide opportunities for developing, learning, and practicing this needed ability.

What does it mean to see ourselves in the face of the other? To some it means empathy or the ability to understand or to feel what others are experiencing. To others it requires the art of perspective taking, grasping the point of view of the other, without judgment. No matter the explanation, seeing ourselves in the face of the other requires a sense of resonance with the perceived other at some level. We need a sense of relatedness and to feel a human bond. The Rx Racial Healing Circle methodology provides opportunities for experiencing such bonds, if only temporarily. To learn more and/or to connect with an expanding network of trained facilitators, please visit http://www.drgailcchristopher.com.

Wise Indigenous leaders who have engaged in racial healing circles remind us that circles of compassion are core to the sensibilities of their cultures. Nature provided the model for circles: The arc of the sun as it moves from rising to setting, the base of mountains and trees, and many animals' homes such as the birds' nests are circular, and the four directions create a full circle (Mehl-Madrona, 2010).

The wisdom of Indigenous leaders is also reflected in Einstein's quote about circles of compassion, "Our task must be to free ourselves from this prison by widening our circles of compassion to embrace all living creatures and the whole of nature in its beauty" (Einstein, 1950, p. 1). This is helpful to environmentalists and naturalists in garnering support for a more holistic relationship with our planet and nature. Einstein's expansive circle of compassion evolved to include a strong stand against racism as well as a deep engagement with African Americans and communities of color.

In their book *Einstein on Race and Racism*, Jerome and Taylor (2005) chronicle Einstein's writings and speeches against racism. They document his private acts of support for civil rights leaders and organizations. Einstein considered racism to be a deeply embedded pathology in America. "The worst disease" in American society, he wrote, is "the treatment of the Negro" (Jerome & Taylor, 2005, p. 33)

This man, the most recognized genius of the 20th century, reminds us that to be biased is to be human. He framed the belief in a hierarchy of human value—racism—as an illness. Like so many of his insights, this understanding was far ahead of his contemporaries in science and in the general public.

There are those who disagree with the idea of describing racism as a disease. Their disagreement stems from a long-standing tension and binary framing of racial justice work as either relational or systemic, as work on individual attitudes and behaviors or work on structural issues such as employment, housing, and poverty. After working for decades in both kinds of work as distinct efforts or approaches, I am clear that they must be done simultaneously by a large and mobilized community.

Mississippi River: A Metaphor for Racism

Whether describing the Nile, Amazon, or Yangtze River, historians know that large rivers became the centers around which civilizations and nation-states have flourished. This is true for the Mississippi River; named by the Indigenous dwellers of the Algonquin Native tribes as the Father of Waters, the Mississippi River is one of the world's longest rivers.

This mighty river provides a good metaphor for the power of a single phenomenon to shape our lives—the belief in a hierarchy of humanity that flows through the American psyche and society like the Father of Waters, the Mississippi. It drove the slavery economy and became the center around which 18th-, 19th-, 20th-, and even 21st-century America flourishes.

Each of the great rivers, including the Mississippi, has a delta, a landform created from the earth and rocks along the banks that it touched while moving rapidly to the ocean beckoning its waters. The river carries this sediment and debris to an end place where movement slows to stagnation in the delta.

The human body has become the delta for the metaphorical river of racism. Sediment and debris from exposures have become socially embodied. Landforms—islands of separation, including residential segregation characterized by political and economic disinvestment—create adverse and toxic experiences and fear of perceived others for some. These deltas help generate chronic stress and traumatic body responses, which cause excess vulnerability to disease and premature death.

But unlike rivers, whose existence and flow are vital for sustaining geographic and human life, racism is manmade. This antiquated belief system and way of seeing/being can be undone. Racism flows like a river, but it is not a river. Racism can and must be eliminated and its harmful consequences healed. When implemented on a large and comprehensive scale throughout the nation, Rx Racial Healing Circles will help move us beyond needless divides toward the wholeness upon which a viable democracy depends.

References

Davis, R. O., & Wilson, D. L. (Eds.). (2008). *The Lincoln-Douglas debates.* Knox College Lincoln Studies Center and University of Illinois Press.

Einstein, A. (1950, March 4). *Condolence letter to Norman Salit, Jerusalem.* The Hebrew University of Jerusalem.

Gardner, H. (2006). *Changing minds: The art and science of changing our own and other people's minds.* Harvard Business School Press.

Jerome, F., & Taylor, R. (2005). *Einstein on race and racism.* Rutgers University Press.

Mehl-Madrona, L. (2010). *Healing the mind through the power of story: The promise of narrative psychiatry.* Bear and Company.

Report of the National Advisory Commission on Civil Disorders. (1968). U.S. Government Printing Office.

Rosenkranz, Z. (2018). *The travel diaries of Albert Einstein: the far east, Palestine, and Spain, 1922–1923.* Princeton University Press.

Thomas, V. T. (1998). *Partners of the heart: Vivien Thomas and his work with Alfred Blalock: An autobiography.* University of Pennsylvania Press.

Williams, D. (2016, November). *David R. Williams: How racism makes us sick.* TED. YouTube. https://www.youtube.com/watch?v=VzyjDR_AWzE

31

Between Us

A Black and White Woman's Conversation About Friendship

Janie Victoria Ward and Becky Thompson

Introduction

At a historical moment of unprecedented worry about the future of progressive education—on the heels of Black Lives Matter organizing and just before the onset of the pandemic—we came together to teach a new course on Black and White women's friendships. While the two of us had been teaching at the university for decades, this was our first chance to coteach, a journey that led us to many honest conversations about how our relationship unfolded in a White-dominant institution and its implications for alliance building.

To our surprise, the course evaluations following the course were off the charts. Throughout the class the multiracial group of students had willingly engaged in deep conversations about themselves, their families, and their communities. While their enthusiasm was partly about the historical, sociological, and multiracial feminist scholarship they read, their big aha moment reflected being in the presence of a Black woman (Janie) and a White woman (Becky) willing to talk openly about their racial experiences. We talked honestly about power dynamics at our university, the mistaken assumptions Becky and Janie had made about each other, and why it took years for us to really communicate. At a historical moment when the murders of Black men and women at the hands of White police had finally shaken the nation to action, we all recognized our hunger for the course and its transformative possibilities.

While we approached the course unsure about the emotional and intellectual connection between relationality and allyship, teaching this class helped us see the two as dialectical (particularly helpful reading on cross-race dialogue included an interview between Audre Lorde and Adrienne Rich in

Janie Victoria Ward and Becky Thompson, *Between Us* In: *Antiblackness and the Stories of Authentic Allies.*
Edited by: Norman Kim, Carolyn Coker Ross, Mazella Fuller and Charlynn Small, Oxford University Press.
© Oxford University Press 2024. DOI: 10.1093/oso/9780197642535.003.0032

Lorde, 1984; Plummer, 2020; and Wilson & Russell, 1996). On the one hand, there is a common (reductionist) assumption that if you have cross-race friendships, that itself is enough to make social change. On the other hand, there is an assumption that it is possible to be an ally without having done the work of making and sustaining relationship. From our perspectives, enduring cross-race relationships are essential components of transformative allyship.

The dearth of literature on cross-race friendships encouraged us to turn to each other as two women who are social scientists, race scholars, and activists. We've been involved with multiple cross-race relationships (good and bad), racial justice activism (before it became "a thing"), and preparing the next generation. We are living in a time when students are told that being an ally is important, yet few young adults have experience working across race. In addition, they seldom see adult women engaged in multiracial alliance building. Although there is a common articulation of the need for Black and White women to trust one another, there is much less attention to how such trust can be built. We realized that allyship starts with honesty, a willingness to be vulnerable, and an awareness of each other's histories. Trust and mistrust are encoded in facial expressions, in a person's tone of voice, and in eye contact and body language. As the writer James McBride (2020) writes, "A (wo)man who doesn't trust can't be trusted" (p. 52). After decades of doing historical and theoretical work on racial justice where we deliberately did not include our own stories, we saw the efficacy of a more dialogical approach (Thompson, 2001; Ward, 2000; Ward & Robinson-Wood, 2022). Our hope is that sharing these conversations will illuminate what stands in the way of, as well as what nurtures, honest friendships, as this is what sustains allyship.

Taking Risks, Telling the Truth

While Janie and Becky taught at the same institution for 30 years, we've only recently worked together. Ironically, what brought us together was a lockdown at Simmons following an active shooter threat on campus. We—along with several students, faculty, and administrators—ended up crammed in a small room with large plate-glass windows and a door with no lock. The moment was filled with panic. We could hear campus police running up and down the hall, though it was unclear what they were saying or who they were pursuing. We crouched silently under desks and tables, some texting loved ones, others watching news feeds about the incident on local TV. Uncharacteristically, Becky, rather than taking charge, was huddling in the corner, clearly upset. Janie had never seen Becky in such a vulnerable state.

Not even 2 hours later, after the all-clear, we found ourselves in a small faculty meeting. In the discussion, Becky asked a White college administrator about a decision he had made that compromised racial justice at the expense of personal ambition. Looking embarrassed, he offered little response to Becky's antiracist principle, muttering that such decisions were outside his responsibility. Later, Janie shared how impressed she was that Becky, who had been so shaken just a short time before, could bounce back and reclaim her warrior mode. Before the conversation Becky had worried that her response during the lockdown had been read as White fragility rather than as an understandable vulnerability in a crisis situation. Now Becky realized that Janie listened to her incisive critique of institutional racism and affirmed Becky's warrior resilience.

Our leaning in began first with letters rather than face to face, and that allowed Janie to pause and think through her responses. Janie wrote Becky back, and rather than breaking or moving away from each other in fear, we found we were actually coming closer. Our conversations built on reactions to each other's reflections. There were still unanswered questions, but they illuminated the path we pursued in our coteaching.

At one point Janie shared with Becky how isolated she felt once the one White feminist faculty member whom she considered her friend died unexpectedly. It had been hard for Janie to admit that she was lonely, frustrated, and resigned to the racial stagnation at the heart of Black and White relational disconnections. She had been reflecting on her own cross-racial relationships, which she knew could be strong, loving, and not always easy.

Hearing this opened a way for Becky to talk about her loneliness and isolation. As Becky spoke, Janie realized that she hadn't thought about what a White warrior sister resister like Becky might be dealing with. Despite her impressive advocacy credentials, Becky was the one White faculty member at the institution who always spoke up. And for that she also became the person everyone else expected to take the hit. Janie hadn't imagined that a White ally would hurt so deeply and require the kind of self-care necessary for people fighting the good fight. Hearing Becky, Janie realized too that it wasn't fair to expect her to be the one that people would always count on and then not offer her the needed support.

Our conversation compelled Janie to flip the script. She wondered, "If Becky were Black, how would I act? How would my expectations have been different? And why hadn't I reached out?" Support isn't simply saying thanks for speaking up. It means acknowledging the cost to the truth teller of raising her voice in a setting where the truth is often maligned or ignored. In supporting White resisters, thought Janie, am I not also supporting myself— my efforts, my beliefs?

The missing communication between Janie and Becky was fed by two forms of alienation: resentment and lack of accountability. Janie acknowledged the resentment she had carried: "Why should I care about the Beckys of the world?" She struggled with an underlying anger and suspicion that Becky, as a White woman, was going to bail at any moment. When Janie was in graduate school at Harvard there were White women who knew how to talk about antiracism and were happy to do so, until they got married and moved to the suburbs with their White husbands and increased class privilege.

Among Black women there is suspicion about how long White women will stay in the battle. And sometimes Black women's understandable hesitation can be prolonged as we wait to see if a White woman is going to flee or cut loose. There are so few White women who hang in there for the long run that we end up asking, "Who is that woman?" There is Gloria Steinem, still looking so good, still out there loudly proclaiming, "this fucking sucks." And there is Jane Fonda, who, at age 82, was arrested each Friday on the steps of the Capitol in support of climate change activism as she told the public, "I want Greta Thunberg to be proud of me." But public iconography has not yet made room for White allies who are in it for the long run. In the absence of that, it is easy to assume they don't exist.

While White women's unaccountability led Janie to hang back, Becky spent years thinking that when she felt isolated and weary, she certainly shouldn't talk with Black women faculty, administrators, or staff about this. In her mind, Black women already have so much to deal with that they certainly shouldn't have to take care of White antiracists' emotions. Many White allies assume that they shouldn't ever want or expect to get Black women's support. The last thing Black women need is an upset White woman complaining about having been slighted or disrespected. Black women certainly should not be asked to talk through complicated dynamics with White allies. White allies should take that labor to other White allies.

"That's legit," Janie explained. But in calling attention to Black women's strengths, Black activists are emphasizing the need for positive mental health. Maybe there's a need among Black activists to value the mental health of White allies too. To do so, Black women must first stop imagining that allies need to be perfect. Black women often talk about how White women are going to betray, hurt, or abandon Black women. But Black women don't think enough about how to protect and hold White women allies when they are doing the work.

We need to figure out how to trust—knowing that it can't be a blanket trust, but also knowing that an "I can't trust any of them" attitude won't do. In the absence of that dichotomy, there is a tired dance taking place, one that is generations, if not centuries, old. Black women check White women out. Black activists try to decide what side a White activist is on and how much she knows. And Black activists anticipate that a White woman will eventually betray us. Every time she doesn't live up to our expectations we can say, "Just as I thought—she's another one who can't be trusted."

Our conversations opened a way for Janie to think about how race had influenced her thinking about Becky. Janie had been wrestling with several contradictions. She figured, "Becky was a resister (good) but she was a White woman (bad, and thus unworthy of Janie's empathy). After all, she's White; she can take care of herself, AND the world is set up to take care of her. AND they'll never hurt her the way they hurt Black women." For those reasons, and as a self-protective gesture, Janie's default position was to just keep moving forward without reaching out to Becky. Our conversation uncovered how the perspective taking and empathizing that sister resisters need each other to do can quickly become out of reach. Upon reflection, this work is what both women want to see in the next generation of resisters.

Bolstering Each Other

Janie's willingness to reach out to Becky ignited a coteaching experience that sparked creative energy that she feared had been long ago extinguished. Viewing the classroom as text, we explored interpersonal relationships as a powerful way to understand the dynamics of oppression and resistance.

One example of creating this generative emotional space occurred when we taught a memoir cowritten by a Black woman and a White woman in which a conflict erupted that nearly destroyed the friendship. At the heart of the conflict was that all-too-familiar silence about race that Black and White women allow to suck up the air in a relationship.

It wasn't until the women did the work of excavating what had gone awry that they realized their pattern. For years they had danced around the topic of race, fearing that breaking the silence would unravel the relationship. Now they better understood: Focusing on their sameness was at the root the problem.

This realization deeply resonated with Janie. She began to think about her undergraduate students of color, who were also navigating cross-racial friendships in predominately White institutions. Despite the endless talk about racial diversity, cultural sameness in many White spaces is what's valued and rewarded, including among U.S. college students. The message is: As long as you are like *us*, we'll accept you, and you'll be okay.

Janie had wanted the students to pick up on the contradiction. After all, her emotional connection to the dilemma was painfully familiar and its effects were still raw. The moral dishonesty left Janie feeling increasingly frustrated. She was concerned that students, especially the Black students, needed to know that they can't trust an institution's articulation that they are welcome and wanted. The trap door that awaits young women is found in the difference between what an institution says and what it does. In class discussions students were identifying institutional racism and the relationships that keep the system intact; yet the students were stymied in their ability to make the connection between silence and complicity, avoidance and dishonesty. A cacophony of thoughts were bumping around in Janie's brain as she thought to herself, "Such lies can get a Black woman hurt."

In previous years, Janie would have gone home, had a drink, maybe shared the story with a friend, and then left it alone. But because we were in a class where both Becky and Janie had made honesty central to their teaching, Janie committed to giving voice to her feelings. Instead of backing away, Janie took a risk and interrupted the flow with a question: "Was anyone else bothered by how the friendship between the women was dependent upon pretending they were the same?"

Haunted by times when she had dodged that contradiction, Janie felt there were lessons she wanted the students to carry with them. After a robust class discussion, Janie told Becky, "I want the Black students to understand that sometimes their best White friend really doesn't understand (even if she says she does). The blizzard of whiteness in their White friends' lives often obscures their ability to see Black people in all our complexity. Black students need to ask, 'What is my friend's life like when I am not there? Am I your only Black friend? Does our relationship depend upon connecting across our sameness and ignoring our differences?' And then ask, 'If I give voice to those differences, will that destroy our relationship?'"

Speaking up, pushing back, taking a stand, and honoring one's truth within the context of cross-racial relationships can be treacherous work. Discussions with Becky reaffirmed for Janie that teaching these resistance strategies is fundamental to their professional studies, to building strong cross-racial friendships, and to supporting students' mental health.

Our course found room for in-the-moment reflection on emotionally charged racial realities, and it allowed Janie to witness Becky's long-standing work of teaching from an embodied perspective.[1] Janie shared that for years she had heard faculty devalue Becky's pedagogy. Some dismissively called her "the toucher." Becky shared that she faced insults, slights, and reprimands from colleagues who resented her innovative approach. Becky's willingness to allow students to bring emotions into the classroom was twisted into labeling her rather than questioning the damage of disembodied classrooms where students are required to leave their feelings and bodies outside the door.

Janie's response was direct and clear: "Becky, as a Black woman I need to ask you, why would you let these labels and criticisms into your psyche? Black women learn to compartmentalize damaging messages. You are letting whiteness diminish you when your work is so important and thoughtful that you need to protect it. And, honestly, if you did back down because of these critiques, I would have less respect for you."

Janie's response was tremendously healing for Becky. Even as she had been asked to speak nationally and internationally on embodied teaching, at her home institution she went underground with her work. To her, somatic work is at the heart of antiracist pedagogy because it assumes that much damage is done at the level of the body as that's where fear, memories, and misconceptions are stored.

---

[1] Embodied teaching, which is the focus of Becky's book (Thompson, 2017), recognizes that learning takes place on multiple levels—the mind, body, and spirit. Making room for emotions allows for deeper learning than is possible when we limit knowledge to abstract thought. Such teaching makes time for healing rituals in classrooms after frightening events including 9/11, university lockdowns, school shootings, and police brutality.

Confronting that damage by thinking alone won't work. Just thinking solidifies the body memories (since they are being ignored). Laughing, moving, stretching, crying, and breathing together can make space for real eye contact and new conversations. It can change how people see themselves and others. Janie reminded her friend, "Stand strong and keep developing your classroom innovations. Do not let whiteness win. Keep resisting even when you are getting your ass kicked. Keep doing what you know is right."

Ways to Support Allies and Be One

In this period of increased national attention to racism, scholars, memoirists, journalists, and policymakers have all added their voices to the question of what makes a good ally and why (Hamad, 2020; Kendall, 2021; Kendi, 2019; McGhee, 2021; Metzl, 2020; Rothstein, 2018; Saad, 2000).

Janie has had a lifetime of starting conversations with White people that went nowhere or ended up with White people doing most of the growth and development with Janie as the teacher and emotional guide. She was ready to have a different kind of conversation. Becky could clearly articulate insights from her emotional life, AND she didn't have to be schooled in basic Racism 101. Janie never switched into cruise control—that sense when words coming out of one's mouth are preprogrammed because they've been said so many times before. Instead, Janie felt the desire to be on her toes, listening attentively and reacting thoughtfully. She allowed Becky's words to deepen her understanding of self and her connections to other White women.

Becky's approach to being a race ally has come partly from what she has wanted from straight people committed to standing alongside queer people. Because Becky has lived a queer-lesbian life for many decades and chooses not to live inside the binds and assumptions of heterosexual consciousness, she sometimes misses how heterosexism operates. As a result, when Janie first let Becky know that faculty at Simmons have long referred to her as a "toucher" and someone who indoctrinates students (to hate White people, to become lesbians), Becky felt a chord of hurt she couldn't fully articulate. As a straight woman, Janie clearly named how those castigations conjured up old stereotypes of lesbians as lecherous and women trying to convert young girls to becoming gay. At an even deeper level of hurt, the claim that Becky was "the toucher" flipped (and invalidated) a painful reality. As a survivor of sexual abuse who has written about it, Becky then became the perpetrator in the rumor mill's castigations.

At first Janie was surprised that Becky could not see this link, but once Janie pointed the insults out, the two could strategize about how to deal with them. For Becky, Janie's response was an example of being friends and allies—friendship in that Janie was outraged about the toll it has taken on Becky to work amid these rumors, and allyship in that she and Becky could then identify steps Becky could take in the face of these rumors. Becky is now taking back her power, and that would never have happened had they not had these honest conversations. Janie said, "You have had many experiences of resisting on behalf of others. Now it's time to turn to resisting on behalf of yourself."

For Becky, being an ally for students of color requires an enduring commitment to identifying White ways of dismissing, belittling, and undermining students of color. That means a sister resister has to be on top of it and not necessarily wait for the students to see the damage themselves. Seeing how oppression operates requires that Becky have a nuanced understanding of students' lives—where they get support, why they are in school, how they have been raised in terms of race consciousness, and the complex dynamics of how White faculty can undermine confidence. Becky can't opt out of learning this about students (based on the rationale that she will never know what it means to be Black). Janie will never know what it means to live a queer life, but the more she knows about queer life, politics, struggles, and joys, the better able she is to see how homophobia attempts to undercut one's humanity.

Years ago, Becky wrote *A Promise and a Way of Life* (Thompson, 2001) because she wanted to find White people across multiple generations who have taken on racism and have in the process grown a backbone. Social movement activism is made possible through love, work, and spiritual relationship building. What she learned is that White antiracists have been trained, supported, and mentored by people of color each step of the way. It's slow work. It's scary work. It's essential work.

Becky and Janie believe that we all need to slow this river right now. As Resmaa Menakem (2017) teaches in *My Grandmother's Hands*, White people need to make room for the pause. In their friendship, both Janie and Becky make room for each other to pause. Their insistence to talk about interactions (whether from 2 decades ago or from 2 weeks ago) in detail, without skipping any steps in how it felt or who said what, when, and why, offers healing on a profound level. Janie has recently retired, and who knows how long Becky will stay at the university, but both of us still insist on "lifting as we climb": educating women with their eyes and hearts open to this complicated multicolored world.

References

Hamad, R. (2020). *White tears/brown scars: How white feminism betrays women of color.* Catapult.

Kendall, M. (2021). *Hood feminism: Notes from the women that a movement forgot.* Penguin.

Kendi, I. (2019). *How to be an antiracist.* One World.

Lorde, A. (1984). *Sister outsider.* Crossing Press.

McBride, J. (2021). *Deacon King Kong.* Penguin Books.

McGhee, H. (2021). *The sum of us: What racism costs everyone and how we can prosper together.* One World.

Menakem, R. (2017). *My grandmother's hands: Racialized trauma and the pathway to mending our hearts and bodies.* Central Recovery Press.

Metzl, J. (2020). *Dying of whiteness: How the politics of racial resentment is killing America's heartland.* Basic Books.

Plummer, D. (2020). Chapter 12. "Some of my friends are . . ."In *Some of my best friends are: The daunting challenges and untapped benefits of cross-racial friendships* (pp. 182–205). Beacon.

Rothstein, R. (2018). *The color of law: A forgotten history of how government segregated America.* Liveright.

Saad, L. F. (2000). *Me and white supremacy: Combat racism, change the world and become a good ancestor.* Source Books.

Thompson, B. (2001). *A promise and a way of life: White anti-racist activism.* University of Minnesota.

Thompson, B. (2017). *Teaching with tenderness: Toward an embodied practice.* University of Illinois.

Ward, J. V. (2000). *The skin we're in: Teaching our children to be psychologically strong, socially smart, and spiritually connected.* Free Press/Simon and Schuster.

Ward, J. V., & Robinson-Wood, T. (2022). *Sister resisters: Mentoring Black women in college.* Harvard Education Press.

Wilson, M., & Russell, K. (1996). Making friends: Relationships on the campus, in the workplace, and beyond. In *Divided sisters: Bridging the gap between Black women and White women* (pp. 157–186). Doubleday.

32

Our Path to Authentic Allyship

Examining Beliefs and Actions to Provide Client Care

Ashley Acle, Alyssa Davis, and Claire St. John

The word "ally" comes from the Latin *alligare*, to bind together. To be an authentic ally, we must do more than reach a hand down or even across; we must bind to the cause and to those it serves, making the struggle our own. Allyship must not be undertaken only in the service of someone considered "other" or "in need of help," but as a moral imperative for humanity. We must recognize how exposing and expunging racism benefits us all.

Black Lives Matter, Antiracism, and Coming Together

In preparing this chapter, we three reflected on our conversations about racism and antiblackness, American history and White supremacy, and how our experiences as mental health clinicians informed our perspectives and authentic allyship. Like many discussions in 2020, ours were sparked by the murder of George Floyd on Memorial Day weekend during the raging COVID-19 pandemic and the Black Lives Matter protests against the endless killing of Black people in the United States and the insidiousness of White supremacy worldwide. We looked at our work in the field of eating disorders, a predominately White-centered field; discussed treating people of color; and challenged each other to be reflective while sharing our experiences. We returned to the importance of self-awareness, examining and interrogating our beliefs, assumptions, and place in society. We discussed our identities of privilege, marginalization, and approaching authentic allyship as individuals and as a collective. We broke this chapter into sections to illustrate how we engaged in these discussions and authentic allyship, individually and together.

Ashley Acle, Alyssa Davis, and Claire St. John, *Our Path to Authentic Allyship* In: *Antiblackness and the Stories of Authentic Allies*. Edited by: Norman Kim, Carolyn Coker Ross, Mazella Fuller and Charlynn Small, Oxford University Press.
© Oxford University Press 2024. DOI: 10.1093/oso/9780197642535.003.0033

Our Positions in Racial Allyship and Mental Health: Who We Are

Our identities influence how we engage and grow in authentic allyship. We begin authentic allyship by briefly naming our positions, which inform our perspectives and biases.

Alyssa Davis is a Black cishet woman and registered dietitian. Her privileged identities include being Christian, straight sized, and a well-educated professional class member. Ashley Acle is a multiracial cishet woman of color and a marriage and family therapist. Her privileged identities include being educated, light skinned, and English speaking. Claire St. John is a White woman and a registered dietitian. Her privileged identities include growing up in a generation whose well-meaning, liberal parents taught us that skin color doesn't matter and being part of a group with greater access to power.

Complexity, Nuance, and Context of Identity in Racial Allyship

Our identities are multilayered, complex, polylithic, and embedded within larger contexts that have individually and collectively socialized us. By knowing the depths of our identities and exploring these independently and in community with others, we can collectively engage in dialogue and learning, assuming a nonexpert stance.

Identity Development, Confusion, and Recognition of Marginalization

Disentangling racism and its impact upon our identities can feel like vivisection. There is an art to removing the poison of racism that is so engrained in our culture from a living, feeling human being. Examining our power and privilege (or lack thereof) and biases and assumptions tied to identity and its development is difficult yet essential to authentic allyship. In our White-centered world, this investigation is often disregarded by White people and one that people of color may associate with painful early othering experiences.

Through discussions and reflection, we recognized several shared and distinct themes in our respective journeys of identity development, noting both individual and collective experiences that shape racial allyship and areas for racial healing.[1]

Alyssa noted incidents of othering and healing from racism, leading to an interest in her perception of herself and how others see her. She shared experiences of feeling like she wasn't different until she was suddenly disabused of that idea. She found herself diminishing the hurdles she overcame as a Black woman, minimizing her pain because others suffered more.

"I realized," said Alyssa, "that I didn't want to paint myself as a victim, and even though my struggles were valid and oftentimes large, I would shrug them off, which only buried my resentment." She recognized the importance of unlearning a socialized instinct to smooth things over and make others feel comfortable.

"I have to allow myself to be angry, sad, frustrated, or disappointed rather than focusing on others in interactions and when talking about racial and social justice issues," said Alyssa.

Ashley shared experiences of covert racial and ethnic othering prompting recognition of her marginalized identities. "I quickly learned that being seen as 'different' meant I was somehow exotic, inferior, or did not belong," said Ashley. She recognized a socialized obligation to code-switch for power proximity but at a personal cost of inner conflict and disconnection from her value of responsibility.

She noted how context, experiences of privilege and marginalization, and the complexity of her identity impact how others see her and her understanding of herself. "I realized," said Ashley, "that my surroundings, those around me, and others' responses can influence my cognizance of different parts of my identity."

She recognized healing opportunities as someone harmed by racism yet also granted unearned advantages from antiblackness, colorism, and immigration status. She shared opportunities for unlearning internalized oppression and socialization to simplify identity, as well as opportunities for embracing an intersectional, historical sociocultural lens.

Claire wrestled with what it means to be part of the often unnamed collective of "White people" and learning about the systemic nature of racism

---

[1] To learn more about racial healing, we recommend Annaleise Singh's *The Racial Healing Handbook* (2019).

in the past and present while holding awareness. "Thinking about how my race has benefited me," said Claire, "becoming aware of this message that I, and other White people, are neutral and raceless, has been a painful process."

She shared moving through a world that centers whiteness through policies and images, recognizing the ghosts of slavery and Jim Crow laws stretching ugly tendrils into the present and affecting who we choose to help or imprison, who law enforcement protects or attacks, and who is worthy of life. She noted being led (without much resistance) to believe success is attainable by anyone with a work ethic, smarts, and savvy, because our country is fair, just, and safe for all, and that it takes minimal research to undo these assumptions. She recognized the ongoing process of looking at herself, her beliefs, and her actions and reckoning with racism and antiblackness.

Taking on the Struggle of Disadvantage

Self-awareness and reflection are the foundation for informed, responsive, authentic allyship. We simultaneously navigate the personal, move toward and uplift marginalized communities, and build relationships as authentic allies.

Navigating the Personal to Become Rooted in Authentic Allyship

Authentic allyship is both intimately personal and relational. In this snapshot of our journeys navigating authentic allyship, we worked through discomfort, fear of complacency, and a recognition that being "nonracist" is insufficient.

Imagery and metaphor were potent in our discussions, with Claire sharing that stopping at "not racist" is akin to feeling satisfied that there is a fire extinguisher on the wall while the house is engulfed in flames. She shared that she, like many White colleagues, hadn't seen how this passive stance was detrimental to everyone and how it perpetuated the avoidance of discussing race or racism.

"Avoidance of racism allowed my biases to go unexamined and hidden away from judgment," Claire said, "preventing me from seeing how much I've benefited from it." Navigating her position and experiences entailed the uncomfortable process of breaking down her previous associations of racism with white robes and hoods firmly located in the past and instead seeing racism presently and systemically and acknowledging her privilege.

Alyssa and Ashley shared tension between navigating their socialized experiences of minimizing the harm of racism to our communities and healing in a world where overt and covert racism, microaggressions, and other oppressive acts persist. Alyssa shared how invalidation of Black perspectives and pain has continued effects on her and her community, noting her experiences of microaggressions, subtle acts of racism, and a lingering struggle with feeling that her experiences weren't harsh or violent enough to warrant concern.

Alyssa saw this pattern of invalidation as a symptom of kowtowing to White fragility and antiblackness. "The Black community has had to get along, not make a fuss, and try not to make too much trouble for White people for so long and I excused insidious acts of racism and the feelings that followed," said Alyssa.

Another component of this tension is the experience of self-silencing, an occurrence that is far too common to the survival of Black, Brown, and marginalized people. Ashley noted that socialization to follow the rules for demeanor and spoken language provided some safety for physical survival yet also contributed to constant contortion and disconnection from ourselves.

"I've learned to seek out safety and security by 'blending in,'" said Ashley, "but I end up fragmented from my community and ancestral roots, and voiceless in creating change." Alyssa added that guilt arose for not speaking up. For Alyssa and Ashley, navigating the personal entailed unlearning a tendency to minimize their own experiences and voices and instead learning to honor and embrace their voices. The importance of voice resonated with Claire also, who recognized she had a responsibility to speak up, especially when a White person said something racist or derogatory.

Navigating our personal experiences allowed our motivations for persevering in authentic allyship and doing good to crystallize. Ashley shared how thinking about her ancestors and legacy motivated her authentic allyship. She connected with a profound appreciation for what her ancestors endured and her wish for our current efforts to uplift future generations into a world of equity.

In our drive to do good, Claire noted the importance of ongoing evaluation, particularly in reassessing how we're living up to our commitments as allies. She found herself momentarily slipping back into the comfort of being White with fewer discussions of racism top of mind, a privilege her coauthors did not share. Claire reminded herself, "Authentic allyship is not a part-time commitment, just as it is not a part-time need." Adopting ongoing evaluation created accountability and allowed her to more fully incorporate allyship into her identity. By navigating our personal experiences, we become rooted in an identity of authentic allyship and ready to move toward taking on the struggle of disadvantage.

Moving From Self to Taking on the Struggle of Disadvantage

Our self-awareness and ability to navigate the personal are symbiotic in taking on the struggle of disadvantage. With personal insight, we are charged with owning our responsibility, ongoing reflection, and recognizing how our experiences influence how we engage with others in allyship. To move from self to taking on the struggle of disadvantage, we think relationally, build community, and respond from a collective.

This experience is awe-inspiring, liberating, challenging, and heavy. We come together to celebrate freedom, change, hope, joy, creativity, and life. We prompt ourselves and each other to racially heal. We use our privilege responsibly, keeping each other accountable and honoring the lived expertise of marginalized people. We grieve racism and the lives and opportunities lost and stand up against injustice. We are honest with each other while owning our part and needs for learning and unlearning. We support each other in navigating our experiences to more actively and genuinely engage in an allyship movement that benefits humanity.

We also honor the leaders whose sacrifices and thought leadership paved our way. We witness and grow in understanding our positions in this movement, surrounded by learning and commitment to equity. Our actions today pave the way for generations to come. Next, we explore relationships, vital components for healing, and allyship in provider–client and supervisor–supervisee relationships.

Relationships of Authentic Allyship

Named and unnamed power dynamics influence with whom we have relationships and the tone of those relationships. Though these dynamics are seemingly less impactful within microcosms, the insidious messages of antiblackness/White supremacy upholding power dynamics prevail. As authentic allies, we have an opportunity to use power responsibly to amplify oppressed perspectives. The very survival of marginalized communities requires deciphering the authenticity and safety of others.

Relationships as authentic allies require genuine respect for marginalized people, a level of vulnerability, openness to feedback, and a willingness to call each other into a space of accountability and growth. These shared values paired with earned trust and community shaped directing, guiding, and challenging each other to delve deeper into areas we avoid. We challenge, but we don't do the work for each other. Accountability and follow-through keep allyship and antiracism active. Our relationships, trust, authenticity, and commitment to equity advance our growth. We are frequently grateful for the open, honest communications we shared while writing and continuously as we move through this process and come together across different experiences, understandings, and assumptions.

Trust, Listening, and Compassion Are Vital for Healing

The body's healing mechanisms are a metaphor for how we must work together to combat antiblackness and racism. When the body is wounded, a cascade effect begins. Our nervous system relays signals to begin the healing process, initiating activity in various blood cells to stop bleeding by clotting, removing dead and injured cells, and repairing damaged tissue with new, healthy cells. Our bodies are incredible machines that are constantly regenerating and repairing.

Racism affects us all, people of color and White people. The body cannot heal itself without all systems participating. Similarly, humans cannot heal from the damage of racism without coming together to cultivate change. This includes learning and unlearning together with openness and willingness to acknowledge our ignorance, flaws, and the impact of our actions on others.

We must also maintain a willingness to listen to people who are different from us, overcoming any ingrained reactions of skepticism, doubt, or judgment. Invalidating emotions and experiences creates an unsafe environment. Defensiveness is likely, and fostering trust becomes impossible. Without trust, there is no repair.

Compassion is imperative for fostering trust and repair, allowing us to connect by empathizing with another's experience. Without empathy and care, there cannot be a proper motive. Without a proper motive, authentic allyship cannot exist. When authenticity is present, actions come from a place of responsibility rather than a place of guilt. This requires continuous mindfulness and internal examination of motive and intentions.

Provider–Client Relationships

Though mental health professionals are familiar with compassion, trust, and repair in therapeutic work, the impact of power dynamics inherent in health care settings is less recognized, particularly between clients and providers. Power dynamics influence rapport, emotional safety, and trust, and may hinder clients from challenging providers' assumptions. We offer an example to demonstrate the crucial importance of the vital components of trust, listening, and compassion within these power dynamics as allies in mental health care.

Many clients with eating disorders report experiences of trauma. Claire noted seeing trauma as specific to an individual, greatly affecting the person in front of her, but limited to that person, like a single flame on a match head. Racial trauma was not in her immediate frame of reference as a White professional. She didn't expand her point of view to see the broader systemic trauma, a symptom and perpetuation of White fragility. Accordingly, her treatment plans were based on individual trauma, which meant she didn't recognize or address these lived experiences.

Claire recalled a specific client she and Alyssa worked with who broke through her perspective on endemic trauma. This client brought her racial trauma into the space, repeatedly and forcefully. She talked about how antiblackness affected her life and made it difficult to feed or value herself when our culture so plainly doesn't. She talked about White standards of beauty, how she was pressing back against them, and how hard that was.

Looking back now, Claire recognized that, as a mental health professional, she was part of invalidating this client's traumatic pain and experiences. She also recalled listening in a predominately White treatment team, noticing the discussion slowly coalesce around the idea that the client was "externalizing" when she talked about race, using race to distract from doing the necessary personal and interpersonal work of recovery. The team agreed the client should be encouraged to fight racism head on, but only once she was well, akin to telling someone to focus on getting their headache under control and find aspirin later.

In hindsight, Claire acknowledged that the client couldn't fix racism by talking about it, but she should have had an opportunity to process the trauma that came from living in a world of White supremacy that neutralizes the harm and trauma inflicted on Black Americans daily. Dismissing the trauma of racism perpetuated that hurt.

"We failed to offer the care she needed," recalled Claire. "This client continued to talk about the impact of anti-black racism, fighting for the intersection of race and eating disorders to be acknowledged. Our predominantly White treatment team started to listen more."

Alyssa's work with this client created a healing space, one where she voiced how meaningful it was to have a Black clinician validating her experience. Alyssa quickly saw the impact racial bias and minimization of racial trauma had, noting the injustice and upsetting nature of separating the client's race from her treatment, thereby excluding her racial trauma and its harmful effects on her life, relationship with food, and body. Witnessing the treatment team dismiss this client's experience and invalidate the client's racial pain was difficult.

Alyssa's similar experiences as a Black woman allowed her to compassionately and intricately conceptualize the client's experiences and recognize that it was not possible to separate racism from her eating disorder. At times, Alyssa questioned her conceptualization, but she refused to exclude race from the client's treatment. Looking back, she wished she and the team advocated for a healing space for this client's experiences to be acknowledged and compassionately integrated into treatment. She saw how meaningful it was to provide a healing space for the client to express herself as a Black woman and have her experiences heard.

Clinicians of color are often tasked with reparative work and creating a healing environment for clients, providing a space we may not have ourselves. As we talked about this case, Alyssa emphasized that all clinicians are capable of and responsible for creating a validating environment; listening without judgment is a mental health professional's job. She challenged thinking about how frequently non-Black clinicians neutralize and bypass experiences of racism, to "make the client feel better," by saying something like, "I'm sure he didn't mean to be racist when he said that."

Denial is problematic. It undermines and invalidates the client's experience and their hurt, giving compassion to the person who made a racist comment. Trusting the hurt person's story and listening with openness and interest make us all better clinicians. This also means examining our racism and the assumptions and microaggressions we may bring to sessions and professional settings with colleagues.

By advocating for and with our clients and colleagues, we can carry the burden of antiracist and antioppression work together, uplifting marginalized people together. Authentic allyship fosters reflection, sensitivity, responsiveness, safety, and trust in provider–client relationships.

Supervisee–Supervisor Relationships

Authentic allyship in the workplace is not only between the clinician and client but also between clinicians. In reflecting on Claire's and Alyssa's experience, Ashley focused on the inexperience of a new clinician, wrestling with assumptions, addressing racial trauma and mental health, and advocating for a different approach. Health care professionals are gatekeepers to clients' continued care, as we are gatekeepers to the profession as supervisors and hiring managers.

Yet many are not trained in allyship or cultural competence. Supervisors' feedback scaffolds supervisees' approaches to discussing race and oppression professionally and personally, offering opportunities to acknowledge power and privilege while working through anxiety about broaching recognized but taboo topics of discussion.

As the topic of culturally sensitive supervision is beyond the scope of this chapter, we encourage readers to explore other published resources for continued learning (e.g., *Culturally Sensitive Supervision and Training: Diverse Perspectives and Practical Applications*, by Ken Hardy and Toby Bobes [2017]). We also encourage supervisors to reflect on their "self of the supervisor" and examine how power, privilege, positionality, and reflexivity can inform their authentic allyship.

Grit and Persistence in Authentic Allyship

Any conversation about allyship would be incomplete without stressing that authentic allyship is a way of being, an ongoing, active process rooted in antiracism and antioppression. Authentic allyship is a countercultural stance and process, and we must remain steadfast and persistent in it. In the moments where we feel particularly raw, we recenter in our relationships and rest.

Our relationships and shared commitment to equity, accountability, safety, and reflection are a significant part of our journey and this snapshot in time. Through relationships, we continue to discover and wrestle with biases and uncover our internalized societal messages. We challenge each other to think critically, take ownership, change behaviors perpetuating racism, and advocate against inequitable policies and practices. Accountability to each other, ourselves, and our motivations keeps us on course. We encourage intentionality and action about who and what foster continued grit and persistence in authentic allyship.

Rest is an integral part of grit and persistence in authentic allyship. We cannot do all the work, all the time. We also cannot stop doing the work, nor can we proceed without caring for ourselves and each other. Rest allows us to recharge, heal, and nurture. Those with marginalized identities may need reminders that rest, nurturing, and healing are also acts of resistance, opportunities to connect with our values and hope for an equitable future.

Those with privilege must not fall into patterns of complacency and avoid this difficult work. It is too easy to take a vacation from racism and other forms of antiblackness when these oppressive forces are not part of our everyday lives.

The Present and the Future

On June 18, 2021, Juneteenth became a national holiday. We each experienced the formal recognition of Juneteenth differently. We were planning and writing this chapter, thinking both that this event was suggestive of change and how a divided response in this country was symptomatic of many of our earlier conversations about antiblackness, racism, and oppression.

The Voting Rights Act, passed in 1965, is under attack at the time of this writing, with minority voting access specifically targeted. The 13th Amendment allows for the unpaid labor of the incarcerated, who are predominantly people of color. Recognizing Juneteenth as a national holiday may open the door for people to educate themselves about the history of Juneteenth and slavery in our country. For those things, we are hopeful.

However, acknowledging slavery is the easy part. Taking responsibility for perpetuating the rippling effects of slavery is more difficult. Too many people avoid responsibility to effect change, worried they'll be labeled racist and preferring to maintain their own "good standing" as "good people." Focusing on self-preservation hinders authentic allyship.

Alyssa questioned the intention behind recognizing Juneteenth as a national holiday: Are we putting yet another bandage on racism in our country, in an attempt to pacify those of us who want to see real change? If our body is bleeding out from several wounds, a Band-Aid won't help. Healing from the multiple wounds of racism on our nation's body will be messy and difficult, requiring time, intentional effort, consistency, and dedication.

Being an ally and truly binding ourselves with the cause means we cannot stop at inward reflection and outward discussion. Follow-through is necessary. Words mean nothing without action. Learning and unlearning will take place continuously over a lifetime, and doing our own work is imperative. But we cannot stop there. If we are *really* going to be authentic allies, let's put our actions where our words are. As it is our human and professional responsibility to do good, let's heal the wound of racism for the benefit of all humanity.

References

Hardy, K. V., & Bobes, T. (Eds.). (2017). *Promoting cultural sensitivity in supervision: A manual for practitioners*. Routledge. https://doi.org/10.4324/9781315225791

Singh, A. (2019). *The racial healing handbook*.

PART VIII
WHITE PRIVILEGE

33

White Fragility

A Prominent Barrier to Antiracist Progress

Anh-Thuy H. Le

White Fragility: What Is It?

White fragility, a term coined by Professor Robin DiAngelo (2011), is defined as a defensive reaction on the part of White individuals to "even a minimum amount of racial stress," which results in an array of defensive responses. Such a reaction is often associated with anger, guilt, and withdrawal as well as corresponding behaviors of silence, arguing, or leaving the situation.

Most notably, this defensiveness results when White people are involved in uncomfortable conversations about race. For instance, triggering situations may include being told they did something racist, confronting the idea that their perspectives are informed by racist values/beliefs, and discussing unequal access to resources based on race.

Ironically, the originator of this term, herself a White woman, demonstrated this defensiveness when she was criticized for taking space from Black scholars who have studied the same issues. In a recent interview, when asked about being one of the leading *New York Times* bestselling authors on antiracism, DiAngelo deflected by maintaining that 29 of the 32 bestselling authors were Black and reiterated that she had been doing this work for 25 years to justify why she made the list (Hill, 2021). By doing so, she implicitly suggests that her success is due solely to her industriousness and experience rather than acknowledging systemic racial disparities that have benefited her and not Black scholars.

As shown, White fragility serves to shut down productive conversations on the systemic oppression faced by individuals who are Black, Indigenous, and people of color (BIPOC) and instead recenters White feelings. Those who continue to enact and stand to gain from White supremacist policies and institutions become the focus once more, diverting from the feelings and

Anh-Thuy H. Le, *White Fragility* In: *Antiblackness and the Stories of Authentic Allies*. Edited by: Norman Kim, Carolyn Coker Ross, Mazella Fuller and Charlynn Small, Oxford University Press. © Oxford University Press 2024. DOI: 10.1093/oso/9780197642535.003.0034 experiences of those actually harmed by White supremacy. In this way, White fragility is another means of preserving the status quo that has been defined by White supremacy—it is another tool in the toolbox of the oppressor.

Importantly, White fragility is coupled with White privilege—it harnesses this privilege to solicit comfort or to elicit support, and it is so insidious that it may even pull this reaction from those harmed by the given behavior. For instance, this may look like a Black individual needing to stop and assuage the guilt or tears of a White colleague during a discussion of how the latter benefits from White privilege.

Personally, there have been many conversations about race that I have been involved in that were stymied due to White individuals expressing discomfort, uncertainty, or guilt about the topic at hand. In turn, classmates, colleagues, and professors devoted time and effort to alleviate these uncomfortable feelings, prematurely ending important discussions.

When we buy into this pattern, what we are saying is that White comfort must be preserved at all costs—including at the expense of authentic change and systemwide progress. We inadvertently reinforce the belief that White people are to be accommodated, protected, and prioritized—a notion that is foundational to White supremacist ideology. Applebaum (2017) illustrates this concern deftly in her reflections on how to effectively teach about White privilege in the classroom, including how comfort can be complicit and the importance of White students staying present with their discomfort rather than escaping it.

Of course, for many BIPOC individuals, the instinct to comfort is ingrained as a result of White supremacist ideology in the first place, which explains why we may feel conflicted for engaging in this cycle. As for the White individuals who are comforted, they successfully avoid further introspection on how they function within and are served by discriminatory systems. As with any form of avoidance, they may reduce their short-term discomfort by sidestepping difficult conversations but, in the long run, will increasingly struggle to engage in race-based discussions. Thus, White fragility not only derails present engagement but also perpetuates White people's difficulty in thinking critically about race.

I clearly recall this occurring at a workshop I attended in 2015, where the purpose was to discuss experiences of racism and their impact on students of color in academia. After a few BIPOC students shared evidence of systemically entrenched racism (e.g., evident in feedback from professors, conversations with colleagues, etc.), the topic quickly diverted to White students explaining how such discussions made them *scared* of sharing their opinions for fear they would say something offensive and be misperceived as racist.

They described wanting to learn and emphasized that they were open to doing so but often remained silent due to the potential backlash. By doing this, White students were seemingly justifying that their opting out of these critical conversations was a result of others' reactions rather than acknowledging how their own discomfort was preventing them from participating in this painful but necessary dialogue.

White fragility, then, allows White people to occupy the role of victim, presenting the narrative that this discomfort is *pushed* upon them by external forces rather than recognizing that they are unequipped or unwilling to have these discussions due to a lifetime of privilege. In line with this, instead of critically examining the White centering that was occurring during this workshop, the moderator engaged with it and validated these experiences by spending the remainder of the time confirming how difficult such conversations could be. Notably, the moderator was a Black man, which illustrates how BIPOC individuals may themselves be conditioned to center White comfort.

We must also consider whether there is an implicit fear that unless White people remain central, comfortable, and happy during race-based discussions, they will withdraw their "allyship" and turn on or leave the social justice movements they claim to support. Jones and Norwood (2017) provide examples of this in describing the accounts of various White women who, upon discussing the need for intersectionality at the Women's March of 2017, expressed concern about bringing race into the demand for gender equality.

Similarly, a Pew Research Center (2020) survey found that White support for the Black Lives Matter (BLM) movement peaked in June 2020 at 60%, following the death of George Floyd due to police brutality. However, just 3 months later, this support had waned to 45%.

At the workshop, after the White students expressed their discomfort, a silencing occurred. The few BIPOC students' voices gradually faded out while the chorus of White voices grew louder in confirming that they felt silenced. I left this event feeling unsurprised, unfulfilled, and also angry. I was not able to articulate then what I felt, but I realize it now: It felt like another space had been co-opted by White people and that they had successfully curtailed any possibility of losing their standing at the center of everyone's story.

This contrasts with the experiences of many Black individuals who, when denouncing systemic racism or expressing the pain they have experienced due to racism, may be told that America is postracial, questioned as to whether their experiences are legitimate, or told to stop playing *the race card*.

Ironically, White people often cite policies such as affirmative action as reasons that Black people who complain of ongoing discrimination are being overly sensitive and searching for a reason to be upset. However, when conversations illuminate how White people benefit from existing discriminatory practices (e.g., bank loans, college admissions, job offers), they may struggle to hear this because of their own sensitivity to being complicit in these inequitable systems.

Strangely, White people seem to bristle more at the idea of being *called* racist than in actually behaving in a racist manner. As examples, we need look no further than former Louisiana justice of the peace, Keith Bardwell, who refused to marry interracial couples as recently as 2009 but subsequently protested that he was not racist. Likewise, in 2020, Miya Ponsetto denied being racist after having attacked a Black teenage boy whom she falsely accused of stealing her phone (in actuality, she had left it in a ride-share vehicle).

In a similar vein, White people are often characterized as "objective" and free from bias, when they actually have the most to lose should the status quo be disrupted. For instance, I have heard many BIPOC academics recount how they have been criticized as "too close" to the subject matter they research as it relates to diversity issues and race, while White scholars are viewed as conducting research from a bias-free lens and therefore given more credibility.

Intertwined with the notion of White fragility is the myth of White innocence (Applebaum, 2017). Where Black people need to prove their innocence daily (e.g., making sure they do not come across as loud or threatening, driving more carefully to avoid being pulled over), whiteness is held up as the standard for morality. White fragility builds on the narrative of White innocence by preventing further examination of how interwoven racism is into the fabric of American society. It blocks discourse about discriminatory systems, policies, and beliefs, thereby minimizing the atrocities of racism and people's awareness of how it persists.

The pervasiveness of the myth of White innocence is evident when we consider how much of history has been sanitized to preserve the notion of White people as innovators, explorers, and saviors. This is illustrated by the following examples: the fact that many American citizens were unaware of the Tulsa Race Massacre (which occurred in 1921) until the television series *Watchmen* depicted it in 2019 (Polowy, 2021) and, similarly, how many Americans did not know what "sundown towns" were (i.e., towns where Black people could be present during the day but needed to leave by sunset or else they risked arrest at the least) until it was highlighted in another television series, *Lovecraft Country* (St. Clair, 2020).

At the national level, White fragility (undergirded by White innocence) is currently on full display in the aftermath of the Capitol riots that took place on January 6, 2021. Some of the perpetrators who have been arrested, denounced on social media, and otherwise held to task for their actions are now maintaining innocence and claiming that they were unaware events would turn violent.

They are rationalizing their participation in the most egregious breach against a government institution in the United States to date by arguing that they did not have malicious intent. This, despite the fact that they were heeding the encouragement of a president who openly characterized Mexicans as "drug dealers" and "rapists," who wanted to build a wall to keep out Mexican immigrants, who continued to proclaim the guilt of Black and Latinx youths who were proven to be wrongfully convicted of rape, and who enacted a ban that prohibited immigration from seven predominantly Muslim countries.

As another example, Kyle Rittenhouse was portrayed as a scared White child protecting himself from angry rioters when, in fact, he was the one who attended a BLM protest with an assault rifle. Despite having shot and killed two protesters, he was not detained when walking by police officers.

In fact, a crowdfunding campaign was started for him and accrued $586,940 in 5 months, with other news reports estimating he raised over $1 million to pay his bail and legal fees. A police officer donated to this fund and was subsequently terminated for the following message that he addressed to Rittenhouse, which perfectly encapsulates White fragility: "You've done nothing wrong."

These widespread narratives reinforce the idea that White people are not motivated by racism despite committing crimes or atrocities; instead, they are given the benefit of the doubt—a leniency that is not afforded to Black people.

White fragility is also juxtaposed against harmful myths about other groups, including the angry Black woman or the dangerous Black man. The former stereotype is invoked when a White aggressor who initiates a confrontation with a Black woman blames her when she dares retort in kind, deflecting fault by latching onto an existing trope of the woman as unruly or belligerent. Further, there is the deifying of Black women as paragons of strength (Donovan & West, 2015). Their ability to withstand suffering and setbacks is glorified and held up as an ideal, when in fact, what it allows for is a means of desensitizing oneself to the abuses they suffer in order to propagate the current system established by White supremacy.

Highlighting the frailty and victimhood of White people while emphasizing the aggressiveness and durability of Black people places Black individuals who call for accountability into the role of aggressor, scapegoating them in their own victimization (Srivastava, 2006). As an example, in July 2021, a White woman hitting a Black woman at a retail store prompted the latter to start recording the encounter in a video that later went viral. In response, the White woman began having a "breakdown," including crying and curling up on the floor, which resulted in bystanders defending her and calling for the (true) victim to leave the store.

Although White fragility has been previously characterized as a defensive reaction when discussions of race cause discomfort, Applebaum (2017) makes the point that White people also *perform* White fragility with an awareness of how it protects them. As an example, take the case in New York City of a White woman, Amy Cooper, calling the police on a Black man, Christian Cooper (no relation), for "threatening" her when he really was asking her to leash her dog in a public park while he birdwatched. She knowingly invoked the stereotype of the angry Black man to preserve her own White innocence. Thankfully, because Mr. Cooper recorded this encounter, it went viral, and Ms. Cooper was subsequently fired from her job. However, she then sued her employees for not investigating the incident thoroughly enough, alleging emotional distress.

This is an important subset of White fragility—White women's tears, which can be (and often are) weaponized to harm Black people. Phipps (2021) argues that White women's tears hearken back to colonial-era power dynamics between Black individuals, White women, and White men, and that these dynamics often centered on sexual violence. Namely, Black women were hypersexualized and raped by White men, but rape was not defined as a crime if it involved enslaved persons. In contrast, accusations of rape by White women against Black men activated White men's rage and protection, leading to brutal retaliation. Emmitt Till and the Scottsboro Boys are likely the most well-known, though unfortunately not isolated, examples of the latter.

Where Does White Fragility Come From?

Imagine never being challenged, never being told you are wrong, and never being shown that you are wrong (for engaging in microaggressions, for holding racist assumptions, for being complicit in racist systems, and the like). Then, imagine a cultural reckoning in which you are *corrected* and called to account for your actions and words.

After any widespread protest movement or civil rights movement in America, there has been a pattern of conservative backlash (Glickman, 2020). Although White fragility existed before this, we are witnessing it to a greater degree, as a response to the nationwide protests that peaked in the summer of 2020 following the police killing of George Floyd.

DiAngelo (2011) argues that society has historically protected White people from race-based stress such that their ability to tolerate racial stress ("racial stamina") is markedly lowered, replaced instead by an expectation of racial comfort. She notes a combination of factors that breeds this mindset, including segregation, pervasive messaging about White superiority, racial arrogance, and entitlement to racial comfort. Thus, when BIPOC individuals voice opinions or behave in ways that challenge Whites people's positions and/or expectations of power, White fragility results.

In thinking about the increasingly multiracial landscape of the United States, we must consider the role of families in teaching and maintaining White fragility. For instance, you may have heard it in White friends who refuse to call out their elders for their racist behavior for fear of rupturing relationships. Many also justify their family's racism by attributing it to generational differences, as though to rationalize this behavior.

Expanding on this, Robinson-Wood and colleagues (2021) discuss the ways that interracial families navigate racial conversations, highlighting how White fragility is evident even in these family systems. In interviews with 30 multiracial/biracial millennials, a common theme emerged of "racially informed disquiet," which referred to the distress and/or invalidation participants experienced due to their parents' denial of racism or their child's multiracial identity. This suggests that, even in families in which a child is actively experiencing discrimination or has questions about their identity,

White fragility can impede meaningful discussion and leave these young adults grappling with the truth of racism on their own.

What to Do About White Fragility?

Taking all of this together, what can we do about this near-automatic defensiveness on the part of many White people when confronted with the reality of racism? DiAngelo proposed that White individuals should foster racial stamina by interacting more with BIPOC individuals and by engaging in these difficult conversations rather than avoiding them. However, critics have pointed out that these recommendations focus more on individual-level changes rather than systemic ones (Frey, 2020).

Applebaum (2017) presents the idea of fostering vulnerability and critical hope to counteract White fragility. She defines the latter as a reframing of how White people think about systemic oppression—namely, that the discomfort associated with racial conversations should be thought of as a growing opportunity and the chance to rectify deeply embedded wrongdoing, rather than as a personal attack. Of note, Applebaum emphasizes that professors should not accommodate or allay the discomfort their White students report. Instead, they should encourage them to sit with it and to use it as a means of examining their own role in these systems to promote personal growth toward "learning to become more human" (Applebaum, 2017, p. 872).

My views on next steps are twofold: Both individual- and system-level transformations are necessary to initiate *and* maintain change that is truly revolutionary and dismantles the status quo established by White supremacy.

White people should be encouraged to change individually, as policy-level changes alone can feel removed and lull people into a false sense of complacency that racism is being adequately addressed. We have seen this dichotomy illustrated in policies such as affirmative action, which many Whites endorse agreement with *conceptually* but not functionally (Newport, 2020). As such, the recommendations from scholars such as DiAngelo and Applebaum are useful in providing ways to work toward meaningful personal change. Obviously, these next steps will be helpful only for those White individuals interested in authentic growth and reflection. For those who are not, changing societal norms and legal repercussions may be the most effective means to curb their behavior.

Given the automaticity of defensiveness, White individuals will need to exercise deliberateness to enact change. For instance, when their worldview or perspective on race is challenged, they will need to consciously pause and refrain from sharing their sentiments and instead truly listen to and practice empathy for the speaker. As noted previously, White fragility recenters the White experience and White feelings, so to counter this, White people will need to willingly center Black people's lived experiences.

Additionally, White people should deeply reflect on what they mean when they express feeling *scared* of talking about race. Do they mean they are experiencing true fear of violent or dangerous outcomes, or do they mean they are uncomfortable? When we accurately label emotions, we are better able to gauge the appropriateness of different responses. That is, if someone expresses fear and begins crying, most people will instinctually want to offer comfort or alleviate their distress. However, if White people could relabel this as discomfort and voice that these were difficult but important topics to discuss, listeners could acknowledge these emotions without the accompanying need to halt further conversation.

Similarly, White people must step outside of their own comfort to actively be antiracist, including challenging their family and friends who say or do racist things. Revolutionary change does not occur alongside a comfortable existence; by its very definition, it entails upheaval in service of something *more*.

White people will also need to grapple with what it means to be a "good" person. There is a deeply ingrained fear of being labeled racist in America, to the detriment of personal growth. In the conversations I have been involved in when White fragility reared up, the White people present were *adamant* that everyone needed to understand they were not racist. They became so focused on this label that it impeded their ability to engage in or process the discussion in a meaningful way. Instead, what they should do is sit with the idea that they did something racist and try to own it and grow; when we make room for missteps and commit to genuine change, that is the epitome of progress.

As far as I know, it is not perfection that BIPOC individuals are seeking when we point out racism; it is acknowledgment of the wounding and commitment to do better. It may help to consider what BIPOC individuals are condemning as well when we protest systemic racism. Similar to arguing that individual men are not each evil but that *patriarchy* and toxic masculinity are harmful, we are not arguing that each White person (YOU) is willfully malicious. Rather, we are asking that White people understand how they engage in and benefit from systems designed to oppress BIPOC people and to take responsibility to stop perpetuating these systems. It will require work at a personal level, but we need White people to stop taking it so personally.

In terms of broader, system-level changes, we need to redefine what it means to be a "good" person *societally* because this idea of infallibility that is connected to White innocence makes it impossible to eliminate White fragility. When White people have only received messages about the good that they have done while none of the atrocities they committed are owned, they are unable to contend with the idea of needing to make amends.

Instead, what we need is an overhaul of the history of this country to more accurately reflect the abuses and suffering inflicted on BIPOC individuals. If our education system taught us earlier on how policies and institutions were designed to privilege White people and to disadvantage BIPOC people, it would be easier for laypeople to admit their own problematic behavior and to redress these wounds. This would require a massive undertaking at the political, legal, and educational levels, but that illustrates how deeply rooted racism and White fragility are in American society.

What this might look like would include acknowledgment from political leaders of this reprehensible history (e.g., California Governor Gavin Newsom's creation of a task force for reparations to Black Americans, Trudeau's apology about the abuse of Indigenous children), as well as sanctions on weaponizing White fragility (e.g., New York's proposed bill to make it a hate crime if someone called the police with false accusations based on someone's race, gender, or religion). Only by acknowledging our history and committing to actionable change can we biexpect these tools of oppression to be dismantled.

References

Applebaum, B. (2017). Comforting discomfort as complicity: White fragility and the pursuit of invulnerability. *Hypatia*, *32*(4), 862–875.

DiAngelo, R. (2011). White fragility. *International Journal of Critical Pedagogy*, *3*(3), 54–70.

Donovan, R. A., & West, L. M. (2015). Stress and mental health: Moderating role of the strong Black woman stereotype. *Journal of Black Psychology*, *41*(4), 384–396.

Frey, W. R. (2020). White fragility: Why it's so hard for white people to talk about racism Robin DiAngelo. *Journal of Social Work*, *20*(1), 123–125. https://doi.org/10.1177/1468017319868330

Glickman, L. (2020, May 21). How white backlash controls American progress. *The Atlantic*. https://www.theatlantic.com/ideas/archive/2020/05/white-backlash-nothing-new/611914/

Hill, M. L. (2021, August 12). *Examining whiteness as a social construct* [Video]. Twitter. https://twitter.com/marclamonthill/status/1425835115276537858

Jones, T., & Norwood, K. J. (2017). Aggressive encounters and white fragility: Deconstructing the trope of the angry Black woman. *Iowa Law Review, 102*(5), 2017–2070.

Newport, F. (2020, August 7). *Affirmative action and public opinion*. Gallup. https://news.gallup.com/opinion/polling-matters/317006/affirmative-action-public-opinion.aspx

Pew Research Center. (2020, September 16). *Support for Black Lives Matter has decreased since June but remains strong among Black Americans*. https://www.pewresearch.org/fact-tank/2020/09/16/support-for-black-lives-matter-has-decreased-since-june-but-remains-strong-among-black-americans/

Phipps, A. (2021). White tears, white rage: Victimhood and (as) violence in mainstream feminism. *European Journal of Cultural Studies, 24*(1), 81–93. https://doi.org/10.1177/1367549420985852

Polowy, K. (2021, May 28). *The Tulsa Race Massacre turns 100: How HBO's "Watchmen" helped teach America a crucial history lesson*. Yahoo. https://www.yahoo.com/now/tulsa-race-massacre-hbo-watchmen-education-history-lesson-224759540.html?guccounter=1&guce_referrer=aHR0cHM6Ly93d3cuZ29vZ2xlLmNvbS8&guce_referrer_sig=AQAAAIT7qET5XW3jO2tAc8cgHvn7m_AosAB5BmKiiyjunFUzn1vvpnKQAv5qKxc1zghTReFmEkuOkrKHKGQ3zc3FJc5RxhX0XqimqaTKsoAfvP5XMght12bfOJ9EaqwIhyVW8IEeeS5oIPlc-05eTFdoe6s_j8F38dYYW5dHSA_zkb72

Robinson-Wood, T., Muse, C., Hewett, R., Balogun-Mwangi, O., Elrahman, J., Nordling, A., Abdulkerim, N., & Matsumoto, A. (2021). Regular white people things: The presence of white fragility in interracial families. *Family Relations*. https://doi.org/10.1111/fare.12549

Srivastava, S. (2006). Tears, fears, and careers: Anti-racism and emotion in social movement organizations. *Canadian Journal of Sociology, 31*(1), 55–90.

St. Clair, J. (2020, August 17). The "sundown towns" from Lovecraft Country were (and still are) a real thing. *Men's Health*. https://www.menshealth.com/entertainment/a33598135/sundown-town-lovecraft-country/

34

In the Wake of White Privilege

Jennifer A. Coleman

I was born on a ship. Not a small yacht or catamaran, no—one of the larger than life, unbelievable, city-on-water, massive ships. At first glance it appears striking. If you walk on board, stained-glass windows illuminate a path of red velvet carpet. You can hear the chandeliers as crystal clinks along with the slight sway of the ocean (barely detectable, mind you). Motionless elevators transport you up and down endless floors. There is a smell of sweetness, of fresh flowers anywhere you turn. You can relax your aching body as you slip into one of the luxury pools or feel the sweat roll down your cheek as you run laps at the gym. You might satisfy your taste buds with a fresh a strawberry, mango, and hibiscus fruit smoothie at a café. At a moment's notice, you can meet any desire. This ship is a Titanic of our generation.

On this ship, we have access to mouthwatering buffets of infinite food, exotic fruit and vegetables, fresh fish, anything prepared with a simple request. Some of us work, but many spend our days relaxing, enjoying the luxuries, or bathing in the sun to darken our complexion. On the rare occasion we feel ill, we are met with concern, care, and inquiry. We are educated by those indoctrinated with knowledge about the glories this ship has produced.

This ship appears grand, but the wake and the debris left behind by this ship are ghastly.

My parents were born on this ship. My parents' parents were born on this ship. This ship has been sailing the ocean for centuries. Everyone on this ship is familiar to me. Many of us share the same language, faith, and cuisine preference. There are others with different tongues, varied religions, and dress of choice. Yet we are all on the same ship. To be clear, some folks are born with less. They have interior housing, with no views of the sky. They have fewer trinkets and reduced access to the grand amenities. Most of them spend their days working in the hopes of someday having a balcony, or at least a window with a view. Yet, they are still protected by the safety that this ship offers all its inhabitants. These

Jennifer A. Coleman, *In the Wake of White Privilege* In: *Antiblackness and the Stories of Authentic Allies.*
Edited by: Norman Kim, Carolyn Coker Ross, Mazella Fuller and Charlynn Small, Oxford University Press.
© Oxford University Press 2024. DOI: 10.1093/oso/9780197642535.003.0035

folks do not fear the storms as those on land might. These folks do not suffer the damage this ship leaves behind.

Naively, it wasn't until my 20s that I accurately saw the people who lived on land. We docked to refuel, and I saw those who came to service our ship—none of whom had ever stepped foot on this ship. I saw and smelled the stench of the mounds of garbage we left behind on their land. They watch as this ship sails by, their beaches and shores filled with the debris from our wake.

Every time I see land, and people living on it, it is as if I am awakening from a slumber, from years of being taught to see that this ship and what lives on it is grand. I was groggy at first. But now, with time, I am compelled to keep my eyes open. I admire the vast land, the contours of the mountains and valleys, while I weep at the pollution we created—the murky water, the dying trees, the rotting vegetation, the sickly wildlife, the humans we have slaughtered. Yet, even with my eyes open I will never understand, fully and completely, how it is to live life on solid ground, to suffer the damage. How can one living on the waves understand the texture of garbage slicing the skin under one's feet?

There was guilt at the beginning. I did not build this ship. Nor did my parents, nor my parents' parents. At birth I did not ask to be granted access to the lifestyle it has afforded me. Every passenger on this ship is reaping the benefits. Yet many, many passengers are oblivious to the reality that they are even on a ship. They are ignorant to the lifestyle of humans living on land, even though these passengers may have read stories about or talked to those who live on land. For some this is purposeful, narcissistic malice. For others it is blissful ignorance. But both contribute to the wake and the debris and the damage, which I have finally realized we are purposefully and systematically leaving behind. These passengers choose to deny their reality and the reality of those on the shore. Yet, knowingly or not, this debris is our responsibility to address.

There is anger at times. We did not choose to be on this ship. I did not choose to be on this ship. I want to dock, set foot on land, and run into the mountains—burn this ship to the ground. I want to fight and argue, and claim bold statements, and wash my hands of the filth. Others on this ship want to rescue those on land. They want to save them. They cannot see that we are the ones who need saving. We are the ones who need to save ourselves.

There is acceptance. There is understanding that the guilt and the anger are about me, and that is not helpful or fruitful, and the focus is incorrect. There is acceptance that whether I have built this ship or not, whether I chose to board this ship or not, I must recognize the life it has afforded me, the life it has not afforded others. I have the responsibility—we have the responsibility—to bring this ship to harbor and offload the inhabitants and tear the entire ship down. This ship was built on the labor and suffering of others, the oppression and genocide of many.

This ship is real. This ship is an illusion.

The Hull

If you are like me, you have lived your entire life aboard the ship known as *White privilege.*

White privilege is a life of benefits based on being born with White-colored skin in a society that tells themselves that White is superior. White scholars have argued for years that there are inherent human differences based on our hue. Differences in intellect. Differences in ability. Differences in aptitude. These are lies. The lies are persistent and bold. These lies are an illusion to create a society in which Whiteness was and is king.

Social psychology teaches that humans have an innate need to group people and things; to understand the world better and feel safer, we have a desire to place things and people into neat and tidy categories. There is the group to which I belong and there is the group to which others belong. The group to which I belong is good and the group to which you belong is bad. We are right and you are wrong. This is called "fast thinking," which has evolved to be adaptive for threats, for example, to help you determine if you should run away from a tiger charging at you. Unfortunately, fast thinking has led humans to group each other based solely on the shade of their skin—and the concept of race was born.

Race itself is a social construct. It is artificial. A sham. And yet it is the golden key or the handcuffs that often determines our fates.

The grouping of races resulted in racism, discrimination based exclusively on the color of one's skin. Humans could have just as easily decided to group others based on height or eye color. Imagine if you were kidnapped and enslaved because you had blue eyes or were left-handed. Discrimination is a pillar of White privilege, giving it legs on which to stand. One group cannot be superior unless others are inferior.

I was better able to see the hull of the ship after being introduced to the seminal piece about White privilege by Peggy McIntosh (1988). This reading was one of many steps toward understanding the ship I was born on and on which I continue to live—and the wake that is left behind.

There is likely no aspect of this world that White privilege does not touch. As a clinical psychologist and a therapist for over 10 years, I have witnessed the wake of this ship of White privilege, particularly in the fields of mental health and higher education. It is prevalent in hospitals and clinics, in the research conducted and the patient–provider interactions. White privilege lives and breathes in the sacred therapeutic relationships we build with clients. Social determinants of health are everywhere. These privileges are visible and invisible.

I, and those who are White, have the privilege of:

> *A net wealth that can be 10 times*
> *that of my Black counterpart (Taylor, 2019).*
> *Being more likely*
> *to be paid more*
> *due to the color of my skin, even if I have the same educational*
>   *attainment as someone*
> *who is Black (Taylor, 2019).*
> *Being more likely*
> *to obtain a college degree (HRSA, 2020).*
> *Being more likely*
> *to own my own home (HRSA, 2020).*
> *Being more likely to*
> *have insurance coverage (AHRQ, 2021; HRSA 2020).·*

White privilege is not only the presence of benefits but also the absence of obstacles and barriers. Living my life on this ship of privilege has afforded me the luxury of avoiding so much. Avoiding:

> *Carrying the weight*
> *of over 200 years of transgenerational trauma,*
> *caused by kidnapping, rape, murder, and cultural genocide*
> *(Degruy, 2017).*
> *A sevenfold risk of homicide compared to White Americans*
> *(HRSA, 2020),*
> *and thus increased risk of suffering the loss of a loved one.*
> *The burden of increased risk of*
> *trauma exposure due to systemic oppression.*
> *Continual anger or rage from historical and ongoing oppression*
> *and trauma (Degruy, 2017).*

A shorter life expectancy (HRSA, 2020; NCHS, 2016).
The burden of worrying my father or partner or son
will be incarcerated
because of the color of his skin,
and the burden and stress of raising my children alone,
due to this injustice.
I do not carry the burden of housing segregation and redlining
(Taylor, 2019).
My children don't face an increased risk of food insecurity,
or poverty rates twofold that of White Americans,
or twofold rates of unemployment (HRSA, 2020).
I do not face increased rates of homelessness (Taylor, 2019).
I am not burdened with suffering constant stress
due to these disparities in wealth and financial assets (Taylor, 2019).

White privilege is often discussed in regard to specific metrics: Objective, measurable, tangible repercussions we can see with the visible eye. Statistics we can measure and graph. The privilege of affordable housing and access to fair housing loans. The privilege of attending schools with resources. The privilege of having the majority of the U.S. government or Congress look like me and make laws that will likely benefit me. The privilege of having those who look like me write the narrative in the media and news, which tends to include a general positive portrayal of my race. The privilege of authors who look like me create the history books that our children read, and rewrite a history that ignores oppression and the injustice of others.

Yet, the wake left behind from White privilege—the wake and filth that ripple and create tsunamis on others' mental health, the debris—fills an ocean. The debris that impairs mental health may appear to be under the surface and thus not be measured or graphed or accounted for.

As I write this, Simone Biles, the greatest gymnast to date, has withdrawn from the team final of the Olympics. The media went wild. A Black woman was putting her needs first, her needs before that of a White privileged nation. One interviewer asked her about her decision to withdraw: "Is it physical, or *just* mental?" As if physical health is the measurable, tangible metric we all can see and the only issue our society cares about, but the mental component is less real.

Why is it so hard for our society to dive beneath the surface and see how damaging White privilege is for everyone's mental health? It is toxic for everyone who swims in these waters and drinks from these rivers. It will kill us all if we let it.

> *I have the privilege of various protective factors to buffer against mental illness.*
> *I have the privilege of being treated well by society because I am White.*
> *Others often assume well of me because I am White.*
>   *I do not fear that*
>   *my child,*
>   *my partner,*
>   *my family,*
>   *or I will be treated unfairly,*
>   *or the worst will be assumed*
>   *every time we interact with the world*
>   *because of the color of our skin.*
>   *I avoid increased stress*
>   *due to discrimination, racism, colorism, and ignorance.*

Mental health is linked to everything. Physical health is intricately linked to your mental health. Mental health is linked to your physical health. Mental health is physical health and physical health is mental health. Racism is linked to inflammation, which is linked with chronic illness (Taylor, 2019). Exposure to violence is linked to worse mental health. Income and wealth affect one's mental health.

Renters have higher rates of mortality and psychological distress compared with homeowners (HRSA, 2020). Housing stability is associated with health and mortality (HRSA, 2020). Employment is linked to mental health. Employment is linked to insurance. Discrimination is associated with worse mental health. Prejudice is linked to worse mental health. Systemic racism is linked to worse mental health. Low socioeconomic status is linked with increased risk of homelessness, incarceration, and substance abuse, which are all linked to mental health (HRSA, 2020).

Research suggests that rates of mental illness may actually be the same or lower in Black people than Whites people (APA, 2017). And yet, since many Blacks are overrepresented in the most vulnerable sections of the U.S. populations (e.g., homeless, in prisons, living in low socioeconomic areas, etc.), these higher rates may be inflated due to health disparities. This could suggest that without such muddy waters, without the toxicity of White privilege, Black Americans may be mentally healthier.

> *My Whiteness affords me better access to health care and better quality of*
> *care (AHRQ, 2021).*
> *I am more likely to be able to afford nutritional food (HRSA, 2020).*
> *I am more likely to be vaccinated for the flu and more likely to receive*
> *needed dental care (NCHS, 2016).*
>
> *I am not burdened with the terror,*
> *a terror I cannot begin to imagine,*
> *of higher risk of preterm birth,*
> *low birth weight,*
> *and more than a twofold risk of infant mortality*
> *compared with*
> *White counterparts (HRSA, 2020; NCHS, 2016).*
> *I do not carry the weight*
> *that my children are more likely*
> *to struggle with obesity,*
> *a public health issue associated with*
> *higher morbidity in adulthood (NCHS, 2016).*
> *I do not have the burden*
> *of being more likely to develop hypertension,*
> *having a six to eight times higher risk of dying from HIV,*
> *being twice as likely to die*
> *from diabetes,*
> *being twice as likely to die*
> *from kidney disease,*
> *developing end-stage renal disease*
> *due to diabetes,*
> *or having a higher rate of dying from cardiovascular diseases (AHRQ,*
> *2021; HRSA, 2020; NCHS, 2016).*[3]
> *Because of my skin color, I am not*
> *facing higher rates of dying from*
> *colorectal (30% higher),*
> *prostate (101% higher),*
> *breast (34% higher),*
> *or cervical (69% higher) cancer than White Americans (HRSA, 2020).*

Is it clear yet just how toxic these waters have become?

The framework for mental health and illness along with mental health care is embedded in a White, Western, privileged schema (HRSA, 2020). Mental health in the United States is rooted in White European practices and ideologies (e.g., those of Sigmund Freud). White privilege is different from culture (i.e., a set of shared values, beliefs, and norms in a group). Both privilege and culture affect how people view the world and, thus, how systems (such as our medical system) are created or utilized. Our culture dictates who has access to good health care, who can afford such health care, and sadly the quality of such health care. White privilege creates its own culture, and it breeds White superiority. White privilege affects the lens through which White people, and often others, view the world. It affects our norms, our beliefs, the institutions we build, the laws we create, and our view of reality. White privilege leads to bias.

If you are a White therapist like me, we have the privilege of:

Learning about others who look like us
during our years of education.
Being taught, trained, and clinically supervised by someone who looks
* like us.*
Being more likely to pass the licensure exam, because it was written for
* people of a similar background.*

I avoided the burden
of almost no one looking like me
throughout my education as a therapist,
because only
6% of psychologists are Black (79% are White; AHRQ, 2021).
I avoid the weight of a history of medical mistrust
(rightfully so, due to historical mistreatment,
racism, and discrimination in the medical and mental health fields),
and minimal research exploring that mistrust (APA, 2017; HRSA 2020).
I do not have the burden of being labeled
by those who have enslaved me
as mentally ill (i.e., drapetomania)
for not wanting to be enslaved.
I am not burdened with having to request
a health care provider who looks like me,
so they might understand me
and my culture and background,
or at least believe what I say is true.

Culture affects symptom presentation. Culture affects conceptualizations and beliefs about health and illness. What is illness and what is health are culturally bound. Culture affects stigma about illness and treatment-seeking behaviors.

As a White person seeking mental health care:

> *I have the privilege that if my "intelligence" is assessed it will be with a tool*
> *that was created, standardized, and normed on people who look like me.*
> *I am more likely to*
> *be accurately diagnosed for a mental health condition (HRSA, 2020).*
> *I am more likely to*
> *use mental health services of any kind (SAMHSA, 2015).*
> *I am more likely to*
> *utilize prescription medication (SAMHSA, 2015).*
> *I am more likely to*
> *have utilized outpatient mental health services, regardless age, regardless*
> *of insurance status (SAMHSA, 2015).*
>
> *I can avoid the burden*
> *of being more likely to face clinician bias*
> *with a mental health diagnosis (HRSA, 2020).*
> *I avoid the weight*
> *of culturally incompetent providers*
> *and poorer quality of mental health care (APA, 2017).*
> *I avoid being less likely to receive medical care due to cost (HRSA, 2020).*

Access to insurance and health care is linked to mental health. Earning a higher income is linked with better-quality health care (AHRQ, 2021). Having a racially diverse health care provider improves access to health care for people of color (AHRQ, 2021). Yet roughly only 5% of physicians are Black, 5% of dentists are Black, 11% of registered nurses are Black (69% are White), 8% of EMTs and paramedics are Black (72% are White), and 6% of physician assistants are Black (73% are White)—despite Black people and African American people making up about 13% of the U.S. population.

Over the last 20 years, the gap between the quality of care for Whites and Blacks has not shrunk (AHRQ, 2021). Only a third of African Americans who need mental health care obtain it (APA, 2017).

Sinking the Ship

So how do we stop this ship, clean up the debris, and get off the boat? It begins with a decision and a commitment to dismantle it. It begins with awareness and insight, education and re-education and unlearning. It starts and continues with action.

I am horrified by the unlearning that must occur. But standing still will not dismantle this ship. I can share what has helped me, while also recognizing that everyone may utilize different tools or have different strengths, and there are many ways to become and be antiracist.

I encourage you to read. Read books by people who look like you and have lived a life on the ship of White privilege. Try Tim Wise, a White, male, American, antiracist activist, writer, and educator who speaks out about White privilege. Read books by people who do not look like you and who may challenge how you see the world. Pick up Michael Eric Dyson's *Tears We Cannot Stop* and reflect on his sermon to White America. Read books that may grant some levity, along with sorrow: *How Not to Get Shot: And Other Advice From White People*, by D. L. Hughley and Doug Moe. Read authors who published recently, and those who were unpublished years ago. If you don't know where to start, consider Audre Lorde, James Baldwin, W. E. B. Du Bois, bell hooks, Ijeoma Oluo, Ta-Nehisi Coates, or Ibram Kendi, to name just a few.

We often cannot unlearn without the help of others who can see it from a different perspective. It is not their job to teach us, but we are often benefactors of the gifts that others' lived experience and knowledge have so graciously provided. Learning about how to be an antiracist from those who have experienced racism first-hand is powerful. Try listening to the podcast Code Switch, or any number of others written and voiced by people who are different than you. Read about how psychology and mental health are imbedded in a White privilege framework. Read a chapter from *Even the Rat Was White: A Historical View of Psychology*, by Robert V. Guthrie.

If you are White, learn how to decenter yourself. Work to promote the voice of people who do not look like you. Center their ideas and their work. Take up less space in the world, space that is assumed to belong to us because we are White and we are privileged. Recognize that your beliefs, values, and practices may not always be best or right. Challenge yourself to see the world from another's point of view.

As White psychologists, White researchers, White doctors, and White therapists, we hold a special burden and a unique privilege. Our clients or research participants give us their trust and their confidence. Our clients often share their darkest moments with us in a sacred space we work to create. But this sacred space is often muddied by Whiteness. White providers must ensure we are not doing harm. We must recognize our conscious and unconscious biases. We must dismantle White privilege in mental health care and medical care. We must support those who are Black, Asian, Indigenous, Latino/a, queer, immigrants, and gender diverse who are seeking a career in mental health, so we can all benefit from a more diverse field of mental health.

Antiracism work is more than just reading some books or listening to a few talks. Antiracism in the mental health world involves purposeful dismantling of a system that will push back and argue in favor of the benefits of White privilege. Antiracism work in the medical field will most likely be uncomfortable and may even get you in trouble—because a system that benefits the privileged does not wish to dismantle itself.

Dr. Lisa Bowleg (2021), a Black social psychologist, provides some concrete ideas for change. She encourages us to research the strengths of Black communities and partner with Black community-based and grassroots organizations. She urges us to stop working to keep White people comfortable and reminds those who do not reap the benefits of White privilege and those doing antiracist work to engage in self-care.

Dismantling the ship of White privilege in mental health is complex and nuanced. It is the job of us who hold the power, and yet we require a different tool set than we're used to. Audre Lorde (2018) explains, "the master's tools will never dismantle the master's house." Are you willing to sink this ship with me?

References

Agency for Healthcare Research and Quality (AHRQ). (2021). *2021 National healthcare quality and disparities report* (AHRQ Pub. No. 21(22)-0054-EF). https://www.ahrq. gov/research/findings/nhqrdr/index.html

American Psychiatric Association (APA). (2017). *Mental health disparities: African Americans.* https://www.psychiatry.org/psychiatrists/cultural-competency/education/ mental-health-facts

Bowleg, L. (2021). "The master's tools will never dismantle the master's house": Ten critical lessons for Black and other health equity researchers of color. *Health Education & Behavior, 48,* 237–249. https://www.doi.org/10.1177/10901981211007402

Degruy, J. A. (2017). *Post traumatic slave syndrome: America's legacy of enduring injury and healing.* Joy DeGruy Publications.

Lorde, A. (2018). *The master's tools will never dismantle the master's house.* Penguin UK.

McIntosh, P. (1988). *White privilege and male privilege: A personal account of coming to see correspondences through work in women's studies* (Working Paper 189). Wellesley Centers for Women.

National Center for Health Statistics (NCHS). (2016). *Health, United States, 2015: With special feature on racial and ethnic health disparities.*

Substance Abuse and Mental Health Services Administration (SAMHSA). (2015). *Racial/ethnic differences in mental health service use among adults* (Publication No. SMA-15-4906). U.S. Department of Health and Human Services.

Taylor, J. (2019). *Racism, inequality, and health care for African Americans.* Century Foundation. https://tcf.org/content/report/racism-inequality-health-care-african-americans/?agreed=1

U.S. Department of Health and Human Services, Health Resources and Services Administration (HRSA), Office of Health Equity. (2020). *Health equity report 2019–2020: Special feature on housing and health inequalities.*

Glossary

ally: Someone who makes the commitment and effort to recognize their privilege (based on gender, class, race, sexual identity, etc.) and work in solidarity with oppressed groups in the struggle for justice, understanding that it is in their own interest to end all forms of oppression, even those which they may benefit from in concrete ways. Allies commit to reducing their own complicity or collusion in oppression of those groups and invest in strengthening their own knowledge and awareness of oppression.

antiblackness: The Council for Democratizing Education defines antiblackness as being a two-part formation that voids blackness of value while systematically marginalizing Black people and their issues. The first form of antiblackness is overt racism. Beneath this anti-Black racism is the covert structural and systemic racism that categorically predetermines the socioeconomic status of Black people in this country. The structure is held in place by anti-Black policies, institutions, and ideologies.

antiracism: The active process of identifying and eliminating racism by changing systems, organizational structures, policies and practices, and attitudes, so that power is redistributed and shared equitably.

authentic allyship: An active and action-based state of taking on the struggles of oppressed groups as one's own, including acknowledging one's own privilege and developing a willingness to share that privilege with those who do not have it, educating oneself about the origins and impacts of systemic inequities as they affect oppressed peoples, recognizing and working to counter one's own biases, and centering the voices and needs of others while decentering one's own.

BIPOC: An acronym that stands for Black, Indigenous, and people of color.

colorism: The allocation of privilege and favor to lighter skin colors and disadvantage to darker skin colors. Colorism operates both within and across racial and ethnic groups.

critical race theory: Critical race theory recognizes that racism is ingrained in the fabric and system of American society. The individual racist need not exist to note that institutional racism is pervasive in the dominant culture. The critical race theory movement considers many of the same issues that conventional civil rights and ethnic studies take up but places them in a broader perspective that includes economics, history, and even feelings and the unconscious. Unlike traditional civil rights, which embraces incrementalism and step-by-step progress, critical race theory questions the very foundations of the liberal order, including equality theory, legal reasoning, Enlightenment rationalism, and principles of constitutional law.

diversity: The state of being composed of dimensions or characteristics that differ from one another, such as race, ethnicity, gender and gender identity, sexual orientation, disability, religion, socioeconomic status, age, and other differentiating dimensions and identities. It has come to refer to a societal value that recognizes that there is intrinsic benefit and merit to respecting and honoring these differences among people and their life experiences.

equity: Equity is the measure of fair treatment or outcomes across race, gender, class, and other dynamics.

feminism: The advocacy of women's rights on the basis of the equality of the sexes.

HBCU: Historically Black college and university.

implicit bias: A mental process that stimulates negative attitudes about people who are not members of one's own group, which leads to discrimination. Also known as unconscious or hidden bias, implicit biases are negative associations that people unknowingly hold. They are expressed automatically, without conscious awareness. Many studies have indicated that implicit biases affect individuals' attitudes and actions, thus creating real-world implications, even though individuals may not even be aware that those biases exist within themselves. Notably, implicit biases have been shown to trump individuals' stated commitments to equality and fairness, thereby producing behavior that diverges from the explicit attitudes that many people profess. The Implicit Association Test (IAT) is often used to measure implicit biases with regard to race, gender, sexual orientation, age, religion, and other topics.

inclusion: The active and intentional practice of providing and ensuring equitable access to opportunities and resources for people who have historically been marginalized, disenfranchised, and excluded. Inclusion recognizes that discrimination is systemic in nature and therefore centers those people and groups who have been marginalized.

intersectionality: Coined by critical race theorist and legal scholar Kimberlé Crenshaw to explain the discrimination experienced by Black women, whose multiple identity dimensions were not adequately captured in existing models of discrimination. It is an analytical framework for understanding how a person's various, overlapping identities can combine to create different levels of discrimination or disadvantage. It acknowledges that everyone has unique experiences of discrimination and oppression, with attendant connections to privilege and power, that cannot be easily reduced to single identity dimensions.

microaggression: Everyday insults, indignities, and demeaning messages sent to historically marginalized groups by well-intentioned members of the majority group who are unaware of the hidden messages being sent.

passing: Passing refers to the ability of someone with a minoritized identity who is able to be perceived to be or accepted as a member of a dominant or privileged group. Originating with African-American slaves who escaped enslavement and were subsequently able to "pass" as white as a means of survival, it has come to encompass individuals with other stigmatized or marginalized identities.

PWI: Predominantly White institution.

race: A social construct that artificially divides people into distinct groups based on certain characteristics such as physical appearance (especially skin color), cultural affiliation, cultural history, and ethnic classification.

racism: A system of structuring opportunity and assigning value based on the social interpretation of how one looks (which is what we call "race").

reverse passing: Passing as Black when one is White.

structural racism: A system in which public policies, institutional practices, cultural representations, and other norms work in various, often reinforcing ways to perpetuate racial group inequity. The normalization and legitimization of an array of dynamics—historical, cultural, institutional, and interpersonal—that routinely advantage Whites while producing cumulative and chronic adverse outcomes for people of color. Structural racism encompasses the entire system of White domination, diffused and infused in all aspects of society including its history, culture, politics, economics, and the entire social fabric. Structural racism is more difficult to locate in a particular institution because it involves the reinforcing effects of multiple institutions and cultural norms, past and present, continually reproducing old and producing new forms of racism. Structural racism is the most profound and pervasive form of racism—all other forms of racism emerge from structural racism.

systemic racism: See structural racism. If there is a difference between the terms, it can be said to exist in the fact that a structural racism analysis pays more attention to the historical, cultural, and social psychological aspects of a currently racialized society.

wealth gap: Wealth gap, or racial wealth gap, refers to the difference in wealth, the measurable assets that an individual or family possesses, between White households and Black and Latinx households. Wealth inequities in the United States stem from the practice of chattel slavery and the resulting institutionalization of laws and practices that ensured that generations of White individuals could build and retain more wealth than non-Whites.

White fragility: A state in which even a minimum amount of racial stress becomes intolerable, triggering a range of defensive moves. These moves include the outward display of emotions such as anger, fear, and guilt and behaviors such as argumentation, silence, and leaving the stress-inducing situation; these behaviors, in turn, function to reinstate White racial equilibrium.

White privilege: The unquestioned and unearned set of advantages, entitlements, benefits, and choices bestowed on people solely because they are White. Generally White people who experience such privilege do so without being conscious of it.

woke: Originating in Black communities, the adjective usage refers to the state of being constantly vigilant and aware of social inequities and social injustice.

References

American Psychiatric Association. (n.d.-a). *APA Presidential Task Force on Structural Racism glossary of terms.* https://www.psychiatry.org/psychiatrists/structural-racism-task-force/glossary-of-terms

American Psychiatric Association. (n.d.-b). *Racism and Black mental health course.* https://education.psychiatry.org/diweb/catalog/item?id=5913368

Calgary Anti-Racism Education. (n.d.). *Anti-racism.* http://www.aclrc.com/antiracism

Georgetown University Library. (2022). *Glossary of terms. Anti-racism toolkit.* https://guides.library.georgetown.edu/antiracism/glossary

International City/County Management Association. (2021). *Glossary of terms: Race, equity and social justice.* https://icma.org/glossary-terms-race-equity-and-social-justice

Index

For the benefit of digital users, indexed terms that span two pages (e.g., 52–53) may, on occasion, appear on only one of those pages.

Tables and figures are indicated by *t* and *f* following the page number